In the Forest of Fontainebleau

KIMBERLY JONES
with
SIMON KELLY
SARAH KENNEL
HELGA AURISCH

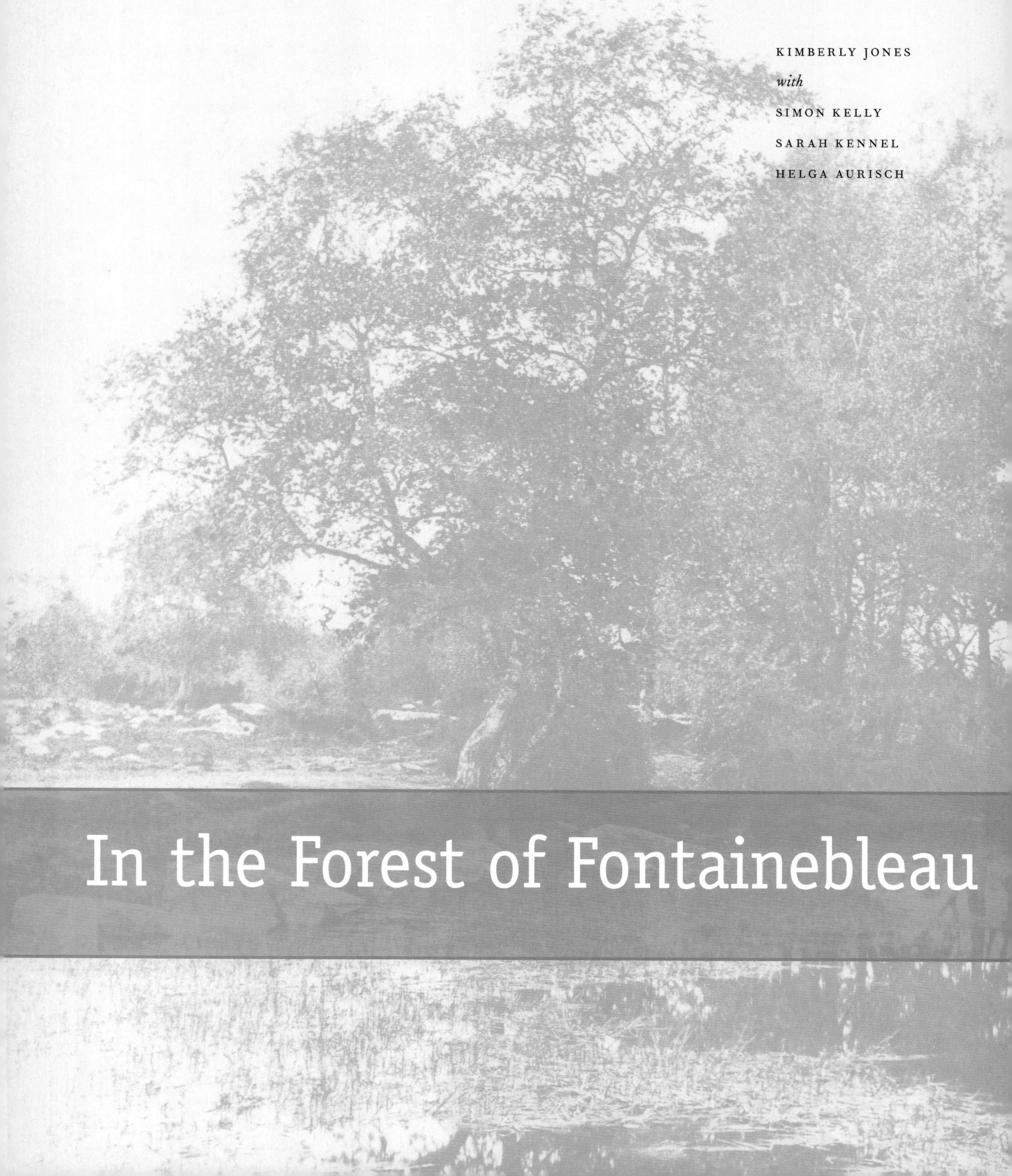

In the Forest of Fontainebleau

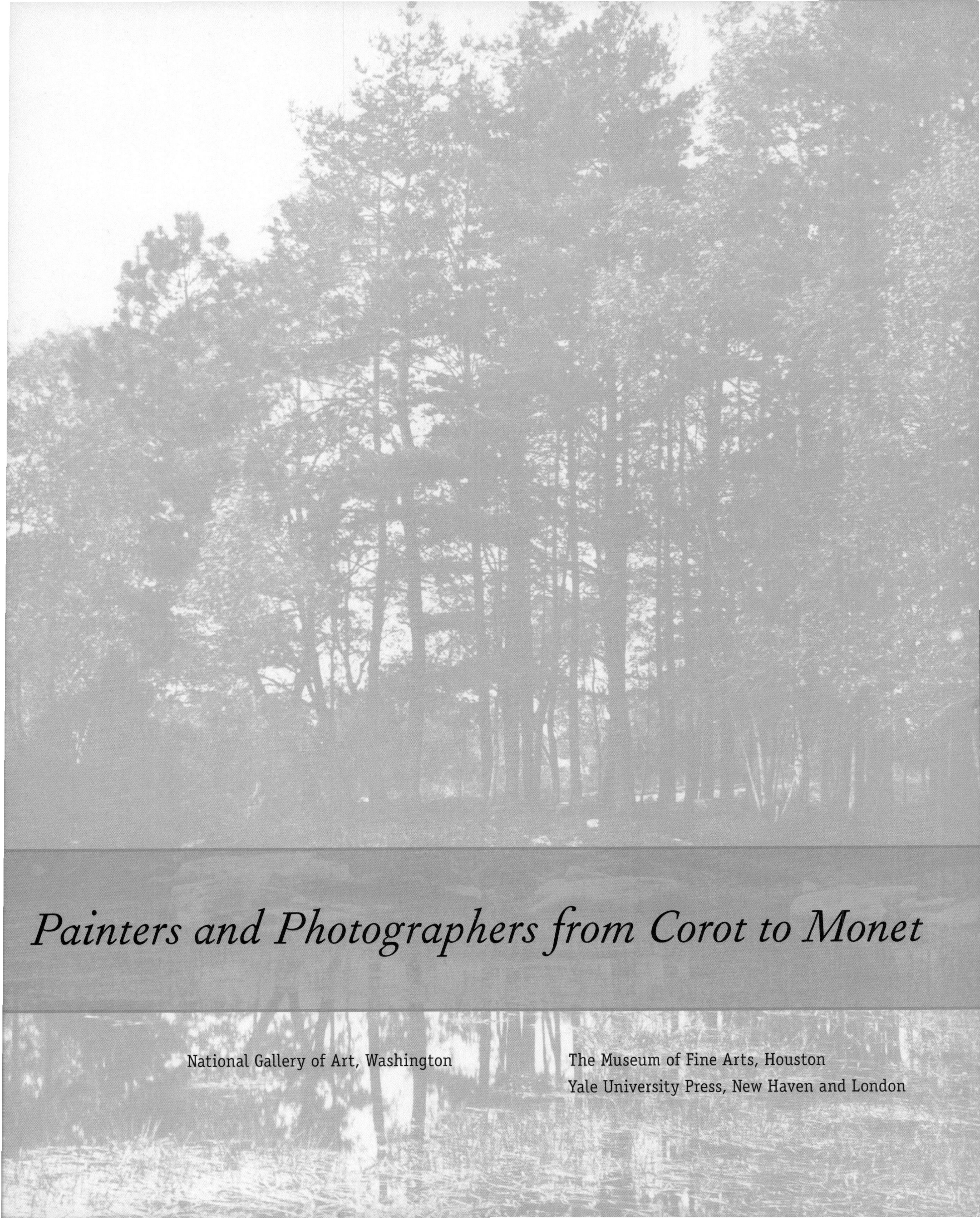

Painters and Photographers from Corot to Monet

National Gallery of Art, Washington

The Museum of Fine Arts, Houston

Yale University Press, New Haven and London

The exhibition in Washington is made possible by The Florence Gould Foundation.

The exhibition in Houston is made possible by grants from the Albert and Margaret Alkek Foundation Exhibition Fund and from the National Endowment for the Arts.

The exhibition is organized by the National Gallery of Art, Washington, in association with the Museum of Fine Arts, Houston.

Exhibition Dates

National Gallery of Art, Washington
March 2 – June 8, 2008

The Museum of Fine Arts, Houston
July 13 – October 19, 2008

10 9 8 7 6 5 4 3 2 1

Produced by the Publishing Office,
National Gallery of Art, Washington
www.nga.gov

Judy Metro, Editor in Chief
Chris Vogel, Production Manager
Wendy Schleicher, Senior Designer
Tam Curry Bryfogle, Senior Editor
Sara Sanders-Buell, Photo Permissions
Mariah Shay, Production Editor

Edited by Mariah Keller, Chicago
Color separations by Robert J. Hennessey

This book was typeset in Fournier MT and ITC Officina Serif by Duke & Company, Devon, Pennsylvania, and printed on PhoeniXmotion Xantur by EuroGrafica, SpA, Vicenza, Italy

---

The hardcover edition is published in association with Yale University Press, New Haven and London.

Yale University Press
302 Temple Street
P.O. Box 209040
New Haven, CT 06520-9040
www.yalebooks.com

Illustrations

FRONT COVER: Augustin Enfantin, *An Artist Painting in the Forest of Fontainebleau* (detail of pl. 1)

BACK COVER: Eugène Cuvelier, *The Forest of Fontainebleau* (detail of pl. 99)

Section openings have been adapted from photographs in the exhibition: title page, pl. 29; Jones essay, pl. 99; plates, pl. 96; Kelly essay, pl. 42; Kennel essay, pl. 90; Aurisch essay, pl. 39; chronology, pl. 32.

Library of Congress Cataloguing-in-Publication Data

Jones, Kimberly (Kimberly A.)
In the forest of Fontainebleau : painters and photographers from Corot to Monet / Kimberly Jones with Simon Kelly, Sarah Kennel, and Helga Aurisch.

p. cm.

Issued in connection with an exhibition held Mar. 2 – June 8, 2008, National Gallery of Art, Washington, and July 13 – Oct. 19, 2008, Museum of Fine Arts, Houston.

Includes bibliographical references and index.

ISBN 978-0-89468-345-9
(softcover : alk. paper)
ISBN 978-0-300-13897-9
(hardcover : alk. paper)

1. Landscape painting, French — 19th century — Exhibitions. 2. Landscape photography — France — Exhibitions. 3. Fontainebleau, Forest of (France) — In art — Exhibitions. I. Kelly, Simon. II. Kennel, Sarah. III. Kessler-Aurisch, Helga. IV. National Gallery of Art (U.S.) V. Museum of Fine Arts, Houston. VI. Title.

ND1356.5.J66 2008
758'.144365074753 — dc22 2007044350

Contents

Foreword

Right Detail of pl. 43

In 1996 the National Gallery of Art mounted the groundbreaking exhibition *In the Light of Italy: Corot and Early Open-Air Painting.* Spanning the years 1780 to 1840 and including artists of diverse nationalities, that exhibition charted the rise and dissemination of plein-air practices that would forever change the art of landscape painting. Although Italy served as the cradle for this new approach, plein-air painting quickly expanded beyond that country's borders as artists returned to their homelands and shared their experiences with friends, colleagues, and students, setting off a quiet but significant revolution in art throughout Europe and the United States.

In the Forest of Fontainebleau: Painters and Photographers from Corot to Monet is, in many respects, a continuation of that narrative, tracking the transmission of this phenomenon in France and the impact it was to have on the development of modern French landscape painting and photography. Here too, Camille Corot is a central figure, a critical link bridging two chapters in the history of plein-air painting. Corot discovered the Forest of Fontainebleau in 1822, three years before his first Italian sojourn. He produced some of his earliest plein-air studies there, then returned in 1829 to explore further the pictorial language of working directly from nature. Thus began a love affair between artist and place that spanned nearly half a century.

Corot was not alone in his deep attachment to the place, however. Other artists, photographers as well as painters, had likewise begun to respond to the allure of the Forest of Fontainebleau. Some, like Corot, who had made the pilgrimage to Italy, found within the precincts of the forest a French surrogate whose topography echoed the rough-hewn terrain they had encountered in the environs of Rome and Naples. Others, perhaps inspired by emergent nationalist sentiment, came to the forest in search of a landscape that was purely, quintessentially French. Despite these disparate and seemingly contradictory objectives, few left disappointed. This was due in no small part to the distinctive character of the Forest of Fontainebleau. While its close proximity to Paris made it a convenient and accessible retreat, its complex topography—which combines magnificent old-growth trees, stark plateaus, and dramatic stone quarries—offered a wealth of motifs to aspiring landscape artists. Fontainebleau encompassed a unique confluence of the beautiful and the sublime, the strange and the familiar, all within the confines of a single forest. It was deemed so remarkable, in fact, that in 1861 a portion of the forest was set aside as a nature preserve, making it the first act of natural preservation in history, more than a decade before the founding of Yellowstone National Park. In the Forest of Fontainebleau, amid ancient oaks and rugged terrain, the practice of plein-air painting took root on French soil and landscape photography became an art. It is the fertile relationship between artists and this unique locale at a crucial point in art history that this exhibition celebrates.

The exhibition owes its conception to Kimberly Jones, associate curator of French paintings at the National Gallery of Art, and was developed in collaboration with Helga Aurisch, associate curator of European art at the Museum of Fine Arts, Houston, and Sarah Kennel, assistant curator of photographs at the National Gallery of Art. Each has written an essay for the catalogue, as has Simon Kelly, associate curator of European painting and sculpture at the Nelson-Atkins Museum of Art.

A major debt of gratitude is owed to our many lenders, both private and institutional in the United States and Europe, who have so graciously agreed to lend their works of art. Without their generosity, this exhibition could not have been realized.

In the Forest of Fontainebleau is made possible in Washington by the generous support of the Florence Gould Foundation. We would like to thank especially John R. Young, president, as well as the trustees of the Florence Gould Foundation for their long-term commitment to the National Gallery of Art and for their continuing support over the past two decades. The exhibition in Houston is made possible by grants from the Albert and Margaret Alkek Foundation Exhibition Fund and from the National Endowment for the Arts.

Earl A. Powell III
Director, National Gallery of Art

Peter Marzio
Director, Museum of Fine Arts, Houston

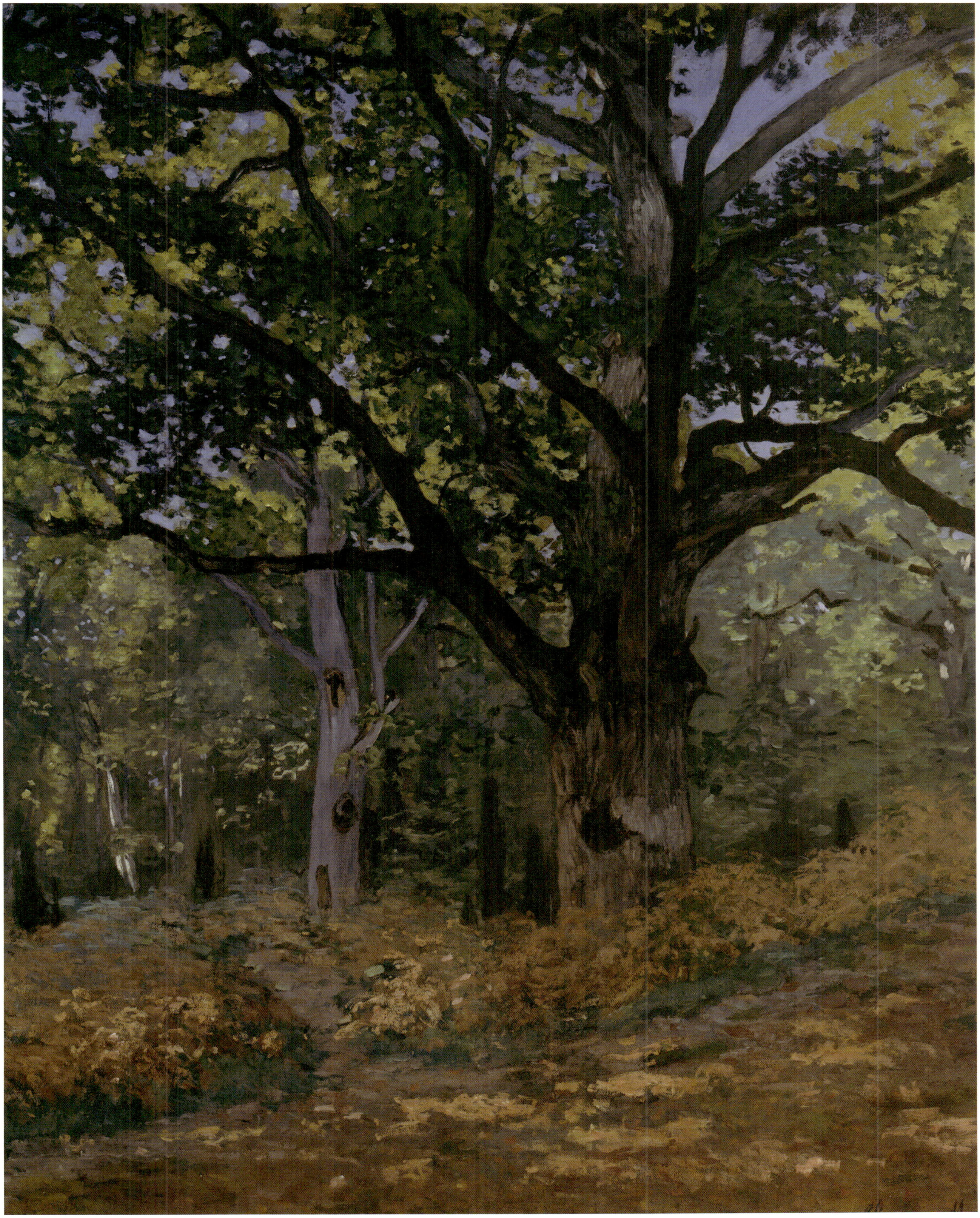

Preface and Acknowledgments

In recent years there has been a renewed interest in mid-nineteenth-century French landscape painting, particularly the work of Barbizon School artists. Antoine-Louis Barye, Jean-Baptiste-Camille Corot, Gustave Courbet, Jean-François Millet, and Théodore Rousseau have all been subjects of monographic exhibitions over the course of the past decade, while other exhibitions — notably those in Munich (1999), Lyon (2002), and Paris (2007) — have focused attention on the Barbizon School and its place within the larger landscape tradition of the nineteenth century. Remarkably, *In the Forest of Fontainebleau* is the first exhibition in the United States since *Barbizon Revisited* (1962) to explore the evolution of modern landscape art in France, from the plein-air practices of Corot and his contemporaries to the most familiar manifestation of that art form, impressionism. It is also the first to consider the place of photography within that narrative.

The Forest of Fontainebleau holds a privileged position in the history of French landscape art, and rightly so. "There is not an artist, among the most celebrated who did not pass by there," Frédéric Henriet observed in 1876, and time has borne out the truth of his statement. From the early 1820s until the early 1870s, the forest was the site of choice among young artists trained in the practice of plein-air painting and active in France. Both sanctuary and subject, the Forest of Fontainebleau served as an open-air laboratory in which artists could carry out their investigation of nature at its purest state, dedicating themselves to the pursuit of its most subtle and ephemeral moods. It became home to an informal and fluctuating artists' colony in the nearby village of Barbizon, where a group of devoted painters gave rise to a new movement that came to be known as "The Barbizon School." Among them were Rousseau and Narcisse-Virgile Diaz de la Peña, who explored and depicted the forest, as well as Millet and Charles-Emile Jacque, who captured the everyday activities of the people living in the surrounding villages.

As the forest's fame increased, so did the number of painters who traveled there, and by the 1850s both French and foreign artists flocked to Fontainebleau and its environs. The forest had become a major site of artistic pilgrimage, and an excursion to Fontainebleau had taken on the obligatory status once associated with the sojourn to Italy. When the future impressionists arrived there in the early 1860s, their presence was both inevitable and ultimately transformative. Years before they would discover Argenteuil, the Forest of Fontainebleau inspired and challenged them, setting the stage for another revolution in the art of landscape painting.

Painters were not the only artists active in the Forest of Fontainebleau, however. As early as 1849, Gustave Le Gray traveled there, producing remarkable photographs of the forest. Other photographers soon joined him, notably Eugène Cuvelier, who was perhaps the most dedicated and sensitive chronicler of the forest and its myriad moods. These artists sought to expand the pictorial syntax of landscape photography, and working side by side with painters, they explored many of the same motifs and shared the same fascination with capturing the transitory effects of light and shadow, weather and season within the confines of the forest. Audacious and experimental, their efforts are analoguous to plein-air painting, reflecting a comparable sensibility and sensitivity in the still nascent medium that underscores the rich and complex dialogue between the two artistic practices. For painters and photographers alike, the Forest of Fontainebleau served as the crucible from which a new modern art was forged.

The National Gallery of Art and the Museum of Fine Arts, Houston, the curators, and the authors of the catalogue would like to thank the many people who have offered valuable information and advice in matters both curatorial and scholarly and who have facilitated the loan of crucial works to this exhibition: Lynne Ambrosini, Nancy Anderson, Glenn M. Andries, Dovinia Angeli, Sylvie Aubenas, Joseph Baillio, Fred Bancroft, Lisa Barro, Graham W. J. Beall, Laura Bennett, James H. Billington, Stephen Bonadies, Marie-Thérèse Caille, Laurence des Cars, Michael Conforti, Tim Craven, James Cuno, Malcolm Daniel, Caroline Durand-Ruel, Anne-Birgitte Fonsmark, Dominique de Font-Réaulx, Josette Galiègue, James Ganz, Bertrand Gautier, Whitney Gaylord, Chantal Georgel, Fabrice Golec, Susan Greenberg, William M. Griswold, Gloria Groom, Torsten Gunnarsson, Violet Hamilton, Dorothee Hansen, William J. Hennessy, Wulf Herzogenrath, Tom Hinson, Rena Hoisington, Perry Hurt,

Charles Isaacs, Eik Kahng, Sheila Klos, Hans Kraus Jr., Mack Lee, Serge Lemoine, Gérard Lévy, David Liot, Russell Lord, François Lorenceau, Linda Lott, Chris Mahoney, Sarah Meister, Marie-Hélène Montout-Richard, Merl Moore, Jane Munro, Monique Nonne, Jennifer Parkinson, Serge Plantereux, Ulrich Pohlmann, Vincent Pomarède, Turner Reuter, Jock Reynolds, Joseph Rishel, Linda H. Roth, Timothy F. Rub, Axel Rüger, Michael Sachs, Marie-Pierre Salé, Alan E. Salz, Polly Sartori, Dr. Hans-Werner Schmidt, Dr. Klaus Schrenk, George Shackelford, John Sillevis, William Stapp, Nancy Thomas, Gary Tinterow, Angus Trumble, Gérard Vallée, Frédéric Valletoux, Charles L. Venable, Lucy von Brachel, Jason Vrooman, Ay Whang-Hsia, Eric Zafran, and John Zarobell.

At the National Gallery of Art we thank Alan Shestack, deputy director; D. Dodge Thompson, chief of exhibitions; Naomi Remes, exhibition officer; Laura Cunningham, assistant for exhibition administration; Susan M. Arensberg, head of department of exhibition programs; Margaret Doyle, assistant curator of exhibition programs; Mark Leithauser, chief of design; Donna Kirk, architect and design coordinator; Bill Bowser, production coordinator; Judy Metro, editor in chief; Chris Vogel, production manager; Wendy Schleicher, senior designer; Tam Curry Bryfogle, senior editor; Mariah Shay, production editor; Sara Sanders-Buell and Ira Bartfield, permissions coordinators for photography; Mariah Keller, freelance editor; Melissa Stegeman, registrar for exhibitions; Kimberly Schenck, head of paper conservation; Ann Hoenigswald, senior paintings conservator; Constance McCabe, senior photograph conservator; Bethann Heighbaugh, associate conservator for loans and exhibitions; Hugh Phibbs, coordinator of preservation services; Steve Wilcox, frame conservator; Jenny Ritchie and Steven Muscarella, matter-framers; Julian Saenz, assistant general counsel; Christine Myers, chief development and corporate relations officer; Patricia Donovan, senior associate for development; Deborah Ziska, chief press and public information officer; Anabeth Guthrie, senior publicist; Neal Turtell, executive librarian; Ted Dalziel and Thomas McGill Jr., interlibrary loan assistants; Lorene Emerson, supervisory photographer; Ken Fleisher, photographer; Andrew Robison, senior curator of prints and drawings; Sarah Greenough, senior curator of photographs; Molly Bloom, staff assistant, department of photographs; Philip Conisbee, senior curator of European art; Virginia Sweet Dupuy, former staff assistant, French paintings; and Michelle Bird, curatorial assistant in the department of French paintings.

At the Museum of Fine Arts, Houston, we extend our thanks to colleagues in various departments, including Edgar Peters Bowron, the Audrey Jones Beck Curator of European Art; Anne Wilkes Tucker, the Gus and Lyndall Wortham Curator of Photography; Teresa Harson and Michelle Packer, European art department; Kathleen Crain and John Obsta, registrar's department; Jack Eby and Bill Cochrane, exhibition design; Karen Bremer Vetter, chief administrator, exhibitions and curatorial; Wynne Phelan, Andrea di Bagno, and Toshi Koseki, conservation department; Diane Lovejoy, publications director, and Phenon Finley-Smiley, graphics manager, and their staffs; Victoria Ramirez, interim education director, and Margaret Mims, public programs manager, education department; Mary Haus, director, communications and marketing, and her staff; Marty Stein and the staff of the Freed Image Library; the staff of the Hirsch Library; and Del Zogg, Works on Paper Study Center. Special thanks go to Cornelia C. Long, chairman, board of trustees; Gwendolyn H. Goffe, associate director, investment and finance; Paul Johnson, associate director, development and membership; and the Brown Foundation Fellows Program at the Dora Maar House, Ménerbes, France, and its director, Katherine S. Howe.

It is with great pleasure that we invite the reader to join us on a journey to this exceptional locale to experience a key moment in the history of art.

Lenders to the Exhibition

Albright-Knox Art Gallery, Buffalo

The Art Institute of Chicago

The Baltimore Museum of Art

Bibliothèque Nationale de France, Paris

Brooklyn Museum

Chrysler Museum of Art, Norfolk

Cincinnati Art Museum

The City of Fontainebleau

Sterling and Francine Clark Art Institute, Williamstown

The Cleveland Museum of Art

The Detroit Institute of Arts

Dumbarton Oaks Research Library and Collections, Washington

The J. Paul Getty Museum, Los Angeles

Mr. and Mrs. Marsh Gibson

Instituut Collectie Nederland, Rijswijk

Hans P. Kraus Jr., New York

Kunsthalle Bremen

Kunstmuseum Winterthur

The Library of Congress

Los Angeles County Museum of Art

Rolf Mayer

The Metropolitan Museum of Art, New York

Middlebury College Museum of Art

The Minneapolis Institute of Arts

Musée d'Orsay, Paris

Musée Départmental de l'Oise, Beauvais

Musée des Beaux-Arts, Reims

Musée du Louvre, Paris

Museum Boijmans Van Beuningen

Museum der Bildenden Künste, Leipzig

Museum of Fine Arts, Boston

The Museum of Fine Arts, Houston

The Museum of Modern Art, New York

The National Gallery, London

National Gallery of Art, Washington

National Gallery of Art Library, Washington

Nationalmuseum, Stockholm

Don Nice

Ordrupgaardsamlingen, Copenhagen

Anthony and Cynthia Petrello

Philadelphia Museum of Art

Private collections

San Diego Museum of Art

John Schlichte Bergen Gallery, Amsterdam, and Jack Kilgore & Co. Inc., New York City

Scully and Osterman Studio

Dietmar Siegert Collection

Southampton City Art Gallery

Staatliche Kunsthalle Karlsruhe

Tel Aviv Museum of Art

Van Gogh Museum, Amsterdam

Victoria and Albert Museum, London

Wadsworth Atheneum Museum of Art, Hartford

The Walters Art Museum, Baltimore

Wilson Centre for Photography, London

Yale Center for British Art, New Haven

Yale University Art Gallery, New Haven

Right E. Jamin, *Fontainebleau* (Paris, 1838). National Gallery of Art Library, Washington

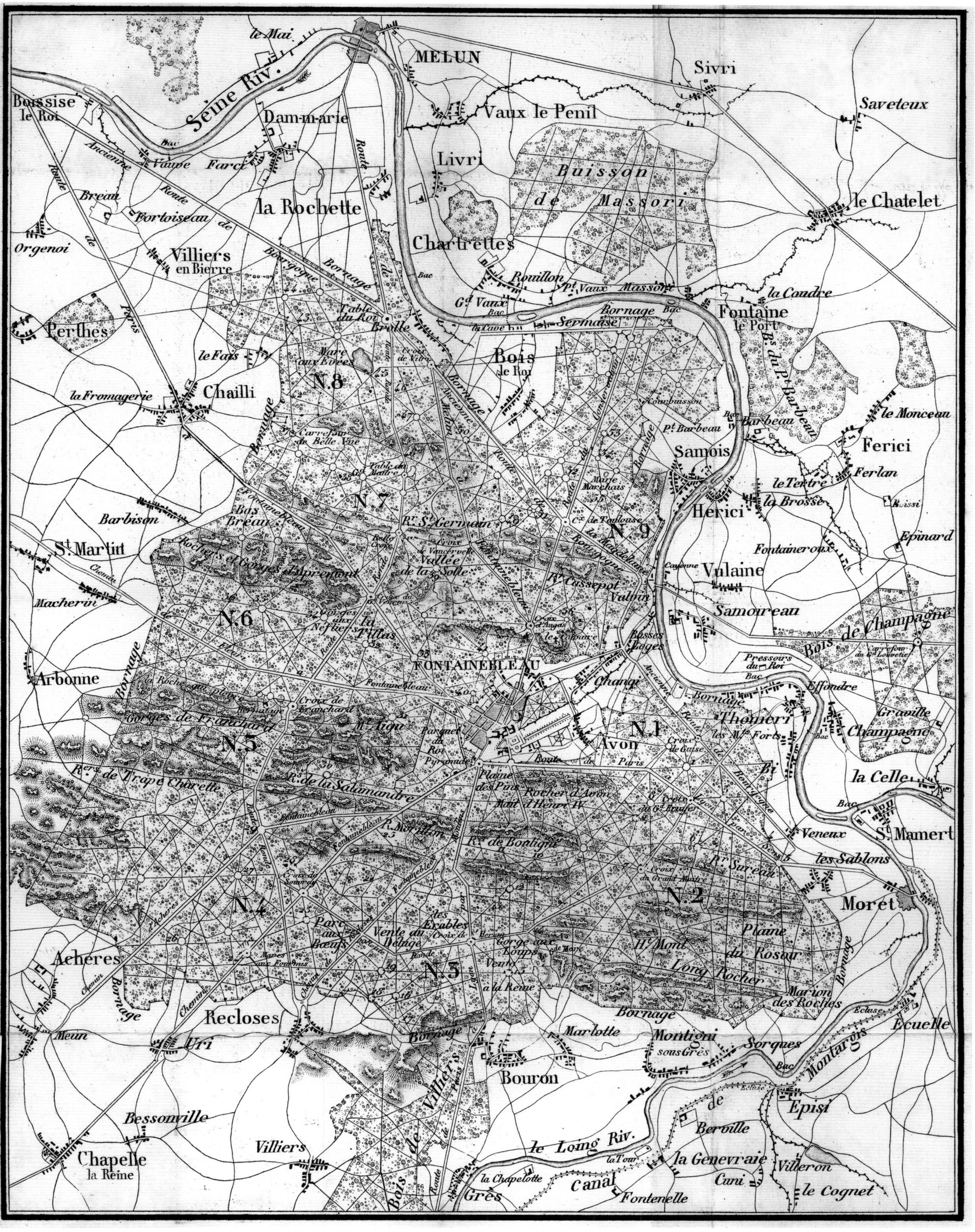
MELUN
Seine Riv.
le Mai
Sivri
Boissise le Roi
Dam-marie
Vaux le Penil
Saveteux
Livri
Farce
Vaupe
Buisson de Massori
la Rochette
le Chatelet
Orgenoi
Villiers en Bierre
Chartrettes
Rouillon
Pt. Vaux Masson
la Condre
Gd. Vaux
Fontaine le Port
Perthes
Table du Roi
Brolle
Sermaise
Bornage
le Fais
Bois le Roi
Mare aux Evées
N.8
Chailli
la Fromagerie
le Monceau
Barbeau
Ferici
Samois
Ferlan
le Tertre
Herici
la Brosse
N.7
Barbison
Bas Breau
Rr. St. Germain
N.9
Epinard
St. Martin
Fontaineroux
Vallée de la Solle
Vulaine
Rr. Cassepot
Valvin
Macherin
Samoireau
N.6
Bois de Champagne
FONTAINEBLEAU
Basses Loges
Changi
Arbonne
Thomeri
Effondre
Gorges de Franchard
Croix de Franchard
Mt. Aigu
N.1
Avon
N.5
Champagne
la Celle
Rr. de la Salamandre
Rocher d'Avon
Mont d'Henri IV
Rr. de Bouligni
Veneux
St. Mamert
les Sablons
N.4
N.2
Moret
Acheres
Parc aux Bœufs
N.3
Plaine du Rosoir
Long Rocher
Marion des Roches
Recloses
Bornage
Marlotte
Montigni sous Grès
Sorques
Ecuelle
Meun
Uri
Bouron
Montargis
Episi
Bessonville
de Beroille
le Long Riv.
Chapelle la Reine
Villiers
Bois de Villiers
la Genevraie
Villeron
la Chapelotte
Canal
Cani
le Cognet
Grès
Fontenelle

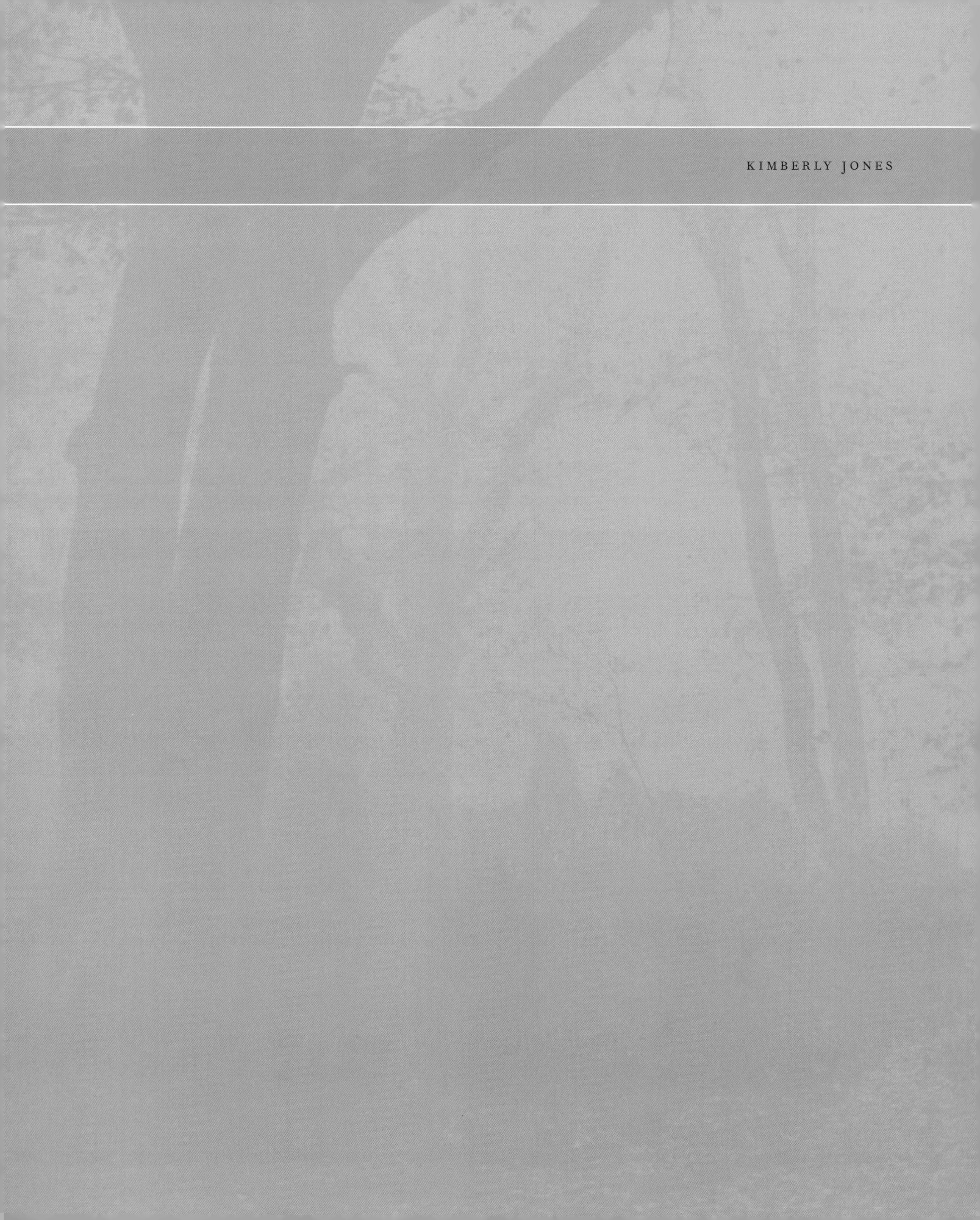

KIMBERLY JONES

Landscapes, Legends, Souvenirs, Fantasies *The Forest of Fontainebleau in the Nineteenth Century*

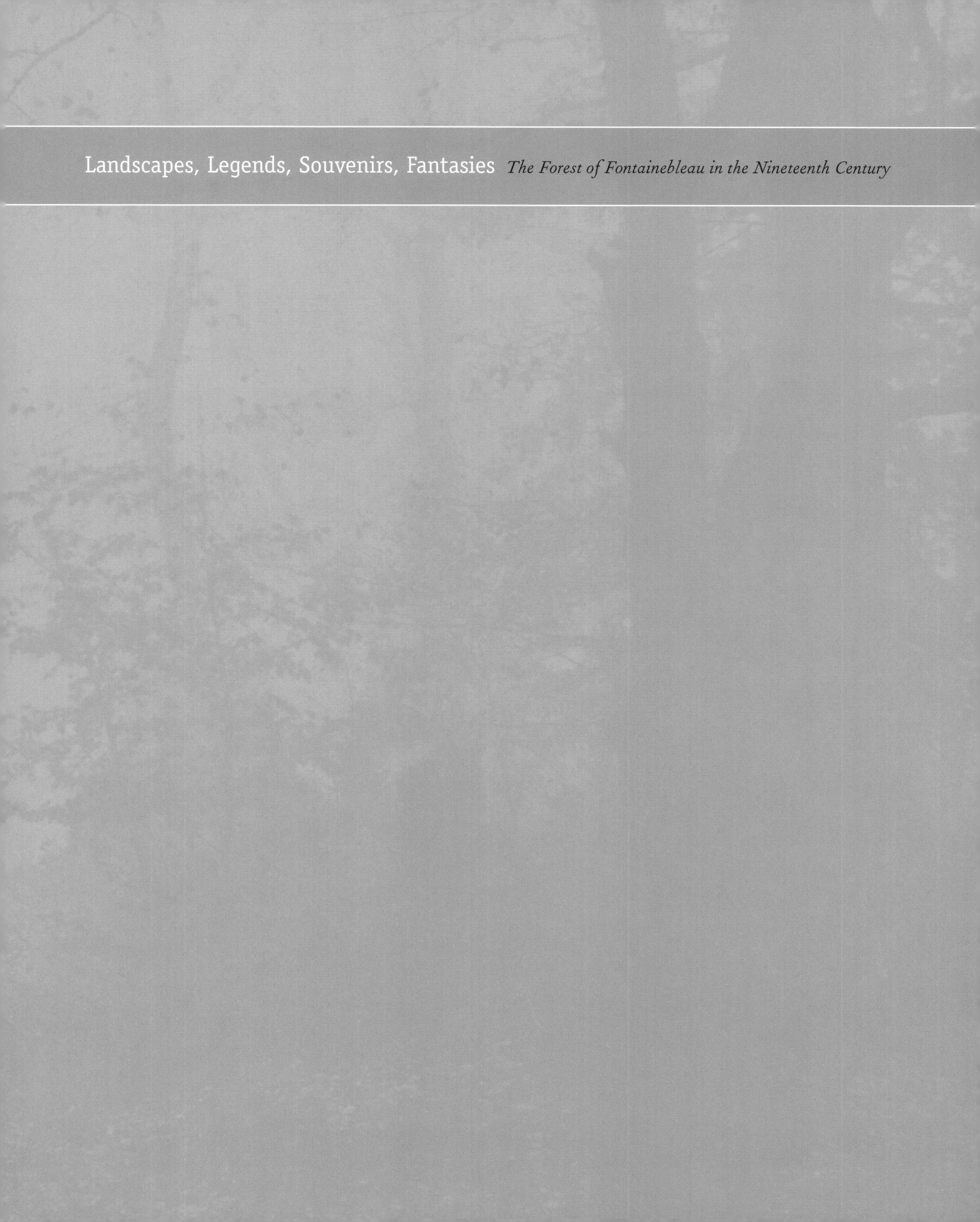

Landscapes, Legends, Souvenirs, Fantasies

The Forest of Fontainebleau in the Nineteenth Century

Right Detail of pl. 40

"Have you ever been in Fontainebleau?" It is with these words that Julia Kavanagh opens her novel *Bessie* (1872).[1] This long-forgotten tale by a relatively obscure British author would seem to have little to offer a modern audience, yet the question Kavanagh posed is one that resonated throughout the nineteenth century. Fontainebleau—or more precisely the Forest of Fontainebleau, the true subject of the narrator's musing—held a singular place in nineteenth-century culture, its mere evocation sufficient to conjure a wealth of images and associations. Once the royal domain and hunting ground of kings and emperors, Fontainebleau is rich with history, stretching back to ancient times. To Chateaubriand, it was the "Desert of the Gauls"; to Théodore Rousseau, it was the home of the Druids. George Sand found echoes of both Switzerland and the Sahara within its precincts, while Victor Hugo considered the Forest of Fontainebleau to be nothing short of a monument.[2] But above all, the Forest of Fontainebleau was home to artists of all nations. Described as the "Parnassus of painters," the "grandam and wet nurse of modern landscape," and "the true school of contemporary landscape," Fontainebleau is uniquely tied to the history of nineteenth-century art, from the romantics to the impressionists and beyond.[3]

Located thirty-five miles south of Paris, Fontainebleau is the largest and most frequented forest in the Paris region, averaging nine million visitors annually.[4] The Forest of Fontainebleau was not always known by that name, however. For much of its history, up until the French Revolution in fact, it carried some variation of the name "Bière," the historical name for the region of the Gatinais that stretched between Melun and Fontainebleau and encompassed the villages of Moret, Arbonne, and Chailly-en-Bière, the latter of which still bears this name.[5] The origin of the name was commonly, albeit erroneously, believed to have derived from a Danish warlord known as Biorn, or Bierra Côte de Fer, who laid siege to Melun in the ninth century and committed unspeakable atrocities upon the local populace, a grim and rather dramatic tale that persisted well into the nineteenth century.[6] The true origin of the name is considerably more mundane and stems from the Medieval Latin *bieria*, meaning "plain": hence its ancient and largely descriptive name *Bieria Sylvia*, or "forest of the plain."

Like Bière, the name "Fontainebleau" presents another curious etymological puzzle. It is not, as earlier historians have suggested, a reference to the beauty of some nearby spring *(fons bellaqueus)* but instead appears to be a derivation of *fontaine de Blaud* and can be found in records dating back to the twelfth century. The meaning of "Blaud" remains uncertain, though the suggestion that it refers to the man or dog who discovered the fountain in the midst of the forest is most often accepted.[7] The two names were subsequently joined by a royal ordinance of 25 October 1573 in which Charles IX officially designated the forest "Bière-les-Fontainebleau."[8]

For all its modern renown, the existence of the forest as a discrete entity is also relatively new. Under the feudal system, the forest was divided into a number of different fiefdoms; Domet indicates that more than twenty such fiefdoms existed at one time. Still other parcels were given to the church, most notably the land ceded for the creation of the hermitage of Franchard in 1194. This longstanding practice had already begun to reverse itself by the eleventh century, when King Robert the Pious began to acquire lands in the forest of Bière for the French crown. An avid huntsman, he is believed to have built the first *rendez-vous de chasse* in the heart of the forest near Fontaine Blaud, the antecedent of the hunting lodge built by Louis VI that eventually became the royal château. Subsequent sovereigns followed the practice of reclaiming the forest for the crown to varying degrees. Some, like Blanche de Castille, purchased fiefdoms, including those at Dammarie and Chailly in 1247, while others, like François I, expanded the crown's holdings in the forest through both acquisition and confiscation.[9] When Henri II signed an edict in 1566 proclaiming the inalienability of the royal domain, he facilitated a process that would continue for the next two centuries.

As the nineteenth century approached, only one enclave, Bois-des-Seigneurs, remained within

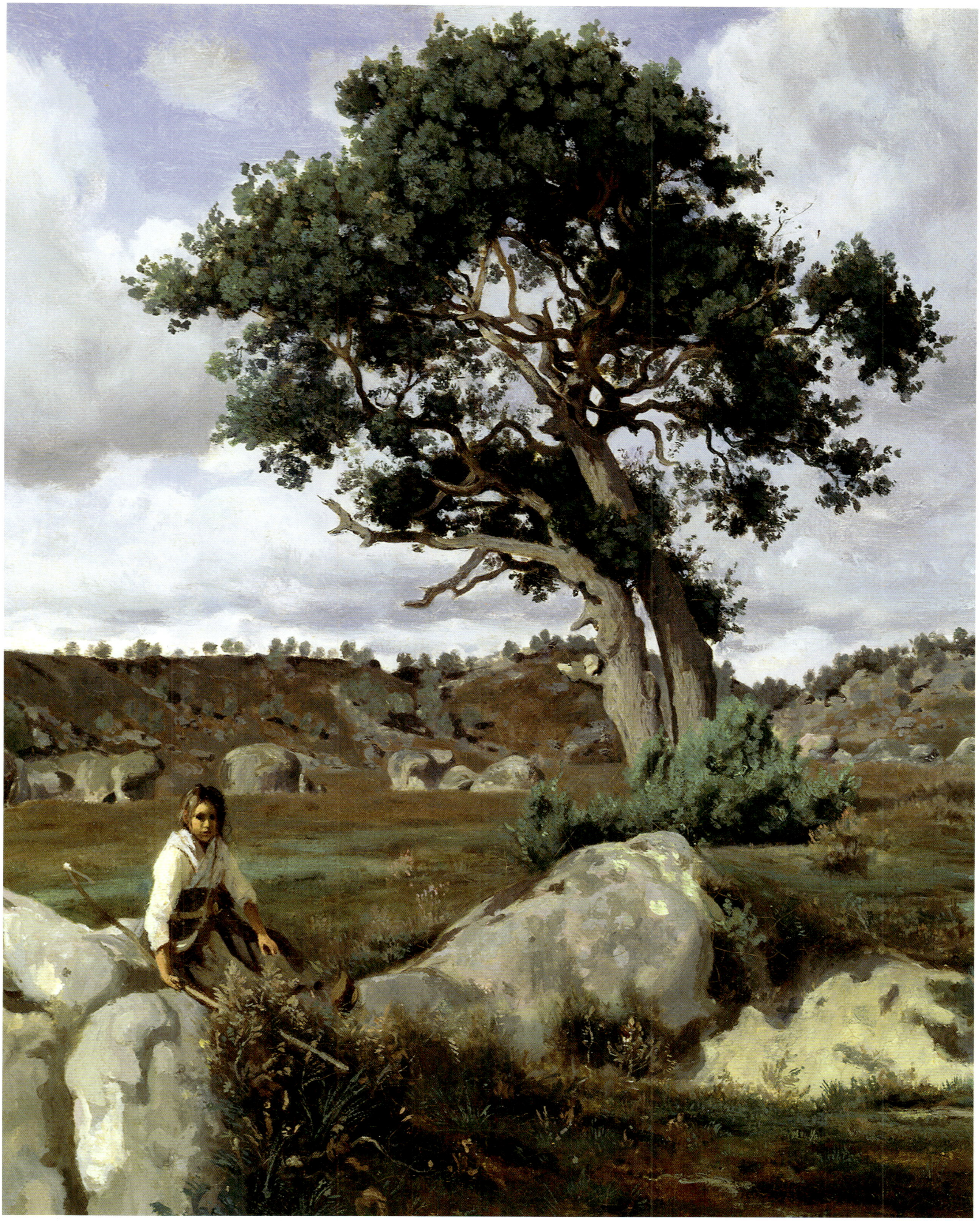

the forest. This would change with the French Revolution when Bois-des-Seigneurs was seized as church property by decree of the National Assembly on 23 October 1790. Declared a *bien national* (national property), the fully restored Forest of Fontainebleau was entered into the *liste civile* along with the Bois de Boulogne, the Bois de Vincennes, the Bois de Sénart, and numerous palaces, including the Louvre, the Tuileries, and, of course, Fontainebleau.[10] Although it was placed under the direct authority of the French state in 1848, in 1853 the Forest of Fontainebleau, which was then estimated to occupy a total of 16,976 hectares, was entered into the *liste civile* of Emperor Napoleon III. It was subsequently restored to the French state by a decree of 6 September 1870, and it remains so today.[11]

The Forest of Fontainebleau differs markedly from other forests in the Ile-de-France region in its sheer size, topography, and the extraordinary variety of vegetation.[12] "On the whole, the forest presents the most diverse appearance and an exceptional mixture of plantings," Jules Clavé remarked in 1863.[13] That is indeed an accurate assessment. The forest is even more distinctive from a purely geological standpoint. It is composed of three basic strata: the plain, which is mostly sand (commonly known as *sable de Fontainebleau*) with an extremely high silica content; large banks of sandstone *(grès)* known as *platières* that rise upward to heights of forty to sixty meters; and plateaus made up of silt *(limon)* and limestone *(calcaire de Beauce)* that are located in the southwest region of the forest at its highest elevation. Further, it is almost completely devoid of water with the exception of a small number of freestanding pools and the occasional stream formed by the accumulation of rainwater.[14] This aridity, surprising given the proximity of the forest to the Seine—which borders it along the northeastern side—is most apparent in the rocky plateaus of the Gorges d'Apremont and Franchard, which are aptly referred to as "deserts" because of their rough-hewn appearance and sparse plant growth.

This unique topography made the forest a site of commercial value, especially during the nineteenth century. Lumber was, of course, its chief commodity. Oak, beech, and later the much-hated, but extremely profitable, pine were cultivated for commercial use. The Forest of Fontainebleau furnished approximately 40,000 cubic meters of wood worth about 400,000 francs per annum, which in turn translated into one million francs on the Parisian market.[15]

Fontainebleau was also an important center for the production of paving stones, an industry that dates back to the fourteenth century.[16] The sheer abundance of sandstone located within the forest, combined with its durability and the relative ease with which the stone can be cut, made it a rich resource for exploitation. At the peak of production in 1829, some 2.9 million paving stones were shipped to Paris, and the forest would continue to provide the majority of paving stones for the French capital throughout the nineteenth century.[17]

Despite such historic and commercial importance, prior to the nineteenth century, the Forest of Fontainebleau was rarely discussed outside of historical texts. Associated with, but ultimately subordinate to, the château that resides deep within its confines, the forest existed almost exclusively as a royal hunting ground. It was, for the most part, ignored and generally viewed less as a locale worthy of contemplation and more as an impediment to travelers journeying to the château. Recounting his journey to the Château of Fontainebleau in 1644, the English diarist John Evelyn famously dismissed the forest, describing it as "so prodigiously encompassed with hideous rocks of whitish hard stone heaped one on another in mountain heights, that I think the like is nowhere to be found more horrid or solitary."[18]

The wildness and unpredictability of the terrain that Evelyn found so displeasing would become a source of fascination for subsequent generations. A half-century later, his countryman Joseph Addison found the forest striking: "It [the Château of Fontainebleau] is situated among rocks and woods that give you a fine variety of savage prospects."[19] Percy Bysshe Shelley and his wife Mary Wollstonecraft Shelley likewise remarked upon this quality when they passed through Fontainebleau in 1814, noting that "the scenery around this palace is wild and even savage.... the hills are low, but precipitous and rough. The valleys, equally wild, are shaded by forests."[20] Twenty years later, Thomas Raikes echoed those sentiments, admiring the forest with its paths "opening at every turn upon the most beautiful pictures of forest scenery, or the wildest views of savage nature. The forest has indeed been called tremendously beautiful."[21]

This insistence on the term "savage" to describe the Forest of Fontainebleau would echo throughout the nineteenth century.[22] Rough, unspoiled, and antediluvian, Fontainebleau was exalted as an example of nature in its purest state, both wild and beautiful by turns, as Raikes observed. In contrast to the more stately forests of the Parisian environs, such as Compiègne and Saint Germain-en-Laye, Fontainebleau's chief virtue was its capacity to startle and surprise. The writer Mary Berry, who traversed the forest in 1790, remarked: "The Forêt of Fontainebleau is one of the most romantic and beautiful parks imaginable, and singular from the large abrupt masses of rocks scattered everywhere in the midst of a flat country."[23] Her choice of the descriptors "romantic," "beautiful," and most notably "singular" reflects the changing sensibility of the age. Where once the unexpected had been considered unattractive, it was now intriguing, compelling, even beautiful. Despite their seeming contrary natures, the sublime and the beautiful coexisted in perfect harmony in the Forest of Fontainebleau.

Of course, not everyone was enamored of the forest. Stendhal in particular, who visited Fontainebleau in 1837, was unimpressed. "The rocks of Fontainebleau are ridiculous," he proclaimed, though he did concede, "in the places where the trees are eighty feet tall, it [the forest] is moving and very beautiful."[24] John Ruskin evoked Evelyn's less-than-flattering assessment in his recollections of his visit in 1842: "The 'hideous rocks' of Fontainebleau were, I grieve to say, never hideous enough to please me."[25]

In 1833, future U.S. secretary of state William H. Seward wrote: "The forest of Fontainebleau is much more imposing in poetry and romance than in reality."[26] This was not an uncommon sentiment, as art and literature shaped many visitors' perceptions of the forest, those of foreigners in particular. Etienne Pivert de Senancour's epistolary novel *Obermann* was one of those literary sources. First published in 1804, *Obermann* chronicles the narrator's exile in Switzerland as well as his youthful excursions in the Forest of Fontainebleau. As the protagonist treks aimlessly through the forest alone, Senancour's descriptions of Fontainebleau are rich and evocative and tinged with sad longing. "I do not orient myself," he recounts in one of his letters. "On the contrary, I stray whenever I can. Often I go in a straight line rather than follow the trails. I make no effort to keep any reference or to know the forest, so that there is always something to discover."[27] In the novel, Senancour established what was to be a central trope of art and literature set within the Forest of Fontainebleau—the solitary man immersed within the perfect solitude of the forest (fig. 1; see pls. 8 and 9). It is an image that resonated throughout the nineteenth century.

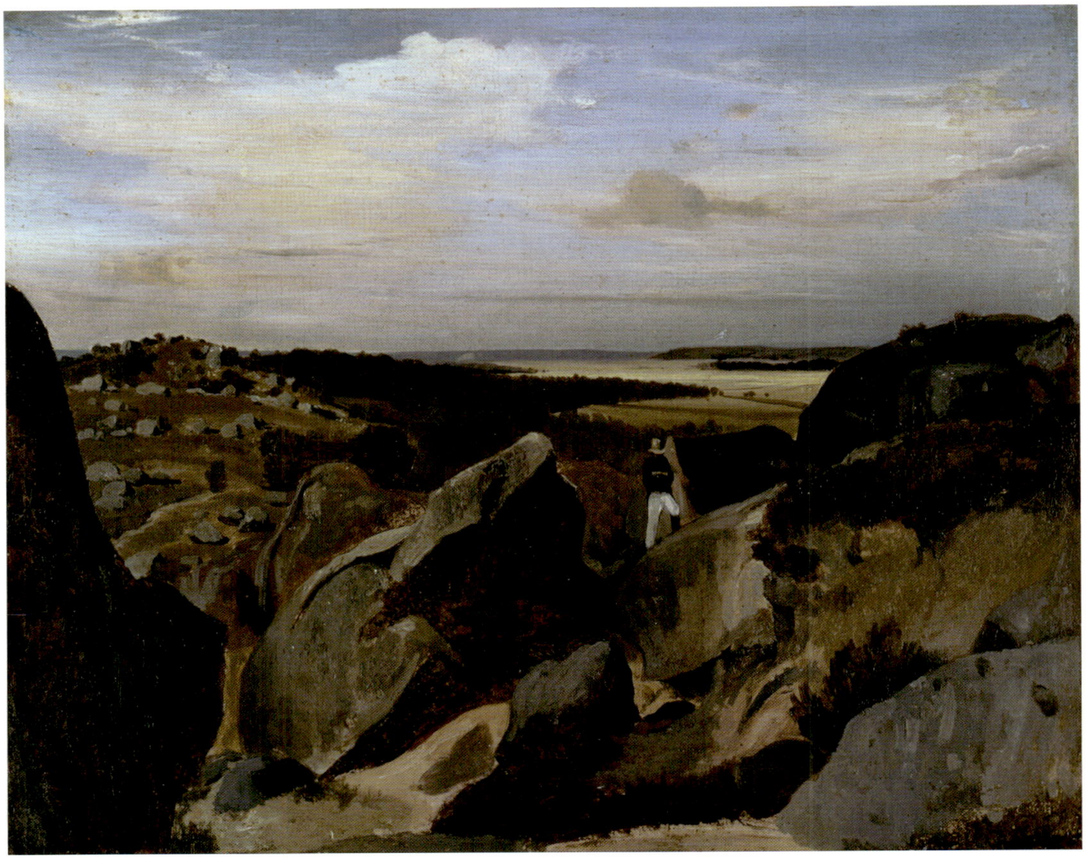

Fig. 1 Jean-Baptiste-Camille Corot, *An Artist Passing through a Chaos of Rocks at Fontainebleau*, c. 1830, oil on canvas, 31.5 × 40.5 cm. Musée d'art et d'histoire, Neuchâtel

Senancour's text was largely ignored when it was first published, but it was subsequently embraced by the romantic literati, who saw in its melancholy narrator a reflection of the age. In 1833, Charles Augustin Sainte-Beuve provided the preface for a new edition of the novel, and the indomitable George Sand wrote a preface that appeared in a number of editions beginning in 1840.[28] Sand herself was a great devotee of both Senancour's novel and the forest in which it was partially set. She is known to have visited the Forest of Fontainebleau as early as 1824 and returned there in 1833, 1837, and 1856.[29] "What a beautiful thing this forest is!" she enthused in 1837, a sentiment that echoes in her later writings, not only in her preface for *Obermann* but also in her novels *La filleule* (1853) and, of course, *Elle et lui*, which includes her own fictionalized account of the nocturnal visit she made to Franchard in the company of Alfred de Musset in August 1833.[30]

Sand's fateful excursion with Musset to the Forest of Fontainebleau was the stuff of romantic legend, inspiring fictional accounts by both writers (*La confession d'un enfant du siècle*, 1836) and, most notably, *L'Education sentimentale* (1869) by Gustave Flaubert. Although published decades after that incident and transposed amid the politically charged days of the revolution in 1848, which toppled the regime of Louis-Philippe, Flaubert's novel is arguably the pinnacle of the romantic fascination with the Forest of Fontainebleau and contains some of the most beautiful descriptions of the forest.[31]

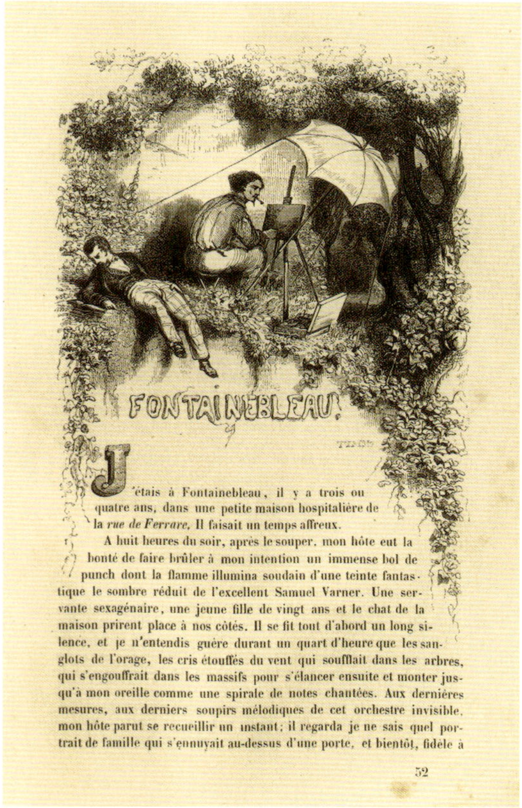
FONTAINEBLEAU.

J'étais à Fontainebleau, il y a trois ou quatre ans, dans une petite maison hospitalière de la *rue de Ferrare*. Il faisait un temps affreux.

A huit heures du soir, après le souper, mon hôte eut la bonté de faire brûler à mon intention un immense bol de punch dont la flamme illumina soudain d'une teinte fantastique le sombre réduit de l'excellent Samuel Varner. Une servante sexagénaire, une jeune fille de vingt ans et le chat de la maison prirent place à nos côtés. Il se fit tout d'abord un long silence, et je n'entendis guère durant un quart d'heure que les sanglots de l'orage, les cris étouffés du vent qui soufflait dans les arbres, qui s'engouffrait dans les massifs pour s'élancer ensuite et monter jusqu'à mon oreille comme une spirale de notes chantées. Aux dernières mesures, aux derniers soupirs mélodiques de cet orchestre invisible, mon hôte parut se recueillir un instant; il regarda je ne sais quel portrait de famille qui s'ennuyait au-dessus d'une porte, et bientôt, fidèle à

52

Fig. 2 Vignette in Charles Nodier and Louis Lurine, *Les environs de Paris: Paysage, histoire, monuments, moeurs, chroniques et traditions* (Paris, 1844), 403

In one of the most famous scenes, Flaubert described the lovers' excursion into the forest. Just as they set out from Bas-Bréau by carriage, they encounter a painter "in a blue smock working at the foot of an oak tree, with his paint box on his knees."[32] This was hardly an unexpected sight. This is the other iconic image associated with the Forest of Fontainebleau: the artist ensconced in the forest with easel, paint box, and parasol at hand as he diligently works "from the motif" (fig. 2).

Few artists worked in the forest prior to the nineteenth century. While the name Fontainebleau had long been associated with art, it was connected first and foremost with the art of the Renaissance: Primaticcio and Fiorentino and the other painters and sculptors who decorated the château that François I had built within the forest. It was the Château of Fontainebleau not the forest that drew artists within its precincts. It was not until the eighteenth century that artists had begun to venture into the forest with purpose. Jean-Baptiste Oudry, Simon Mathurin Lantara, and Lazare Bruandet all worked there, as did less-familiar artists like Jean-François Hue, who has the double distinction of exhibiting the first pure landscape of the forest at the Paris Salon as well as being the first to choose the forest as the subject for his reception piece to the Academy.[33] Others soon followed: Jean-Joseph Bidauld was there in 1783, as was the Belgian artist Jean-François Le Gillon.[34] Eventually, more paintings of the forest began to appear on the walls of the Salon, including those by Bruandet, Le Gillon, and Louis Gadbois, but Fontainebleau still remained largely undiscovered in the early years of the nineteenth century. In fact, between the years 1781 and 1819, only eighteen works depicting the Forest of Fontainebleau were shown at the Salon, fewer than one per exhibition; however, this was soon to change.

In his *Le guide du voyageur à Fontainebleau* (fig. 3), Charles Rémard advised: "The landscape artist can also come and make studies in the forest. Trees and rocks in all kinds of forms will provide abundantly for the practice of pencil or brush, whether he interests himself in some of these objects individually or wishes to group several of them together."[35] Rémard was not the only author to propose the Forest of Fontainebleau as a worthy arena

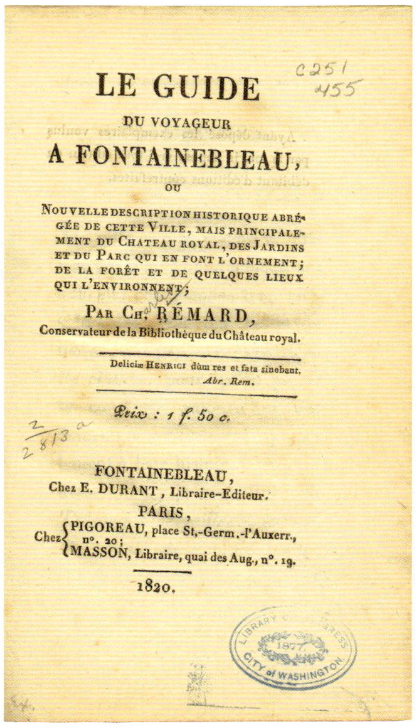
LE GUIDE
DU VOYAGEUR
A FONTAINEBLEAU,
OU
NOUVELLE DESCRIPTION HISTORIQUE ABRÉGÉE DE CETTE VILLE, MAIS PRINCIPALEMENT DU CHATEAU ROYAL, DES JARDINS ET DU PARC QUI EN FONT L'ORNEMENT; DE LA FORÊT ET DE QUELQUES LIEUX QUI L'ENVIRONNENT;
PAR CH. RÉMARD,
Conservateur de la Bibliothèque du Château royal.
Deliciæ Henrici dùm res et fata sinebant.
Abr. Rem.
Prix : 1 f. 50 c.
FONTAINEBLEAU,
Chez E. DURANT, Libraire-Editeur.
PARIS,
Chez PIGOREAU, place St.-Germ.-l'Auxerr., nº. 20; MASSON, Libraire, quai des Aug., nº. 19.
1820.

Fig. 3 Charles Rémard, *Le guide du voyageur à Fontainebleau* (Fontainebleau, 1820). The Library of Congress

for the aspiring landscape painter. In 1806, François-Hippolyte Paillet had also counseled artists to go to Fontainebleau, as had Jacques-Antoine Dulaure in 1825.[36]

Yet all of the texts from the period ultimately echo the sentiments already espoused by Pierre-Henri de Valenciennes in his celebrated treatise on landscape painting, *Eléments de perspective pratique, à l'usage des artistes* (1800): "the forests of France are another vast field offering detail studies for the landscape artist . . . those of Ardennes, Compiègne, Fontainebleau, Villers-Cotterets and Navarre."[37]

Valenciennes was a pivotal figure in the development of plein-air painting in France. He advocated the practice of working directly from the motif in order to gain a truer understanding of nature and its fleeting effects. Even though for Valenciennes *études*, as such spontaneous sketches were known, were simply a means to an end rather than finished works themselves, his underlying principles of close observation and immediacy of response were to have a profound impact on landscape practice for generations to come.[38]

Achille-Etna Michallon, who had studied with Valenciennes at the Ecole des Beaux-Arts, took Valenciennes' philosophy to heart, embracing both his advocacy of open-air painting and his recommendation of working in the Forest of Fontainebleau (see pl. 34). Michallon encouraged his students to do the same. The most famous of these students was, of course, Jean-Baptiste-Camille Corot. It was almost certainly under Michallon's guidance that Corot first journeyed to the Forest of Fontainebleau, beginning a relationship between artist and place that would span five decades.

Michallon's tutelage was brief, cut short by the artist's death, and Corot subsequently entered the atelier of Jean-Victor Bertin, who had been one of Michallon's teachers as well as a pupil of Valenciennes. The older and more established painter was renowned for his historical landscapes that were faithful to the classical tradition. Nevertheless, Bertin advocated open-air practice. He himself had produced a number of relatively informal paintings of the environs of Paris and, like Michallon, advised his students to do the same.[39]

Painted shortly after entering Bertin's atelier, Corot's sketch of a shattered tree trunk in the Forest of Fontainebleau (dated October 1822) is among the artist's earliest known works (pl. 35).[40] Hearkening back to Michallon's earlier sketch, the painting is very much in keeping with Valenciennes' own studies of trees (fig. 4), even as it acknowledges Bertin (between 1816 and 1824, Bertin published *Recueil d'etudes d'arbres*, a collection of tree studies designed for artistic instruction).[41] Corot's inexperience is apparent in the painting; the brushwork is clumsy and there is little sense of spatial recession, but it is clear that he benefited both from Bertin's influence (see fig. 5) and from his time spent in the Forest of Fontainebleau (see pl. 2).

Corot was not the only student in Bertin's atelier to take to the forest. Antoine-Félix Boisselier, Jules Coignet, François-Edouard Bertin (no relation), and Théodore Claude Félix Caruelle d'Aligny also worked

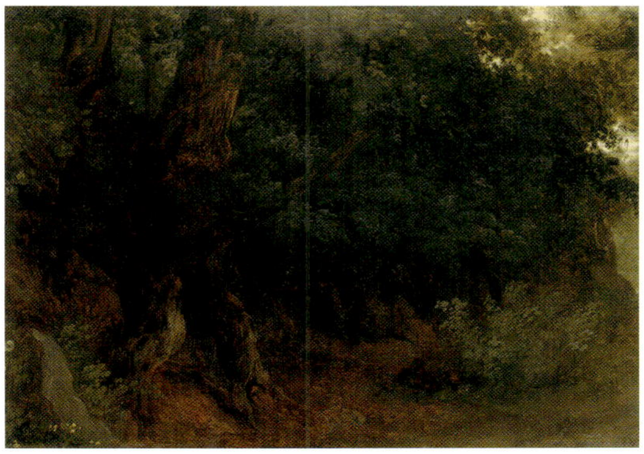

Fig. 4 Pierre-Henri de Valenciennes, *Tree Trunk, Roots, and Leaves*, late eighteenth/early nineteenth century, oil on paper, 23.7 × 33.5 cm. Musée du Louvre, Paris

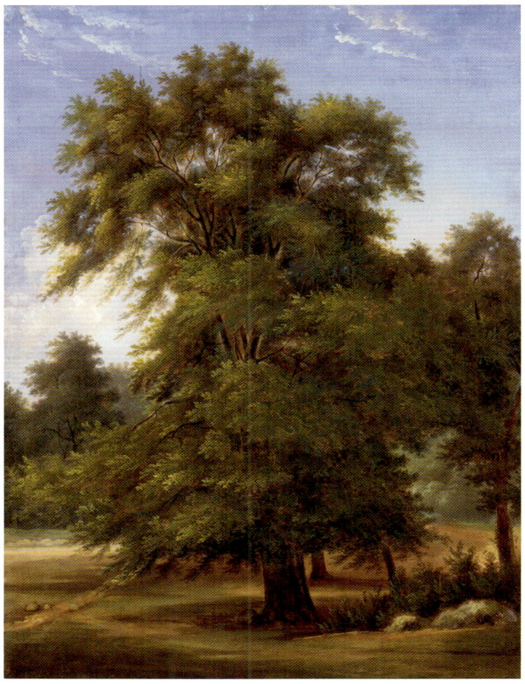

Fig. 5 Jean-Victor Bertin, *Study of a Tree*, c. 1800–1805, gouache, 50.5 × 39.7 cm. Los Angeles County Museum of Art, Wallis Foundation Fund in memory of Hal B. Wallis and Graphic Arts Council Fund

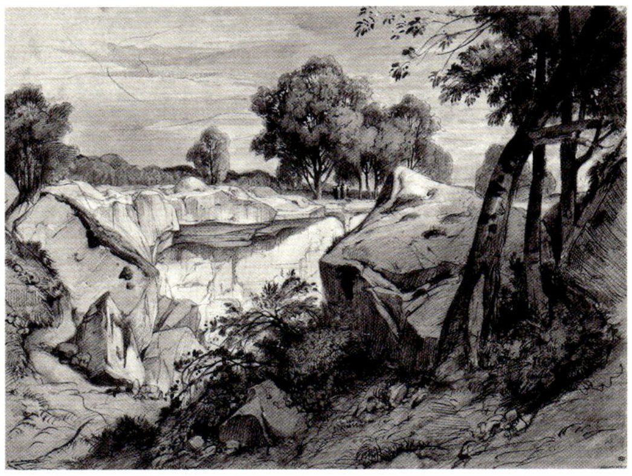

Fig. 6 François-Edouard Bertin, *Fontainebleau Landscape*, c. 1830, pen, brown ink, watercolor, graphite, and wash on paper, 40.8 × 54.4 cm. Musée du Louvre, Paris

there (see pls. 8, 45, 52, and 54; fig. 6). Aligny in particular would develop a lifelong attachment to the Forest of Fontainebleau and would produce some sixty paintings and fifty drawings of the forest over the course of his career.[42] A number of other artists also worked in Fontainebleau at this time, including Jacques-Raymond Brascassat, Alexandre Desgoffe, Richard Parkes Bonington, Augustin Enfantin, and the brothers Auguste-Xavier and Robert-Léopold Leprince (see pls. 1, 3, 25, 41, 46, 49, and 53). Even Théodore Rousseau, who would become one of the giants of the next generation of Fontainebleau artists, passed through the forest in 1828/1829, years before he discovered the village of Barbizon (see pl. 50). They were the first generation of artists to embrace the Forest of Fontainebleau fully as their own, and their growing presence reflects a nascent shift as Fontainebleau began to challenge Italy's undisputed position as the premier center for open-air painting on the Continent.

A sojourn in Italy had long been de rigueur for any aspiring artist, but the country's eminence as the center of open-air painting was of relatively recent vintage, dating to around 1780 when landscape artists from across Europe began traveling to Italy in growing numbers.[43] For many of these artists, it was not the museums or the palaces that most drew their attention; it was the countryside around Naples and the Roman *campagna* that offered stunning vistas and distinctive terrain. Equally important was the presence of a vibrant artistic community that allowed for the exchange of ideas and information. It was a dynamic environment in which artists flourished, learning from nature and each other. Not surprisingly then, artists did not abandon Italy entirely with the discovery of Fontainebleau. Corot made the obligatory pilgrimage there in September 1825 and remained for three years. During that time, he became a close associate of Aligny and François-Edouard Bertin, both of whom were Bertin's students, and he also became acquainted with Brascassat, Coignet, Léon Fleury, and André Giroux.[44] He may also have encountered Enfantin and Louis-Auguste Lapito, both of whom traveled to Italy in the mid-1820s. What is most striking about this, of course, is the fact that all of these artists made their way to Fontainebleau either before or after their Italian sojourns, leading Moreau-Nélaton to call Fontainebleau "a branch office of Italy."[45]

His description was apt. By the late 1820s, Fontainebleau had indeed begun to rival Italy, even giving rise to its own informal community of artists centered in Chailly (fig. 7). The choice of Chailly was largely a pragmatic one; on the road between Paris and Fontainebleau, Chailly was relatively accessible and could offer lodging, thanks to the presence of a number of inns that serviced travelers passing through on the stage or mail coaches. From Chailly, artists would go out into the forest alone or, more often, in small parties to sketch from the motif as Valenciennes and his disciples advocated. Stamati Bulgari, who was a student of Jacques-Louis David and traveled to Chailly in July 1821, recounted venturing into the forest in the company of a fellow artist, equipped for a day's work out of doors: "In one hand he held a large painting canvas; in the other, a pike for fastening his parasol while he paints; on his back he carried a paint box and easel in a knapsack."[46] This image is echoed in a number of contemporary paintings that evoke both the camaraderie and the sense of discovery fundamental to the experience of open-air painting in Fontainebleau (fig. 8; see pls. 1 and 3).

Some years later, H. Mion would comment on this community of artists at Chailly: "For some time, artists have adopted the sojourn to Chailly in

Fig. 7 Auguste-Xavier Leprince, *Village Street with Diverse Figures (Road from Paris to Chailly)*, 15 September 1825, sketchbook (Album Leprince Anne-Xavier-8, folio 52), graphite on paper, 10 × 16 cm. Musée du Louvre, Paris

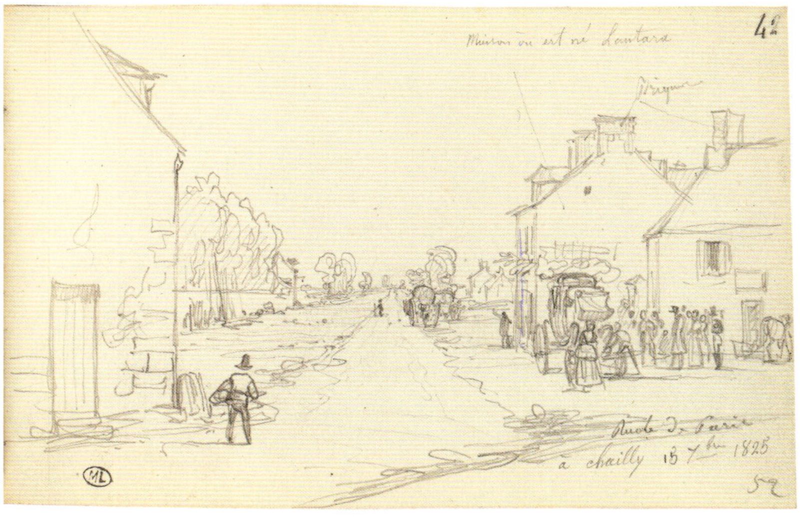

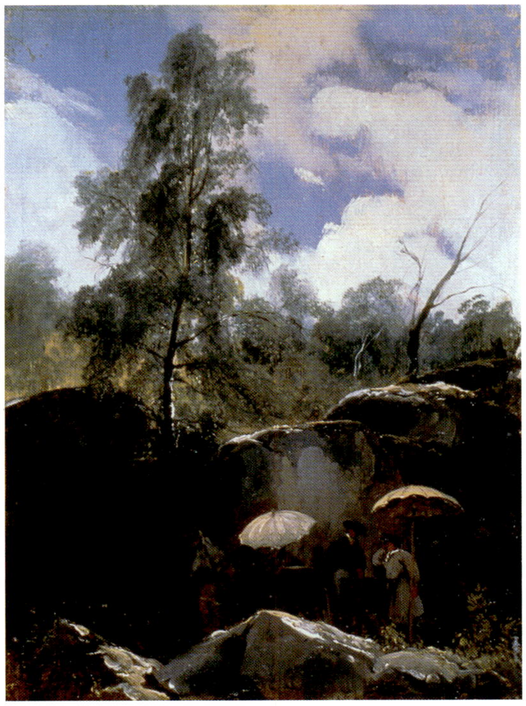

Fig. 8 Jules Coignet, *Painters in the Forest of Fontainebleau*, c. 1825, oil on canvas, 23.5 × 17.5 cm. Musée départemental de l'Ecole de Barbizon, Auberge Ganne

order to study the admirable forms of the old trees and the rustic irregularities of the forest's terrain.... Soon they settle into place, shaded by a large parasol. Nearby artists pass by, offer an observation; but they speak only a few words because the sun moves rapidly, because the sun's effects that they wish to capture with their brush disappear; all their attention is concentrated upon their canvas; it's not the moment for leisurely chats or drawing room gossip."[47]

It was in Fontainebleau that open-air painting became a truly French phenomenon, taking root on French soil amidst the rocks and oaks of the forest. By the 1830s, a new generation of artists had begun to gravitate to the Forest of Fontainebleau, artists who, in contrast to Corot and many of his contemporaries, had not made the pilgrimage to Italy. Chief among them was Théodore Rousseau, a regular visitor to the forest throughout the 1830s and 1840s, beginning with his first extended sojourn at Chailly from November 1833 to February 1834.[48] Louis Cabat was at work there by 1835, and Narcisse-Virgile Diaz de la Peña began to frequent Fontainebleau in 1836, making his debut at the Salon the following year with the first of many Fontainebleau subjects.[49] By 1841, Antoine-Louis Barye was also there, as was Gustave Courbet.[50] Yet there is one notable change from years past, namely the shift away from Chailly to the nearby village of Barbizon, which had become the center of the community of artists.[51]

"Barbizon is nothing remarkable; to speak plain and frankly, it is fair to say that it's a rather ugly hamlet, dependent of the commune of Chailly, composed of a single street," commented one contemporary guidebook (fig. 9; see pls. 65 and 69).[52] Based on this unflattering description, the village of Barbizon seems to have been an unlikely locus for the popular artists' colony it became; however, it did boast other charms, chief among them the Auberge Ganne. This establishment in its most basic form dates to 1824 when François Ganne, the village tailor, and his wife Edmée, the village grocer, first opened their home to visiting artists.[53] Recognizing the need for more substantial accommodations, they subsequently acquired a large barn, transforming it into the two-story inn that bore their name. The Auberge Ganne catered specifically to an artistic clientele, offering simple, dormitory-style accommodations that were both inexpensive and very congenial. For the modest sum of three francs per day—the price varied depending on length of stay, with a discount given to long-term guests—a visitor received lodging, dinner (including wine and bread), and a lunch packed in a little cloth sack that the artist could take with him when he went into the forest to paint from the motif.[54]

In Henry Murger's novel *Scènes de campagne; Adeline Protat* (1854), the character Père Protat recounts the virtues of Barbizon and its inn to the painter Lazare: "Go to the other side—Chailly, or Barbizon. The trees there are more beautiful than here.... You can lodge at Père Ganne's; everyone

Fig. 9 Narcisse-Virgile Diaz de la Peña, *Cottages at Barbizon*, c. 1838–1839, oil on canvas, 25 × 32.5 cm. Private collection, courtesy of Brame and Lorenceau, Paris

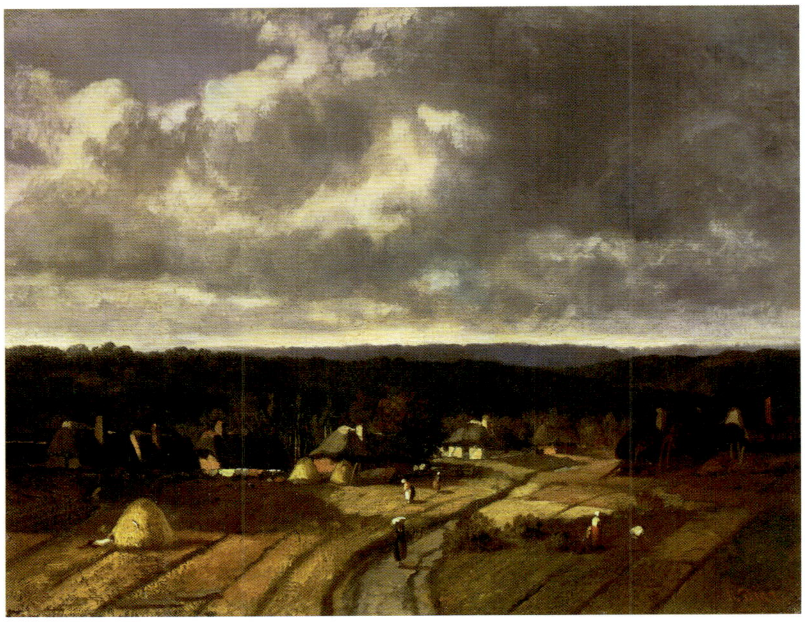

goes there. You'll meet friends."[55] Murger rightly identified the twin charms of Barbizon: proximity to striking landscape motifs and a thriving artistic community based at the Auberge Ganne. The inn's registry reads like a "Who's Who" of nineteenth-century artists: Corot, Aligny, Brascassat, Rousseau, Diaz, Barye, and Cabat were all guests there, as were Honoré Daumier, Charles Daubigny, Alexandre Decamps, François Français, Jean-Léon Gérôme, Eugène Laveille, and Constant Troyon among others.[56] Several of those artists eventually settled in Barbizon on a more or less permanent basis; Rousseau rented a house on the Grand Rue beginning in the summer of 1847 (fig. 10), and Jean-François Millet and Charles-Emile Jacque both settled there in June 1849. Diaz, Barye, Daubigny, Karl Bodmer, and Georges Gassies all had residences on the Grand Rue. They were to become the established and tight-knit nucleus of this burgeoning artists' colony, and the Auberge Ganne served as their lively portal and way station to the forest.[57]

In his article "Les auberges illustrées" (1853), Albert de la Fizelière remarked that "Barbizon has given birth to a new science of painting."[58] La Fizelière's use of the word "science" here is illuminating, for it underscores the growing emphasis on naturalism, which is the hallmark of what became known as "the Barbizon School."[59] For the group of artists who colonized Barbizon, Fontainebleau was more than an open-air studio; it was a laboratory in which they examined the subtle shifts in time of day, season, and atmospheric change with an almost scientific rigor.

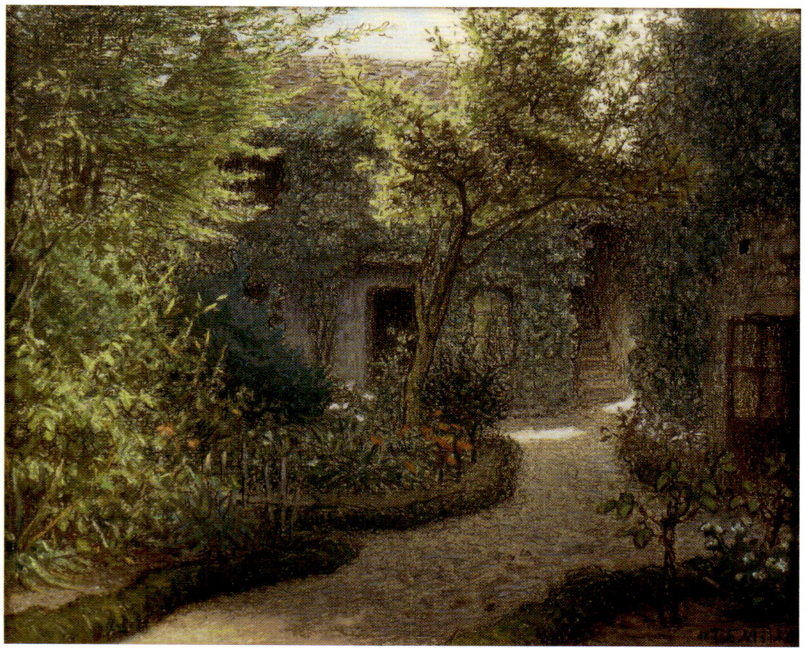

Fig. 10 Jean-François Millet, *Théodore Rousseau's House at Barbizon*, 1868, pastel, 25 × 31 cm. Brame and Lorenceau, Paris

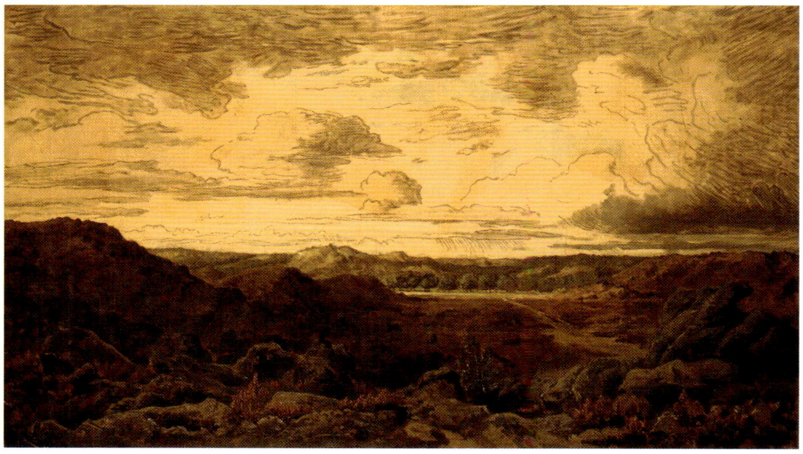

Fig. 11 Théodore Rousseau, *The Gorges d'Apremont*, c. 1859, oil on canvas, 79 × 143 cm. Ny Carlsberg Glypotek, Copenhagen

"At all hours, in all seasons, Fontainebleau always offers impressions that penetrate the human soul and excite a lively poetry," Théophile Thoré wrote in 1847.[60] Artists embraced that sentiment, none more so than Rousseau, who returned repeatedly to his preferred sites (the Gorges d'Apremont and Belle-Croix were particular favorites). He depicted them over and over under diverse conditions, including fog, rain, and snow, and at varying times of day, chasing nature at its most ephemeral (fig. 11; see pl. 101).[61]

A contemporary caricature depicting a group of artists heading into the forest to work offers an intriguing echo of the artists' dedication. Strapped to their backs is the expected artist's paraphernalia—paint box, parasol, and luncheon—but, in addition, they each carry not one but four canvases for the "four customary studies" of morning impression, midday impression, underbrush, and sunset (fig. 12). That this was not entirely exaggeration is evidenced in the works exhibited at the Salon. From 1833 to 1875, twenty-nine autumnal landscapes, seventeen winter or snow scenes, fifteen sunsets, and nineteen morning landscapes—all set within the Forest of Fontainebleau—were shown at the Salon. Years before Monet discovered Argenteuil and the impressionists held their first exhibition, the painters of Fontainebleau had already begun devoting themselves to the pursuit of the transitory moods of nature. Perhaps then it is no surprise to find the impressionists in Fontainebleau as well. Monet, Bazille, Renoir, and Sisley all traveled to the forest in the mid-1860s, the next generation of open-air artists carrying forward the lessons of the previous generation.

By the mid-nineteenth century, artists and writers found themselves sharing the forest with another category of visitor: the tourist. Despite

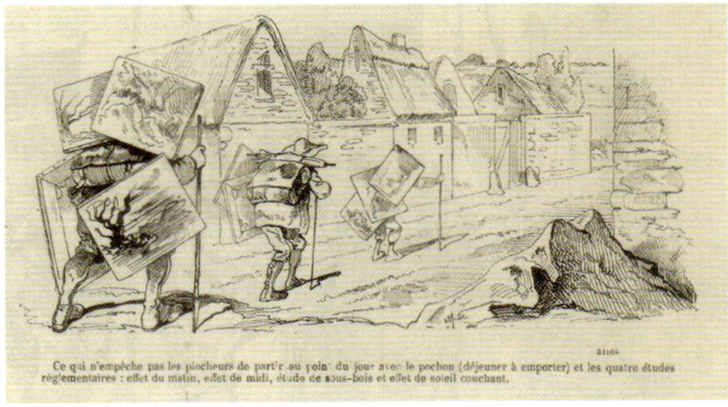

Fig. 12 G. La Fosse, *Caricature of Artists Heading for the Forest of Fontainebleau,* from "Train de plaisir à Fontainebleau," *Le journal amusant,* no. 994 (18 September 1875): 2

its proximity to Paris, traveling to Fontainebleau was a fairly time-consuming activity. There were a number of methods for making the excursion, including private carriage, stagecoach, or the mail coach, which transported both mail and travelers along major routes, stopping along the way to change horses and allow passengers the opportunity to disembark and take food and drink.[62] Visitors also had the option of traveling on a steamboat that ferried visitors between Paris and Fontainebleau via the Seine. Unfortunately, none of these methods was especially rapid, and a traveler could expect a journey of anywhere from six to eight hours depending on the mode of transport, point of departure, and number of intermediary stops.[63]

The introduction of the railway radically transformed the way in which visitors could experience the forest and opened it to a wider audience. The Paris-Corbeil branch of the Paris-Orléans line, which opened in 1840, brought visitors within the vicinity of Fontainebleau (fig. 13), but it was not until 1849, when the Paris-Tonnerre section of the Paris-Lyon rail line was inaugurated, that visitors could travel directly by rail from the capital to the forest, transforming a full day's trek into an easy jaunt.[64] "One hour five minutes," the advertisements proclaimed, enticing visitors with the speed and effortlessness of the journey.[65] During the summer, when attendance was at its peak, eight trains operated daily between Paris and Fontainebleau.[66] By 1856, the number of daily trains had risen to twelve, and by 1867 there were sixteen trains a day between the months of May and November. In the year 1857 alone, some 135,877 visitors passed through the Fontainebleau station.[67]

Given both the popularity and profitability of Fontainebleau as a railway destination, it is no surprise that the first *trains de plaisir* were introduced in 1850, just one year after the rail line was established. Relatively inexpensive, these trains transformed the tourist trade by making daylong excursions beyond Paris and its direct environs both practicable and affordable to the general public. The enormous

Fig. 13 Itinerary map from Paris to Fontainebleau, 1842, 45.4 × 66 cm. Private collection

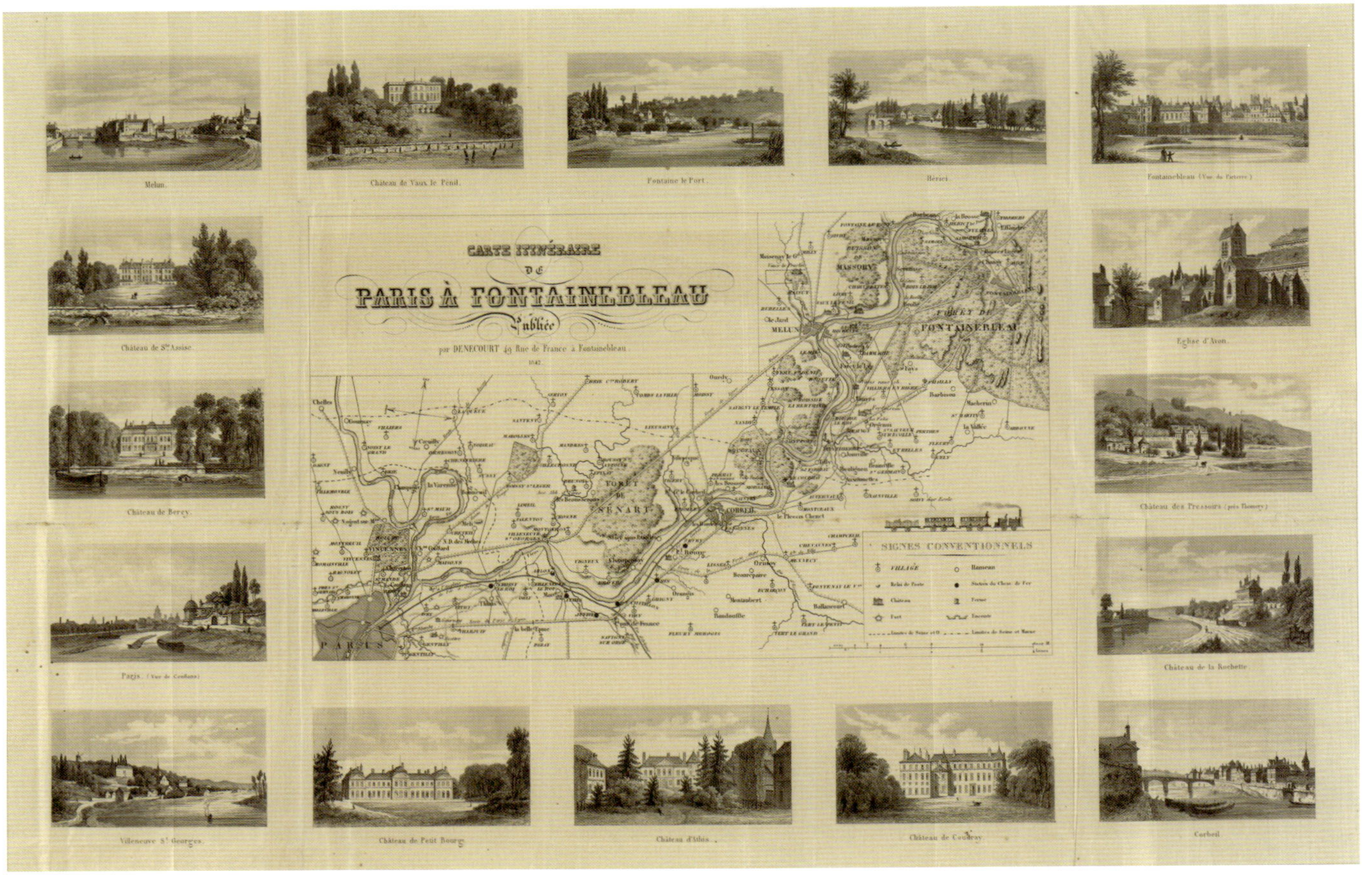

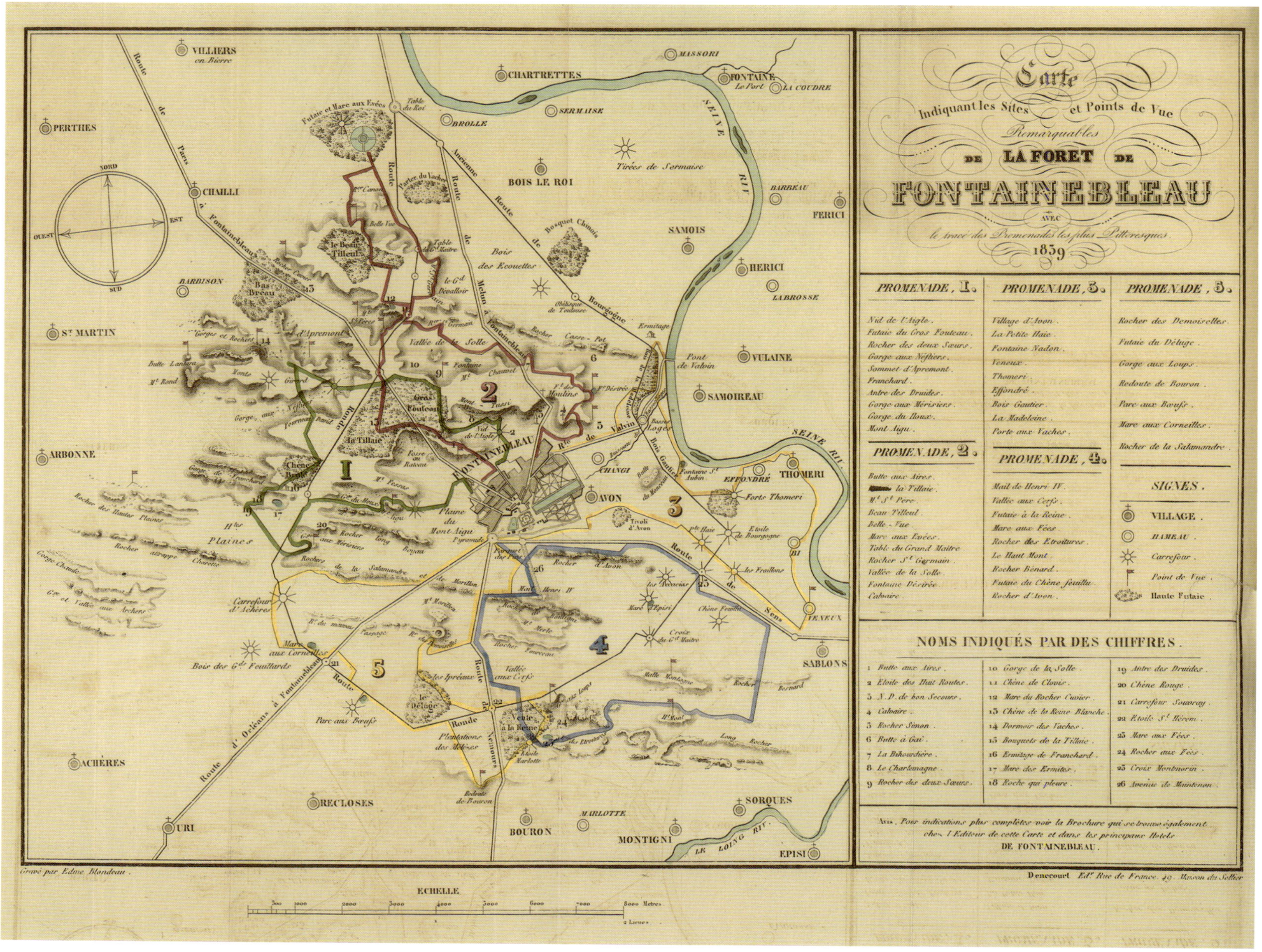

appeal of these excursion trains brought difficulties of another kind, as departure quays on Sunday mornings were transformed into scenes of chaos, with passengers jostling for a place on the crowded trains.[68] Such inconveniences, however, were trifling. For the Parisian seeking to escape the bustle of Paris for the relative tranquillity of nature, the *trains de plaisir* were a godsend.

The allure of the Forest of Fontainebleau as a tourist destination was not merely tied to issues of proximity and accessibility; there were after all a number of other forests in the environs of Paris. But Fontainebleau had two advantages: the forest itself, with its distinctive rough-hewn beauty and rich historical associations, as well as a tireless champion in the form of Claude-François Denecourt. It is not an exaggeration to say that no other individual had a greater impact on the Forest of Fontainebleau during the nineteenth century. Denecourt almost single-handedly transformed the physical landscape of the forest, even as he promoted a new, highly romanticized vision of Fontainebleau, one that was crafted to appeal to a mass audience. Denecourt's enterprise — for there is no other term that truly describes both the scope and intent of his undertaking — was highly controversial, earning him both detractors and ardent supporters, but there is no denying the profound mark he left upon the forest.

Fig. 14 Map identifying the remarkable sites and viewpoints of the Forest of Fontainebleau, 1839, 30.8 × 40.6 cm. Private collection

Following his father's death and his mother's subsequent remarriage, Denecourt's family moved to a small town at the foothills of the Vosges. There he worked as a guide for the travelers who hired carriages from his uncle. In 1809, he enlisted in the army, serving until a leg wound forced his retirement in 1812. He reenlisted, albeit briefly, in 1814 but was wounded once more at Verdun. Upon hearing of Napoleon's return from exile in 1815, he attempted to reenlist a third time but was thwarted by his old injuries. He eventually took a modest position in the department of war administration, and in 1832, after fourteen years at Versailles, he was transferred to Fontainebleau but was dismissed soon after. Embittered by those events, Denecourt found solace and a vocation in the forest. Namely, he devoted himself to celebrating the beauty of the Forest of Fontainebleau and rendering it accessible to visitors both through his words and through the physical transformation of the forest itself.[69] To this end, Denecourt dedicated himself to that most popular of literary forms: the guidebook.[70]

Although such texts already existed, including Rémard's *Le guide du voyageur à Fontainebleau* (1820) and Jamin's *Fontainebleau, ou notice historique et descriptive sur cette résidence royale* (1834), the focus of early Fontainebleau guidebooks is invariably the royal château, with the forest treated almost as an afterthought, if at all. One exception is Jamin's *Quatre promenades dans la forêt de Fontainebleau* (1837), which provided both the inspiration and the model for Denecourt's own endeavors.[71] Jamin's influence is apparent in the first of Denecourt's many guidebooks devoted to the forest, *Guide du voyageur dans le palais et la forêt de Fontainebleau*.[72] Published in 1839, it draws on Jamin's work even as it expands on it. Along with the accompanying map, it presents five promenades, each one associated with a different area of the forest. The promenades identify the sites most worthy of admiration, with an eye toward the motifs and viewpoints that would most appeal to artists (fig. 14). "The forest of Fontainebleau, this charming travelers' rendezvous, this vast artists' studio . . . offers such a variety of surprises that the painter, full of admiration, won't know where to stop his paintbrush," Denecourt proclaimed in the 1840 edition.[73] While the artist might feel overwhelmed by possibilities, Denecourt was more than happy to guide and counsel.

The Denecourt guides are both numerous and varied and include not only longer, more complete guides (figs. 15 and 16) but also less expensive guides devoted to a single promenade, which he published under the title *Les délices de la forêt de Fontainebleau*.[74] More than three dozen titles published under Denecourt's name exist, some in multiple editions. The most popular is his *L'Indicateur de Fontainebleau*, which had been published in no fewer than seventeen editions by the time of Denecourt's death in 1875.[75] Always attuned to his potential audience, Denecourt even produced an English-language edition in 1856, a nod to the increasingly international audience that had begun to frequent the forest.[76]

Denecourt's guidebooks set the standard for such publications for the remainder of the nineteenth century, and elements of his work (such as the maps so painstakingly produced with his collaborator F. Hardy or the *sentiers* [trails] he established in the forest) found their way into other competing publications.[77] For example, Adolphe Joanne, in his *Guide de Fontainebleau*, makes liberal reference to Denecourt's work, using it as the basis for his own more polished and richly illustrated editions.

The guidebooks were only one part of Denecourt's overall strategy. What made his enterprise so audacious, and ultimately so enormously successful, was the manner in which he packaged and promoted the Forest of Fontainebleau to a mass audience, literally from the ground up. In lieu of simply recounting the history of the forest and identifying

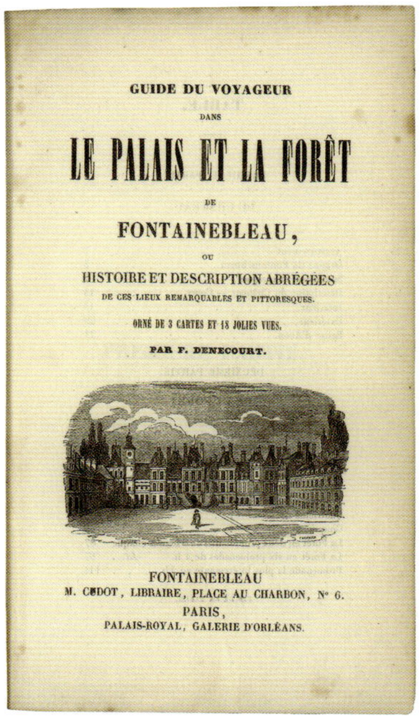
GUIDE DU VOYAGEUR
DANS
LE PALAIS ET LA FORÊT
DE
FONTAINEBLEAU,
OU
HISTOIRE ET DESCRIPTION ABRÉGÉES
DE CES LIEUX REMARQUABLES ET PITTORESQUES.
ORNÉ DE 3 CARTES ET 18 JOLIES VUES.
PAR F. DENECOURT.
FONTAINEBLEAU
M. C[illegible]DOT, LIBRAIRE, PLACE AU CHARBON, N° 6.
PARIS,
PALAIS-ROYAL, GALERIE D'ORLÉANS.

Fig. 15 Claude-François Denecourt, *Guide du voyageur dans le palais et la forêt de Fontainebleau* (Fontainebleau, 1843). Private collection

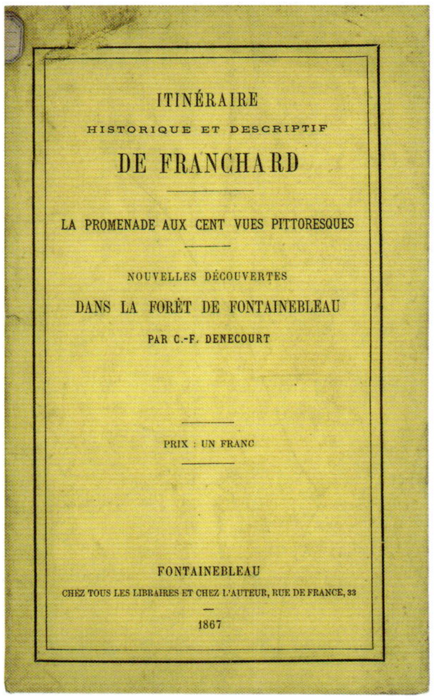
ITINÉRAIRE
HISTORIQUE ET DESCRIPTIF
DE FRANCHARD
LA PROMENADE AUX CENT VUES PITTORESQUES
NOUVELLES DÉCOUVERTES
DANS LA FORÊT DE FONTAINEBLEAU
PAR C.-F. DENECOURT
PRIX : UN FRANC
FONTAINEBLEAU
CHEZ TOUS LES LIBRAIRES ET CHEZ L'AUTEUR, RUE DE FRANCE, 33
1867

Fig. 16 Claude-François Denecourt, *Itinéraire historique et descriptif de Franchard: La promenade aux cent vues pittoresques. Nouvelles découvertes dans la forêt de Fontainebleau* (Fontainebleau, 1867). Private collection its most remarkable sites, Denecourt peddled his own unique vision of the Forest of Fontainebleau, one in which every rock, tree, and clearing was a place of wonder, in which history and fantasy, nature and art merged into an extraordinary, if fictitious whole.

Like his predecessors, Denecourt began by singling out the most famous sites in the forest, including the most dramatic vistas and the oldest and most venerable trees. Many of them were well known long before Denecourt arrived at Fontainebleau. Some, such as La Roche Qui Pleure, had been singled out for their distinctive appearances; others, such as the Mail d'Henri IV, boasted historical associations; and still others, like the Rocher des Deux Soeurs, were the stuff of local legends.[78] But Denecourt went further still by "discovering" new and previously unrecognized wonders. He sought out unusual rock formations and imposing oak trees that were centuries old and christened them with grandiose names, imbuing them with a pseudohistorical import. Not surprisingly, Denecourt also chose to celebrate France's history: the names Pharamond and Charlemagne became associated with two of the oldest oak trees in the forest (fig. 17);[79] and Henri IV and his minister of finances, the Duke of Sully, were commemorated with a pair of oaks that purportedly had once sheltered them during a storm in the midst of a hunting party, a tale that is absent from his *Guide du voyageur* of 1840 but is present in the 1845 version.[80] Other trees bearing evocative names like Goliath, Majestueux, and Les Deux Frères had no claim to fame beyond their striking appearance.[81]

New marvels swelled the rolls in short order. By 1845, Denecourt was touting an extensive litany of ancient trees worthy of admiration, including Trois-Hercules, the Superbe, the Hardy, the Fouchu, the Impérieux, the Nestor, the Rustique, the Briarée, and the Neptune, while historical and modern figures, such as Marie-Antoinette, Napoleon, and even the poet Pierre-Jean de Béranger, were likewise enshrined.[82]

The notable sites continued to multiply, their nomenclature becoming increasingly outlandish and capricious as the years passed and Denecourt's enterprise expanded. Artists were a particular favorite of Denecourt. There were trees named for Giulio Romano, Lebrun, and Girodet and rocks named for Claude-Henri Watelet, Jean Goujon, and Valentin de Boulogne. Poussin lent his name to a belvedere, Claude Lorrain to a gorge, Meissonier to a grotto, and Delacroix to an oasis. Every tree, rock, and vantage point of even nominal interest was graced with a name, connotation, or unique identity unto itself as Denecourt gave free rein to his not inconsiderable imagination. A fantastic outcropping of rocks became the Passage de Cyclopes, a rock with an odd imprint became the Pas de Diable, and a ponderous block of sandstone became the Hippopotame, Léviathan, or Poire des Druides depending on Denecourt's fancy.[83] Poets, writers, politicians, and military heroes joined the ranks of the great historical figures. In Denecourt's fantastical realm, Charles VII could flank Dagobert, Montesquieu could stand beside Schiller, and Shakespeare could keep company with Spartacus.[84] That few of these figures had ever entered the forest was inconsequential. Denecourt appropriated their glory and bequeathed it to his beloved forest, much to the delight of the tourists who visited in ever growing numbers (fig. 18).

In his novel *L'Education sentimentale*, Flaubert recounted what would have been a fairly typical carriage ride through the forest to see the glories of Fontainebleau: "After breakfast, they were led to an open carriage. They left Fontainebleau at a point where several roads diverged, then climbed at a walking pace up a sandy road amidst a wood of small pines. The trees became larger; the coachman saying from time to time 'There are the Siamese Twins, there is the Pharamond, the Bouquet-du-Roi . . .' never omitting any of the famous sites and sometimes even stopping so that they would be sufficiently admired."[85]

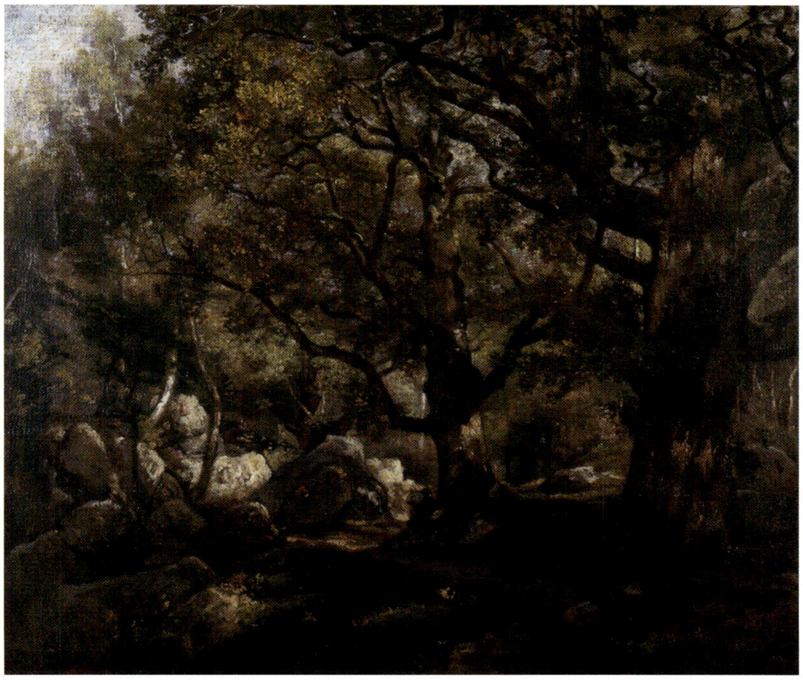

Fig. 17 Constant Dutilleux, *Le Charlemagne*, c. 1860–1861, oil on canvas, 54.5 × 65.5 cm. Musée des Beaux-Arts, Arras

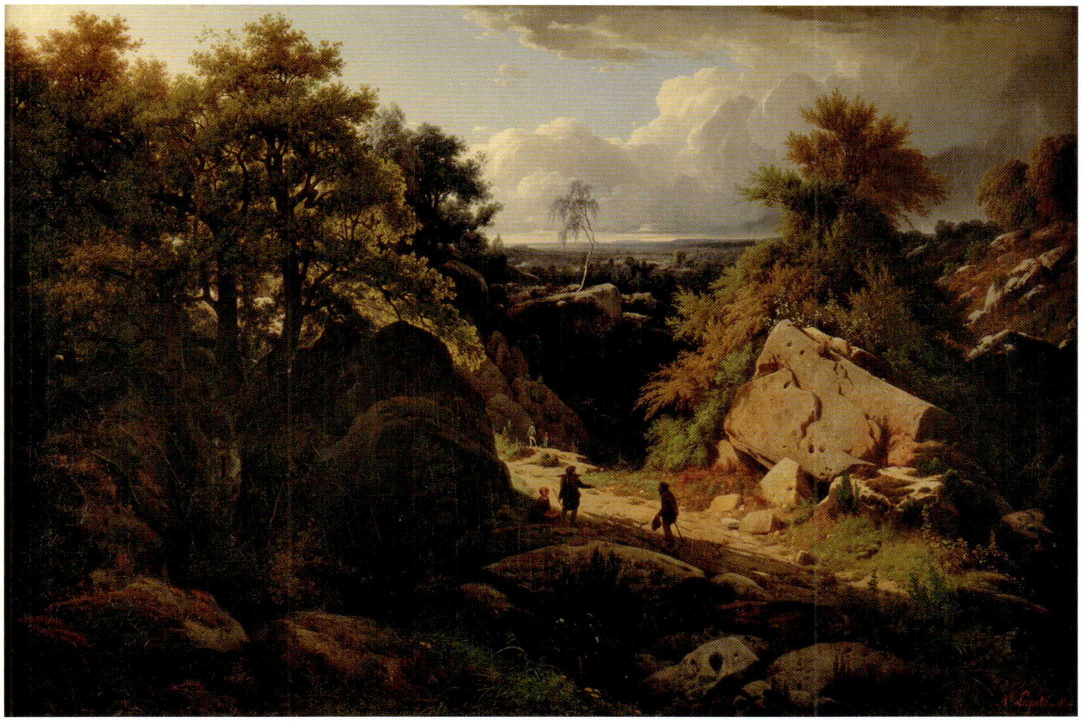

Fig. 18 Louis-Auguste Lapito, *View of the Forest of Fontainebleau, "Les Quatre Fils Aymon,"* 1846, oil on canvas, 108 × 163 cm. Musée Paul Dini, Villefranche-sur-Saône (Dépôt du Musée du Louvre)

This process of identifying and naming sites of interest was merely part of a larger agenda. Denecourt did not merely wish to introduce the wonders of the Forest of Fontainebleau, he literally wanted to guide, even control, the manner in which they were experienced. To this end, in 1842 Denecourt established his first *sentier* (trail) in the forest, a promenade through Mont Chauvet.[86]

The creation of these sentiers is perhaps Denecourt's most lasting and controversial contribution to the forest. By 1850, he had already expanded the number of promenades to eight, plus an excursion.[87] Over the course of his self-imposed career, Denecourt established three hundred kilometers of sentiers throughout the forest.[88] More than simple trails that provided visitors access to the forest, the sentiers were designed specifically with an eye to beauty, with the intention of providing the maximum aesthetic experience. Part historian, part tour guide, Denecourt was the master architect of the typical visitor's perception of the Forest of Fontainebleau. Put in more direct terms, Denecourt was an artist, and the Forest of Fontainebleau was his creation. He molded and shaped the visitor's experience; the small blue arrows he placed throughout the forest to guide visitors were like bold brushstrokes against an otherwise virgin canvas.

Denecourt was adamant that only by following his sentiers precisely and completely could the visitor experience the forest properly:

It is with a certain method, a certain art that one undertakes to penetrate within this vast, this inextricable labyrinth and be able to find oneself. This art, we possess, we humble guide: we have learned it from twenty years of study and laborious research; we have learned it by planning, by tracing all these delightful promenades that one can travel today; we have learned it by adding a thousand new sites, a thousand charming perspectives to these promenades, practically all of them made accessible by us, at our expense.[89]

In many respects, Denecourt was the very antithesis of the romantic ideal presented in *Obermann*. Whereas Obermann explored the forest at random, prizing unexpected discovery over familiarity, Denecourt insisted on rigorous adherence to a preestablished route, dictating the manner in which the landscape should be experienced. Thus, even though his enterprise exploited romantic notions of nature, his underlying principle was fundamentally anti-romantic.

Denecourt's name is forever linked with the Forest of Fontainebleau. Julia Kavanagh gave a nod to his influence in her novel *Bessie*. "The whole forest belongs, not to the Crown, as you might imagine, but to an old soldier," recounts one of the characters, M. de Luisgnan. "He took possession of them. This oak he called Pharamond, that beech he named Alexandre Dumas: and so, toying with literature and history, he peopled this ancient forest with the dead and the living and made it his own."[90]

Denecourt's presence was indeed pervasive—and arguably invasive. Along with the creation of his sentiers, Denecourt introduced a number of other monuments into the landscape. The most distinctive of these was the Fort de l'Empereur (later renamed the Tour Denecourt), which was inaugurated on 23 November 1853 by Emperor Napoleon III and Empress Eugénie (fig. 19).[91] Built on the western summit of the Rocher Cassepot, the fort provided an exceptional vantage point for viewing the forest. Still other monuments seem remarkably gratuitous: the Fontaine Sanguinède, for example, a "pseudo fontaine," as Félix Herbet described it, which was constructed in 1852 near the Vallée de la Solle and which Denecourt graced with the name of one of his subscribers.[92] Its origins might have been spurious, but that seemed irrelevant to his contemporaries. The Fontaine Sanguinède took its place in Denecourt's guidebooks right alongside more authentic natural and historic sites and was even illustrated in the *Album Genévrier*, which was sold to tourists in local shops (see fig. 21).

Fig. 19 Tour Denecourt, c. 1900, postcard, 9 × 14 cm. Private collection

Fig. 20 Caverne des Brigands, c. 1900, postcard, 9 × 14 cm. Private collection

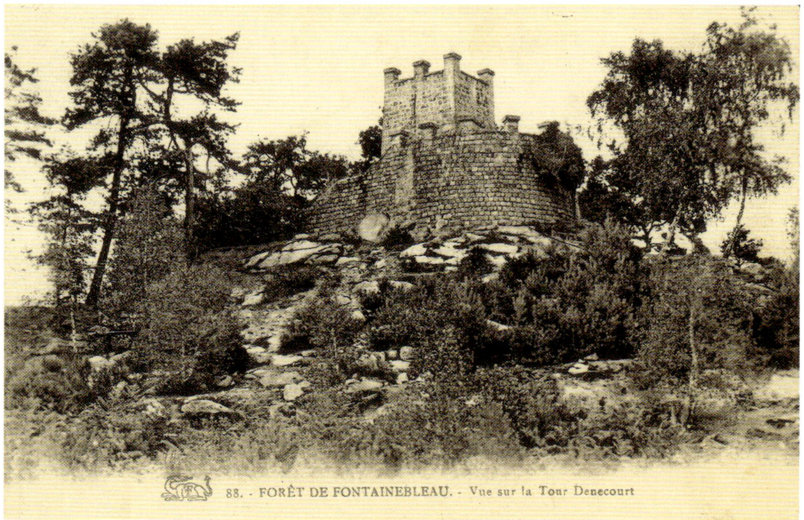

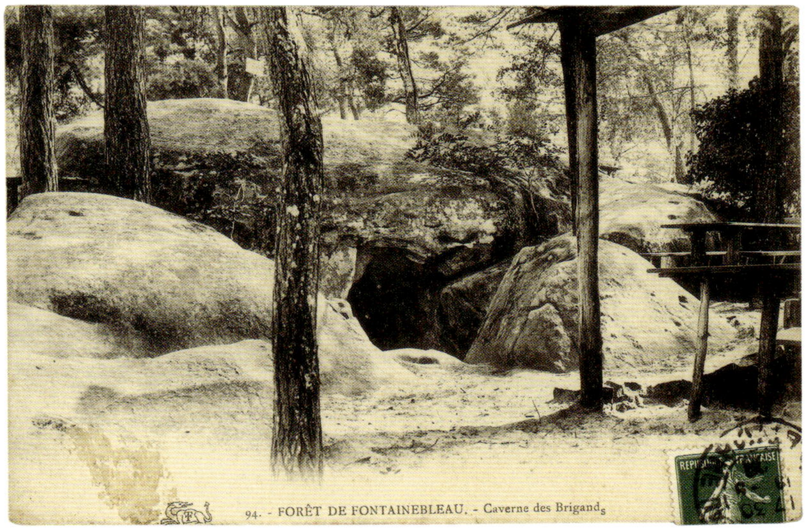

Even more striking is the history of the Caverne des Brigands, perhaps the most famous of Denecourt's inventions (fig. 20). Located in the vicinity of the Gorges d'Apremont and relatively near the village of Barbizon, this cavern, according to Denecourt, was reputed to have been the hiding place of a group of assassins led by a man named Tissier during the reign of Louis XV. Yet, remarkably, there is no mention of this site in any of the early guidebooks about the forest. It is also notably absent from Denecourt's map of 1839 as well as early editions of his own guidebooks. In fact, the first reference to this site is on the map published by Denecourt and Hardy in 1844 and in his *Promenades dans la forêt de Fontainebleau* (1845), in which it is called the Caverne des Voleurs.[93] It finally appears under its definitive name in the third edition of *Les délices de la forêt de Fontainebleau* (1845) and then in all subsequent editions of Denecourt's guidebooks.[94] It became one of the most popular sites in the forest, and its highly romantic—and completely fictional—origins are recounted in dozens of later texts with all the gravity of a true historical account. Denecourt knew his audience well and had no qualms about fabricating tales to feed their hunger for the romantic and the sensational. Nor did he limit himself to fabricating tales: Herbet recounted that a former barkeep claimed to have excavated the cavern at the behest of Denecourt.[95] This was far from an isolated case. Denecourt was known to have engaged quarrymen to construct other caverns to serve as tourist attractions, further blurring the line between natural and man-made wonders.[96] For Denecourt, such distinctions were moot. All that mattered was the vision of the Forest of Fontainebleau he strove to create and disseminate.

Denecourt's influence extended into every aspect of the booming tourist trade. Along with his guidebooks celebrating the forest, he also published texts such as the *Petit indicateur du voyageur à Fontainebleau*, which cheerfully provides the visitor with a wealth of practical information, including train schedules, hotel and restaurant recommendations, carriage rentals, and the names and addresses of reputable guides bearing Denecourt's official approbation.[97] He also helpfully directed the visitor to the various gift shops where they might avail

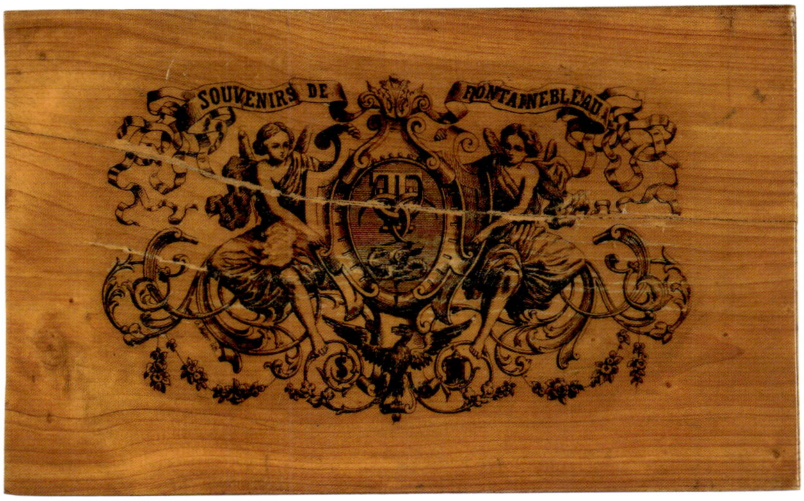

Fig 21 C.H. Walter, *Souvenirs de Fontainebleau. Album Genévrier*, c. 1855. Dumbarton Oaks Research Library and Collections

themselves of the range of souvenirs offered by local craftsmen, including carvings and souvenir albums (familiarly known as "genévrines") made from juniper wood harvested from the forest (fig. 21), maps and, conveniently enough, various publications by Denecourt himself. He gave pride of place to the shop of Madame Cudot, who, perhaps not coincidentally, was the publisher of a number of Denecourt's guidebooks.[98] Beginning in 1840, he also began editing a number of lithographic albums featuring Fontainebleau and other scenic locales in the outskirts of Paris.[99]

Others followed Denecourt's lead. One enterprising soul set up a hut near the Caverne des Brigands, selling "beer and other refreshments at high prices" as well as other objects of interest such as walking sticks, carved wooden objects, and live reptiles.[100] By 1875, there were also a variety of refreshment stands scattered throughout the forest near the popular attractions.[101] Under Denecourt's guidance, the Forest of Fontainebleau became the accessible, attractive, and ultimately trite playground of the bourgeoisie. As one contemporary article crowed: "The forest of Fontainebleau is celebrated throughout Europe, and Americans visit it to admire its wild and picturesque beauty. Beautiful it certainly is, and every one of its charms are mapped out and ticketed, so that the most indolent and careless passenger cannot fail to observe them."[102] Ordered, catalogued, and slickly packaged, the Forest of Fontainebleau was a masterpiece of modern marketing. The once savage forest had been tamed and offered up for public consumption.

Not surprisingly, not everyone applauded Denecourt's influence. George Sand was less than pleased by the changes she saw at Franchard during a visit in 1856: "The surroundings have become a bit too like a pleasure garden. There are too many names and emblems on the rocks. There are too many of them everywhere."[103] Jules Levallois likewise bemoaned the changes that tourism had brought to this once untrammeled portion of the forest: "At present, Franchard is a café by day, a restaurant by evening and hired carriages ceaselessly carry Parisians to the bottom of the valley of Apremont."[104]

How starkly these accounts contrast to earlier images of the region. Auguste-Xavier Leprince, who sojourned in the Franchard region in 1824, painted a group of artists taking their rest at the heights of the Gorges de Franchard (pl. 3). With its low horizon and sweeping panoramic view, it is an image of pristine nature in which the artists, their figures dwarfed by the surrounding landscape, are bold explorers seeking to penetrate the mysteries of the forest. There is a sense of hushed expectancy, a solitude that permeates the place that decades later would be trampled beneath the steady patter of thousands of boot heels.

Philippe Burty, who had known the forest in his youth, was horrified by the changes he encountered when he returned there in 1872: "Man can be felt everywhere. Large red and blue arrows shoot forth from the intersections of all the trails, as if a forest wasn't made for getting lost in! They've attached a caricature in bronze called Nemorosa to the side of a rock. You find a refreshment stand in the desert of Franchart [*sic*], a track in the Vallée de la Salle [*sic*]. There is a 'Viewpoint Victor-Emmanuel,' a Rossini oak, and a descent of Orpheus. It's execrable!"[105] Robert Louis Stevenson, who made his first trip to Fontainebleau in 1875, echoed Burty's opinion that "the *forest has been civilized* throughout. The most savage corners bear a name, and have been cherished like antiquities; in the most remote, Nature has prepared and balanced her effects as if with conscious art; and man, with his guiding arrows of blue paint, has countersigned the picture.... *It is not a wilderness; it is rather a preserve*.... it is truly but a pleasure ground" (Stevenson's emphasis).[106]

The massive influx of tourists inevitably changed the quotidian experience of the forest for all its residents, but perhaps none more so than the artists who inhabited its precincts. For the majority of artists who resided there, the Forest of Fontainebleau was more than a series of motifs to be exploited; it was also a refuge in which they could devote themselves completely to experiencing nature, "a sacred, necessary oasis in the midst of the impious invasion of a destructive and improvident civilization."[107] Within the confines of the forest, surrounded by ancient oaks and rocky gorges seemingly untouched by time, the artist could immerse himself completely in the splendor of nature, sheltered from the distractions of modern life and the world beyond the forest. Or so it had been before the arrival of the train and the flourishing tourist trade.

In a caricature by Cham published in 1864, a furious artist is shown chastising a hapless tourist for moving a tree branch midpose (fig. 22). While admittedly tongue in cheek, Cham's caricature nevertheless evokes the tensions that existed between the artists who had taken up residence in the forest and the tourists who descended upon it en masse each summer.

None felt this more keenly than Rousseau, whose acquaintance with the Forest of Fontainebleau was both long and intimate, dating to his first brief stop there in 1828/1829 to sketch the Pavé de Chailly.[108] The forest was a fecund source of inspiration for him and a touchstone in his work over the course of four decades. In his famous account of their shared trek through the Forest of Fontainebleau in 1847, Thoré related Rousseau's encounter with a woodsman who was hunched over a felled tree that Rousseau had drawn the previous year. Outraged, Rousseau reportedly queried, "But do you know what is the difference between an oak and a board? It is that an oak makes a million boards, while a million boards can never make an oak."[109] For Rousseau, the Forest of Fontainebleau was

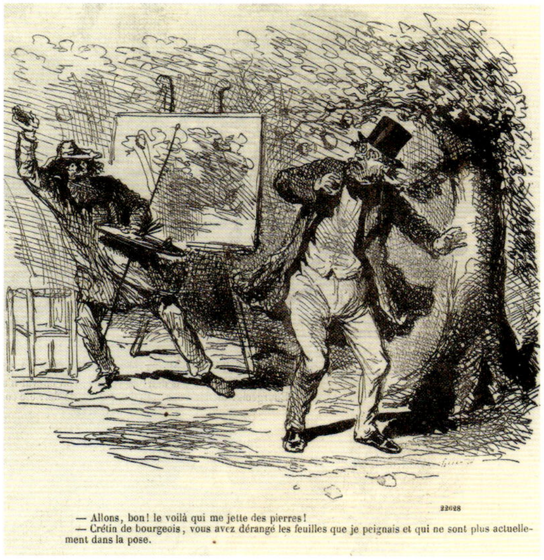

Fig. 22 Cham, caricature from "Excursions à Fontainebleau," *Le journal amusant*, no. 461 (29 October 1864): 2

sacred ground to be admired, cherished, and above all protected from the forces that were, in his opinion, systematically destroying the unique and treasured site.

In 1852, Rousseau took the extraordinary measure of submitting a petition to Emperor Napoleon III through the Duke of Morny, the emperor's half brother who had recently purchased works by Rousseau.[110] The petition, apparently written jointly by Rousseau and Alfred Sensier but presented on behalf of all artists, asked the emperor to protect the forest from further destruction at the hands of the forest administration. Critical of depredations carried out under the reign of Louis-Philippe, Rousseau chastised the current administration for continuing the abhorrent practices. The administration, he wrote, "indiscriminately cuts down trees whose great age, fame, and artistic beauty should make them respected." Equally appalling in Rousseau's estimation was the abundance of pine trees that, he decried, "are wiping out this forest's old Gaul character and will soon give us the severe and sad look of Russian forests."[111]

These criticisms were hardly new. Logging in the Forest of Fontainebleau was an emotionally and politically charged subject during the nineteenth century, especially during the reign of Louis-Philippe, which witnessed one of the most aggressive replanting campaigns in the history of the forest. Between 1830 and 1847, 6,000 hectares were replanted, more than twice the area replanted during the previous three decades.[112] The regions of Erables-Déluge, Mare aux Evées, and Monts-de-Fays had particularly suffered, and contemporaries lamented the loss of old-growth trees as "shameful and clandestine."[113] Decades later Burty still decried it as an irreparable loss.[114] Thoré was scathing in his condemnation of the perceived destruction of the forest by the woodsman's axe. He referred to the downed trees as "noble victims" and described their felling with terms like "death sentence" and "massacre." His words were visceral and blatantly provocative, reflecting the passion that the subject sparked among lovers of nature.[115]

Rousseau's petition touches on another controversial topic, the introduction of pine trees into the forest. Although there is evidence of pine trees in the forest as early as the end of the sixteenth century—a number of such trees estimated to be 120 years in age had been killed in the severe frost of 1709—it was not until the end of the eighteenth century that any systematic attempt was made to introduce such trees into the Forest of Fontainebleau.[116] While initial efforts to introduce maritime pines in 1785 had mixed results, the introduction of the Scots pine the following year proved successful.[117] Louis-Guillaume Lemonnier, botanist and royal physician to Louis XV, imported seedlings from Switzerland that were planted on the northern slope of Mont-Chauvet where they flourished. In 1792, more pines were planted in Mont-Ussy and Fort-des-Moulins.[118]

Hardy, adaptable, accustomed to dry and sandy soil, and resistant to cold, including the severe frosts to which the Forest of Fontainebleau was prone, Scots pine proved to be particularly well suited to the unique climate of the forest, thriving where so many other trees had not. The commercial value of pine provided further incentive for its use in replanting. Scots pine in particular is known for both the quality and versatility of its wood, which makes it suitable for shipbuilding, carpentry, and woodworking. It also produces high-quality charcoal *(charbon de bois)*.[119]

Pine was the predominant species used during the extensive replanting of the forest between the years 1830 and 1847, and the trees soon began to appear throughout the entire forest.[120] By mid-century, as many as twenty-five varieties of pine were introduced into the Forest of Fontainebleau, some through grafting with the already proven Scots pine.[121] And by 1863, pine trees covered some 4,000 hectares, nearly a quarter of the forest's entire area.[122]

At first, the introduction of the pine was heralded as an accomplishment. In his poem "La forêt de Fontainebleau," René Castel praised Lemonnier for bringing the "ornaments of the North" to Fontainebleau.[123] But as the number of pines grew, so did disapproval. There was no small degree of outrage at what one author disparaged as "pinomania," warning, "if they could, they would tear out the entire forest and replace it with pine seedlings."[124]

Thoré was a vocal detractor of this development. "If I were king," he declared, "I would never cut down the great oak trees that the centuries have bequeathed to my country.... Go look at the fir-tree seedlings with which they have poisoned the healthy beds of heather that separate Apremont from Macherin" (Thoré's ellipses).[125] His assertion that pine trees had "poisoned" the landscape was a common one. The fervor of the response is quite extraordinary, reflecting a kind of botanical xenophobia in which the pine tree insinuates itself into the forest like a foreign invader, destroying the purity of the landscape.

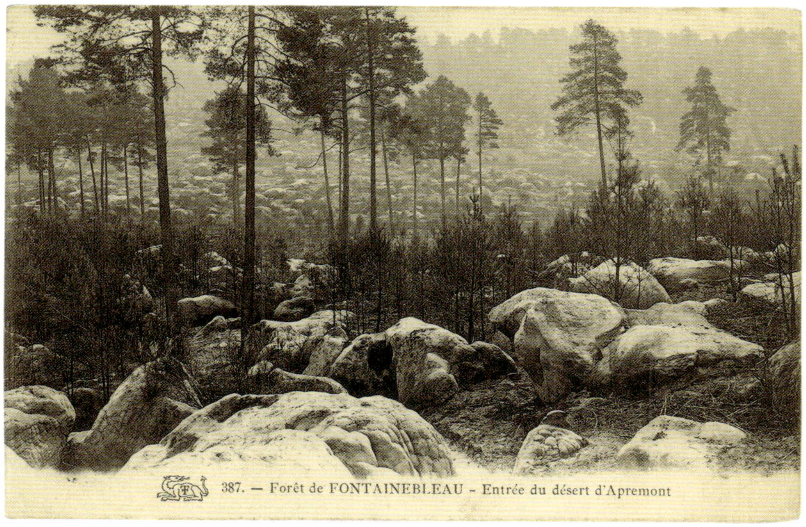

Fig. 23 Entrance to the Désert d'Apremont, c. 1900, postcard, 9 × 14 cm. Private collection

There is no denying that the introduction of pine trees into areas once devoid of vegetation changes the character of the landscape, and not necessarily for the better (see fig. 23). As one author commented, "The pine seedlings, by spreading a uniform mantle of greenery across these arid deserts [of the Gorges d'Apremont] have robbed them of their character. At the end of summer days, the sunsets pour forth the same splendor, but the coloring and the impression is deadened by this curtain of young pine trees; and the painter will search in vain for the spectacle of poetic sadness that this site once offered in its harsh nudity."[126] As these remarks suggest, the distinctive character of the forest itself was at risk from the "invasion of monotonous pines," as one contemporary described them.[127] The "harsh nudity" of Apremont, once its defining trait, had been compromised, softened, and irrevocably altered by the introduction of a foreign element.

But Rousseau did not limit his criticism to the forest administration alone. He also took aim at the burgeoning tourist industry and at the "maniacal old man" Denecourt. Rousseau found Denecourt's activities offensive and scorned his "useless trails" and "ridiculous lookout platforms" as well as the numbers and inscriptions that were "despoiling and dishonoring" the most beautiful sites of the forest.[128] Rousseau had little tolerance for Denecourt's fabrications or for the physical toll tourism in general had exacted upon his beloved forest. Describing an excursion into the forest during the final months of Rousseau's life, Sensier recorded Rousseau's reaction to the Sully, one of the great oaks made famous by Denecourt: "There! A giant in decline, I saw it when it was much more beautiful, but each year they attack it, wound it. They have amputated the strongest branches, so that the veils of the women traveling by carriage don't get caught upon them; they have cut the magnificent roots that solidify the path, in order to make it into a paved road."[129] This was Denecourt's legacy in Rousseau's eyes: a magnificent forest ruined for the ease and enjoyment of the uncaring Sunday tourist.

Denecourt was well aware of his growing coterie of detractors and, though he does not mention him by name, Rousseau clearly topped the list.[130] In response to growing criticism, Denecourt published his defense, a brochure entitled "La guerre déclarée à mes sentiers" in which he vehemently denied the charge that he had "ruined" the forest for artists:

But, certain artists say, we don't like your trails precisely because they have civilized the forest too much and they lead too many unwanted visitors so that we can no longer paint either a site or even the most minor study without distraction....

In truth, these artists would be more comfortable if our sites were forbidden to the 80 or 100,000 tourists and walkers who visit this lovely area of Fontainebleau annually; but in general they are too just to want to keep the enjoyment of our picturesque deserts to themselves and equally too intelligent to reprove someone who, I repeat, has furnished so many subjects, so many treasures for their brushes to explore.[131]

While there is some validity to his claims, it is also undeniable that the influx of tourists had a detrimental effect on the forest. In 1856, Joanne lamented the ruination of the once admirable La Roche Qui Pleure (fig. 24): "This rock, cited as one of the picturesque marvels of the forest, is now one of the most vile places, all dusty and trampled underfoot by incessant visitors, completely covered with the names of men and women."[132] That same year a fire, believed to have been started by careless tourists, destroyed the oak tree dubbed La Reine Blanche.[133] There is a certain irony in the fact that, in his campaign to ensure that no wonder was overlooked, Denecourt may well have hastened the forest's decline by failing to take into account the damage caused by the steady stream of eager and often thoughtless tourists in regions that had once been known only to locals and the most dedicated of artists.

Rousseau could not reverse the damage already done either at the hands of the forest administration or at the hands of Denecourt. He could, however, work to stem the tide, which was the ultimate purpose of his daring petition. Rousseau requested that part of the forest be spared from future cultivation and intervention of any kind for the sake of art. He cited four regions that he deemed most worthy of protection: Bas-Bréau, the Gorges d'Apremont and the nearby Monts-Girards, the Plateau de Belle-Croix, and the Gorges aux Loups: "I ask you for protection, Monseigneur, for these old trees which for artists are the source from which they derive

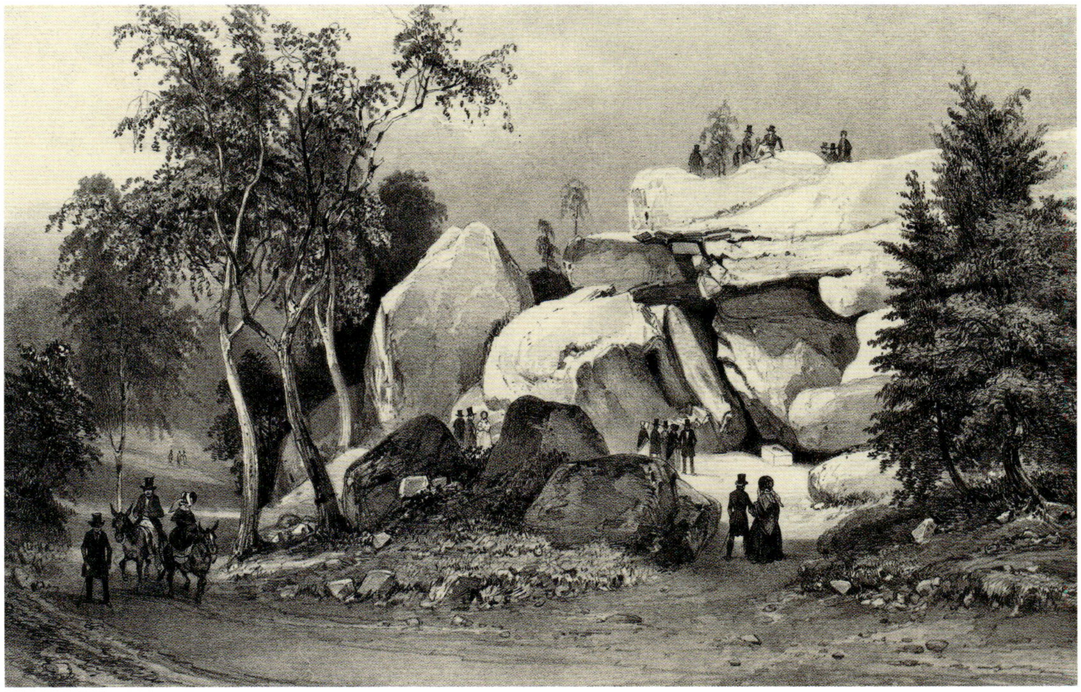

Fig. 24 *View Taken at the Roche Qui Pleure,* nineteenth century, lithograph, 34.6 × 55 cm. *Souvenirs de Fontainebleau,* Château of Fontainebleau

their inspiration, their joy, and their future and which are for all visitors, venerable souvenirs of ages past."[134]

The areas proposed by Rousseau for preservation were among those most frequented by artists and, with the exception of the Gorges aux Loups, were all near the village of Barbizon. They were also sites recommended by Denecourt in his guidebook of 1840. Despite the extraordinary suggestion that these areas be left completely untouched not only by the woodsman's axe but also by efforts at regeneration, Rousseau's appeal ultimately proved successful, though years would pass before he saw its fruition. On 14 April 1861, Napoleon III signed an imperial decree setting aside 1,631 hectares of the forest as a preserve free from cultivation of any kind, of which 1,097 hectares was specifically designated as a "partie artistique."[135] In addition to the areas identified by Rousseau in his petition, portions of Franchard, Rocher Saint-Germain, la Tillaie, Gros-Fouteau, and Ventes à la Reine were also set aside as part of the artistic preserve.[136] It was a tremendous victory, not only for Rousseau and his fellow artists but also for all lovers of nature. With this decree, the Forest of Fontainebleau became the first nature preserve in history, eleven years before the creation of Yellowstone National Park. For more than a century, this region of Fontainebleau would remain inviolate, nature in its most pristine state.[137]

The success of Rousseau's petition set an important precedent and became the model for similar campaigns in years to come. The most important of these was undertaken by the Committee for Artistic Preservation of the Forest of Fontainebleau. Formed in 1872 in response to the administration's plan to cull a significant portion of the forest in the wake of severe deforestation during the Prussian occupation in 1870–1871, the committee's stated goal was "to oppose by all moral means the devastation of the Forest of Fontainebleau," though its ultimate objective was to expand the artistic preserve that had been established in 1861.[138] Following Rousseau's example, the committee, composed largely of artists (Millet was the president of honor, and Daubigny and Corot were also members), campaigned vigorously against the destruction of the forest and addressed a new petition in 1874 to both President Patrice de Mac-Mahon and the director of fine arts, Philippe de Chennevières, proposing that the nature preserve created in 1861 be expanded by 1,000 hectares. They also made impassioned public appeals to gain support for their efforts. Philippe Burty, George Sand, and Victor Hugo were among those who published letters of support in the press. Hugo's letter contained the now-famous declaration: "A tree is an edifice; a forest is a city, and amongst all the forests, the Forest of Fontainebleau is a monument."[139] Burty stated the case even more forcefully: "I ask that the Forest of Fontainebleau be classed among the historic monuments. It is as worthy as the château inhabited only by ominous phantoms. Could the wooden floor stained with the blood of Monadelschi replace its sun-filled clearings? Would you trade the oaks of Bas-Bréau for the acajou table upon which Napoléon signed his abdication?"[140] It was not enough that the forest be protected from exploitation; the committee members wanted nothing less than for Fontainebleau to be classified as a national monument. It was a bold declaration, and the debate continued for years, though to little effect. The artistic reserve was eventually expanded to 1,692 hectares in 1892 and to 1,892 hectares in 1904, but it never attained the official status of a historic monument.[141]

Even as Rousseau and his successors were lobbying for the protection of the forest, artists continued to arrive in Fontainebleau in ever growing numbers. "Every spring or autumn," wrote one author in 1844, "an emigration of artists takes place in Fontainebleau: the most accomplished young landscape artists go there in search of inspiration. The Forest of Fontainebleau, like a good mother, lavishes her most precious treasures to all, from the king's oak to the Rocher des Deux Soeurs."[142] Three years later, Thoré echoed this sentiment, observing, "The painters, however, discovered Barbizon like the promised land and for the past ten years a colony of landscape artists has taken up residence there."[143]

Spring, summer, or autumn, the forest was filled with a steady stream of aspiring landscape artists who came to Fontainebleau in order to learn the art of open-air painting. Like Italy before it, Fontainebleau had become an obligatory destination for any serious landscape artist: "They, the young [artists] burst upon the Forest of Fontainebleau in wild bands, this landscape school of Saint-Cyr where so many painters, arriving as simple soldiers, depart with the epaulet."[144] Fontainebleau had truly become the premier center for open-air painting, eclipsing Italy's historic supremacy.

In his novel *Scènes de campagne*, Henry Murger offered a contemporary perspective on the influx of artists. In the novel's most famous scene, the protagonist, a landscape painter by the name of Lazare, traverses the forest in search of his motif accompanied by his easel carrier, a boy from the village of Montigny, where he has taken up residence each summer.[145] Upon reaching the Mare aux Fées, Lazare warns, "Let's not stop there. . . . In an hour all the hacks from these parts will come and plant their parasols around the pool, and the plateau will look like a mushroom patch."[146] It is an amusing image to be sure, but it is also one that by all accounts is a fairly accurate reflection of the Forest of Fontainebleau at the height of summer (fig. 25).

"Each summer the nearby villages are invaded by legions of artists," Clavé wrote in 1863.[147] Invasion is all too accurate an assessment. Nearly seven hundred artists were guests at the village inns in the environs of Fontainebleau, not just the Auberge Ganne, but others as well, including the Auberge du Cheval Blanc in Chailly—which hosted Corot, Rousseau, Diaz, and Barye—and the disreputable Auberge de la Mère Anthony in Marlotte (fig. 26; see pl. 6).[148]

This invasion was not strictly domestic. From the 1850s onward, Fontainebleau was besieged by artists of all nationalities in growing numbers, including those from Germany (Ludwig Knauss, Max Liebermann, and Georg Eduard Otto Saal; see pl. 55), Holland (Willem Roelefs, Johan Hendrik Weissenbruch, Martinus Antonius Kuytenbrouwer, and Jacob Maris; see pls. 63 and 64), Sweden (Carl Frederick Hill and Oscar Törnà; fig. 27), Denmark (Valdemar Schønheyder Møller), Belgium (Joseph Coosemans, Camille van Camp, and César and Xavier de Cock), Italy (Serafino de Tivoli and Nino Costa), Romania (Ion Andresco and Nicolai Grigoresco), Hungary (Ladislas de Paal and Mihály Munkácsy), and Scotland (John Lavery).[149]

It was the American artists who constituted the greatest foreign presence in Fontainebleau during the second half of the nineteenth century. One of the first and most important was William Morris Hunt, who traveled to Barbizon in the company of William Babcock in late 1852 or early 1853 to meet Millet, whom Babcock had befriended and Hunt admired. It proved a happy encounter; Hunt soon became one of Millet's most devoted followers and important patrons, acquiring and commissioning numerous paintings, including *The Sheep Shearers* (Museum of Fine Arts, Boston), which Hunt himself copied (fig. 28).[150]

In the years that followed, other Americans also made their way to Fontainebleau, including George Inness, who was strongly influenced by the loose brushwork and dark palette that dominated the work of artists of the Barbizon School, and John William Casilear (fig. 29) and Christopher Pearse Cranch, who were there in 1858. Cranch is a figure of particular interest. A friend of the transcendentalist poet Ralph Waldo Emerson, Cranch was the first American artist to exhibit a Fontainebleau work at the Paris Salon. He exhibited two such landscapes there in 1857 and would go on to exhibit Fontainebleau works in both New York and Washington, DC, upon his return to the United States.[151] His friend William Cullen Bryant, who was in Paris at that time, recounted how Cranch would eschew the nearby Bois de Boulogne ("too trim a place," he observed) and head instead to Fontainebleau "where he finds wild nature—rocks and declivities and majestic trees—many of them named after old French monarchs."[152]

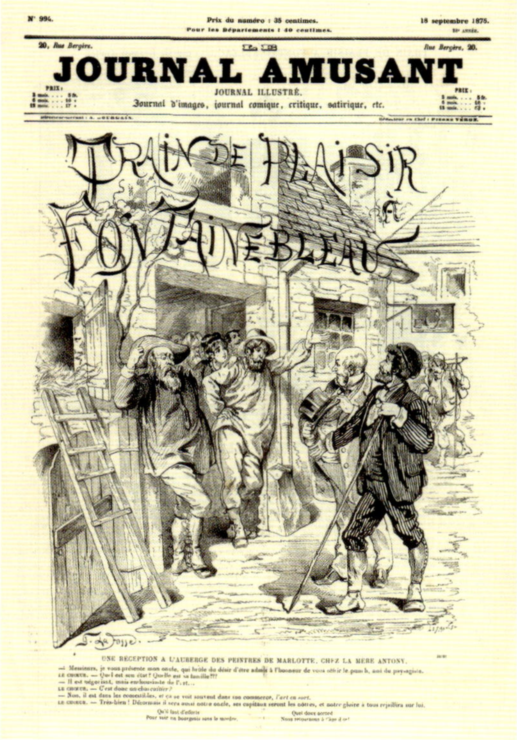
N° 994. Prix du numéro : 35 centimes. Pour les Départements : 40 centimes. 18 septembre 1875.
20, Rue Bergère. LE Rue Bergère, 20.
JOURNAL AMUSANT
JOURNAL ILLUSTRÉ.
Journal d'images, journal comique, critique, satirique, etc.
TRAIN DE PLAISIR À FONTAINEBLEAU

Fig. 26 G. La Fosse, *Reception at the Artists' Inn at Marlotte, at Mère Anthony's,* from "Train de plaisir à Fontainebleau," *Le journal amusant,* no. 994 (18 September 1875): 1

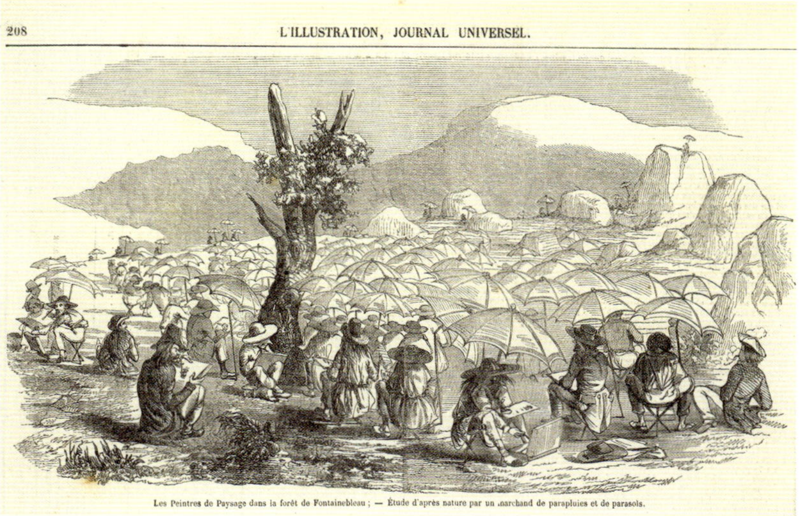
208 L'ILLUSTRATION, JOURNAL UNIVERSEL.
Les Peintres de Paysage dans la forêt de Fontainebleau ; — Étude d'après nature par un marchand de parapluies et de parasols.

Fig. 25 *Landscape Painters in the Forest of Fontainebleau: Study after Nature by a Merchant of Umbrellas and Parasols,* from *L'Illustration* 14, no. 352 (24 November 1849): 208. Research Library, The Getty Research Institute, Los Angeles

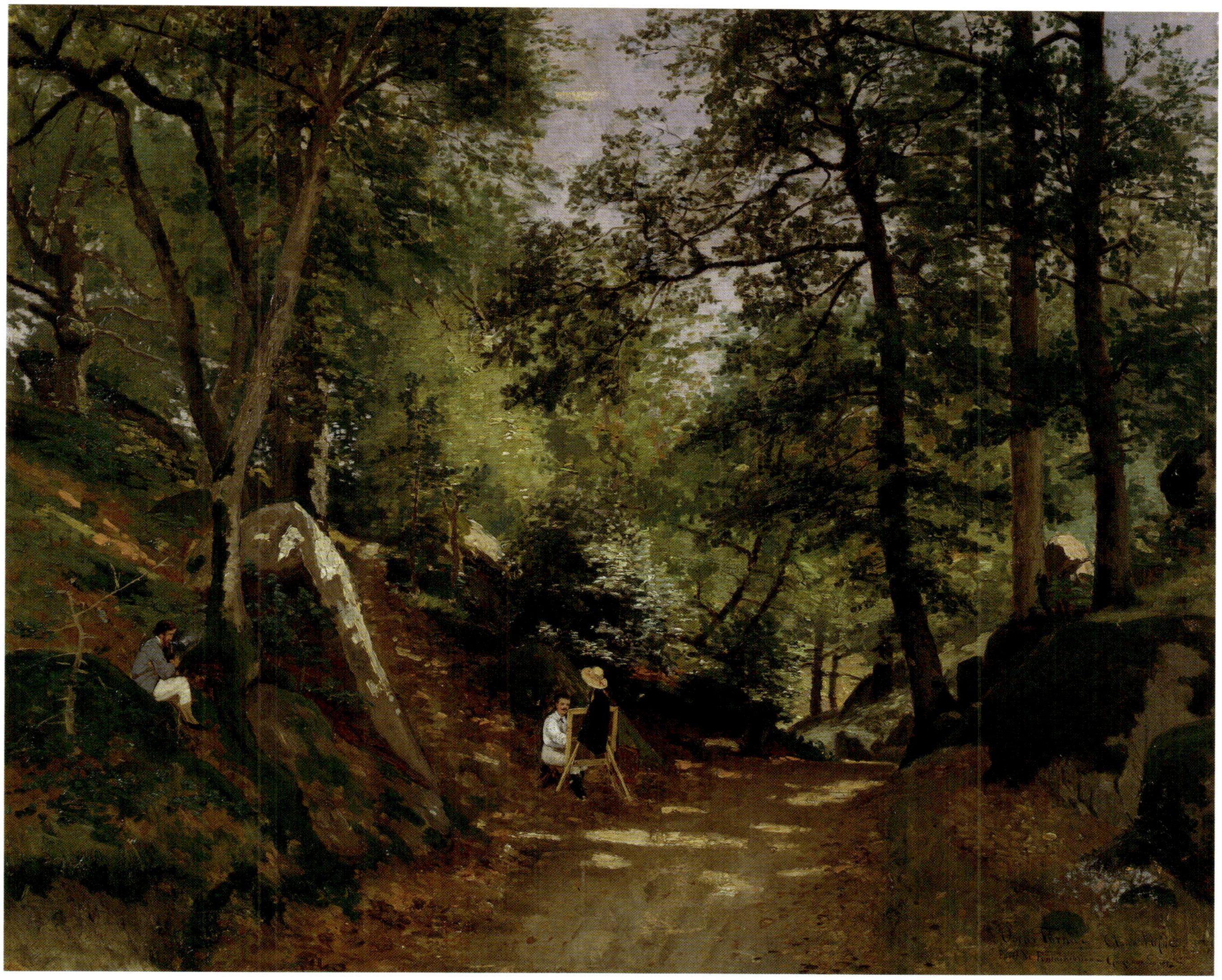

Fig. 27 Oscar Törnà, *Summer Landscape at Fontainebleau,* 1876, oil on canvas, 73 × 92 cm. Nationalmuseum, Stockholm

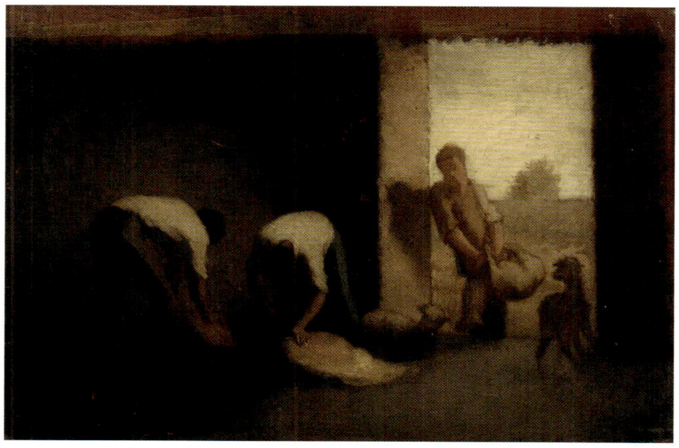

Fig. 28 William Morris Hunt, *Sheep Shearing at Barbizon,* c. 1852, oil on panel, 25.1 × 39.4 cm. Museum of Fine Arts, Boston, Bequest of Mrs. Edward Wheelwright

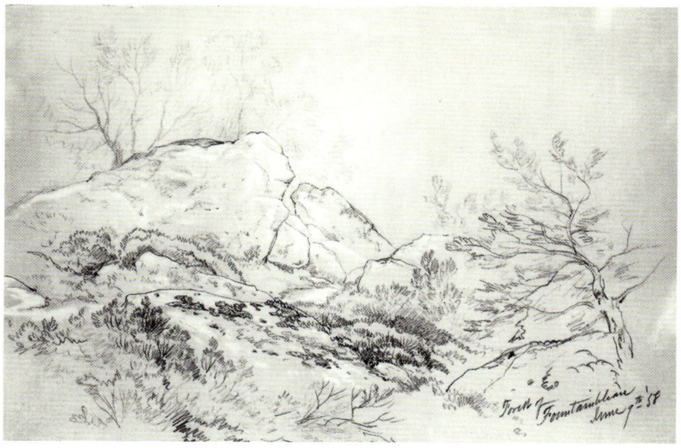

Fig. 29 John William Casilear, *Forest of Fontainebleau,* 9 June 1858, graphite with wash on light brown paper heightened with white, 22.9 × 36.5 cm. Museum of Fine Arts, Boston, Gift of Maxim Karolik

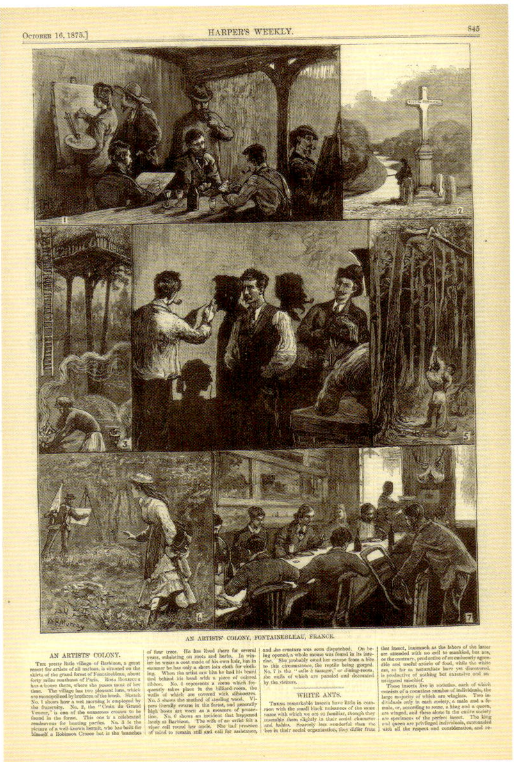
October 16, 1875.] HARPER'S WEEKLY. 843

AN ARTISTS' COLONY, FONTAINEBLEAU, FRANCE.

AN ARTISTS' COLONY.

WHITE ANTS.

Fig. 30 *An Artists' Colony, Fontainebleau, France,* from *Harper's Weekly,* 16 October 1875, 843

Like Cranch, Thomas Moran was drawn to the savage corners of Fontainebleau. He made a number of sketches there in late 1866 and 1867, years before he discovered the untamed wilds closer to home in Yellowstone.[153] But it was not until the 1870s that the true "advent of the Anglo-Saxon"—as the painter Will Hickok Low, himself a regular visitor since 1873, called the first major flood of English-speaking artists—truly took place.[154] Initially, Barbizon was their preferred headquarters, with artists lodging either at the now-respectable Auberge Ganne or at the slightly less reputable Auberge Siron (fig. 30). However, the growing reputation of the village, combined with the wave of tourists following Millet's death, rendered Barbizon too congested and ultimately too banal for serious artists and by the summer of 1875, a new artists' colony had sprung up at Grez-sur-Loing.[155] Located on the opposite side of the Forest of Fontainebleau, Grez and the nearby village of Montigny were picturesque and blissfully unspoiled, much like Barbizon had been a half century prior. Low was there, as was his friend Wyatt Eaton, the Scottish painter Robert Alan Mowray Stevenson, and his cousin Robert Louis Stevenson. Other artists traveled there as well, including Robert Vonnoh, Frederic Porter Vinton, Willard Leroy Metcalf, Theodore Robinson, and George de Forest Brush.[156]

Grez had more to offer than the absence of tourists and the nearby Loing River; it also presented the possibility of new motifs for artists to exploit. As early as 1833, the critic Charles Lenormant had described Fontainebleau as "the locality with the appearance of being the most worn-out by the works of modern painting."[157] That perception would only become more pronounced with the passage of time, as more artists made the pilgrimage to the forest. The most popular sites—the ones touted by Denecourt and, not coincidentally, also typically near the village of Barbizon—were depicted with some frequency. The much-admired old-growth forest of Bas-Bréau appeared in no fewer than forty-five works exhibited at the Paris Salon between the years 1834 and 1875, while the Plateau de Belle-Croix appeared thirty-five times and the Gorges d'Apremont thirty-three times. Grez and its environs, while far from virgin territory, did have the advantage of relative novelty with which to tempt the aspiring artist.

Of course, novelty is fleeting, as the example of the Mare aux Fées proves. Off the beaten path because of its distance from Barbizon, the Mare aux Fées did not even warrant a mention in the earliest Denecourt guidebooks, and paintings of the subject would not appear at the Salon until 1850.[158] Yet as Murger's novel *Scènes de campagne* indicates, its obscurity was short-lived, and by 1875, the Mare aux Fées had graced the walls of the Salon twenty-two times. For the artists who descended on the Forest of Fontainebleau in ever-increasing numbers, the search for fresh inspiration was far from easy. A caricature from 1875 depicts a rather novel approach for achieving this end (fig. 31). While the tone of the caricature is humorous, the crisis it foreshadows is not.

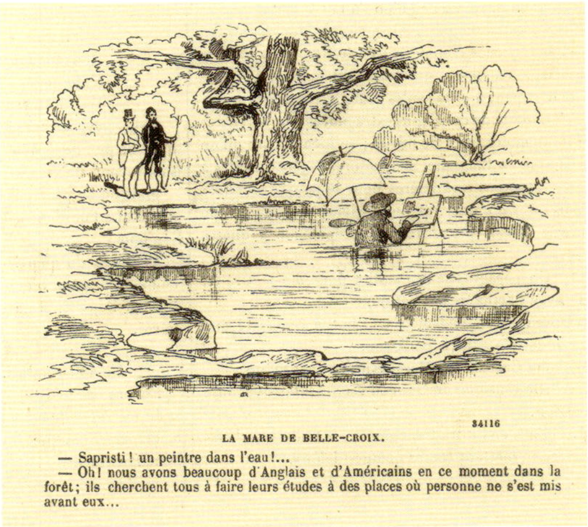

Fig. 31 G. La Fosse, *La Mare de Belle-Croix,* from "Train de plaisir à Fontainebleau," *Le journal amusant,* no. 994 (18 September 1875): 4

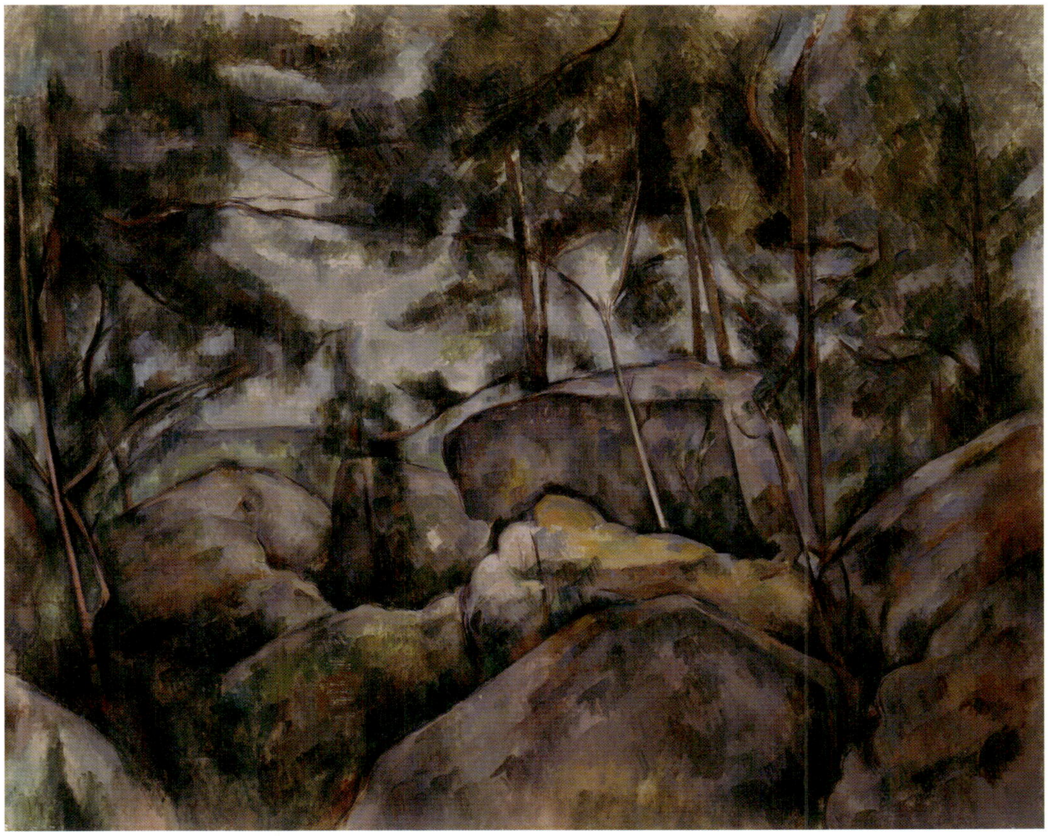

Fig. 32 Paul Cézanne, *Rocks in the Forest,* 1890s, oil on canvas, 73.3 × 92.4 cm. Metropolitan Museum of Art, H.O. Havemeyer Collection, Bequest of Mrs. H.O. Havemeyer, 1929

As so often happens, Fontainebleau began to fall victim to its own popularity. The sustaining myth of the forest—that of a pure, untrammeled landscape in which the man of feeling could lose himself, captivated by the eternal wonder of nature—had begun to collapse, crushed beneath the weight of too many artists, tourists, and distractions. Fontainebleau had become mundane, its mysteries revealed to all. There was nothing new left to discover.

Like Italy before it, Fontainebleau's heyday had passed. The forest would remain a site of pilgrimage for artists for decades to come—Paul Cézanne (see fig. 32), Georges Seurat, Odilon Redon, Félicien Rops, and Pablo Picasso are among those who would make the trek to the forest, following the same trails as generations of artists before them—but much of its glory had faded along with its novelty. In time, artists began to drift to other locales, such as Giverny in France and Old Lyme in America, in a quest for new vistas to explore, new motifs to depict, and new history to be made.[159]

None of this can diminish the legacy of Fontainebleau. For a half century, the Forest of Fontainebleau had been the premier center for artistic experimentation, the crucible in which the modern landscape was forged. It is there that the art of open-air painting first took root on French soil; there that the artists of the Barbizon School introduced a new sense of naturalism into landscape painting; and there that the young impressionists carried out their own experiments in open-air painting, honing their skills and laying the foundation for a new revolution in art. In the course of a single century, the Forest of Fontainebleau had gone from near obscurity to being a site of international renown, its fame eclipsing that of the château in its midst. The forest was indeed the monument that Victor Hugo proclaimed it to be, its influence lingering long after visitors had departed its precincts.

As Stevenson wrote, "Many of us have passed Arcadian days there and moved on, but yet left a portion of our souls behind us buried in the woods.... One generation after another fall like honey-bees upon this memorable forest, rifle its sweets, pack themselves with vital memories, and when the theft is consummated depart again into life richer, but poorer also. The forest, indeed, they have possessed, from that day forward it is theirs indissolubly, and they will return to walk in it at night in the fondest of their dreams, and use it for ever in their books and pictures."[160]

That is the true legacy of the Forest of Fontainebleau.

Plates

Discovery

Artists first began to visit the Forest of Fontainebleau in earnest during the early 1820s. Fontainebleau had much to offer the aspiring landscape artist —proximity to Paris, topography that was both striking and diverse, and a loose community of like-minded artists centered in Chailly—and it quickly became the preeminent center for open-air painting in France, one that rivaled and eventually eclipsed Italy in reputation.

Corot, who was among the earliest and most ardent visitors to the forest, described a typical day at Chailly: "I depart early for the forest; I return late, a bit tired.... I seek the nature of the beautiful oaks of the forest."[1] In the years prior to the introduction of the railway, a sojourn to Fontainebleau remained something of a grand adventure as artists made excursions deep within the forest, their equipment strapped to their backs, the wooden pole of their parasols serving as a walking stick. Some would even hire locals to assist them. In his novel *Scènes de campagne*, Henry Murger described his fictional painter trekking through the forest while a young peasant boy trailed behind him "hunched beneath the weight of a heavy box upon which is strapped a travel easel and one of the large white linen parasols used by artists to maintain even lighting while working out of doors" (see pl. 2).[2]

Drawn by its growing reputation as a center for open-air painting as well as the presence of a number of prestigious painters, including Rousseau, Diaz, and Millet, aspiring artists began to gravitate to the nearby village of Barbizon in growing numbers. Once there, they would lodge at one of the local inns—the Auberge Ganne, Auberge de la Mère Honoré, or Auberge Siron, "that excellent artists' barrack"—which would serve as a base of operations from which they could launch their forays into the forest.[3] There were other inns in nearby villages that were also frequented by artists: in Chailly, the Auberge du Lion d'Or (see pl. 7) and Auberge du Cheval Blanc—an "excellent tavern... where, for 3F75 per day, one is well fed and lodged"—and in Marlotte, the Auberge de la Mère Anthony. The Mère Anthony was a popular gathering place for artists, but it was less reputable than its counterparts and was somewhat unsavory, with its walls "entirely slathered in caricatures... as if house painters had dried their hands there" (pl. 6).[4]

With the advent of the railway, the forest became even more accessible, bringing with it a new generation of painters as well as photographers. In 1849, Gustave Le Gray became one of the first photographers to travel to Fontainebleau, where he produced luminous open-air studies of the forest and its environs. Other landscape photographers, who, like their painter counterparts, adopted Fontainebleau as a privileged site for artistic exploration, soon joined him. "There is no forest in the world more traveled, more drawn than this one," observed one contemporary, "none has inspired more artists."[5]

However, artists were not the only ones who took advantage of this newfound accessibility. Already by the mid-nineteenth century, tourism was a booming industry, and locations such as Fontainebleau that were within easy reach of Paris became popular destinations for Sunday excursions. Tourists flocked to the forest for picnics and promenades, touring Fontainebleau by carriage or on foot and armed with maps and guidebooks that made the forest even more welcoming for a mass audience. Fontainebleau had ceased to be the largely exclusive province of artists and had become a true pleasure ground open to all.

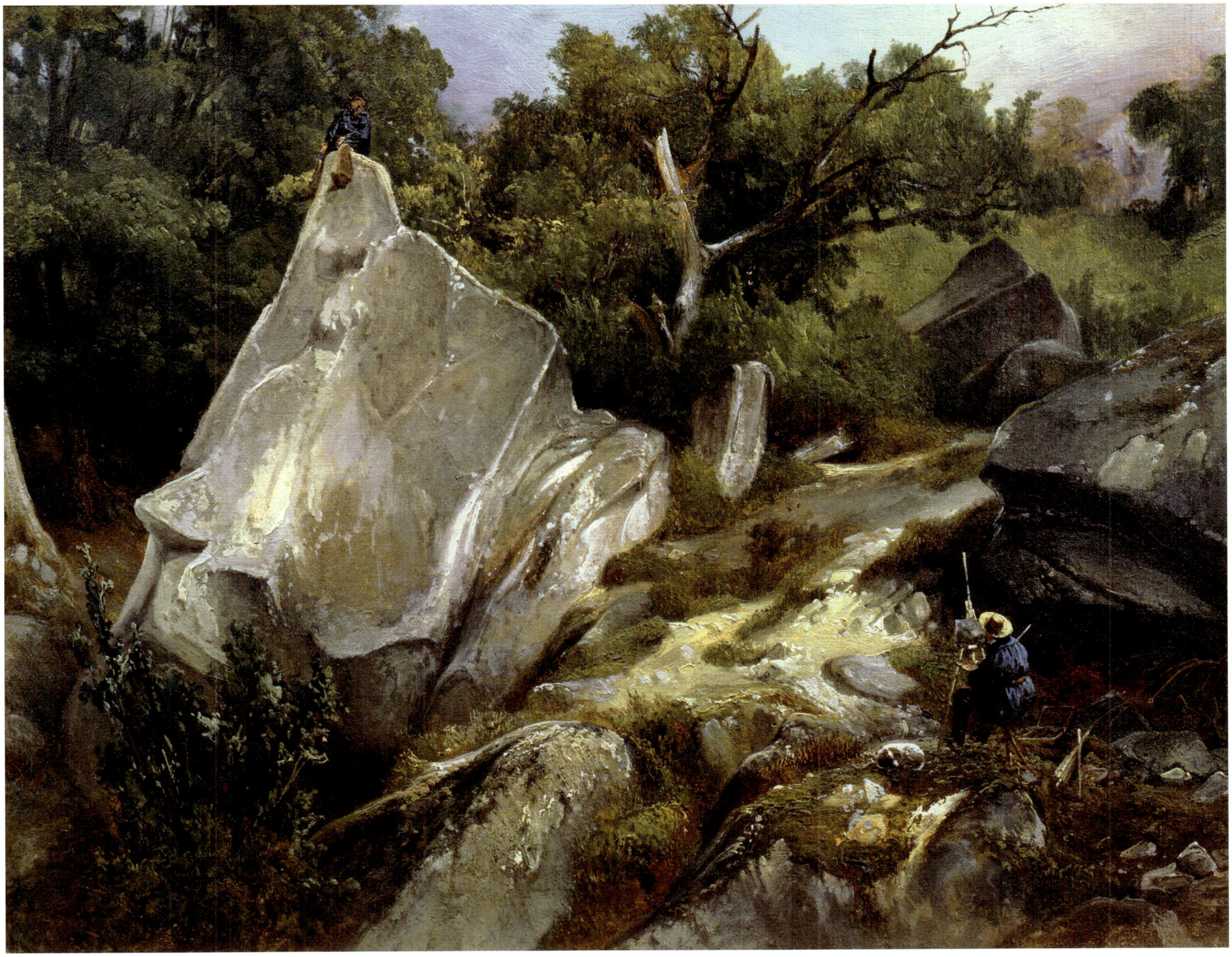

I

Augustin Enfantin

An Artist Painting in the Forest of Fontainebleau, c. 1825, oil on paper mounted on canvas, 26.7 × 34.3 (10½ × 13½). Private collection

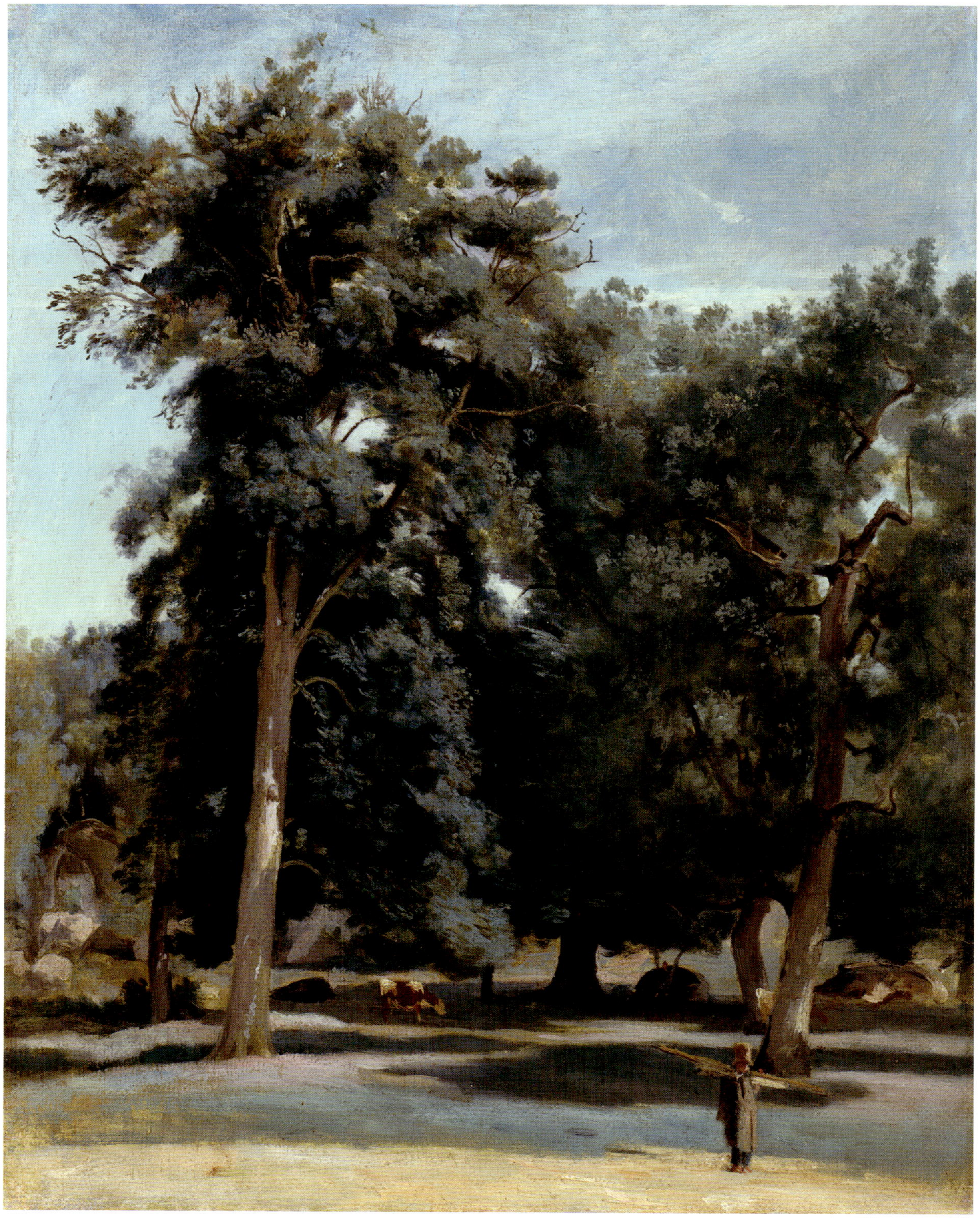

2

Jean-Baptiste-Camille Corot

The Little Easel Carrier, Fontainebleau, c. 1823–1824, oil on paper mounted on canvas, 44.5 × 35.5 (17 ½ × 14). Private collection

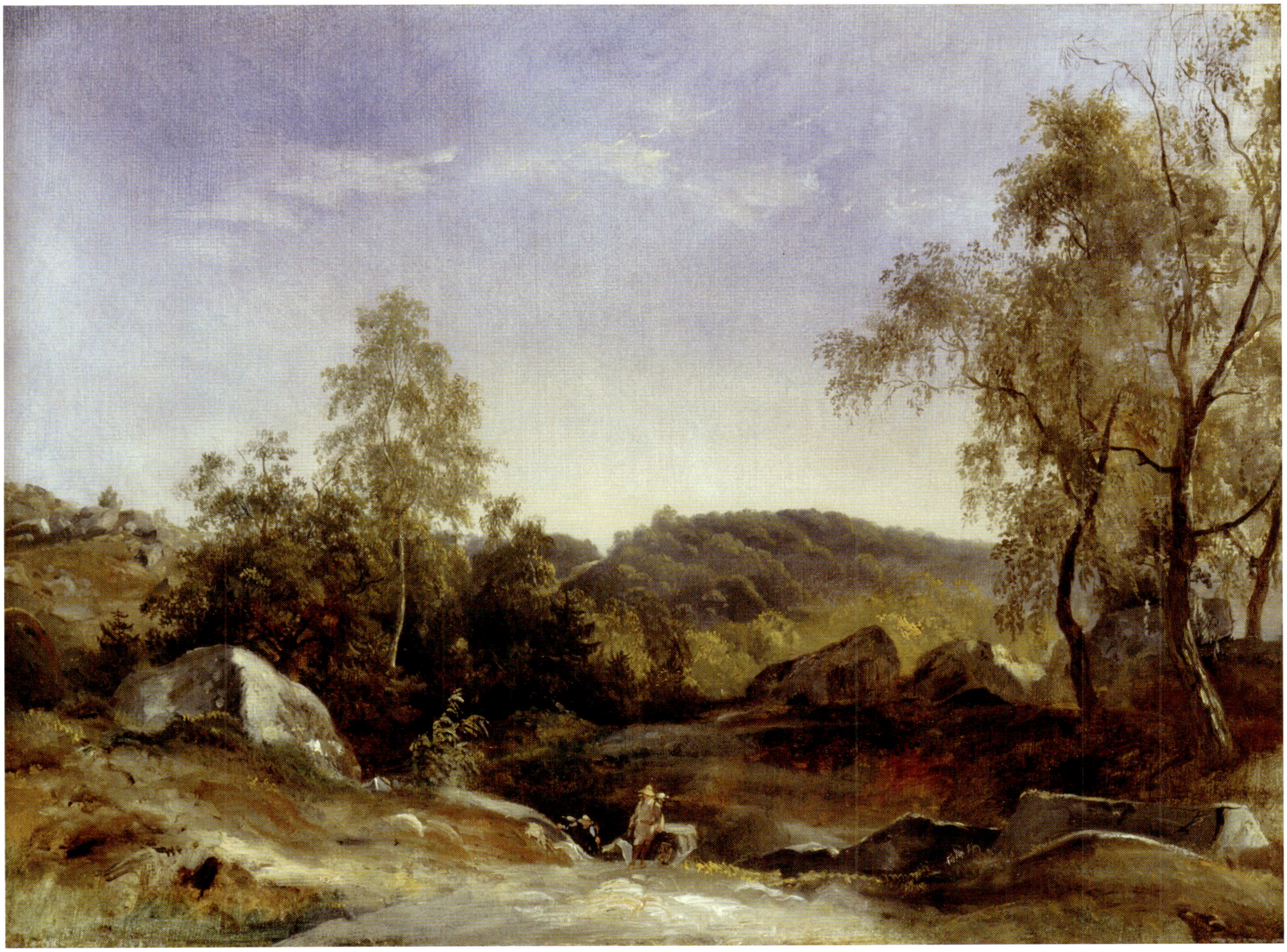

3

Auguste-Xavier Leprince

Painters at Rest, Fontainebleau, c. 1824, oil on paper on canvas, 35.5 × 50 (14 × 19 11/16). Musée Départmental de l'Oise, Beauvais

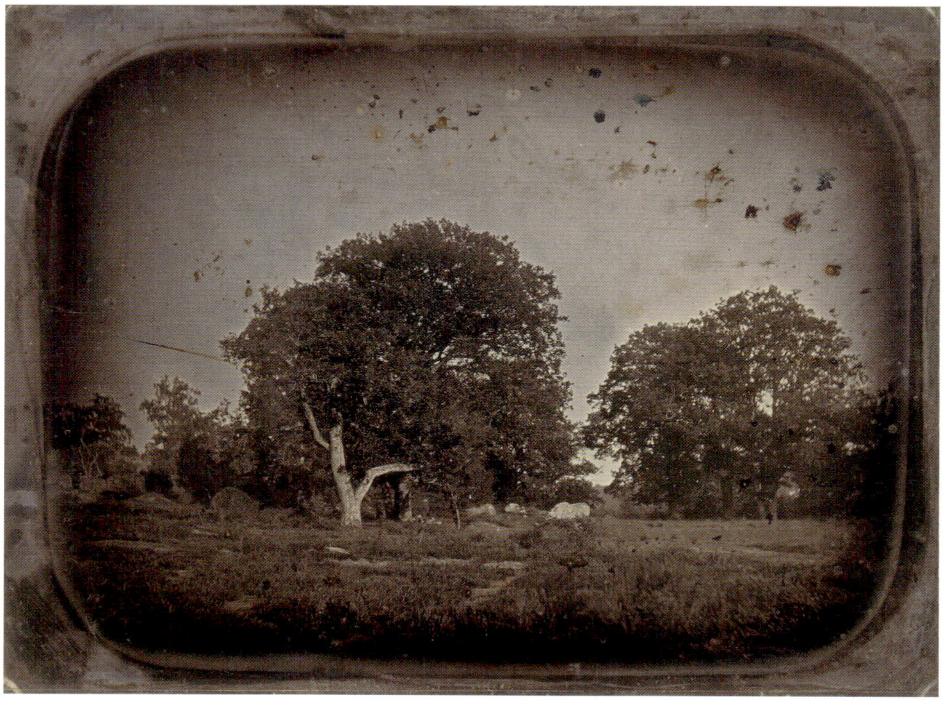

4

Unknown artist

Great Oaks, Forest of Fontainebleau, c. 1845, daguerrotype, 12 × 16 (4 ¾ × 6 5⁄16). Musée d'Orsay, Paris

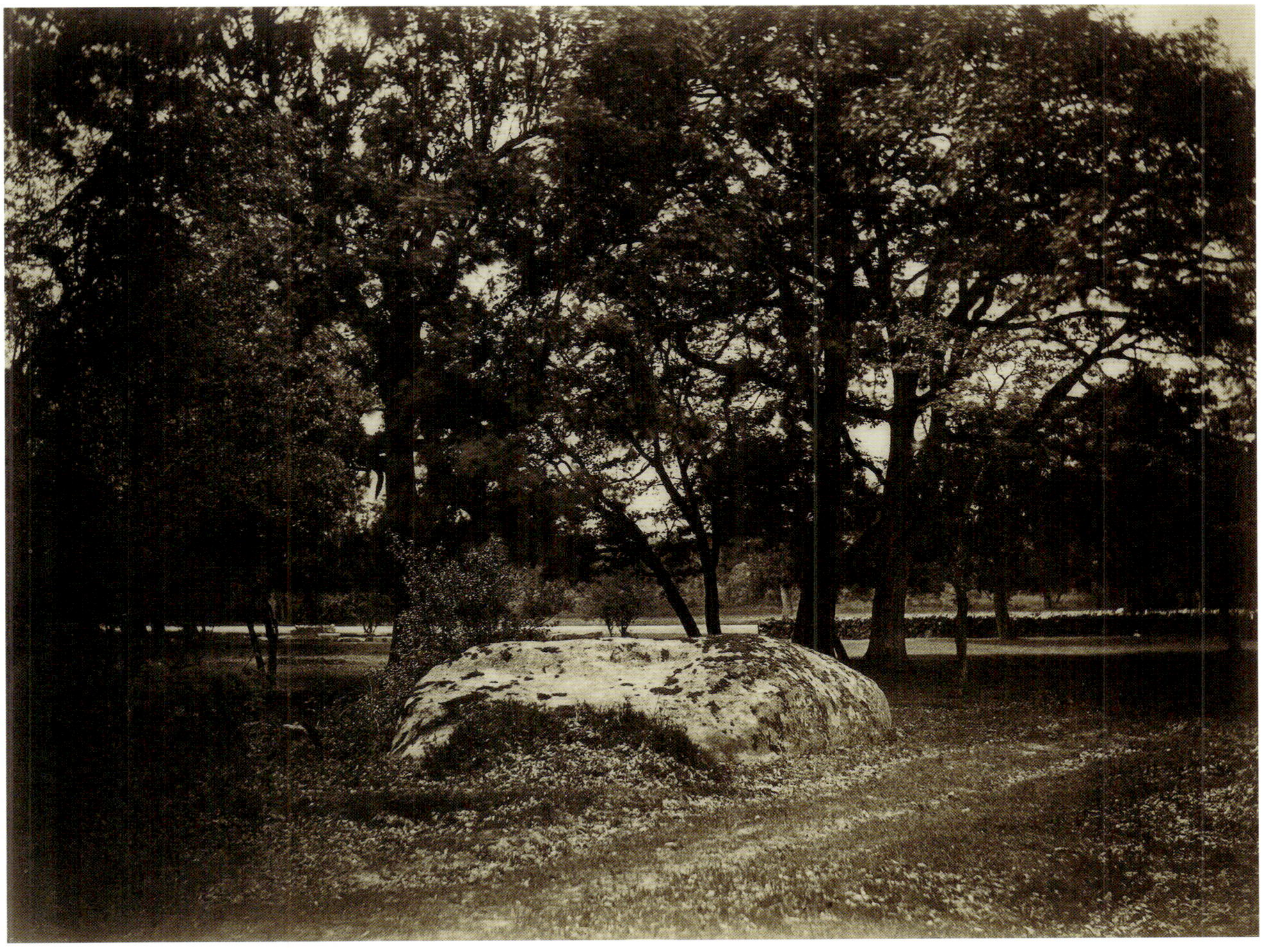

5

Gustave Le Gray

Road Past a Boulder, Forest of Fontainebleau, c. 1852, salted paper print from paper negative, 29.7 × 37.3 (11 11/16 × 14 11/16). Courtesy of Hans P. Kraus Jr., New York

6

Auguste Renoir

The Inn of Mother Anthony, 1866, oil on canvas, 194 × 131 (76 ⅜ × 51 9/16). Nationalmuseum, Stockholm

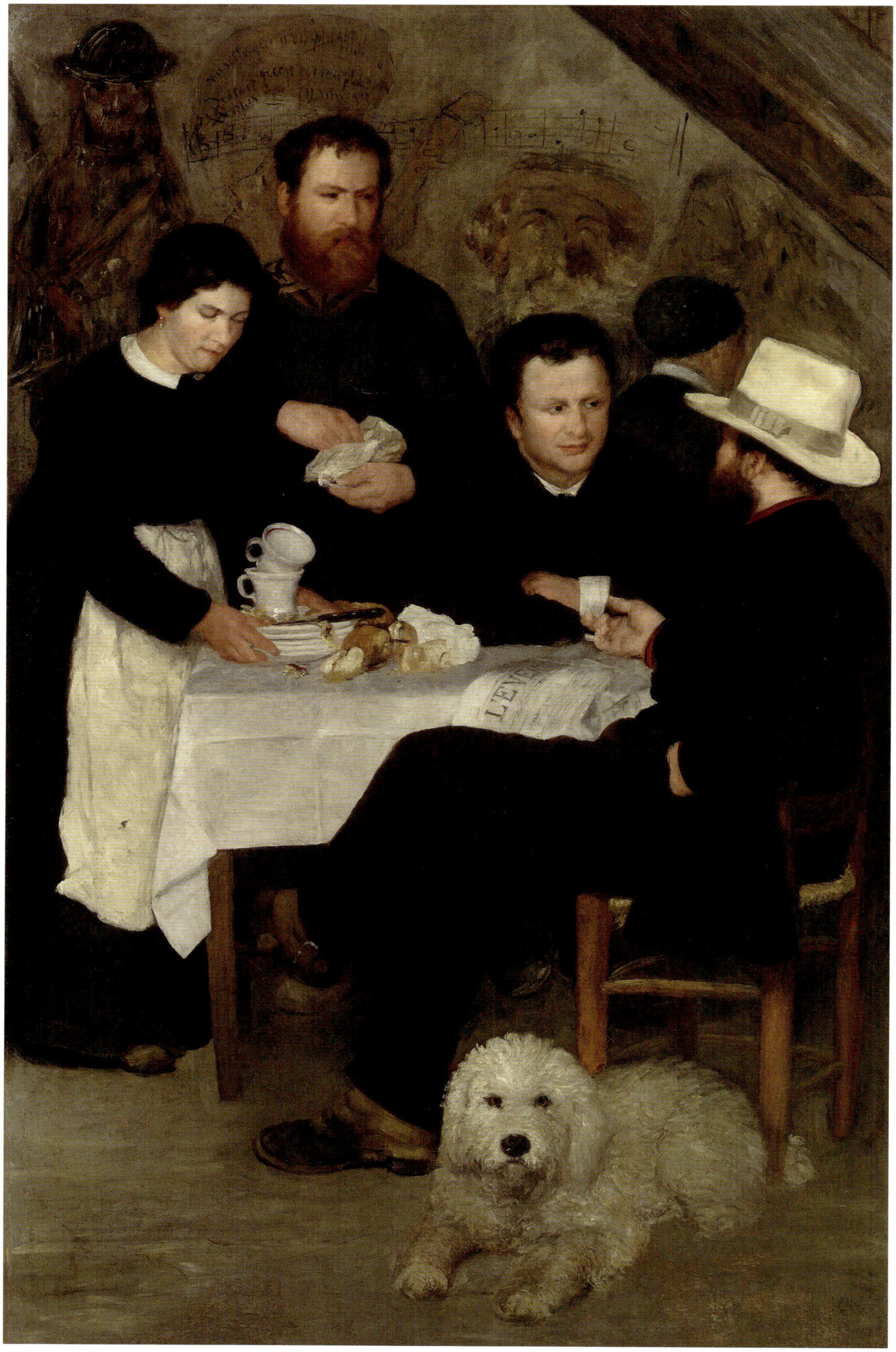

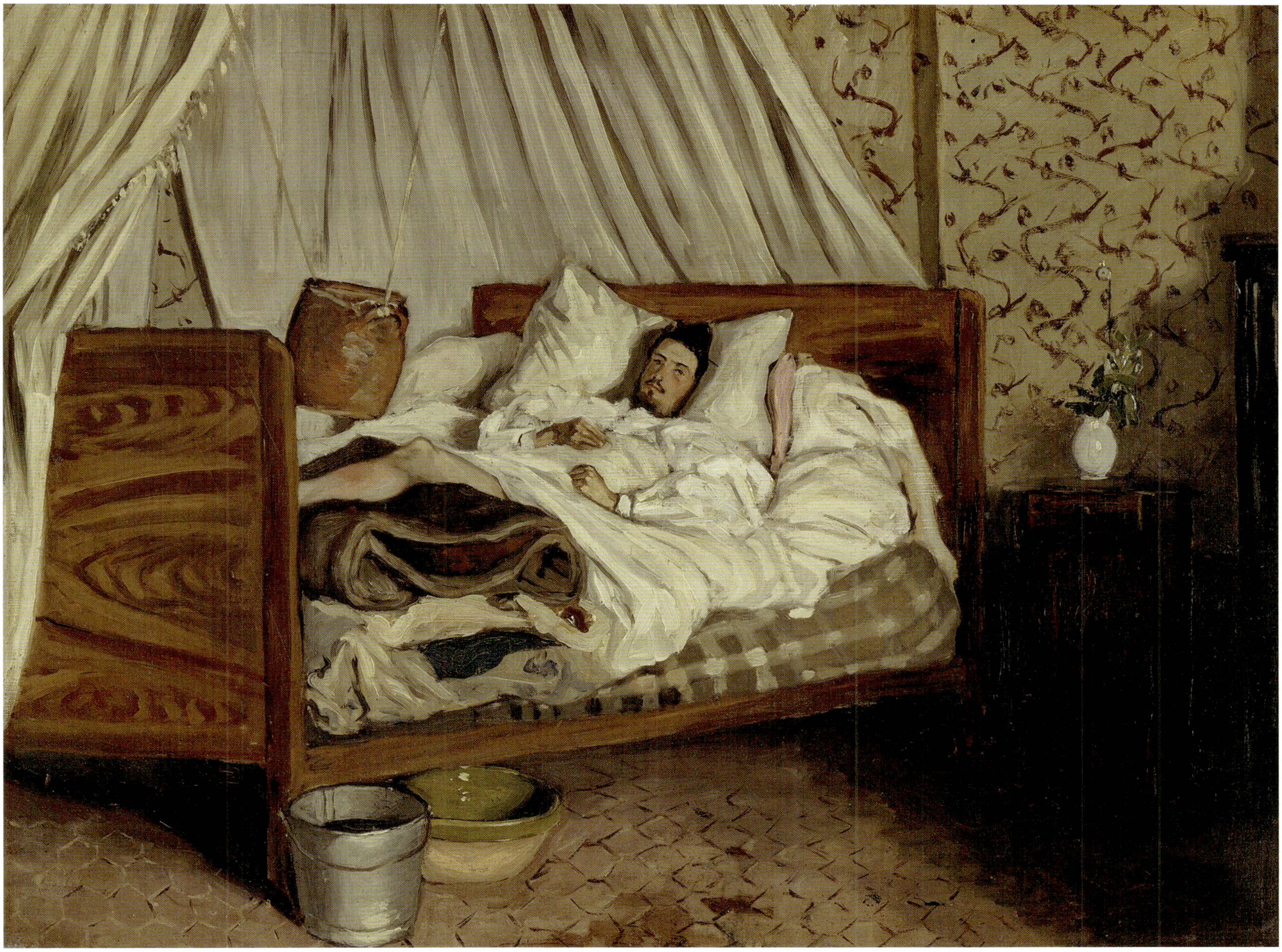

7

Frédéric Bazille

The Improvised Field Hospital, 1865, oil on canvas, 47 × 65 (18 ½ × 25 ⁹⁄₁₆). Musée d'Orsay, Paris

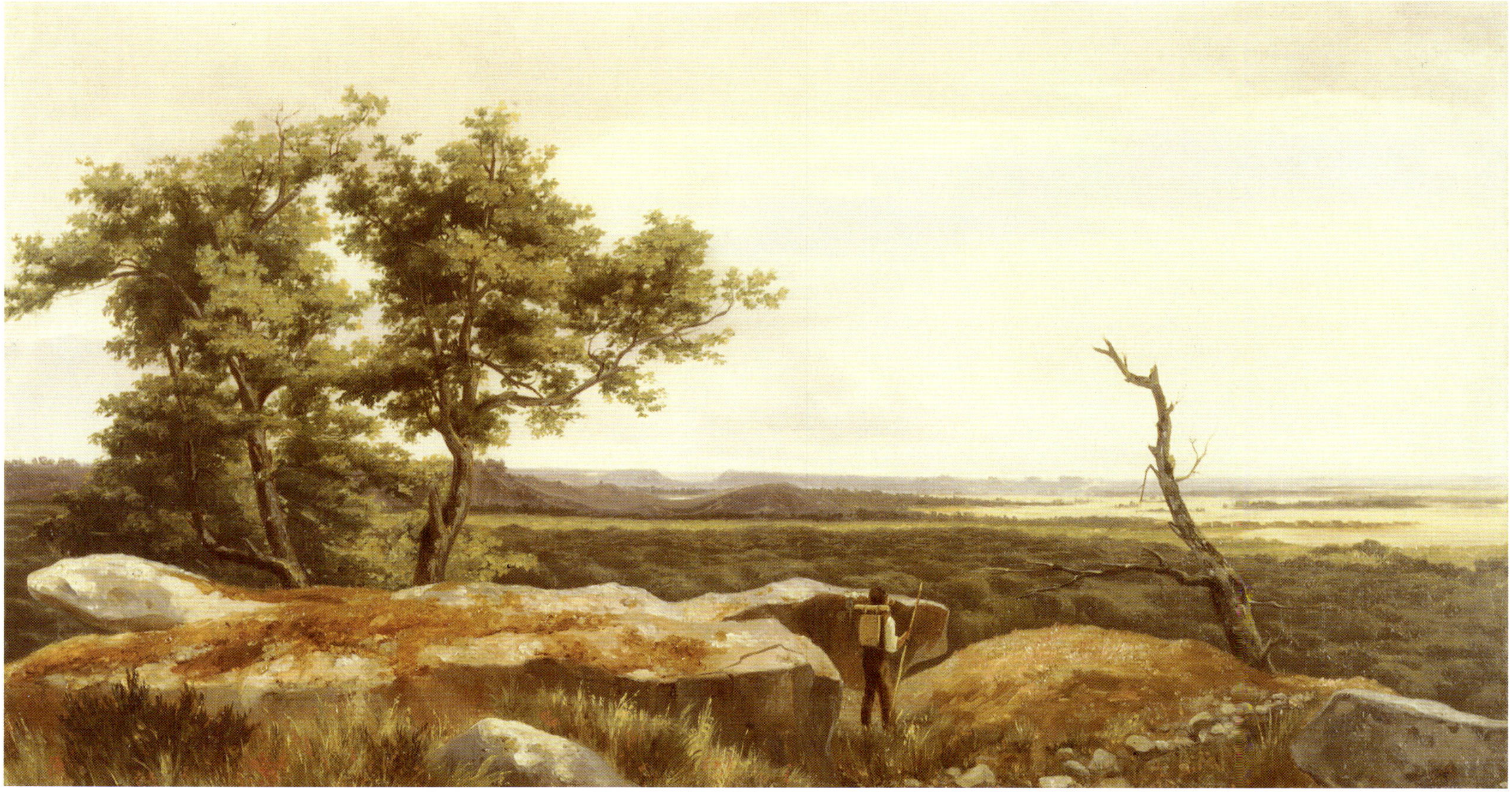

8

Théodore Claude Félix Caruelle d'Aligny

View of Fontainebleau, c. 1850, oil on canvas, 35 × 65 (13 ¾ × 25 ⁹⁄₁₆). Bibliothèque-Musée Marmottan, Boulogne-Billancourt

NOT IN EXHIBITION

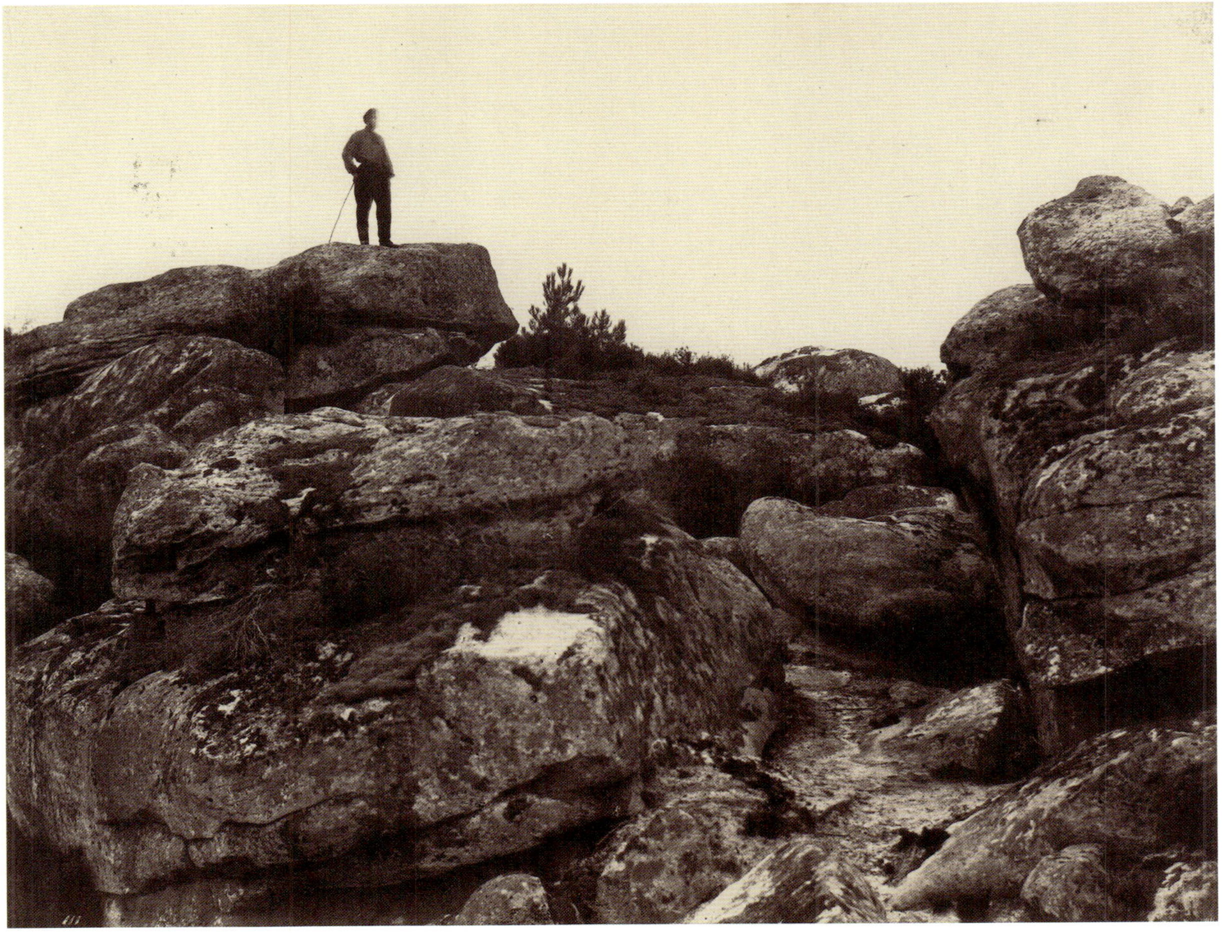

9

Eugène Cuvelier

Franchard, 20 October 1863, salted paper print from paper negative 19.7 × 26 (7 ¾ × 10 ¼). Courtesy of Hans P. Kraus Jr., New York

10

Claude Monet

Bazille and Camille (Study for "Le Déjeuner sur l'herbe"), 1865, oil on canvas, 93 × 68.9 (36 5/8 × 27 1/8). National Gallery of Art, Washington, Ailsa Mellon Bruce Collection, 1970

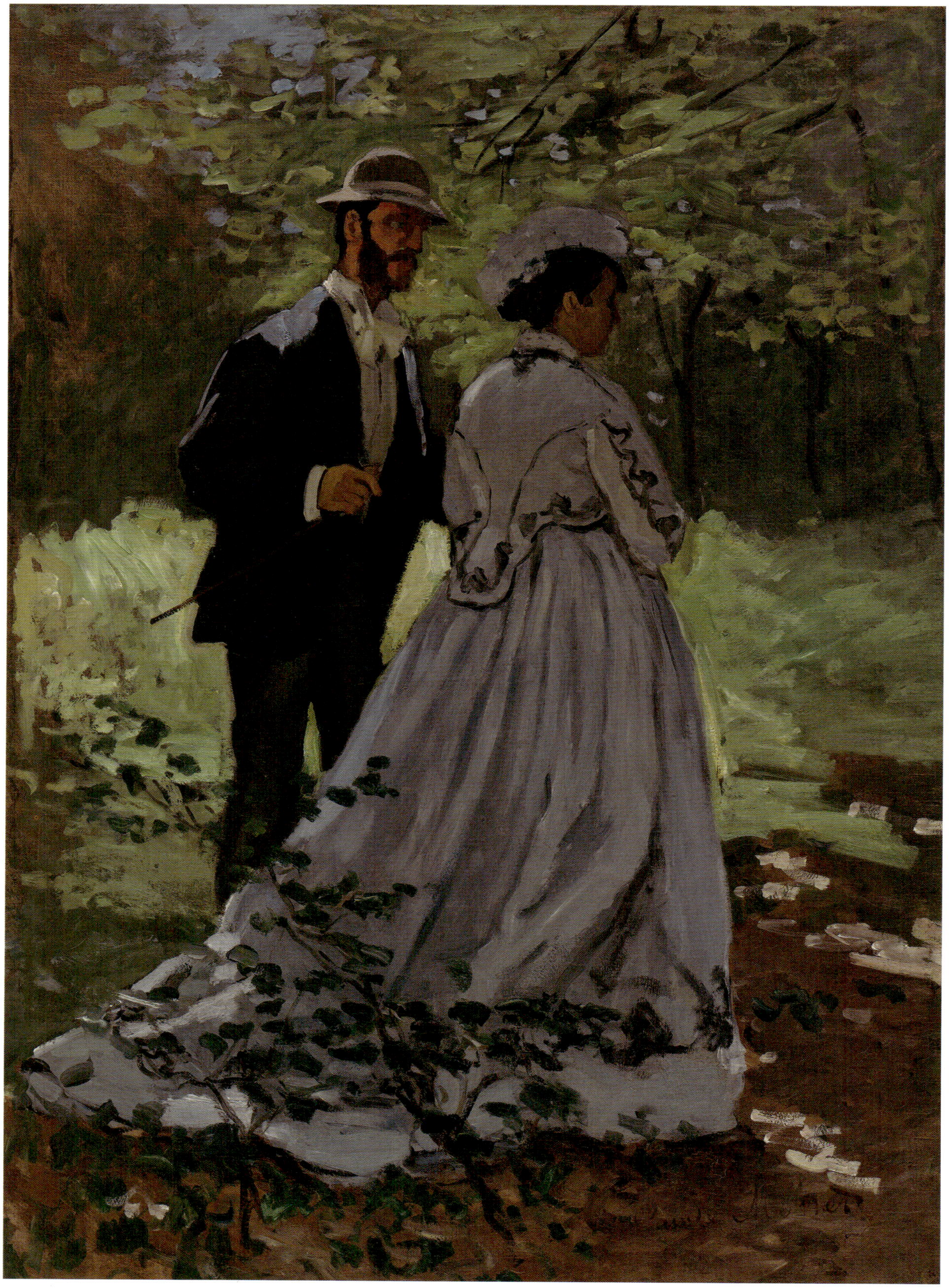

11

Jules Hereau

Monsieur Lafontaine Visits Barbizon, September 1859, oil on canvas, 45 × 35 (17 11/16 × 13 3/4). Private collection, Courtesy of Douwes Fine Art (since 1805), Amsterdam

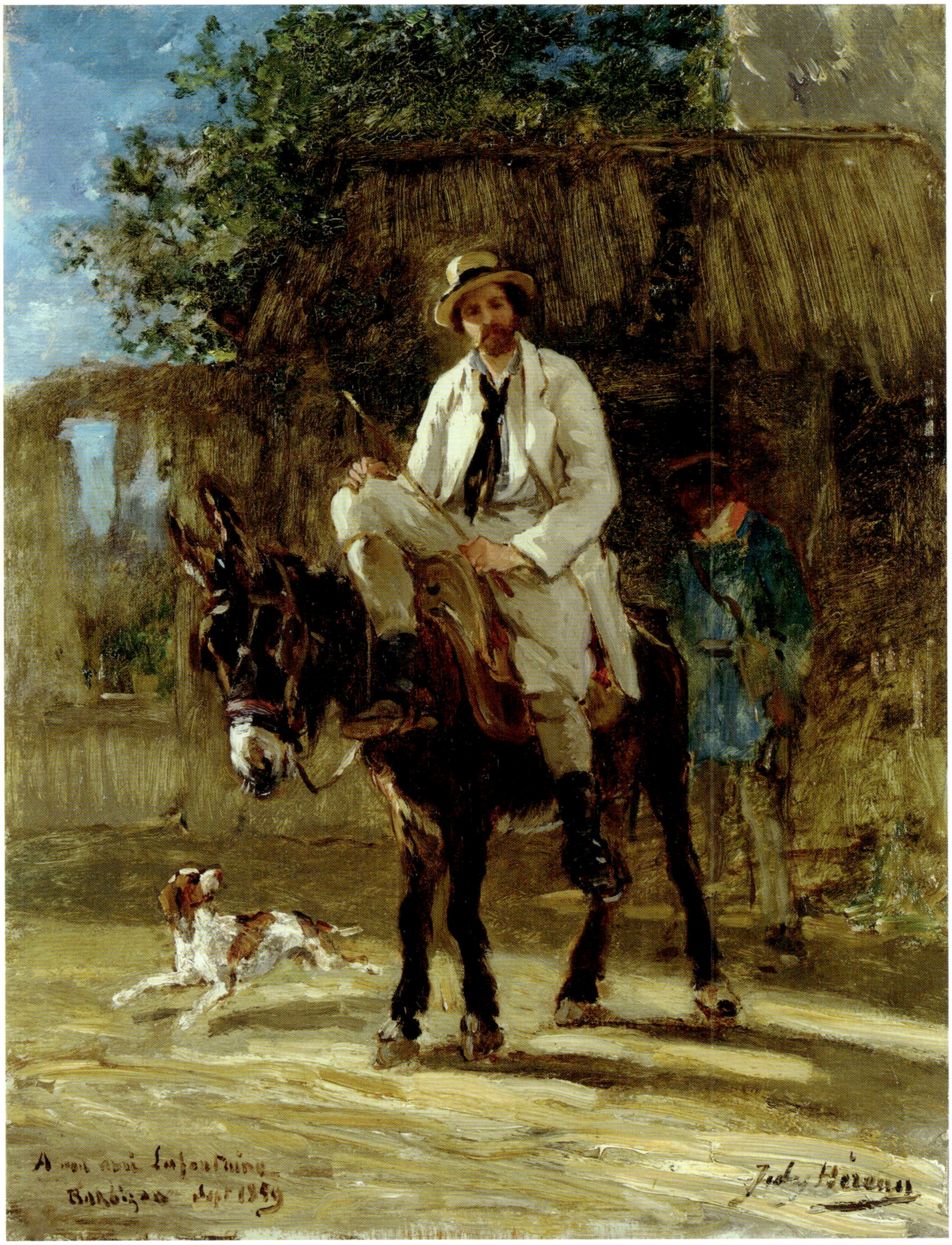

Topography

The Forest of Fontainebleau is remarkable in the richness and diversity of its topography, in terms of both its vegetation and geological phenomena. Among its more unexpected characteristics is the extreme aridity of the forest. Because of the high silica content in the soil and the preponderance of limestone and sandstone, both of which are porous in nature, Fontainebleau is almost completely devoid of water, with the exception of the small number of freestanding pools and the occasional stream formed and maintained through the accumulation of rainwater. Although smaller pools often evaporate in the heat of summer, others remain all year round, including the Mare à Piat, the Mare aux Evées (formerly an infected marsh), and the Mare aux Fées (known by the name of Grande Mare until 1809) (see pls. 29, 32, and 33).[1] During the nineteenth century, such pools were invaluable, providing water to the indigenous animal life of the forest as well as domestic animals, primarily cows, from nearby villages.

Yet despite this aridity, the Forest of Fontainebleau is rich with plant life and accommodates both deciduous and coniferous trees with equal ease. Fontainebleau's fame, however, resides in its old-growth forest. In the mid-nineteenth century, there were 1,000 hectares of *haute-futaie*, old-growth forest that spanned the cantons of Bas-Bréau, La Tillaie, Gros-Fouteau, Grands-Feuillards, and Monts-de-Fays. Oak, beech, and hornbeam dominate there, with some trees estimated to be between five and six centuries old.[2] Bas-Bréau is considered particularly noteworthy in this regard and as early as 1664 had been recognized for the age and grandeur of its trees (see pls. 24 and 25).[3] Located at the northwestern edge of the forest and flanking the Pavé de Chailly, the principal road between Paris and the town of Fontainebleau, Bas-Bréau provided most visitors with their first taste of the forest in the days prior to the establishment of the railroad, and it rarely failed to make an impression. Generally considered to be the most beautiful stand of trees within the forest, it was a favorite haven of artists who claimed it as their domain.[4]

Known alternately as the Grand Route Royale, the Route de Paris, and the Chemin de Chailly, the Pavé de Chailly was an important artistic motif in its own right.[5] Corot painted it in 1822, and during a trip to Moret in 1828, Rousseau stopped there to make a study of the road.[6] Many others would follow suit, including Monet and Le Gray, both of whom were attracted to the dramatic contrast of the open roadway and the massive trees rising up along its side (see pls. 12, 13, and 14).[7] This was not the only road in the forest, however. Contrary to the popularly held belief that Fontainebleau constituted wild, untamed nature, the forest was actually crisscrossed by roads and pathways. The Route des Ligueurs, which had been built expressly to facilitate travel between Paris and the hunting lodge at Fontainebleau, already existed by 1304, and in time other *grands chemins*, as the royal roads were known, would link Fontainebleau with the surrounding villages of Bourron, Chailly, Melun, Moret, and Ury.[8] Over time, more roads were introduced, including the Route Ronde built by Henri IV and some 300,000 *toises* of roadway that were constructed during the reign of Louis XIV.[9] The nineteenth century also saw the introduction of numerous *sentiers*, trails created for the benefit of tourists who visited the forest in ever-growing numbers. Claude-François Denecourt, who was the mastermind behind these sentiers, oversaw the creation of some three hundred kilometers of trail during his lifetime.[10] These various trails and paths increased accessibility to and within the forest, facilitating travel and exploration within the very depths of Fontainebleau.

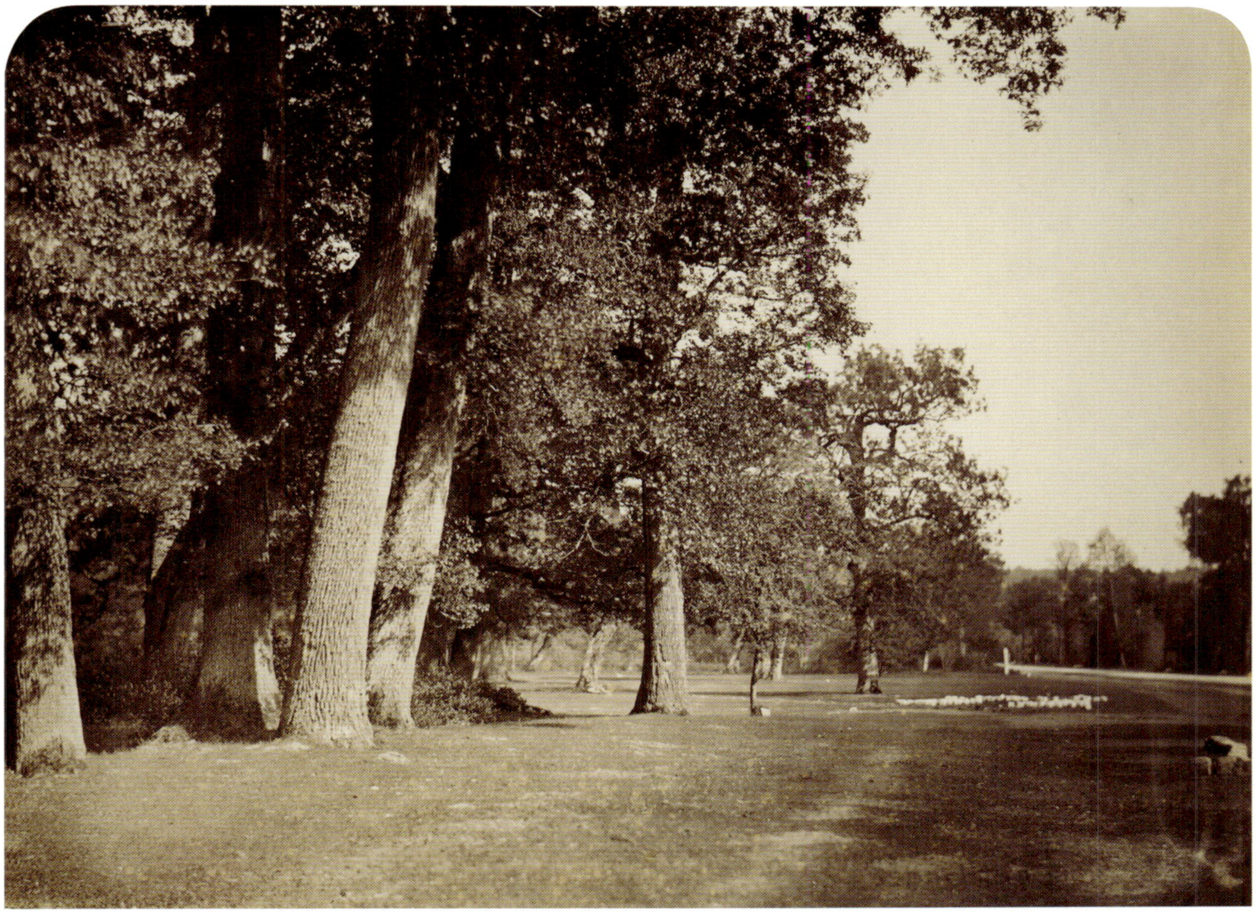

12

Gustave Le Gray

Trees along the Pavé de Chailly, 1852, salted paper print from paper negative, 23.9 × 33 (9 7/16 × 13). The Museum of Fine Arts, Houston, Gift of the Brown Foundation, Inc., The Manfred Heiting Collection

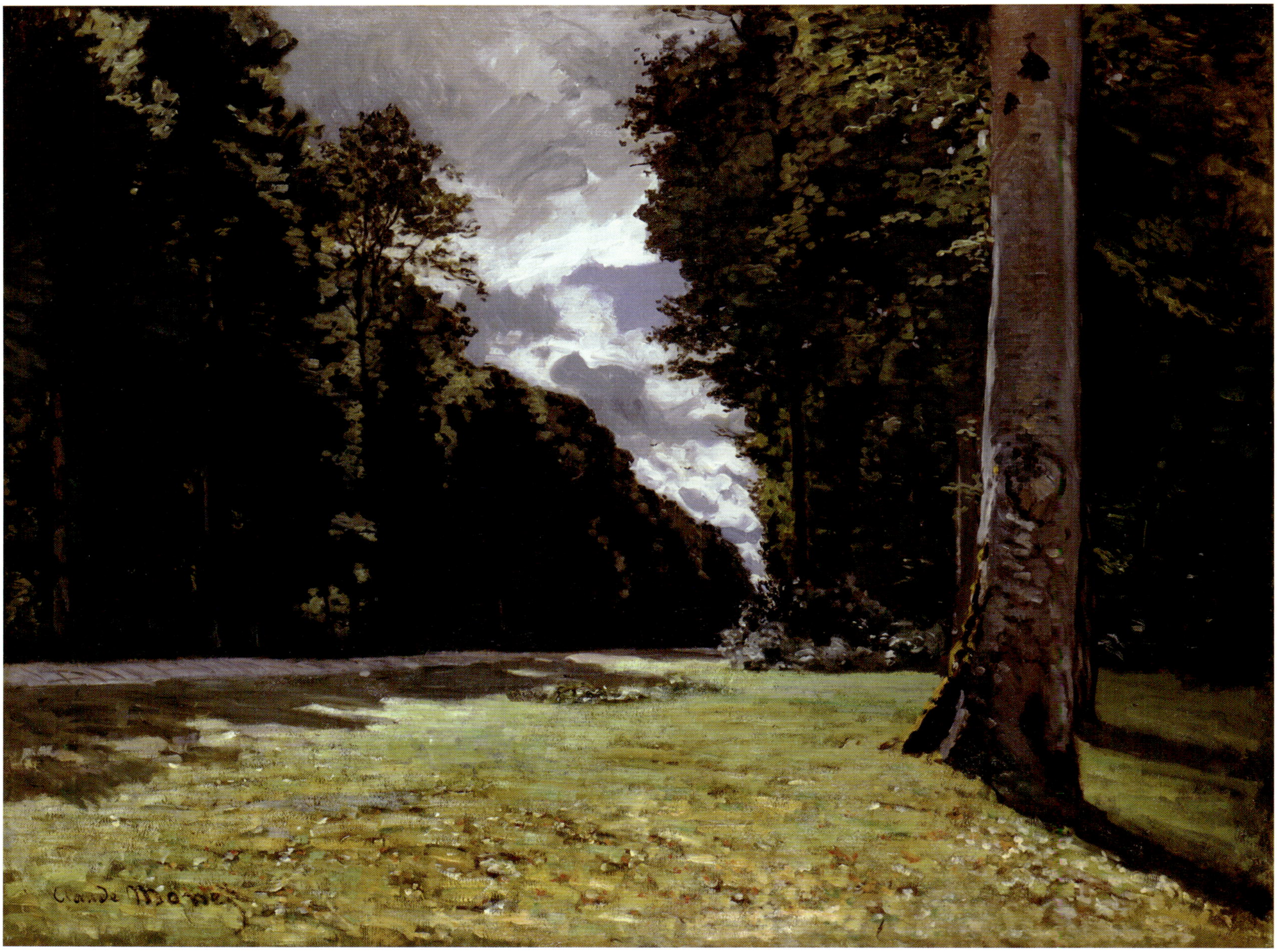

13

Claude Monet

The Route to Chailly (Pavé de Chailly), 1865, oil on canvas, 97 × 130 (38 3/16 × 51 3/16). Ordrupgaard, Copenhagen

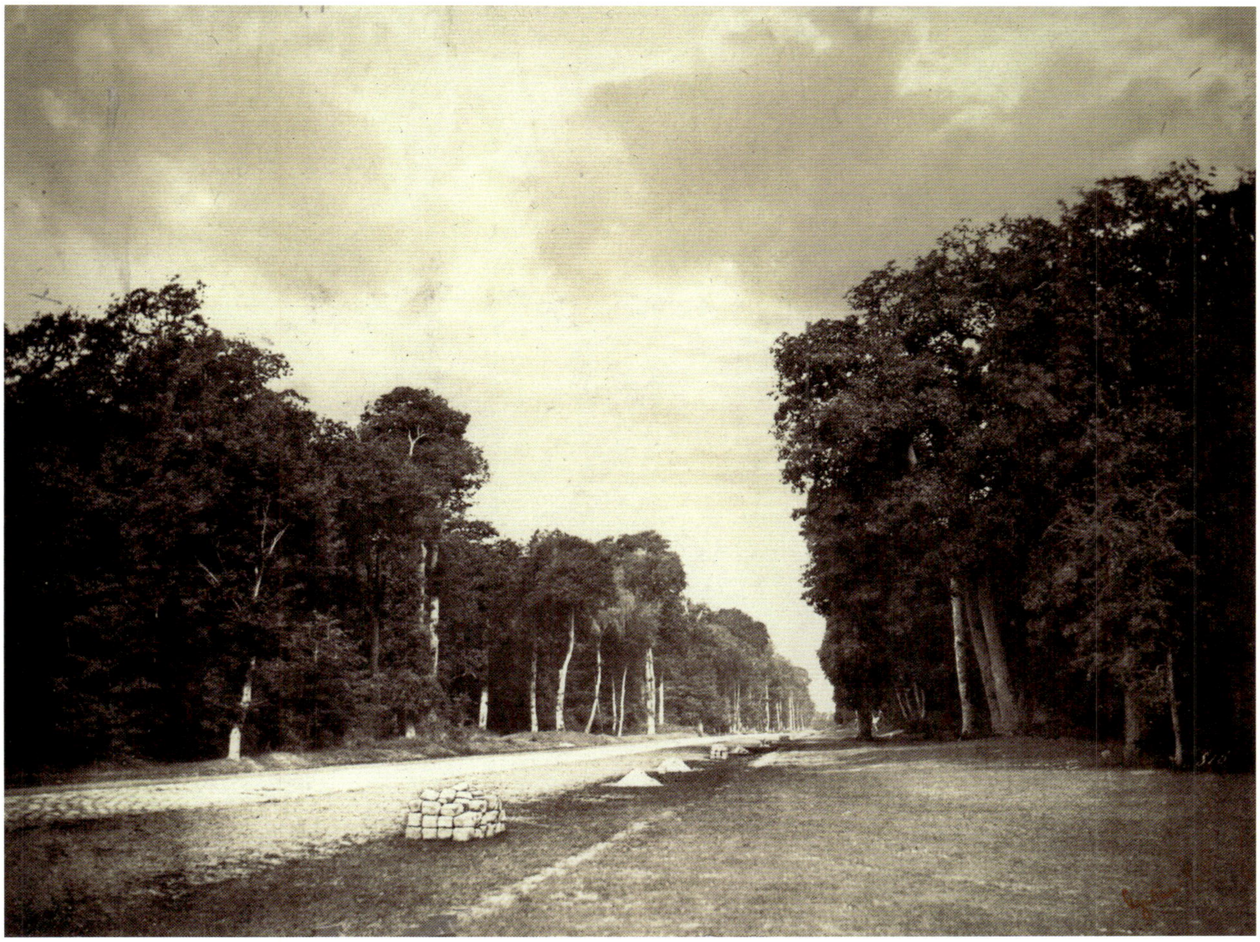

14

Gustave Le Gray

The Road to Chailly, Forest of Fontainebleau (Pavé de Chailly), c. 1852, salted paper print from waxed paper negative (landscape) and collodion glass negative (sky), 28.2 × 38.8 (11 ⅛ × 15 ¼). Victoria and Albert Museum, London, Part of the Townsend Bequest

15

John Beasley Greene

Trees, Forest of Fontainebleau, c. 1852, salted paper print from paper negative, 23.2 × 30.3 (9 1/8 × 11 15/16). The Museum of Modern Art, New York, Gift of Jerome Powell, 1992

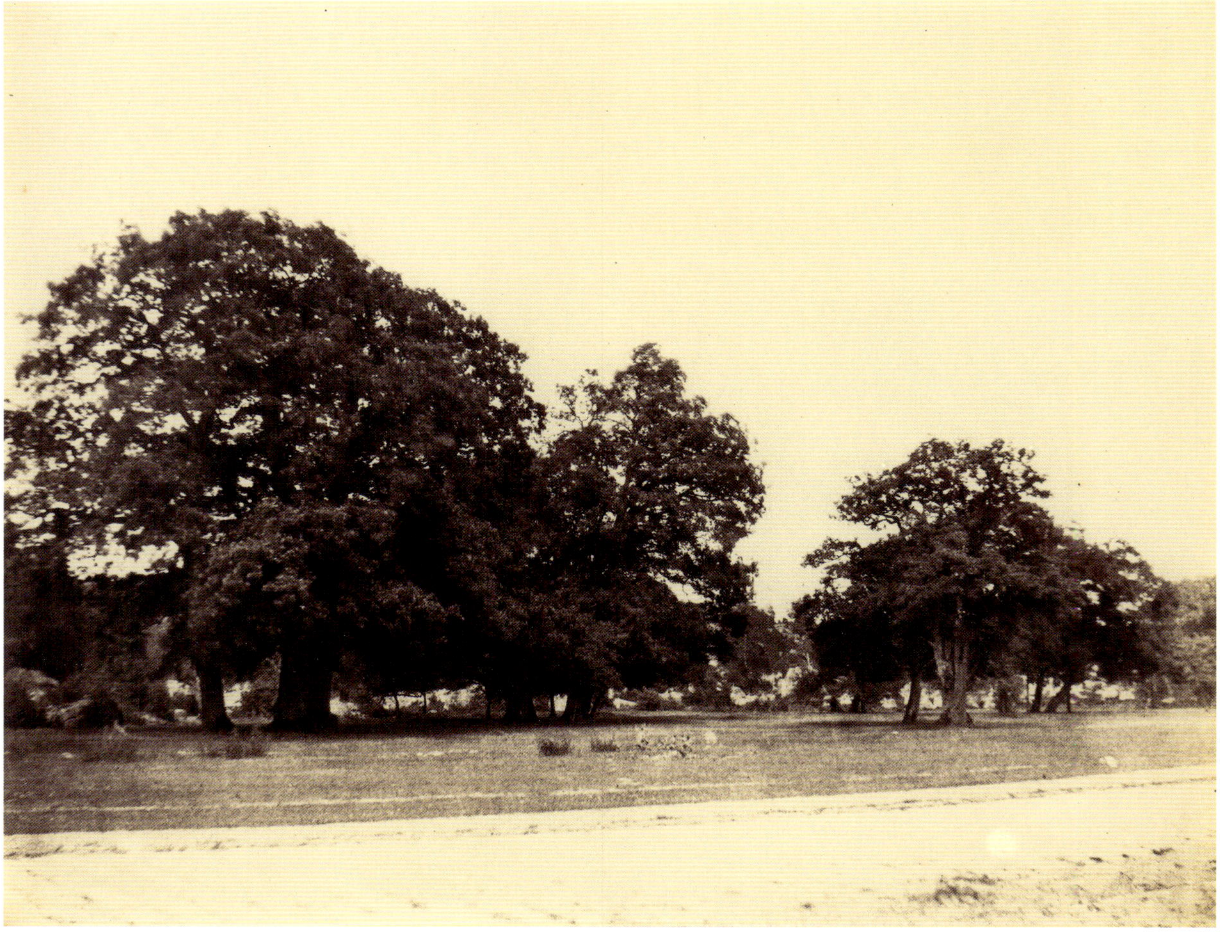

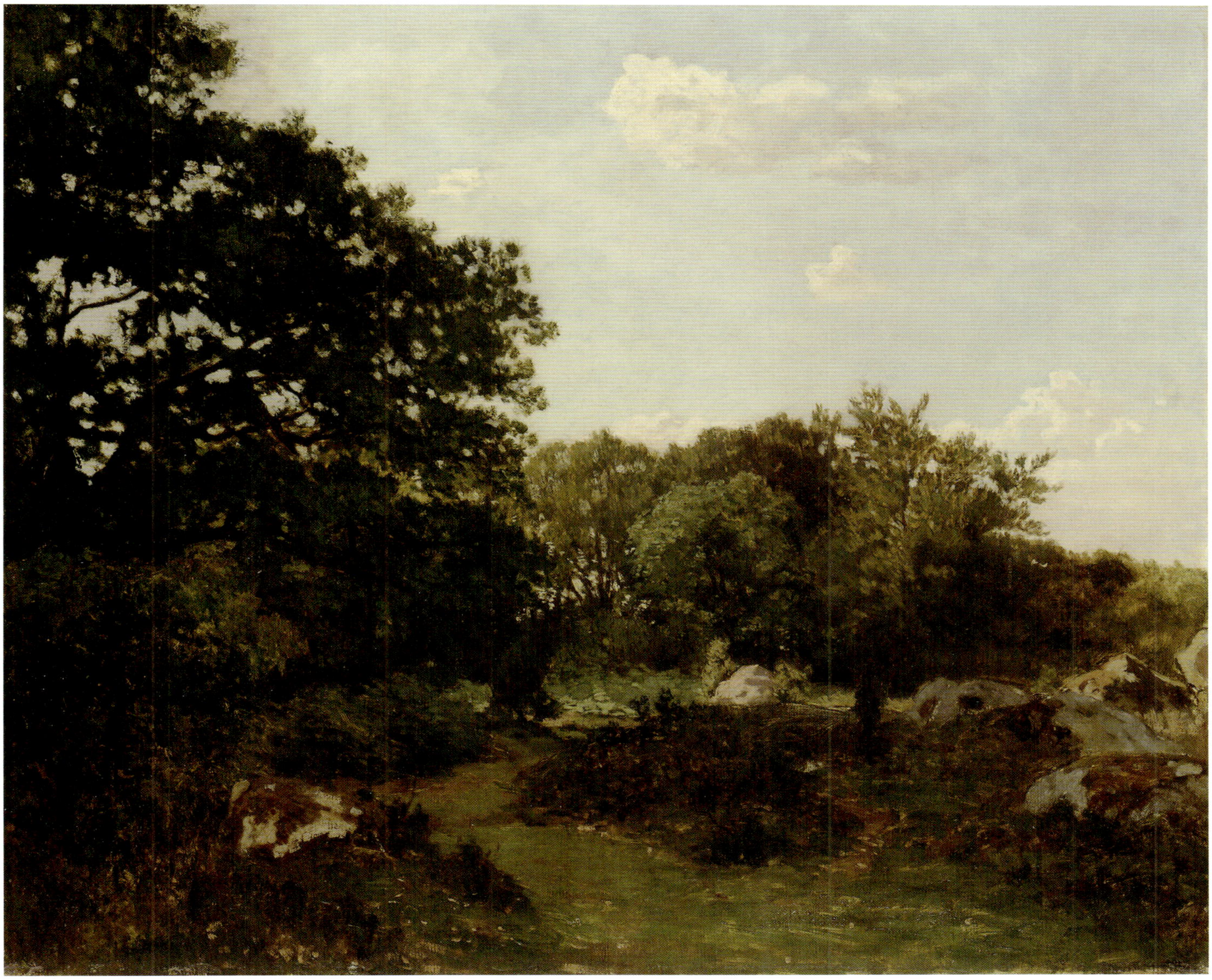

16

Frédéric Bazille

Forest of Fontainebleau,
1865, oil on canvas,
60 × 73 (23 ⅝ × 28 ¾).
Musée d'Orsay, Paris

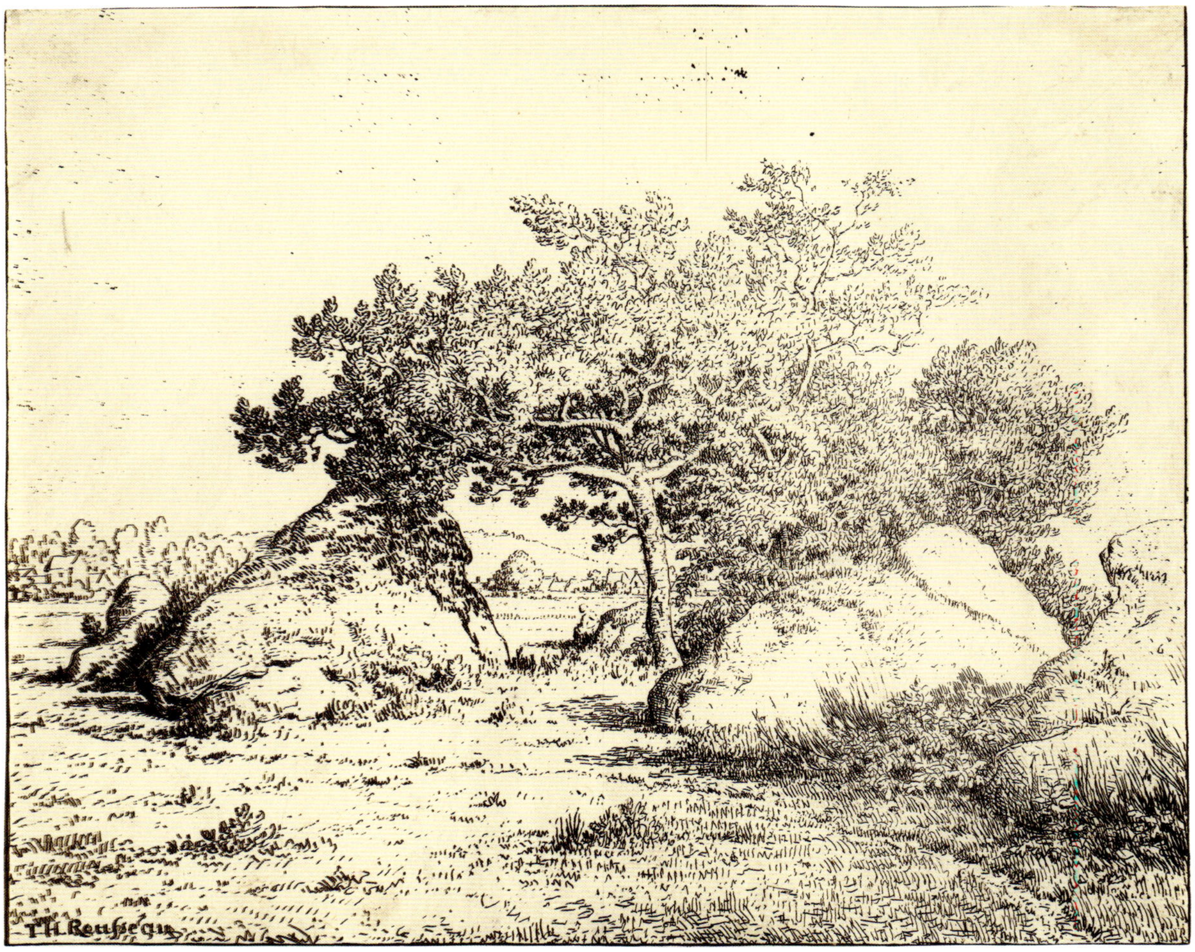

17

Théodore Rousseau

Cherry Tree at Plante à Biau, 1855, cliché-verre, 21.6 × 27.4 (8 ½ × 10 13/16). National Gallery of Art, Washington, Andrew W. Mellon Fund, 1978

18

André Giroux

Untitled (Scene of Fontainebleau), c. 1853, salted paper print from waxed paper negative, 21.3 × 27.5 (8 ⅜ × 10 13⁄16). The Cleveland Museum of Art, John L. Severance Fund, 1996

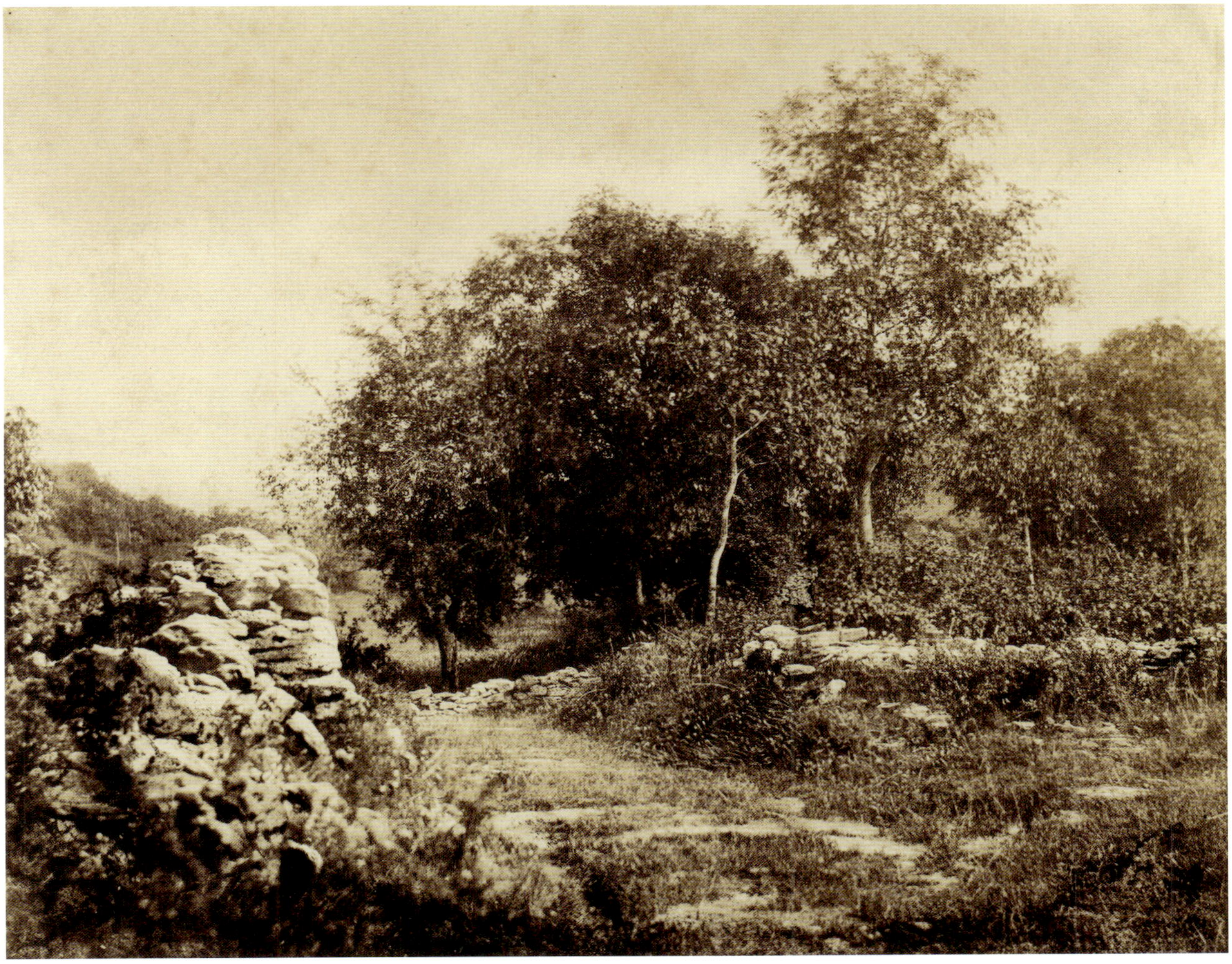

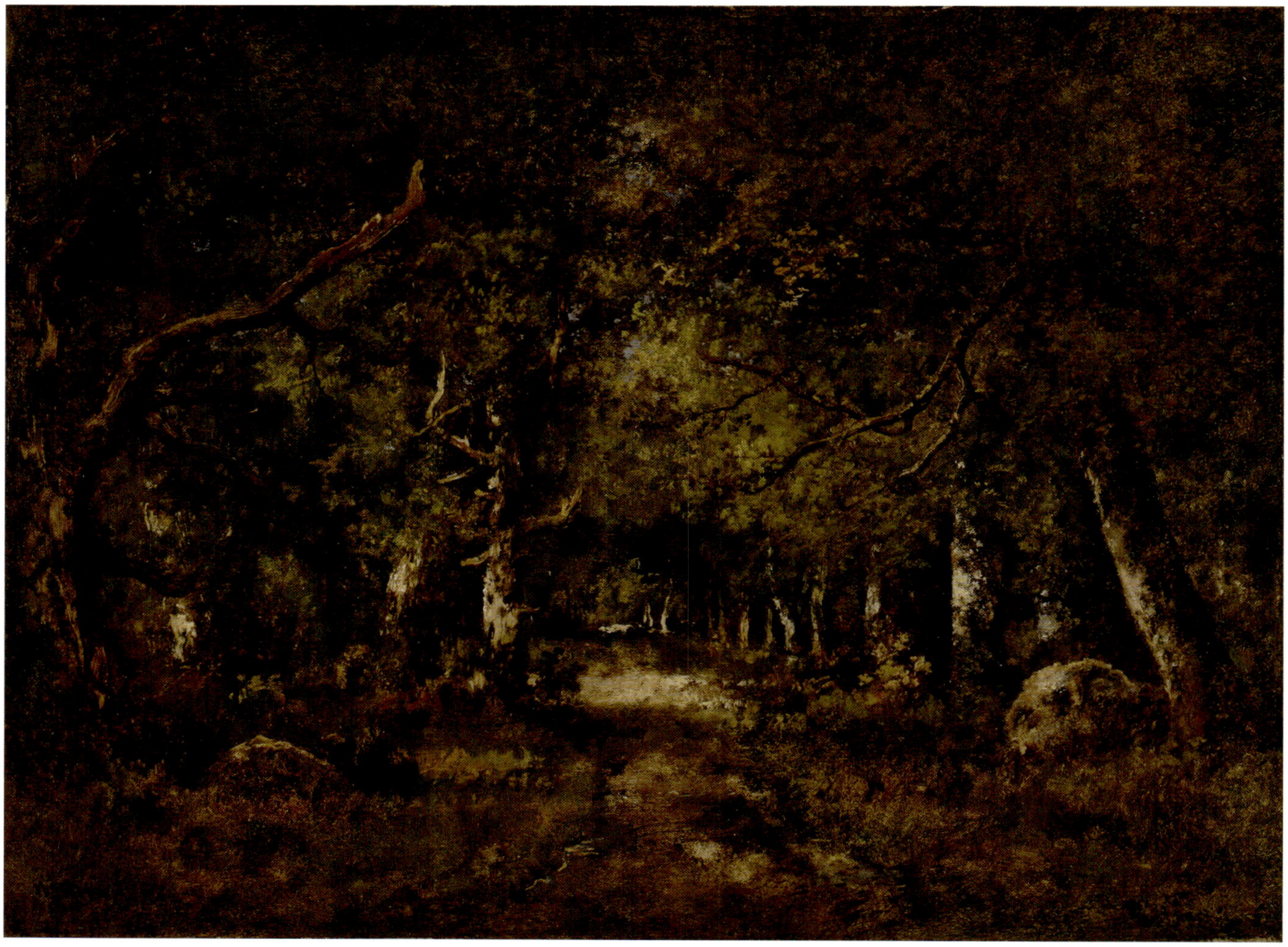

19

Narcisse-Virgile Diaz de la Peña

Forest Scene, 1874, oil on wood, 32 × 44 (12 ⅝ × 17 ⅜). National Gallery of Art, Washington, Gift of R. Horace Gallatin, 1949

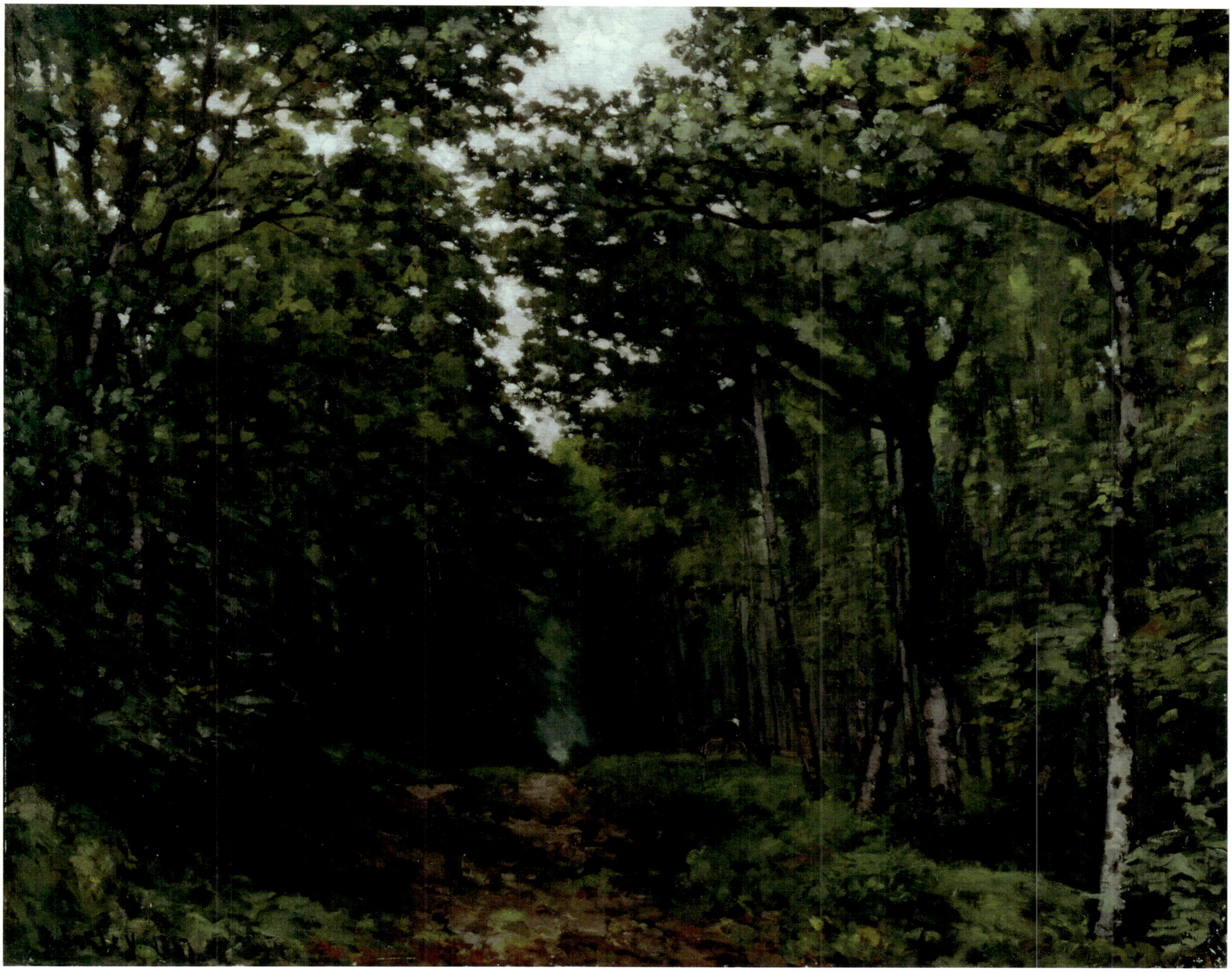

20

Alfred Sisley

Avenue of Chestnut Trees near La Celle-Saint-Cloud, 1867, oil on canvas, 95.5 × 122.2 (37 ⅝ × 48 ⅛). Southampton City Art Gallery

57 D2 W of Paris

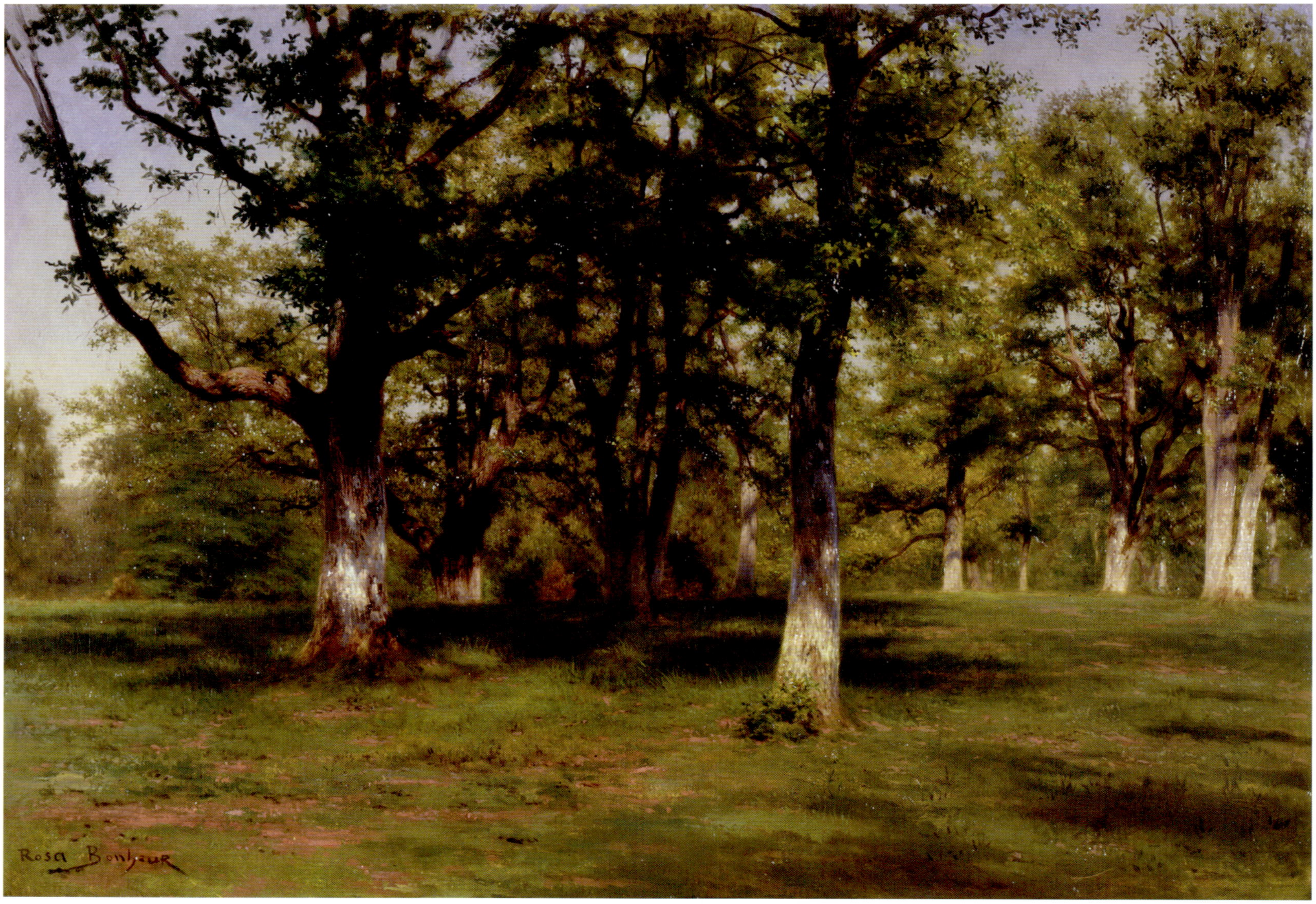

21

Rosa Bonheur

Forest of Fontainebleau: Spring in the Woods, 1860–1865, oil on canvas, 68 × 100.3 (26 ¾ × 39 ½). Private collection

22

Gustave Le Gray

Study of Trees and Pathways, 1849, salted paper print from paper negative, 18.3 × 26.4 (7 13/16 × 10 3/8). The J. Paul Getty Museum, Los Angeles

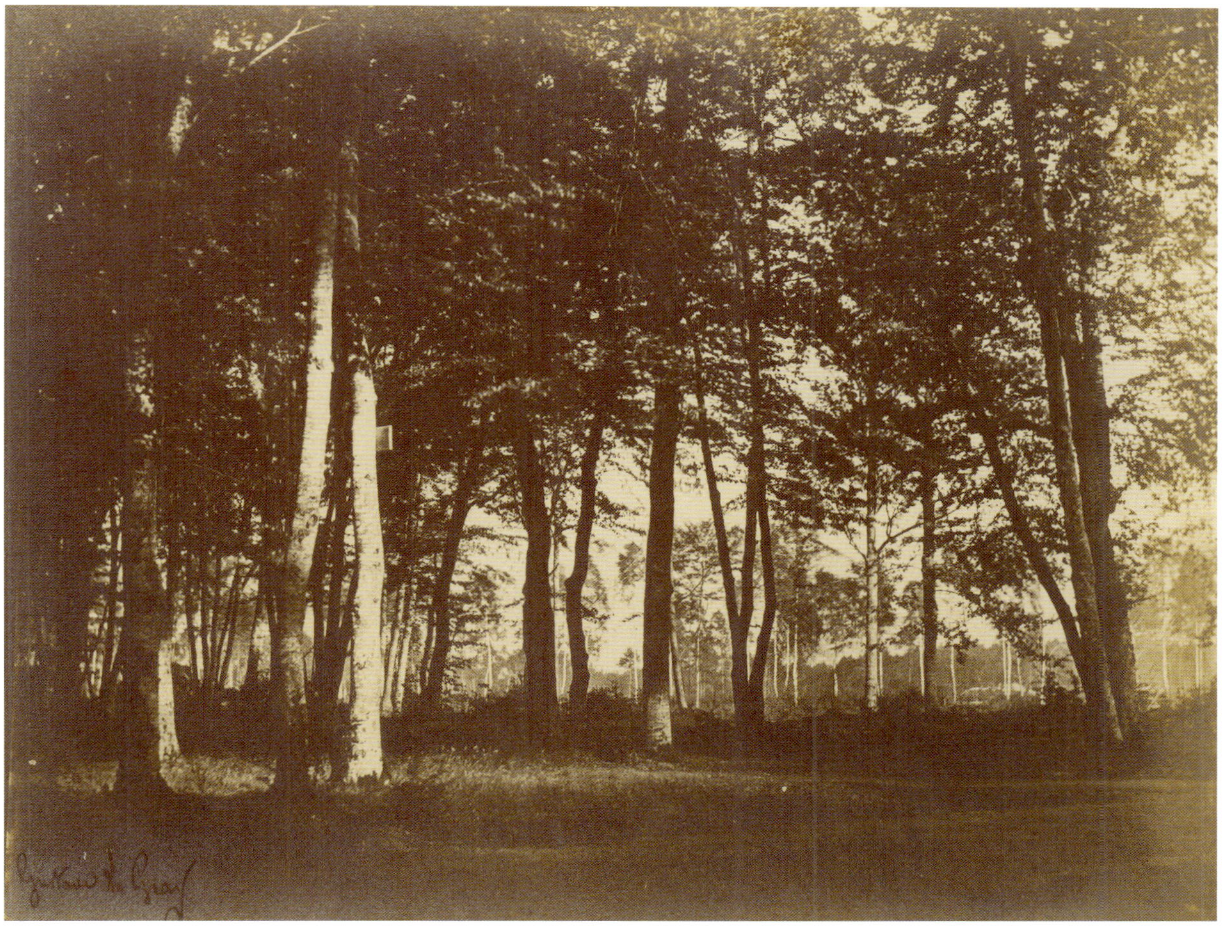

23

John Beasley Greene

Forest of Fontainebleau, c. 1852, salted paper print from paper negative, 24.9 × 30.3 (9 13/16 × 11 15/16). The Museum of Modern Art, New York, Gift of Jerome Powell, 1984

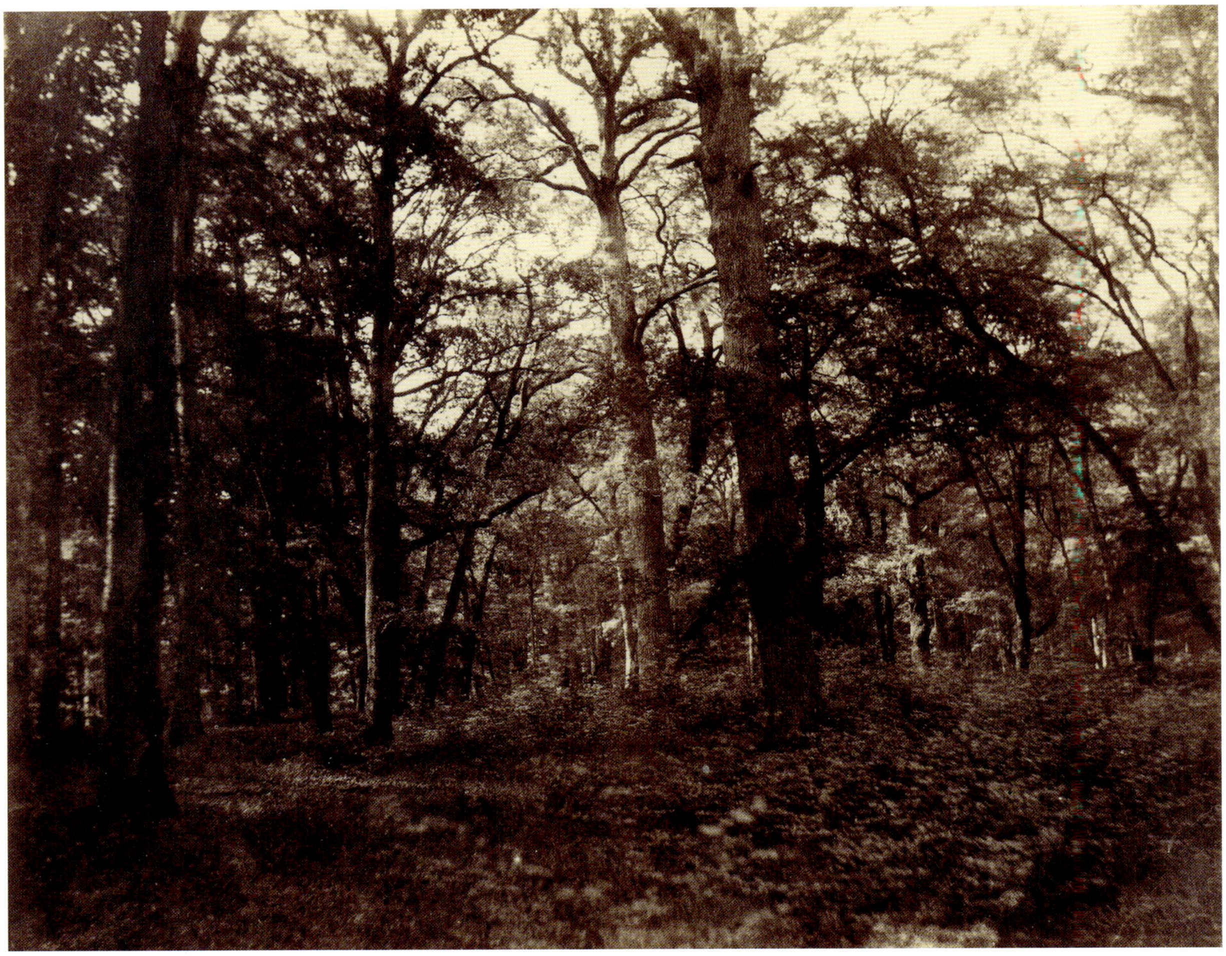

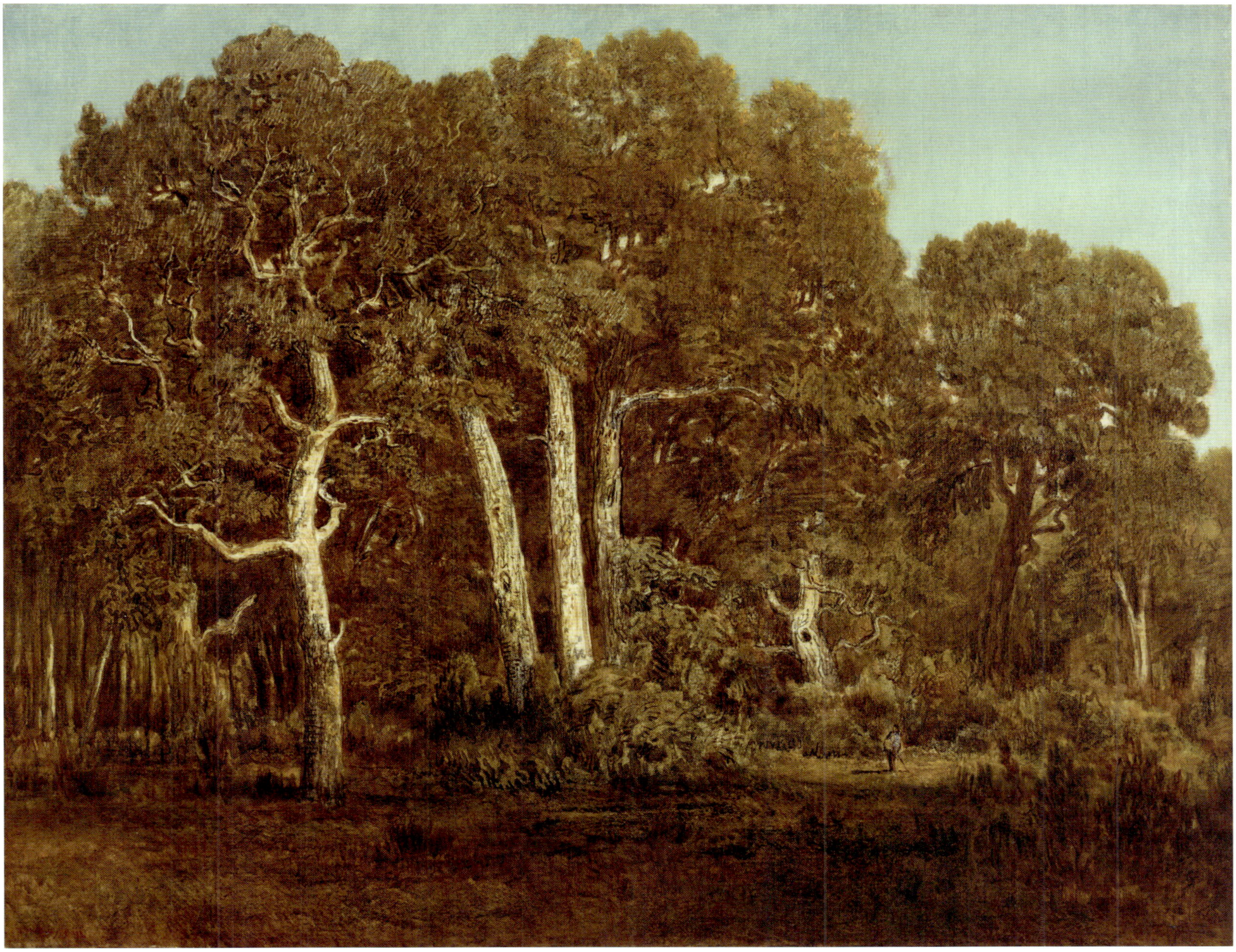

24

Théodore Rousseau

The Great Oaks of the Vieux Bas-Bréau, 1864, oil on canvas, 90.2 × 116.8 (35 ½ × 46). The Museum of Fine Arts, Houston, Museum Purchase with funds provided by the Agnes Cullen Arnold Endowment Fund

25

Robert-Léopold Leprince

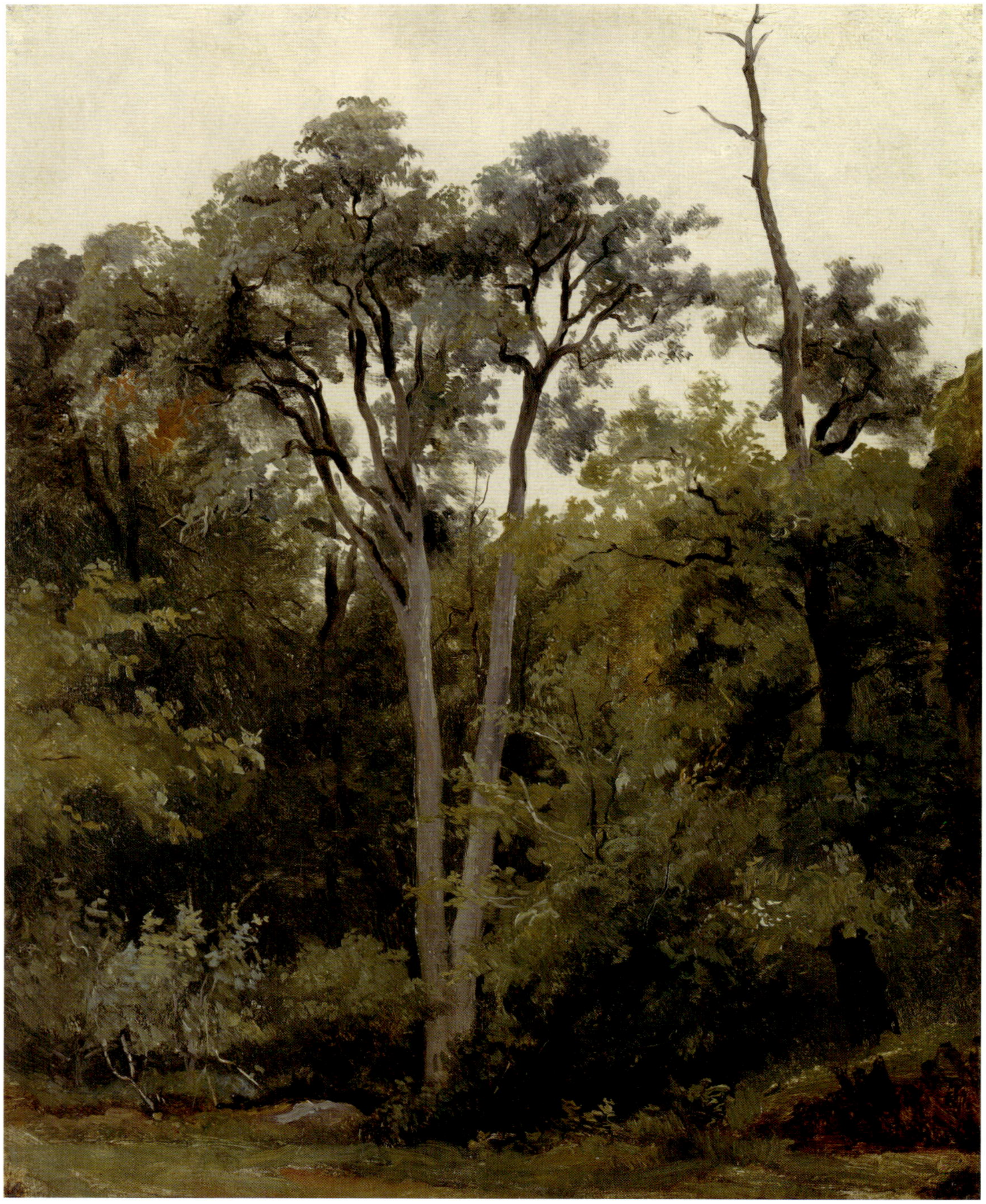

Bas-Bréau at Chailly, 1825, oil on paper mounted on cardboard, 31 × 38 (12 3/16 × 14 15/16). Musée du Louvre, Paris, Gift of the Institute of Industrial Development, 1996

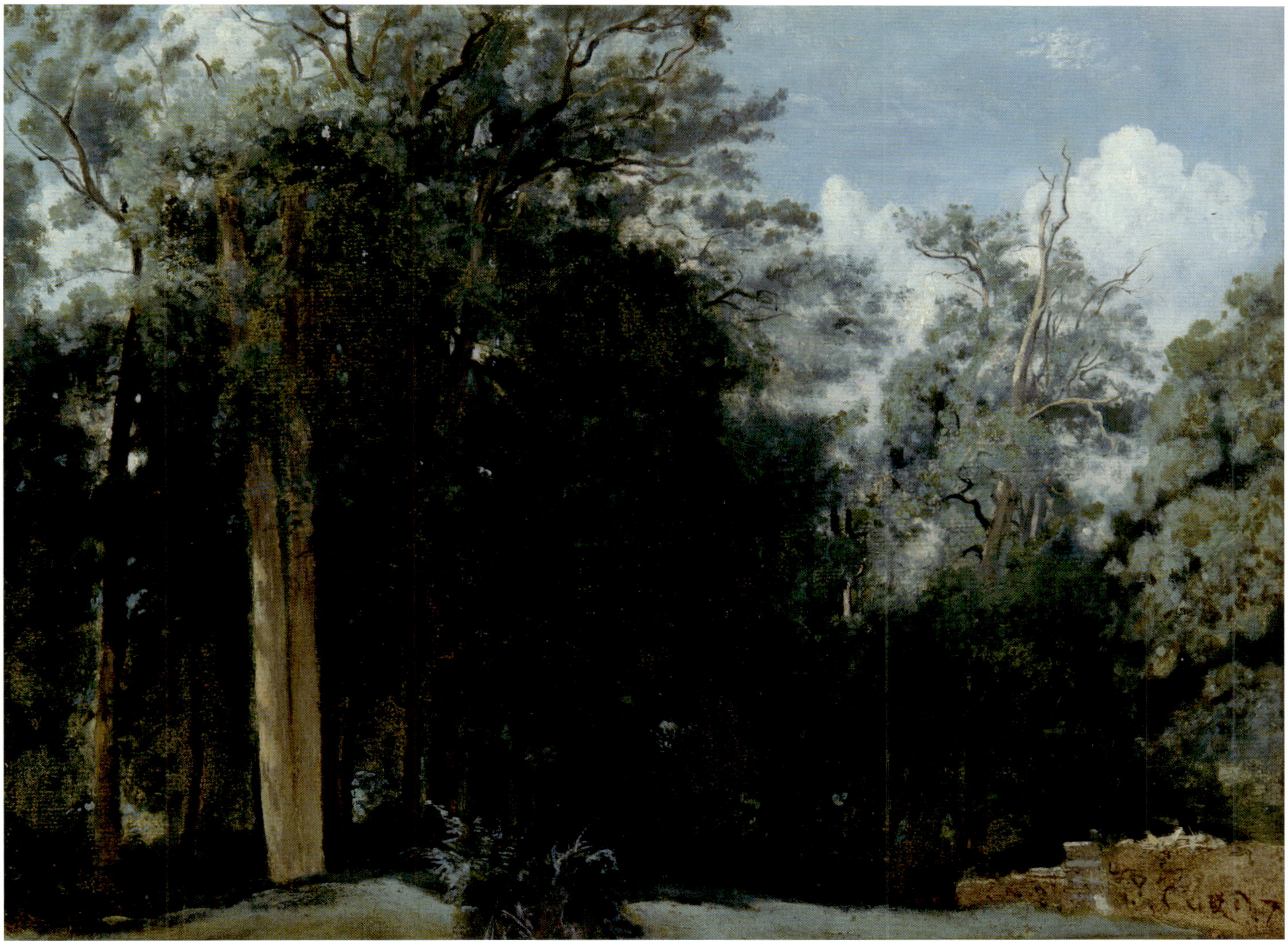

26

Jean-Baptiste-Camille Corot

Clearing in the Forest of Fontainebleau, c. 1830, oil on canvas, 32.5 × 44 (12 13/16 × 17 5/16). Kunsthalle Bremen — Der Kunstverein in Bremen

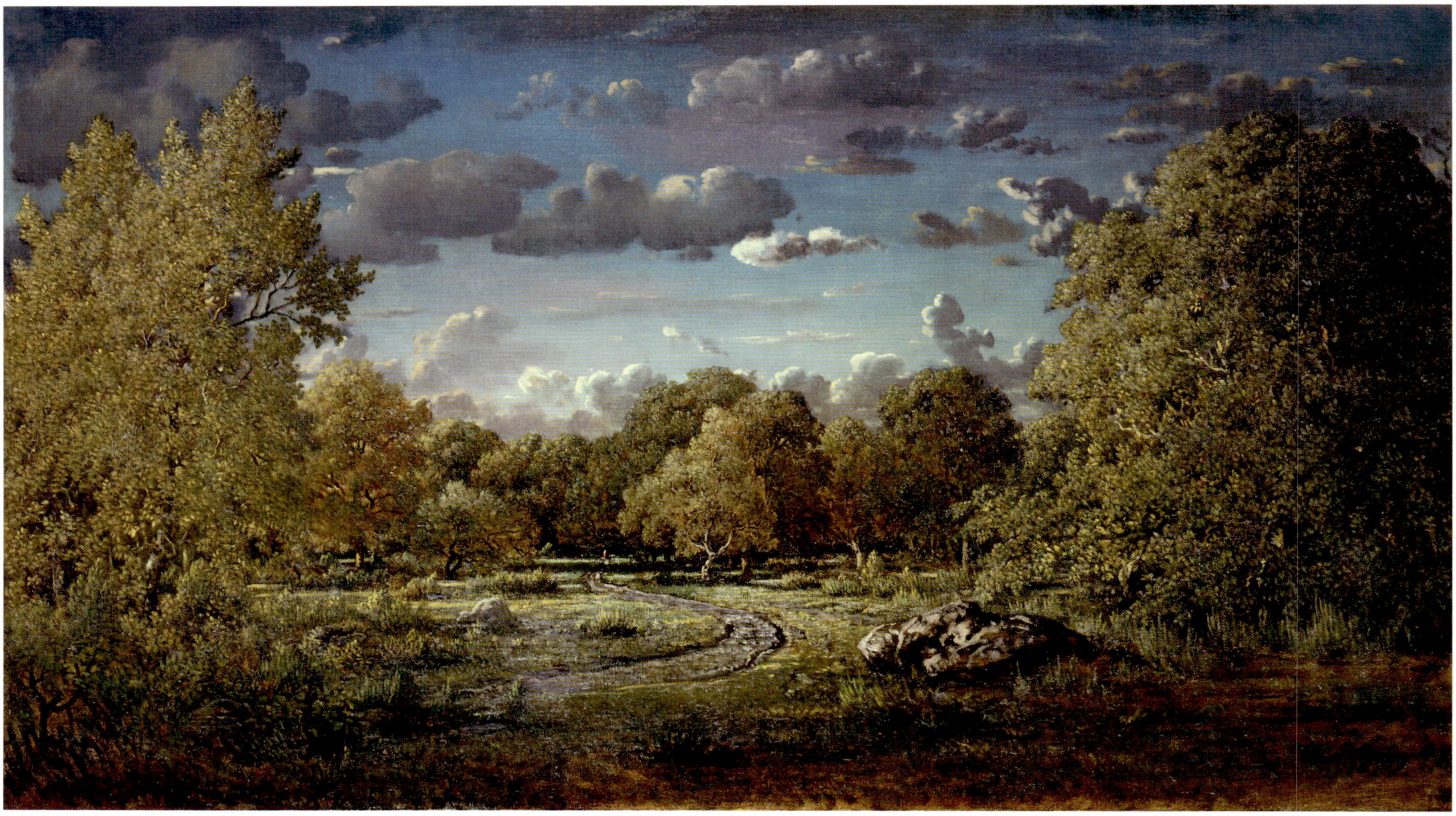

27

Théodore Rousseau

A Clearing in the Forest of Fontainebleau, c. 1860–1862, oil on canvas, 82.6 × 145.4 (32 ½ × 57 ¼). Chrysler Museum of Art, Norfolk; Gift of Walter P. Chrysler Jr.

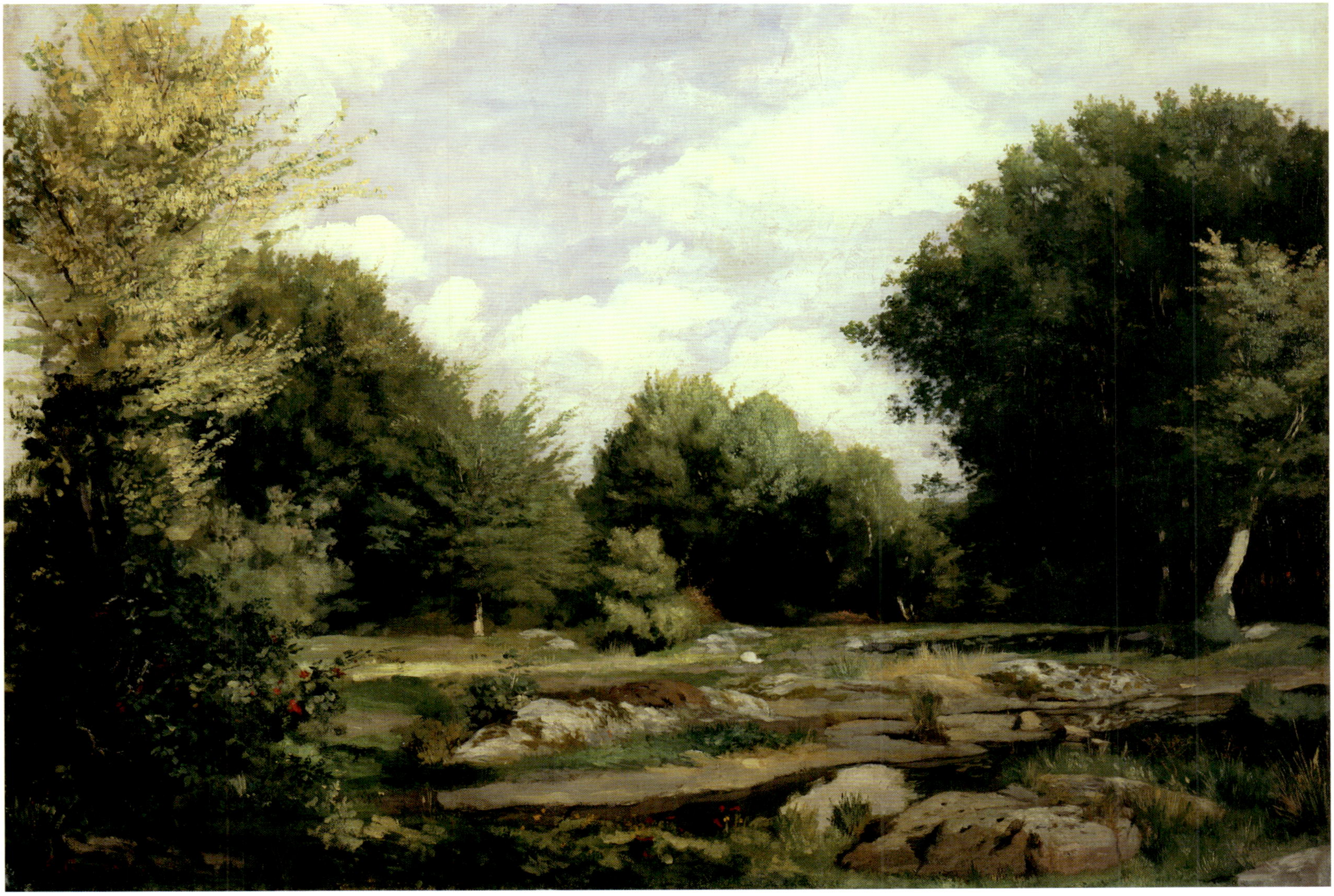

28

Auguste Renoir

Clearing in the Woods, 1865, oil on canvas, 57 × 83 (22 7/16 × 32 11/16). The Detroit Institute of Arts, Bequest of Ruth Nugent Head, in memory of her mother, Anna E. Kresge, and her husband, Henry W. Nugent Head

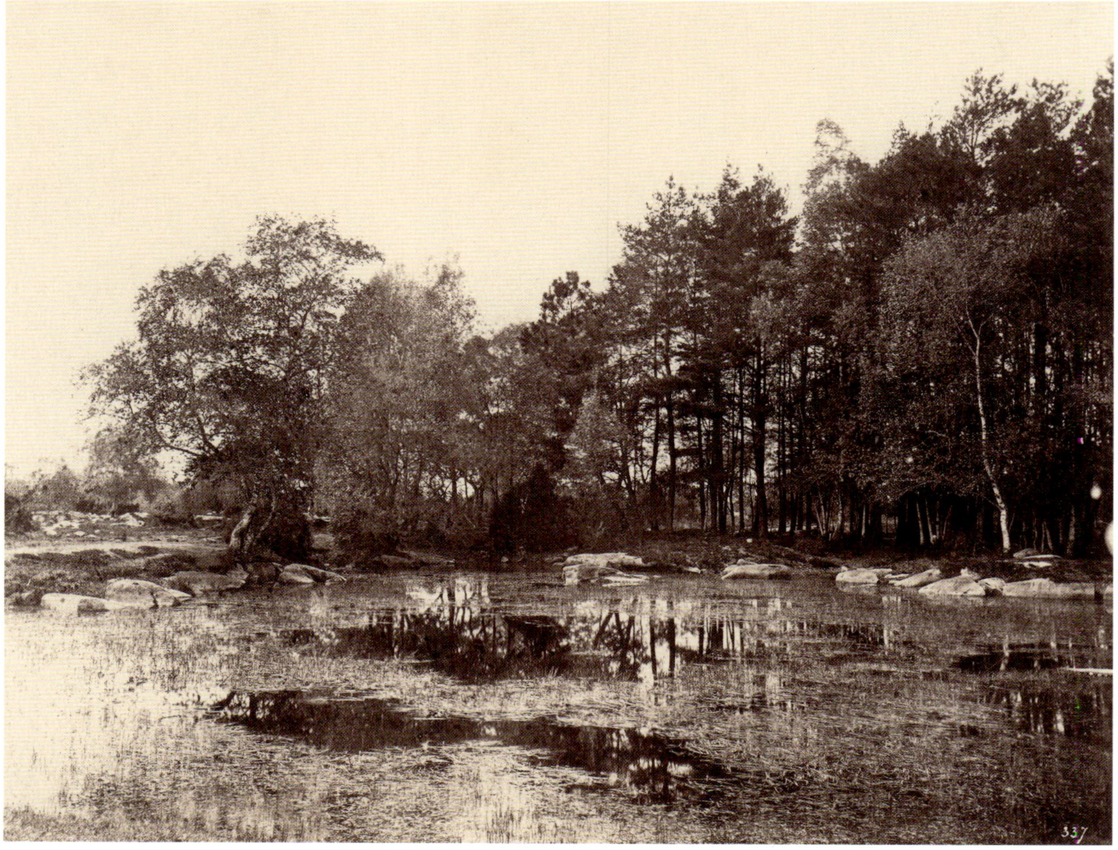

29

Eugène Cuvelier

Mare à Piat, c. 1863, salted paper print from paper negative, 25.7 × 34 (10 ⅛ × 13 ⅜). National Gallery of Art, Washington, Gift of Dan and Mary Solomon and Patrons' Permanent Fund, 2006

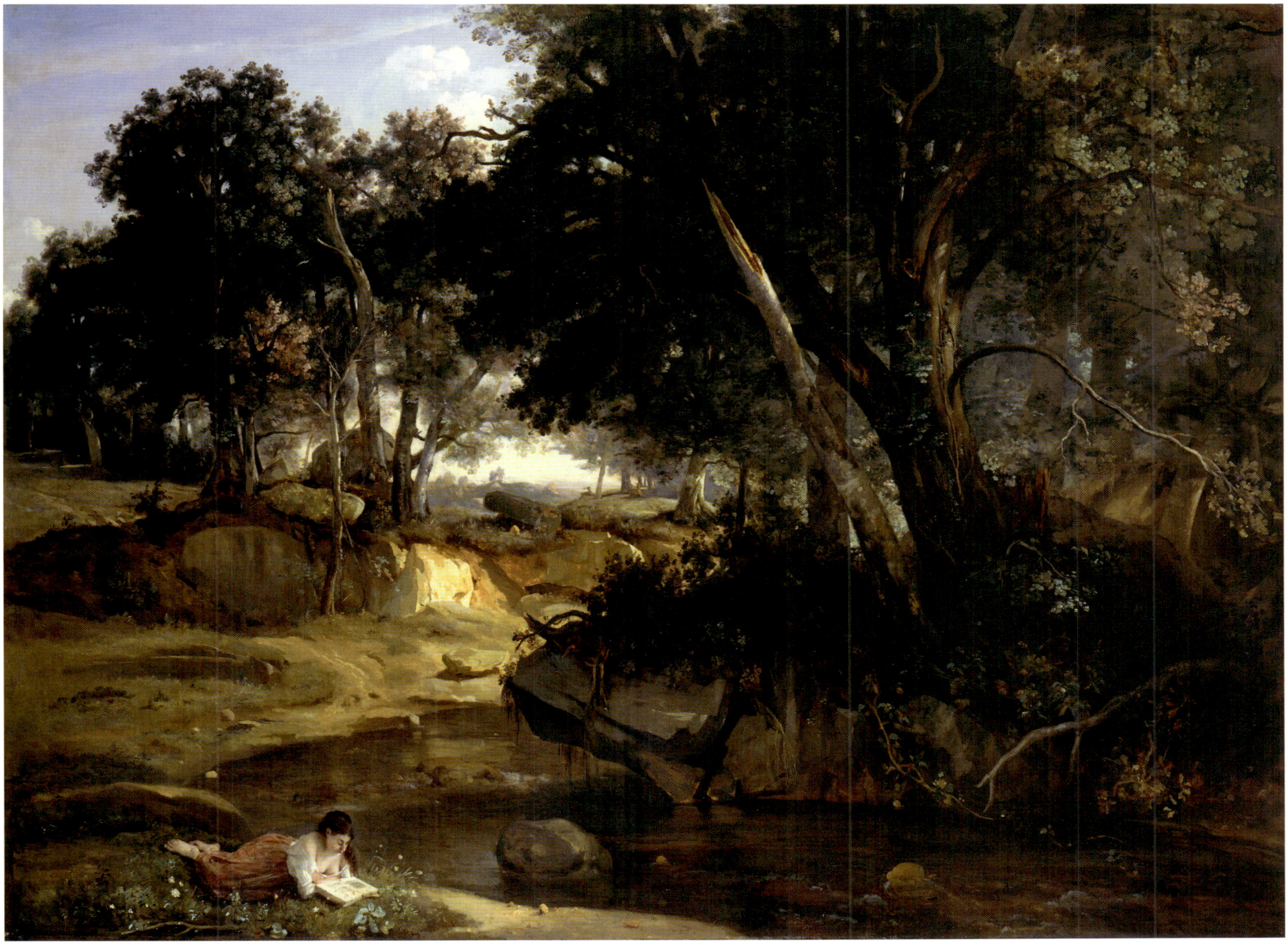

30

Jean-Baptiste-Camille Corot

Forest of Fontainebleau, 1834, oil on canvas, 175.6 × 242.6 (69 ⅛ × 95 ½). National Gallery of Art, Washington, Chester Dale Collection, 1963

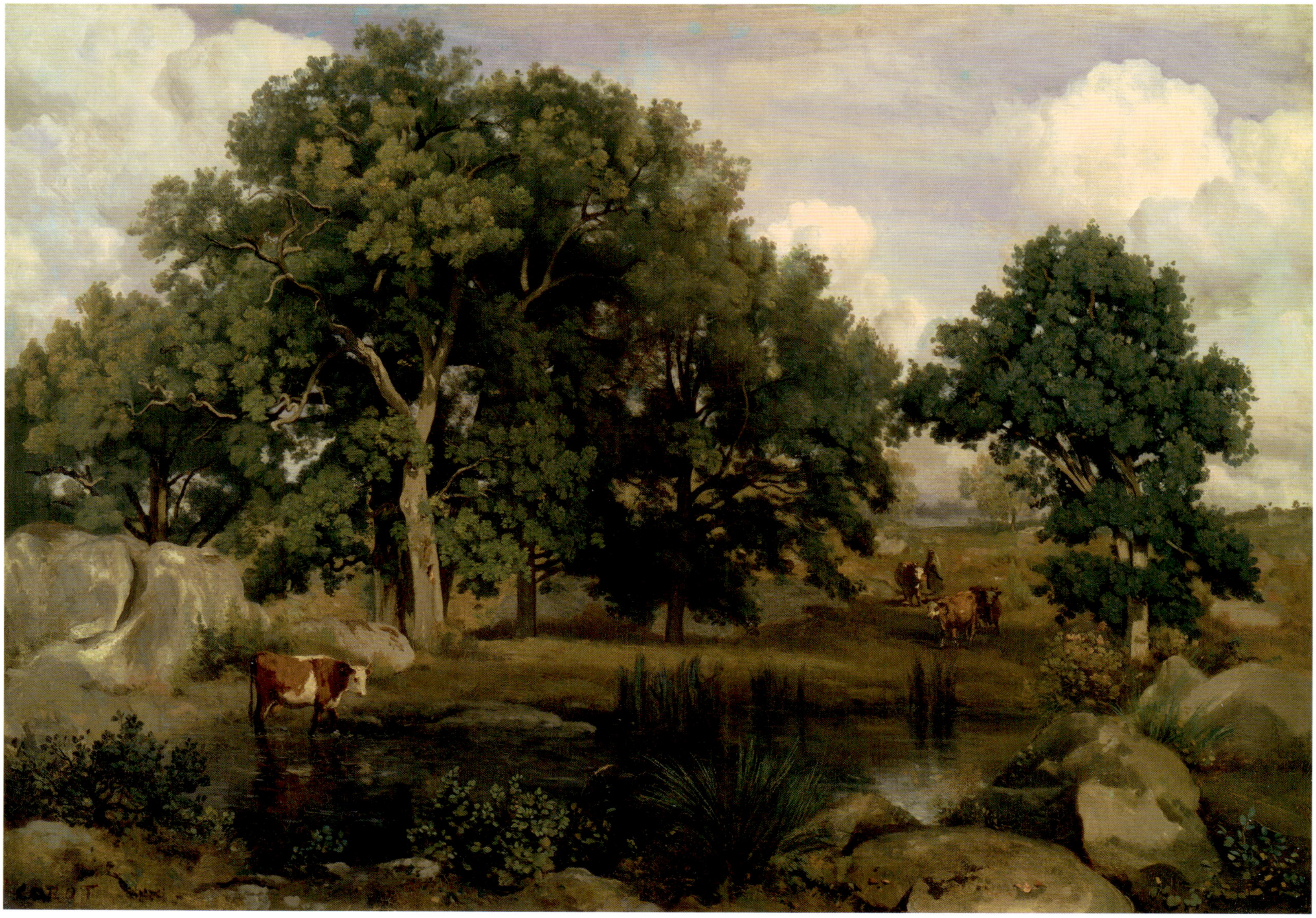

31

Jean-Baptiste-Camille Corot

The Forest of Fontainebleau, 1846, oil on canvas, 90.2 × 128.8 (35 ½ × 50 11/16). Museum of Fine Arts, Boston: Gift of Mrs. Samuel Dennis Warren

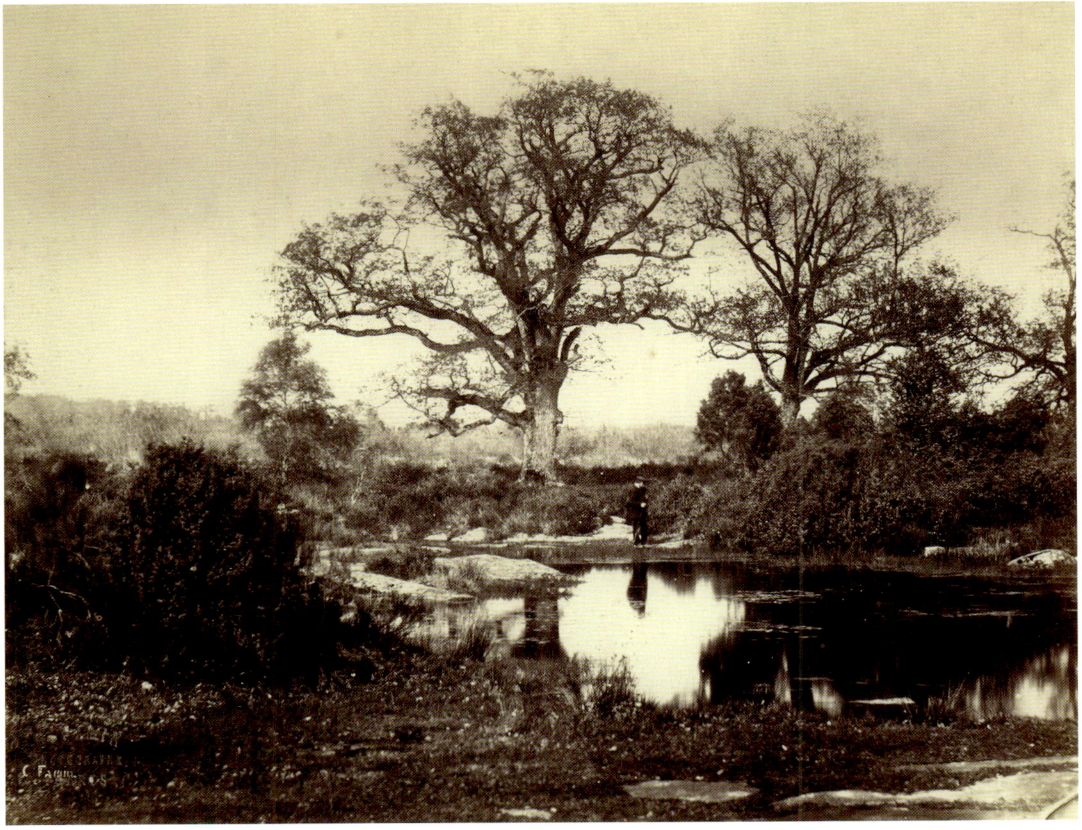

32

Constant Famin

Théophile Chauvel near the Mare aux Fées, 1865–1870, albumen print from collodion negative, 19 × 24.6 (7 ½ × 9 11/16). Dietmar Siegert Collection

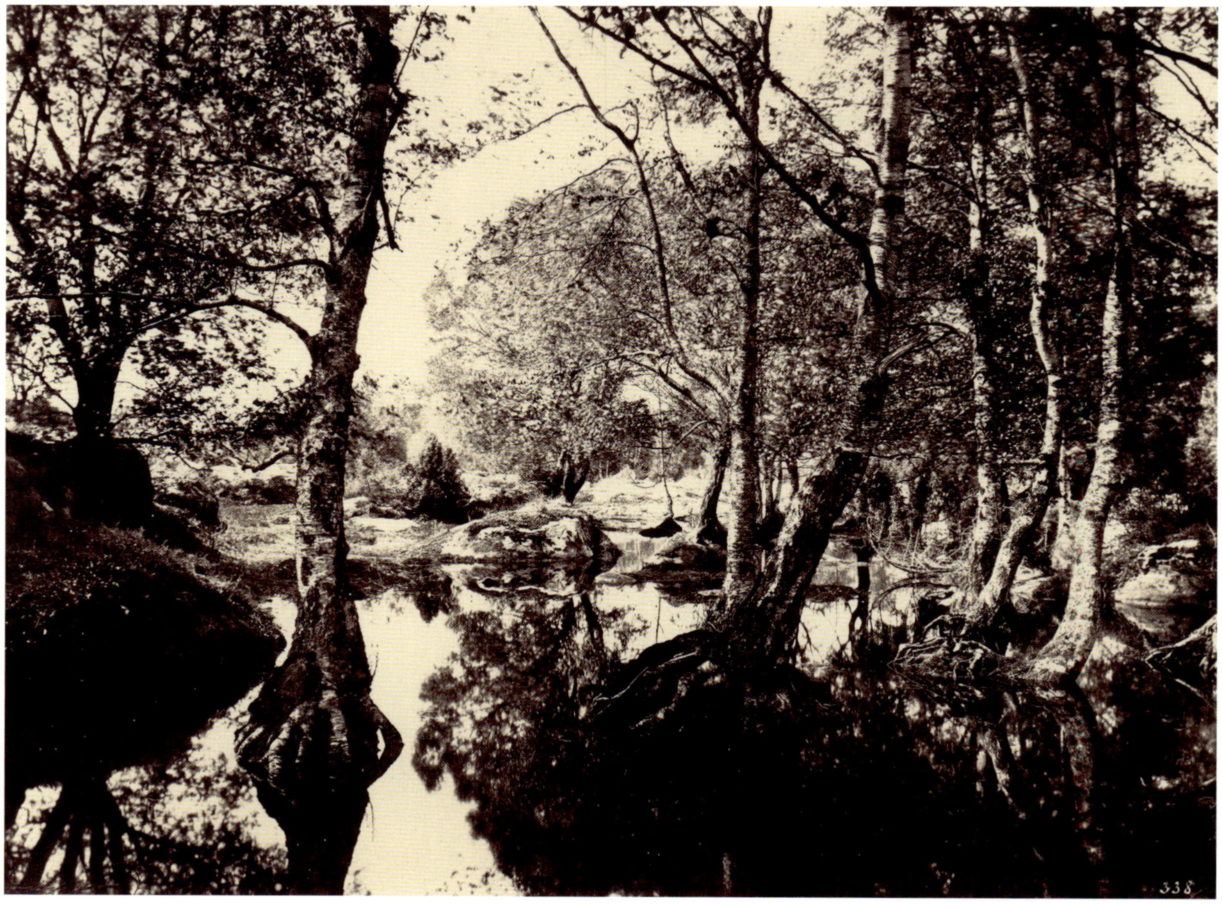

33

Eugène Cuvelier

Belle-Croix, 1860s, albumen print from paper negative, 25.4 × 34.3 (10 × 13 ½). National Gallery of Art, Washington, Ben and Gail Jacobs for the Millennium Fund, 2007

Trees

Fontainebleau is home to a wide variety of trees. While oak, beech, and hornbeam are the dominant species, there are dozens of others, both native and imported, pure and hybrid, including chestnut, maple, and birch; the much-contested pine that brought with it both profit and controversy; and the utilitarian juniper, prized by locals both for the wood from which they carved handicrafts and for the berries used to create a liqueur known as *pissat du lapin*.[1] There are also fruit trees of every variety as well as the Alisier de Fontainebleau (service tree), a unique hybrid that is found only in the Forest of Fontainebleau and was first discovered during the eighteenth century.[2]

The oak trees of Fontainebleau are its great pride, and they have been a source of nearly universal awe for artists and tourists alike. "The forest is truly admirable in certain parts; we have no idea down in Montpellier of such oak trees," Bazille recounted to his mother in a letter of April 1863.[3] Much of the fascination with the oak trees stems from their remarkable longevity. With life spans that stretch over centuries, they serve as silent witnesses to history "that have outlived a thousand political vicissitudes."[4] For nineteenth-century artists, this connection to the past was both palpable and profound. Thoré called the oak "the sacred tree . . . the national tree which served our ancestors as a natural cathedral in the celebration of their mysteries."[5] To walk among the oaks of Fontainebleau is to catch a glimpse not only of France during the ancient times of the Druids and Gauls but also of the origins of the French nation.[6]

Recognizing the fascination these ancient oaks held, Denecourt actively sought them out during his perambulations through the forest, gifting them with august names and incorporating them into his promenades and guidebooks alongside other more established sites. Their visual charm was sufficient to justify their status as objects of veneration. With their massive trunks and gnarled, twisted limbs, these ancient oak trees held a tremendous appeal for the romantic sensibility, embodying nature at its most vigorous and chaotic. As Flaubert wrote in his novel *L'Education sentimentale,* "There were rough, enormous oaks, convulsing, stretching the earth, embracing one another and, resting firmly upon their trunks, similar to chests, launching outward with their naked arms in calls of despair and furious threats, like a group of Titans immobilized in their anger."[7] His vivid prose encapsulates the instinctive power such trees embody.

A number of trees gained widespread fame owing to their popularity as artistic motifs. The Pharamond, the Charlemagne, and the Henri IV were all prized for their age, while others were celebrated for their striking appearances. La Reine Blanche, the "spoiled child of the painters," was one of those trees (see pl. 39), as was Le Rageur, a dead oak with twisted, weather-beaten limbs that stalwartly remained upright through storm and rain (pl. 40).[8] And, of course, the most famous was the Bodmer Oak, named for the Swiss painter Karl Bodmer, who portrayed it in a number of paintings and prints beginning in 1850.[9] Dramatic and distinctive, this knotty oak tree became the signature motif that helped cinch Bodmer's reputation, attracting other artists for years thereafter (see pls. 43 and 44).

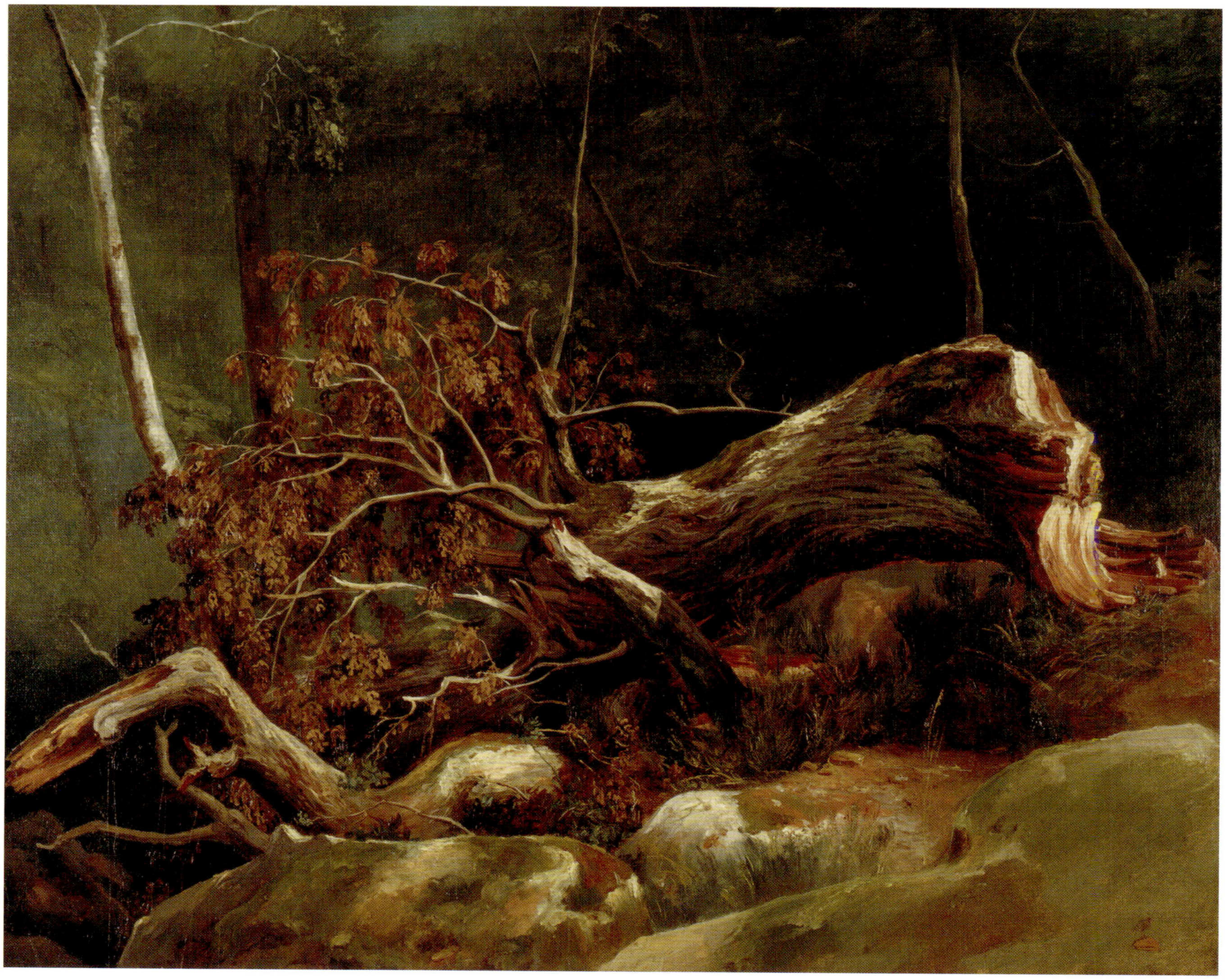

34

Achille-Etna Michallon

The Fallen Oak Branch, Fontainebleau, c. 1816, oil on canvas mounted on card, 41.9 × 52.1 (16 ½ × 20 ½). Lent by the Minneapolis Institute of Arts, The Margaret G. Deal Fund and Gift of funds from the Paintings Council

35

Jean-Baptiste-Camille Corot

Study of a Tree Trunk in the Forest of Fontainebleau, October 1822, oil on paper mounted on canvas, 24.4 × 32.5 (9 ⅝ × 12 $^{13}/_{16}$). John Schlichte Bergen Gallery, Amsterdam, and Jack Kilgore and Co. Inc., New York City

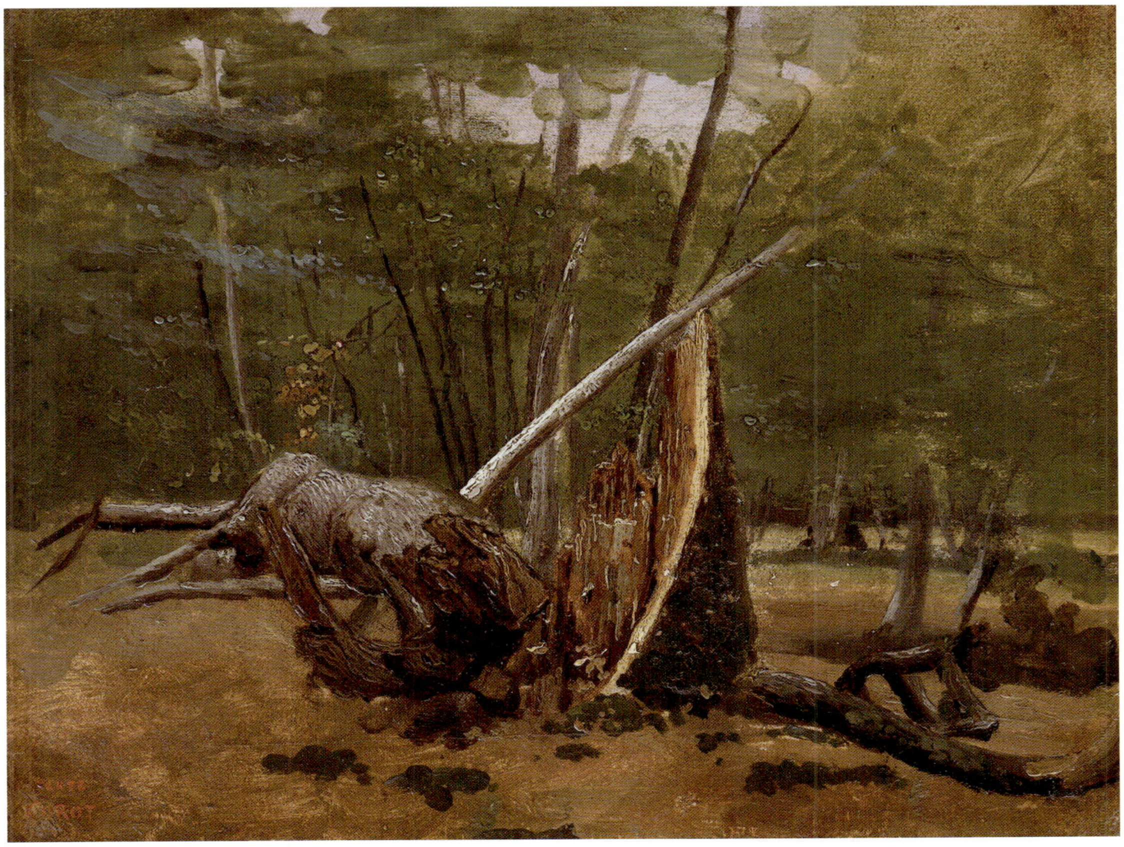

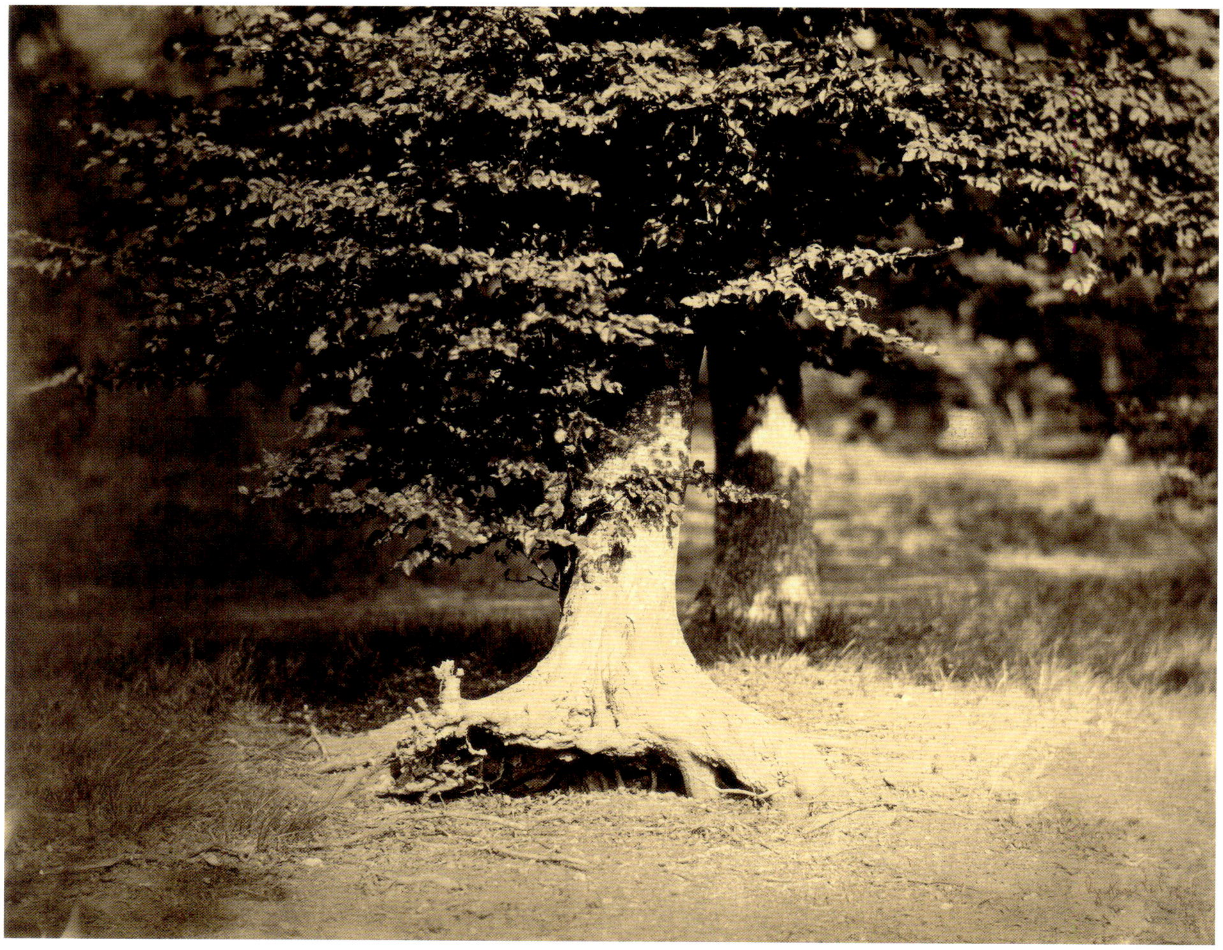

36

Gustave Le Gray

Beech Tree, Forest of Fontainebleau, c. 1856, albumen print from collodion negative, 31.8 × 41.4 (12 ¾ × 16 ¼). National Gallery of Art, Washington, Patrons' Permanent Fund, 1995

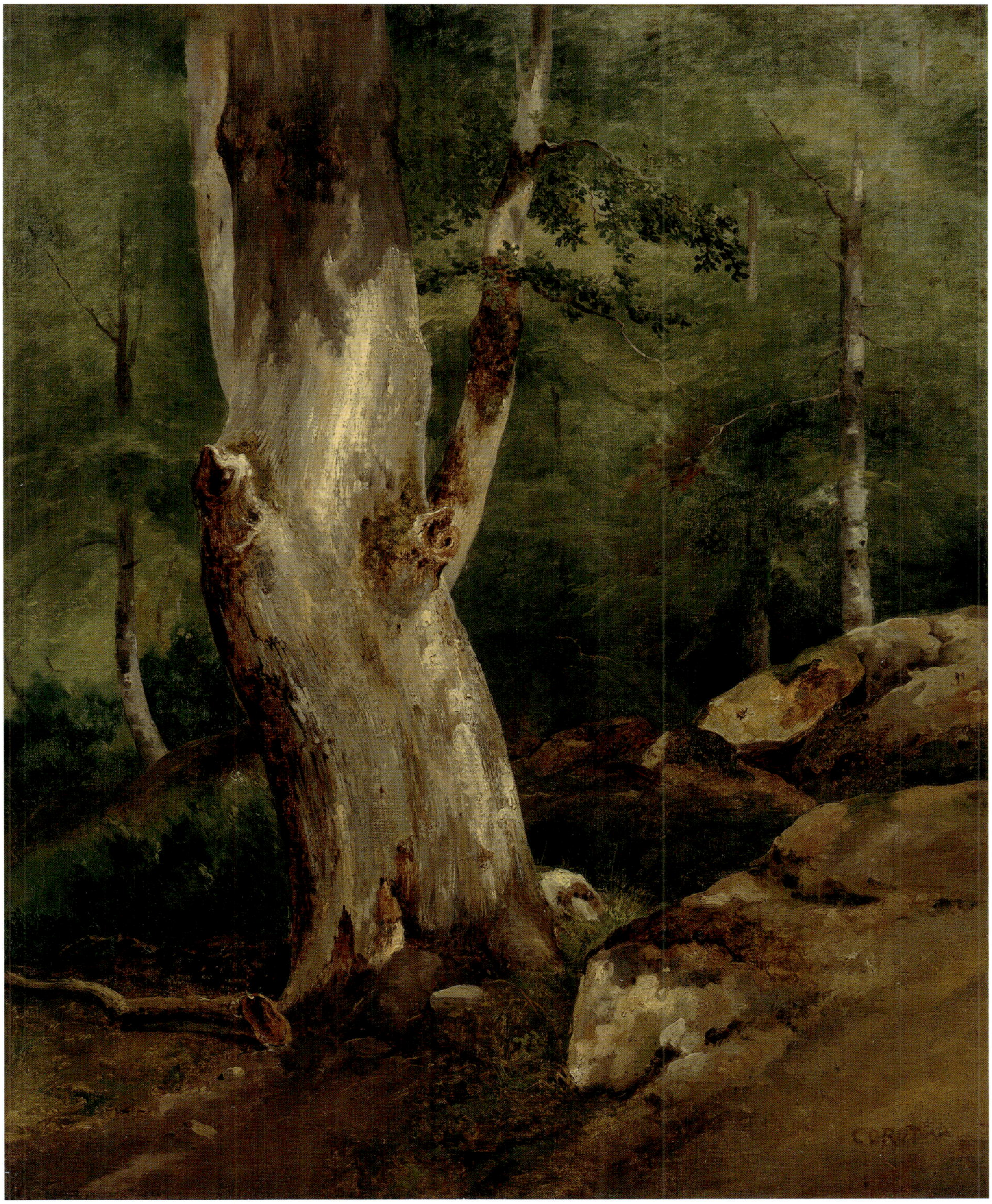

37

Attributed to Jean-Baptiste-Camille Corot

Old Beech Tree, 1828–1830, oil on paper mounted on canvas, 55.9 × 46 (22 × 18 ⅛). Museum of Fine Arts, Boston: The Henry C. and Martha B. Angell Collection

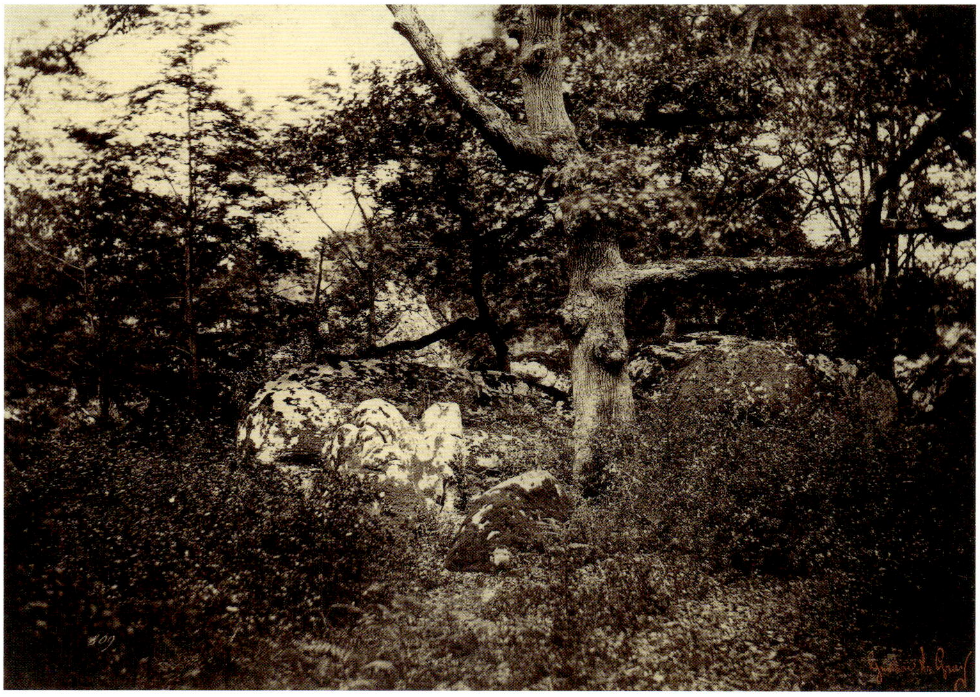

38

Gustave Le Gray

Knotty Oak near the Carrefour de l'Epine, c. 1853, albumen print from waxed paper negative, 15.4 × 20.7 (6 1/16 × 8 1/8). Wilson Centre for Photography, London

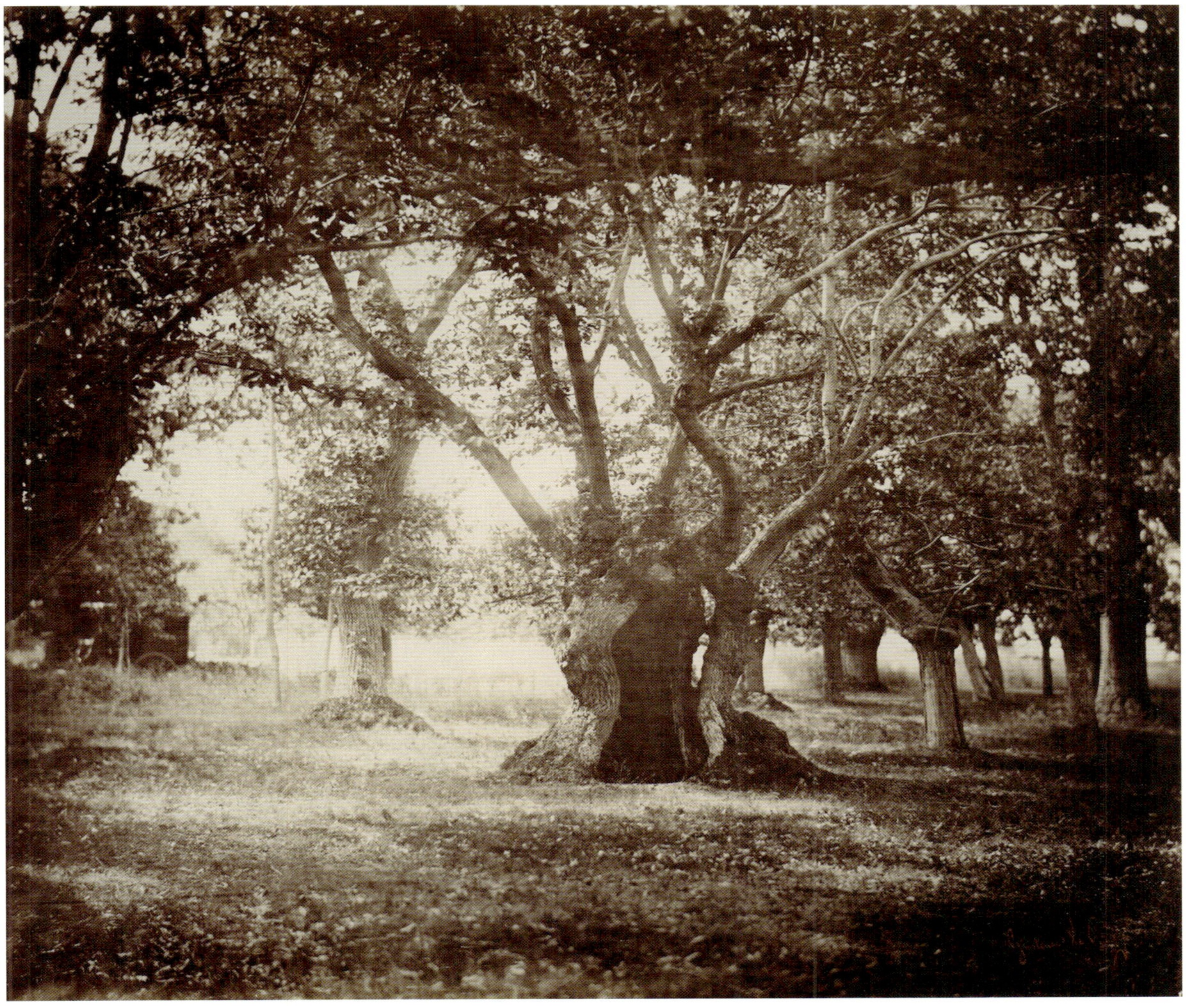

39

Gustave Le Gray

Tree, Forest of Fontainebleau, c. 1856, albumenized salted paper print from wet collodion glass negative, 31.9 × 37.6 (12 9/16 × 14 13/16). The Museum of Fine Arts, Houston, Museum Purchase with funds provided by the Brown Foundation Accessions Endowment Fund, The Manfred Heiting Collection

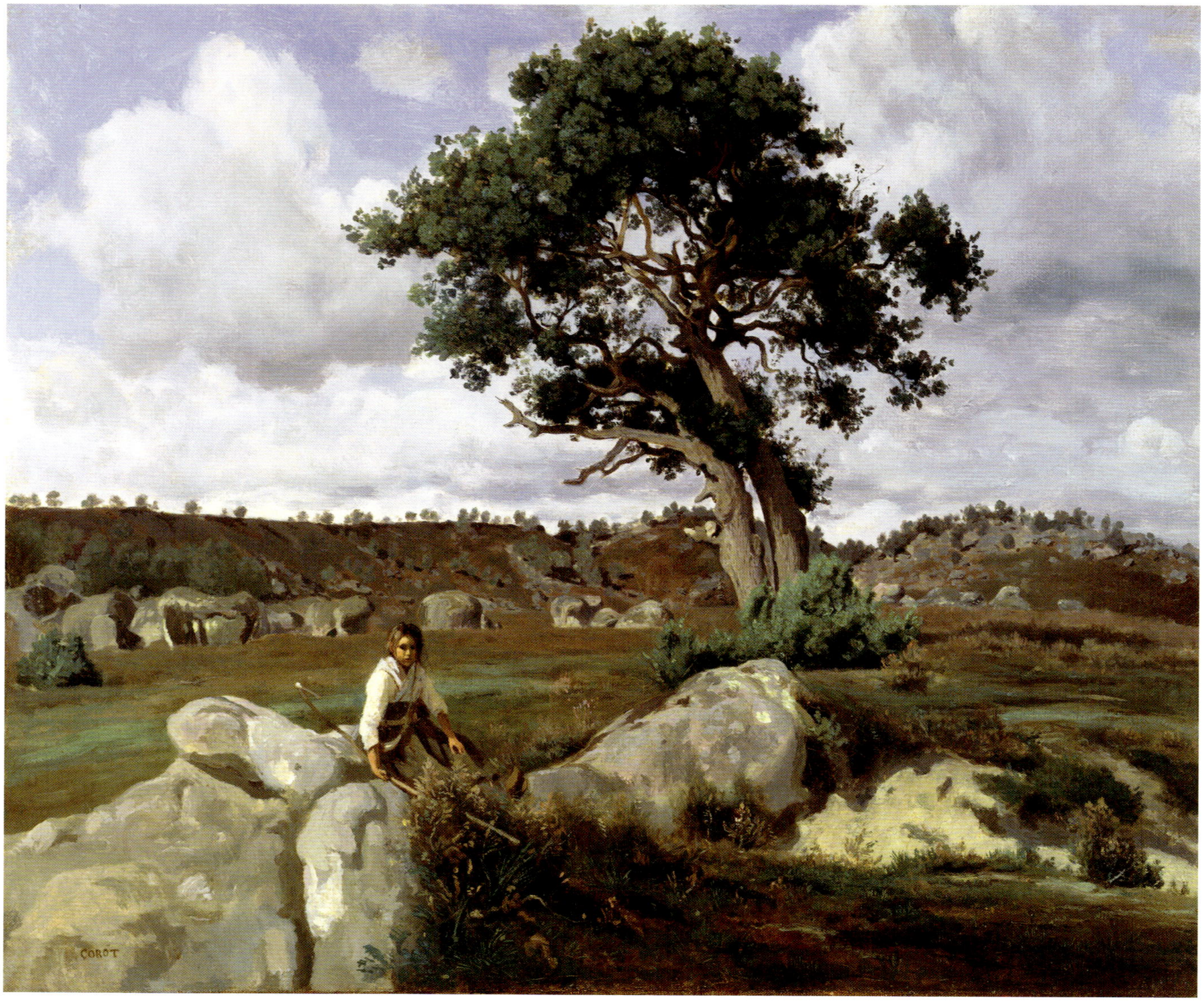

40

Jean-Baptiste-Camille Corot

Le Rageur, Forest of Fontainebleau, c. 1830, oil on canvas, 50.8 × 61 (20 × 24). Private collection

Angry Passionate

41

Jacques-Raymond Brascassat

The Oaks, c. 1830, oil on canvas, 50 × 40.3 (19 11/16 × 15 7/8). Musée des Beaux-Arts, Reims

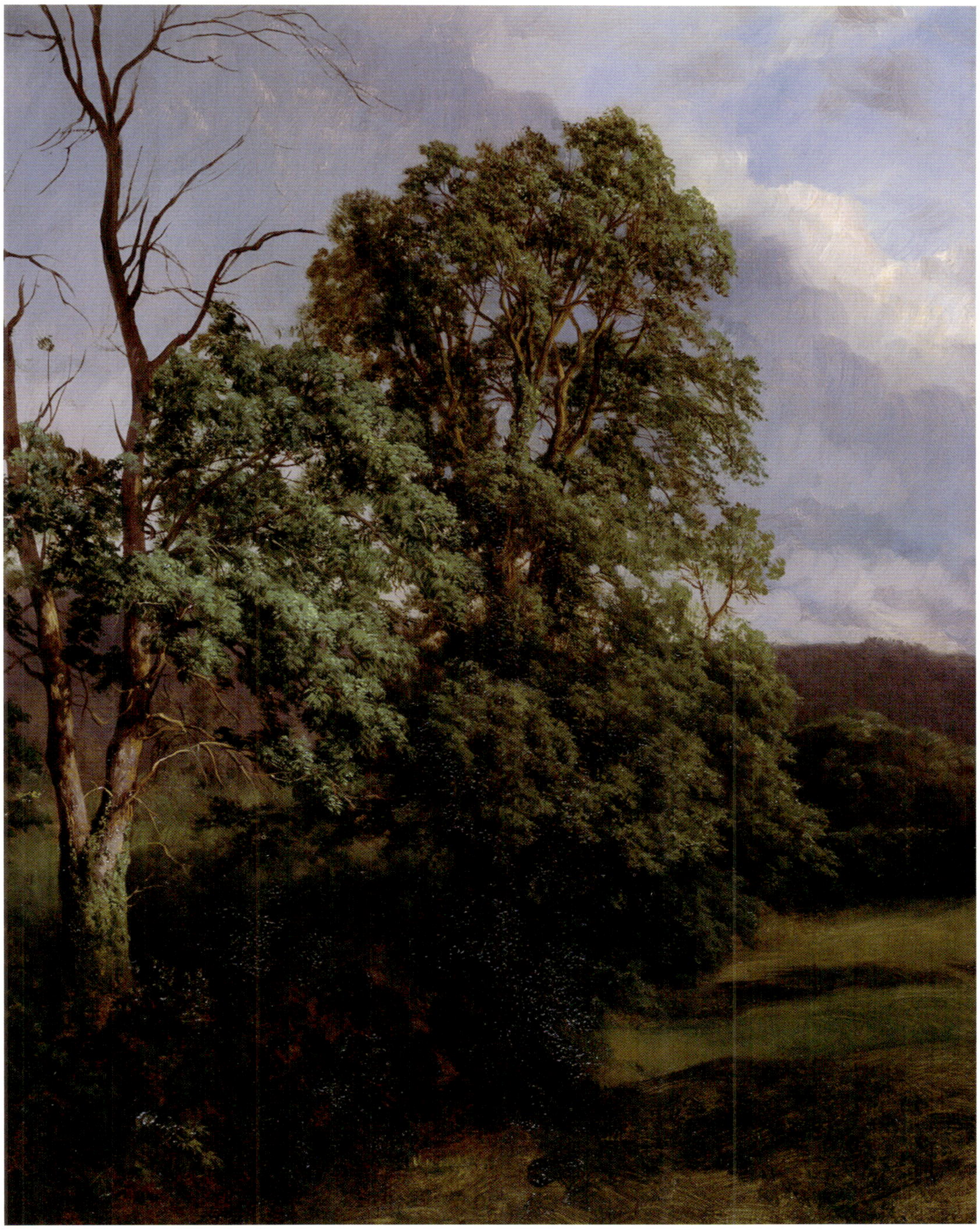

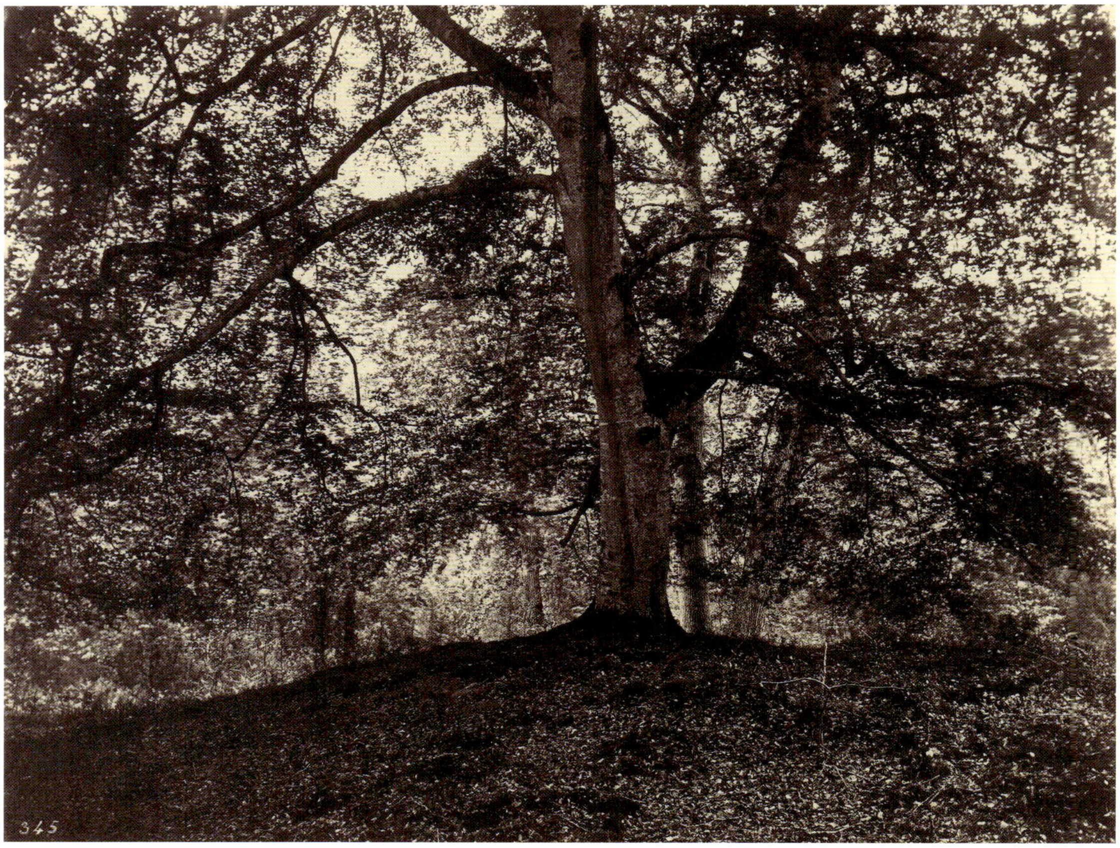

42

Eugène Cuvelier

Beech Tree near Bodmer Oak, early 1860s, salted paper print from paper negative, 26.5 × 33.8 (10 7/16 × 13 5/16). Private collection

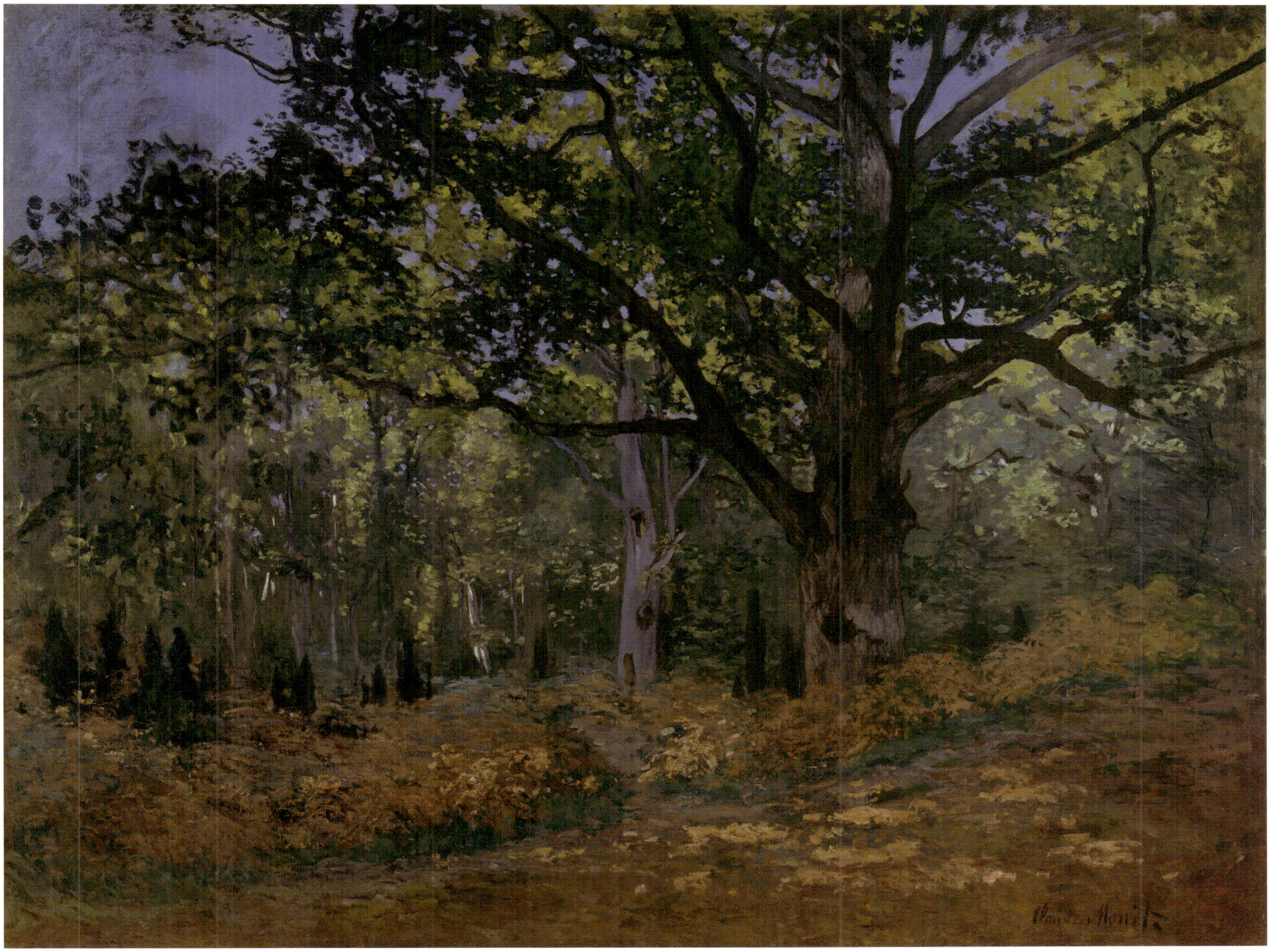

43

Claude Monet

The Bodmer Oak, Fontainebleau Forest, 1865, oil on canvas, 96.2 × 129.2 (37 7/8 × 50 7/8). Lent by The Metropolitan Museum of Art, Gift of Sam Salz and Bequest of Julia W. Emmons, by exchange, 1964

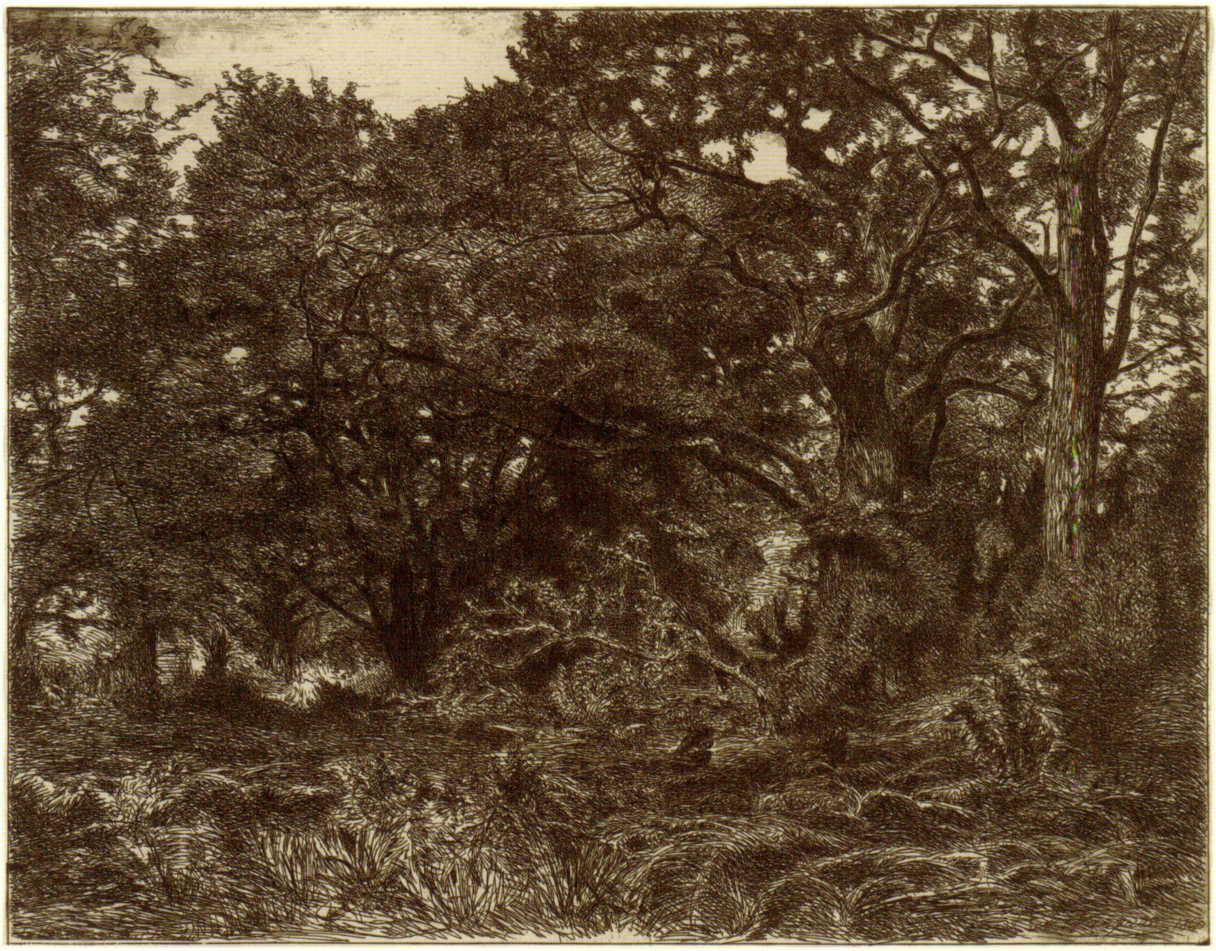

44

Adolphe-Andre Wacquez

The Bodmer Oak at Bas-Bréau, 1860, cliché-verre, 22.7 × 29.1 (8 15/16 × 11 7/16). National Gallery of Art, Washington, Andrew W. Mellon Fund, 1978

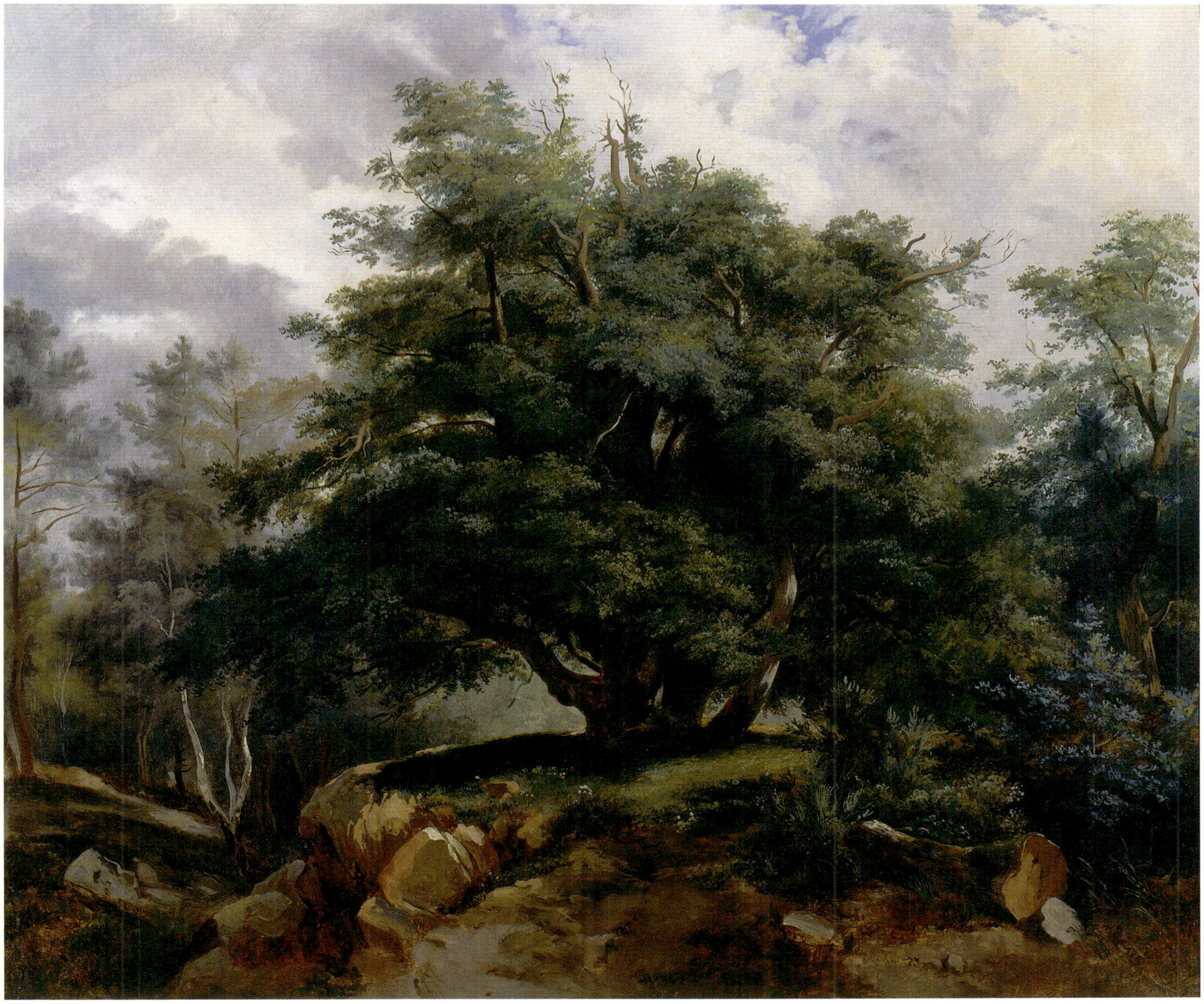

45

Jules Coignet

The Old Oak in the Forest of Fontainebleau, c. 1830, oil on canvas, 54 × 65 (21 1/4 × 25 9/16). Private collection, courtesy of Brame and Lorenceau, Paris

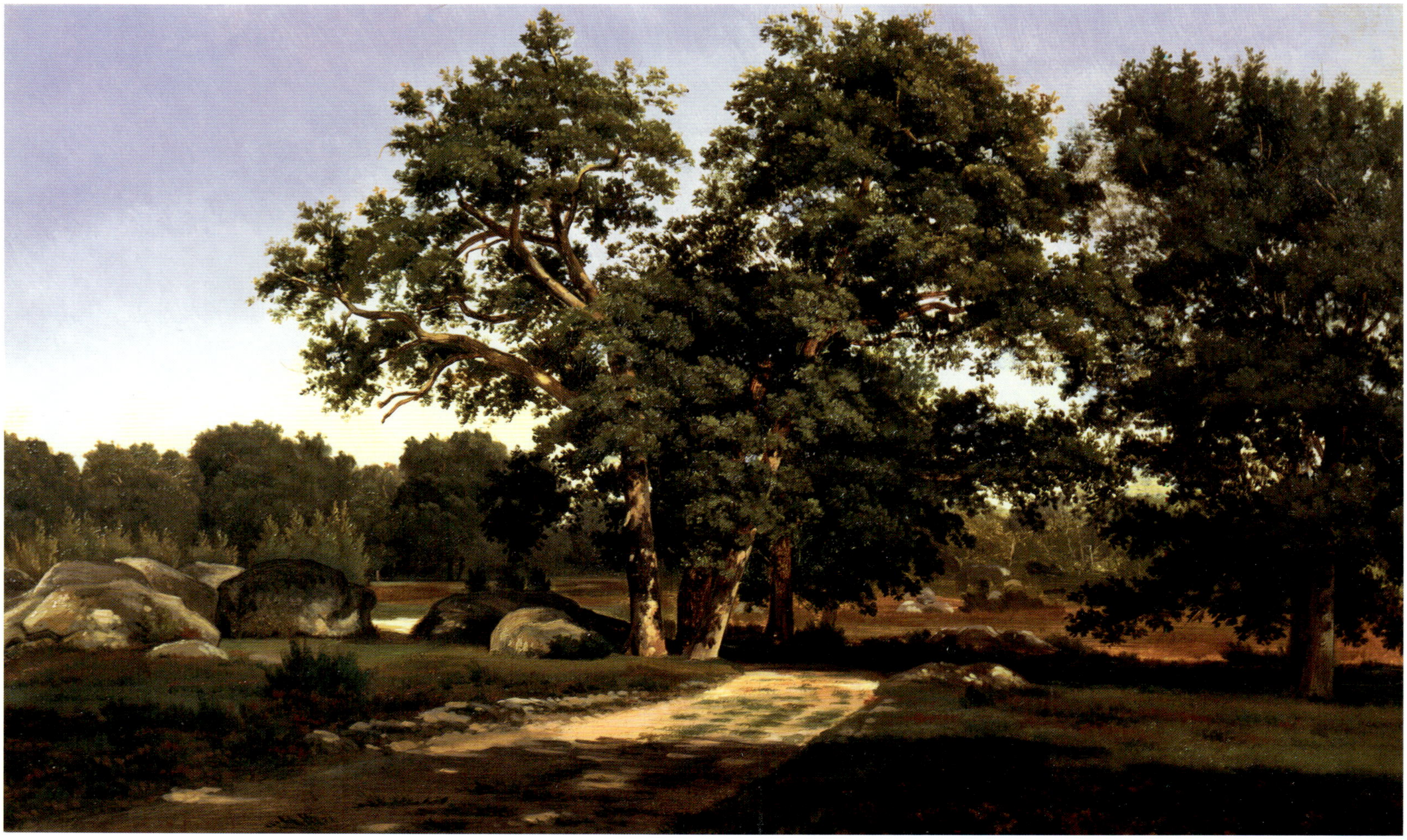

46

Alexandre Desgoffe

The Oaks of Fontainebleau, c. 1850, oil on paper mounted on canvas, 41.3 × 68.6 (16 ¼ × 27). Private collection, New York

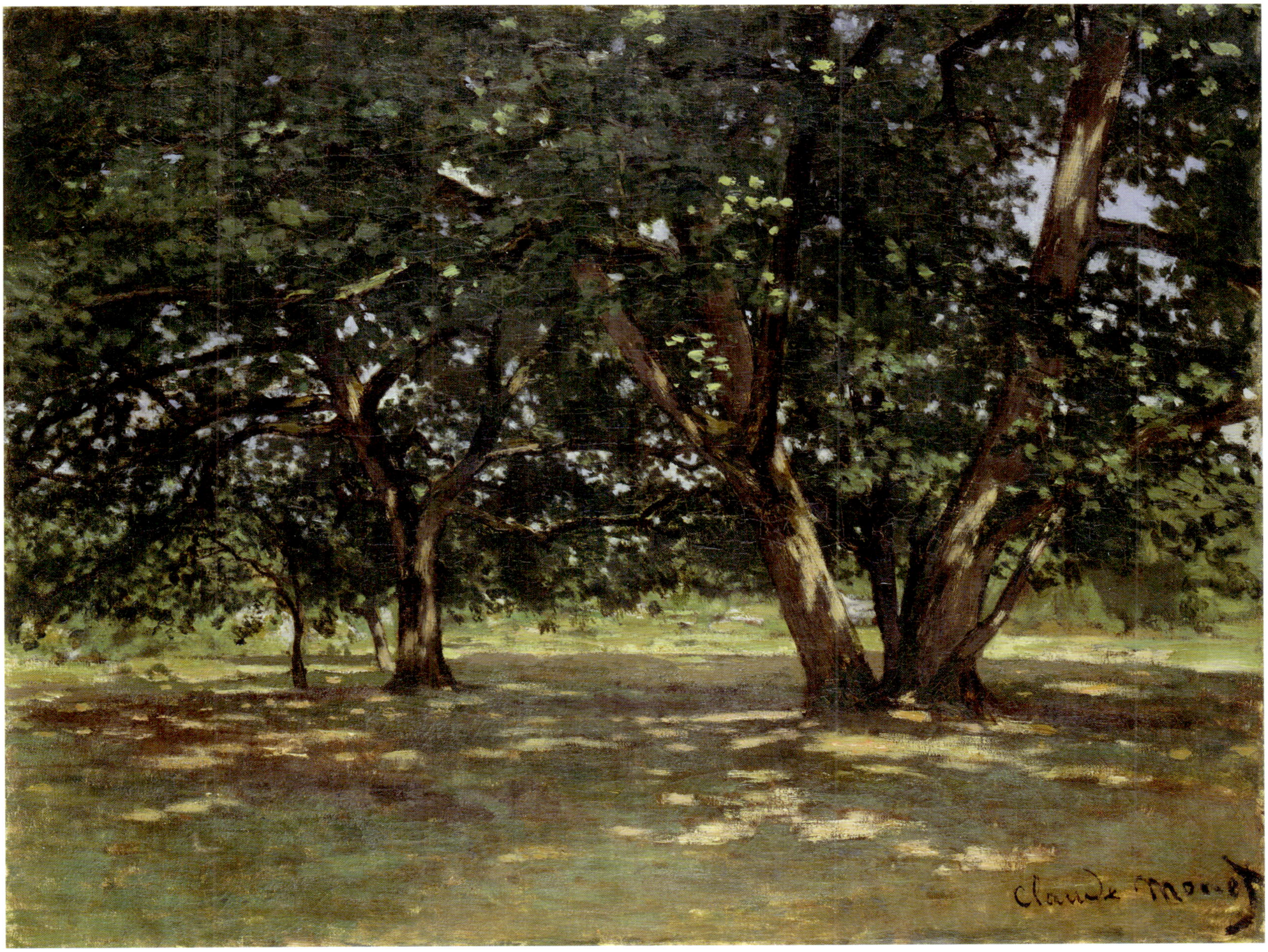

47

Claude Monet

Fontainebleau Forest, 1865, oil on canvas, 50 × 65 (19 11/16 × 25 9/16). Kunstmuseum Winterthur, Presented by the Galerieverein, Friends of the Kunstmuseum Winterthur, 1934

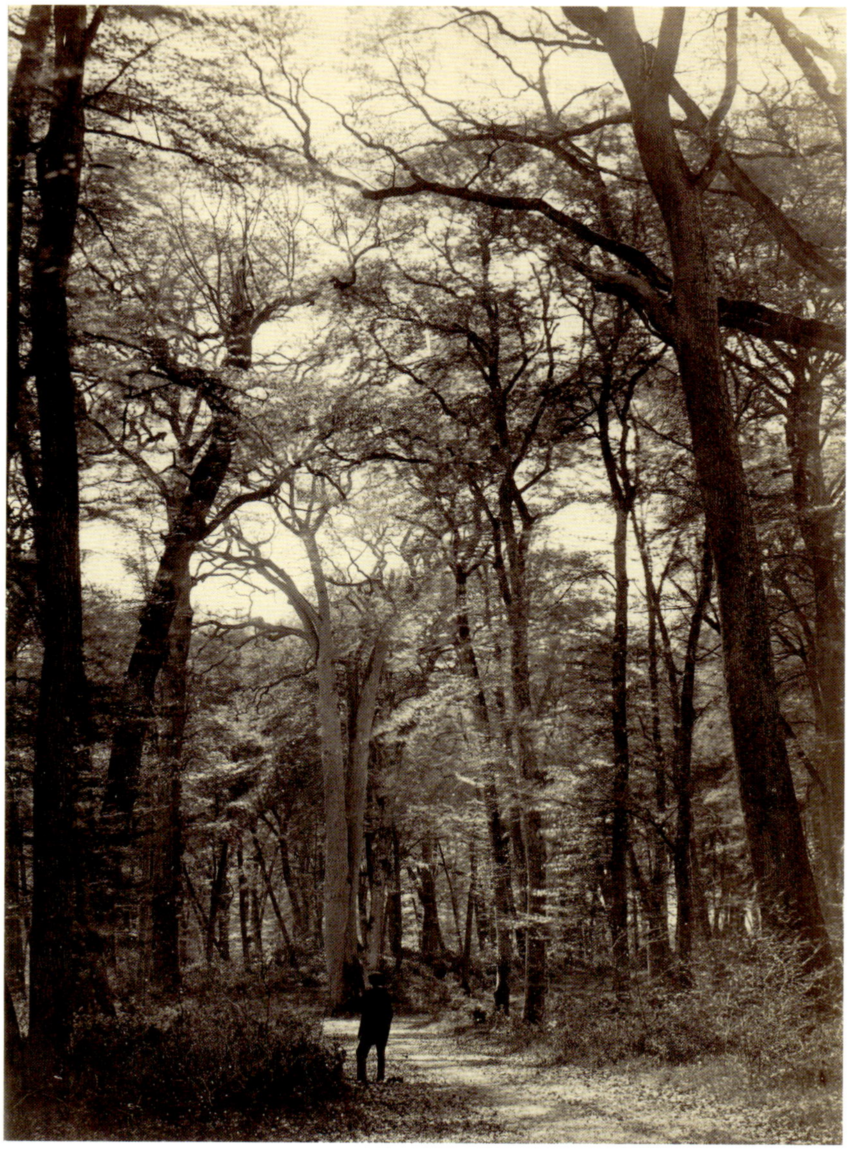

48

Constant Famin

Forest Scene, c. 1865, albumen print from collodion negative, 24.8 × 18.4 (9 ¾ × 7 ¼). National Gallery of Art, Washington, The Horace W. Goldsmith Foundation through Robert and Joyce Menschel, 2004

Rocks

The other distinguishing characteristic of the Forest of Fontainebleau is the profusion of rocks within its precincts. Fontainebleau contains large deposits of both limestone and sandstone, the latter of which was quarried from the fourteenth century onward for the production of paving stones, a lucrative business that reached its peak during the nineteenth century (see pls. 61 and 62). Altogether, rock formations occupy some 4,000 hectares of the forest, nearly one-quarter of its area, with the tallest plateaus extending as high as 140 meters above the level of the Seine.[1]

The extraordinary geological spectacle of Fontainebleau captivated scientists as well as more casual visitors. The French naturalist Georges-Louis Leclerc, Count of Buffon, included a study of the sandstone of Fontainebleau in his *L'histoire naturelle des minéraux* (1783), describing it as among the purest and most homogenous of its type.[2] The Scottish geologist Sir Charles Lyell, who visited Fontainebleau on at least two separate occasions beginning in 1818, expressed delight at his sojourn through the forest: "We had the satisfaction of discovering some new geological facts, and I gained a pretty correct knowledge of most of the formations of the environs and of the position of the grès, or sandstone of Fontainebleau."[3] Lyell's interest was not limited to the scientific, however. He was equally fascinated by the visual drama of the rocks themselves, observing, "In the Forest of Fontainebleau a (limestone) rock bursts up in huge masses through the soil, and presents a very singular appearance, not in any way in character with so tame and flat a country."[4]

The most impressive rock formations in Fontainebleau are found in the various gorges throughout the forest, including the Gorges aux Merisiers to the west and the Gorges aux Loups to the south, with rocks whose "capriciously grouped masses simultaneously offered the most picturesque and most imposing appearance" (see pls. 52 and 54).[5] The most spectacular of these, however, are the Gorges d'Apremont (pls. 63 and 101) and the Gorges de Franchard, which were widely considered the most "savage and desolate" areas of the forest.[6] Located in the northwest quadrant, their proximity to Chailly and Barbizon combined with their rugged terrain and arresting vistas made them particularly appealing to both artists and tourists.

In addition to the gorges, striking configurations of rock are scattered throughout the forest at random. Some of these have the appearance of stylized animals: an elephant, a hippopotamus, and a tortoise, for instance.[7] During a trek through the forest, Thoré observed "a lioness crouched atop a rock" face to face with "a crocodile low to the horizon."[8] Other rocks recall objects both familiar and strange—a jockey's cap, a pear, an anvil, the pillars of Hercules, a sphinx, or a dragon. Denecourt's guidebooks are filled with such fanciful identifications that in turn were immortalized in prints and postcards for a mass market.[9]

Finally, at the highest elevation of the forest are the plateaus. Known as "deserts" because of their barren appearance and lack of vegetation, they seem to recall the terrain of the Holy Land in their extreme aridity and desolation, which added to their exotic appeal for the visitor.[10]

Although such fancies enticed tourists, it was the visual impact of the terrain that most fascinated artists. "Worn, shattered, and covered with piles of enormous, menacing rocks," as one contemporary described the forest, its rough, unexpected topography sets Fontainebleau apart from its more sedate surroundings and gives the forest its strange and dramatic character.[11] In 1872, George Sand neatly summarized the attraction that this aspect of the forest held for generations of artists: "These hodgepodge of rocks offer at every turn a magnificent setting, austere or delectable."[12]

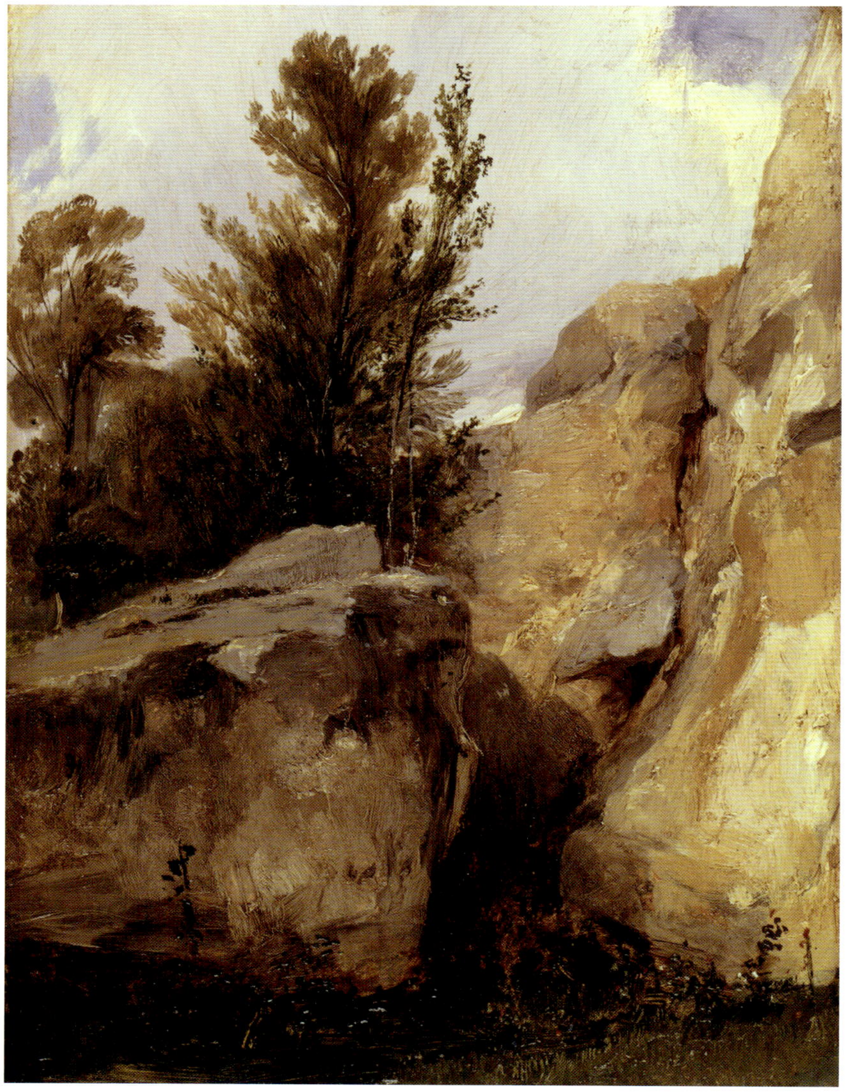

49

Richard Parkes Bonington

In the Forest of Fontainebleau, c. 1825, oil on cardboard, 32.5 × 24 (12 13/16 × 9 7/16). Yale Center for British Art, New Haven, Paul Mellon Collection

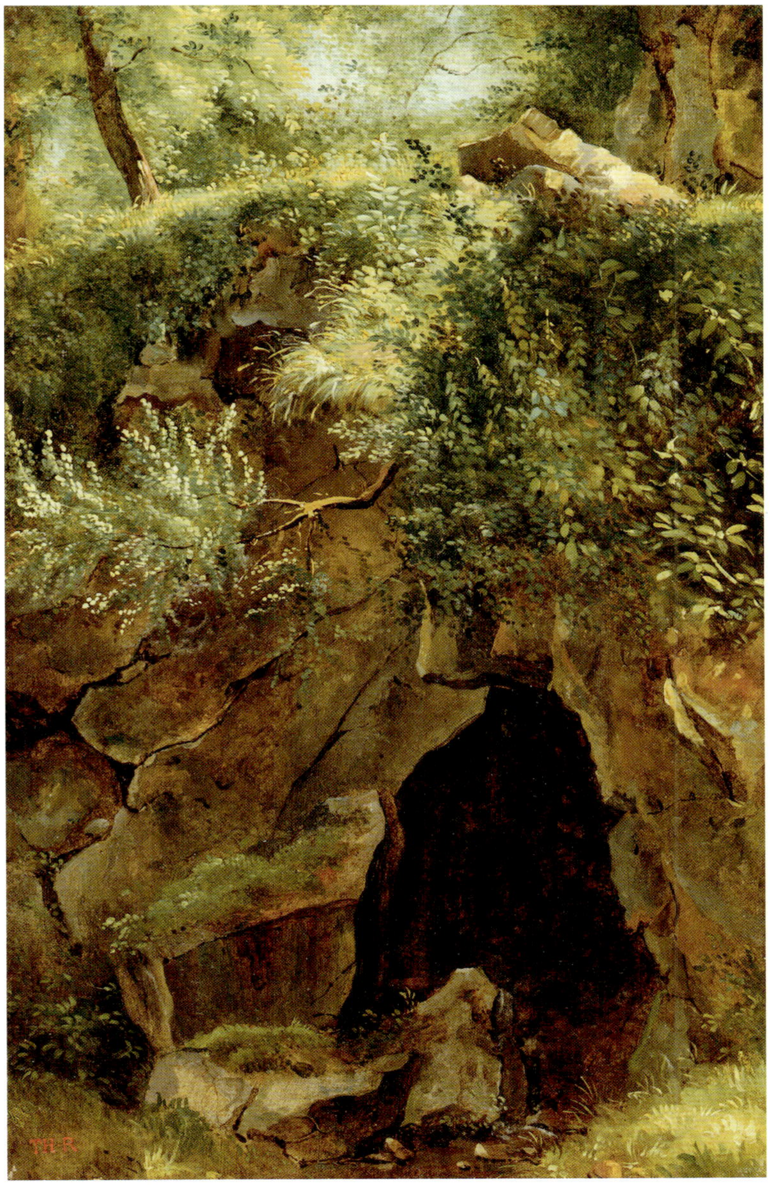

50

Théodore Rousseau

The Cave, 1828–1830, oil on paper mounted on canvas, 36.8 × 24.8 (14 ½ × 9 ¾). Los Angeles County Museum of Art, Gift of Frank Heller and the European Painting Acquisition Fund

51

Narcisse-Virgile Diaz de la Peña

The Rocks of the Belle Epine, Barbizon, c. 1840–1845, oil on wood, 22 × 35 (8 11/16 × 13 3/4). The City of Fontainebleau

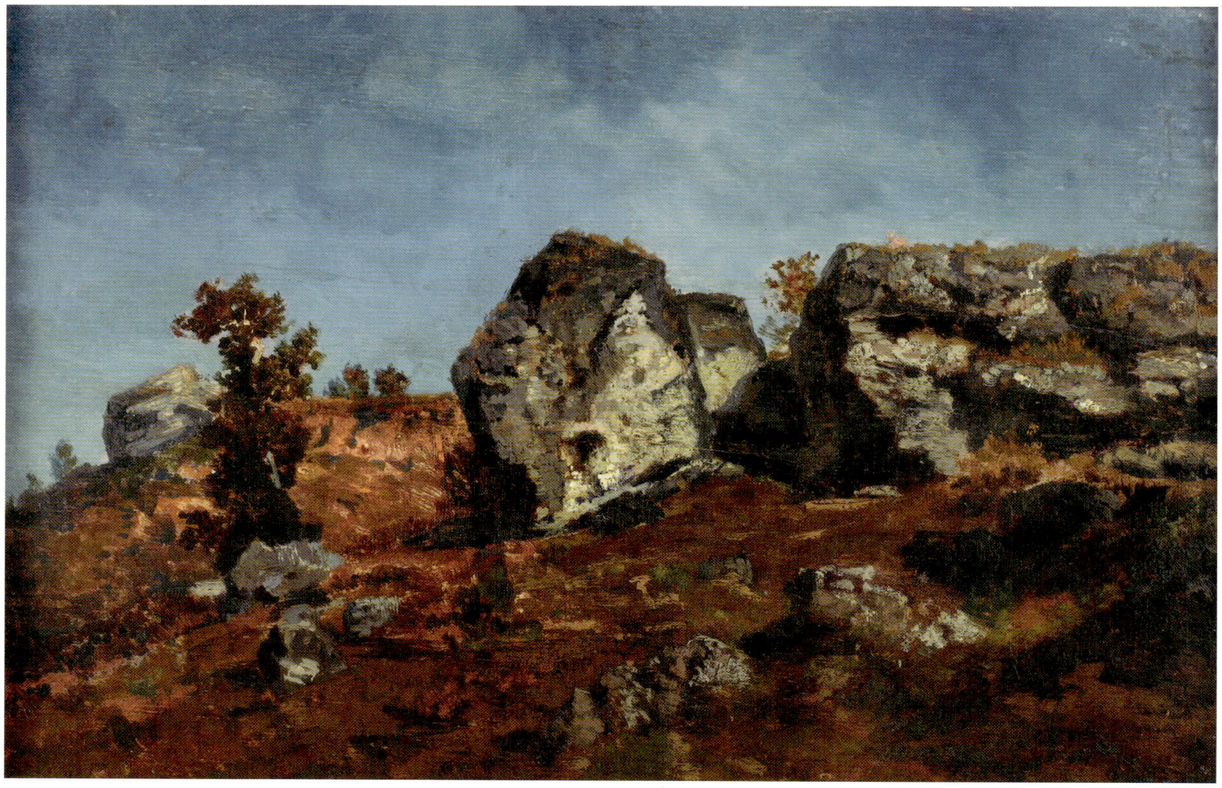

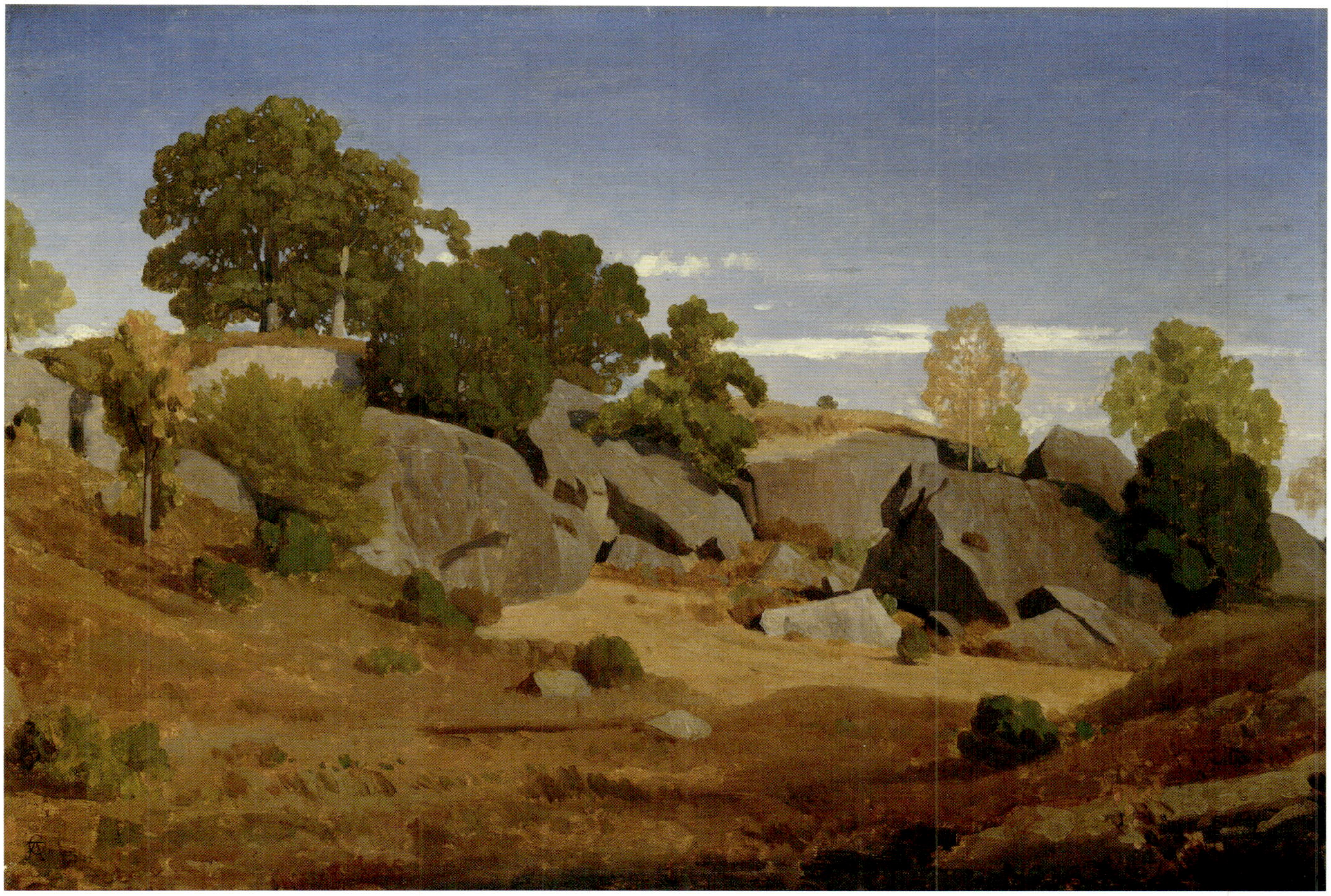

52

Théodore Claude Félix Caruelle d'Aligny

Rocks at Fontainebleau, c. 1842, oil on paper mounted on canvas, 33.4 × 49.2 (13 ⅛ × 19 ⅜). Musée du Louvre, Paris, Gift of Maurice Bourdot-Lamotte, 1951

53

Jacques-Raymond Brascassat

Rocks in a Forest, 1828, oil on paper mounted on canvas, 32.6 × 39.8 (12 13⁄16 × 15 11⁄16). Musée des Beaux-Arts, Reims

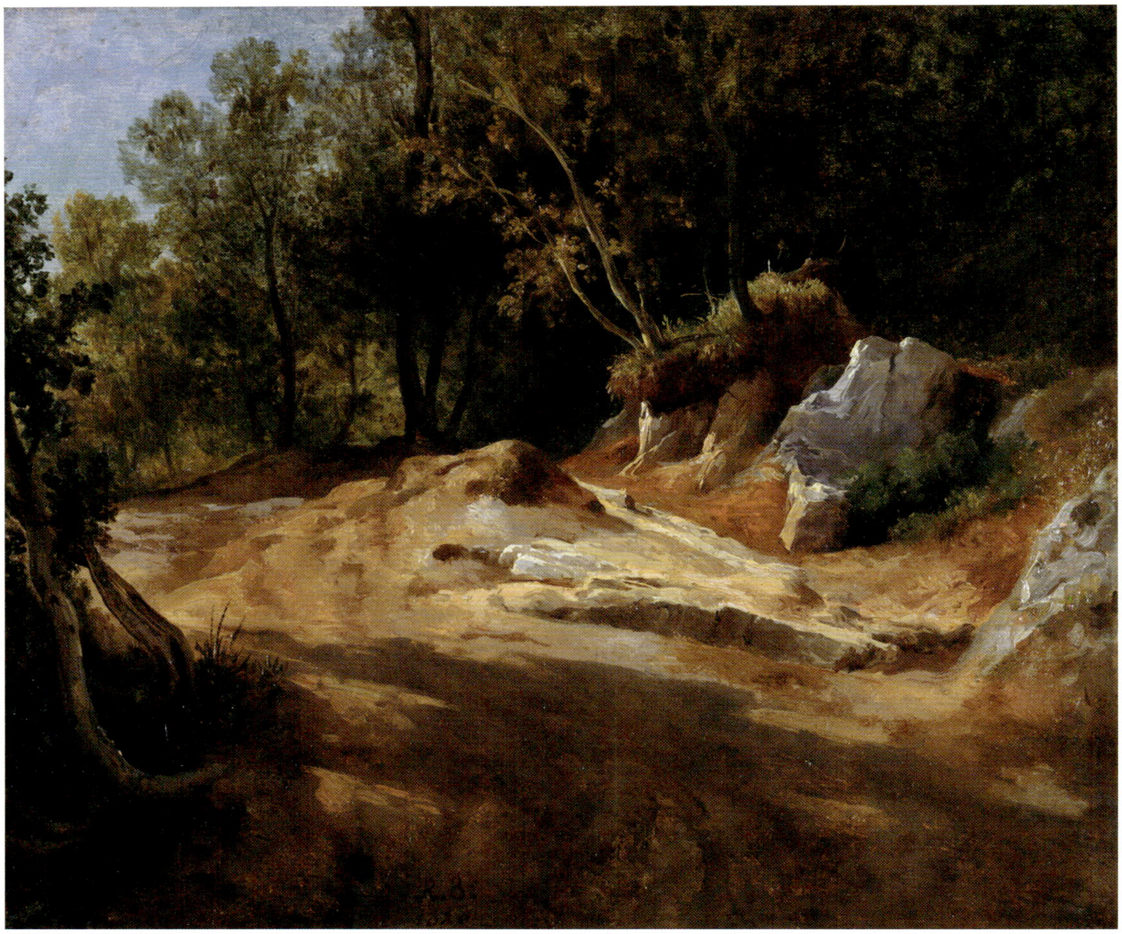

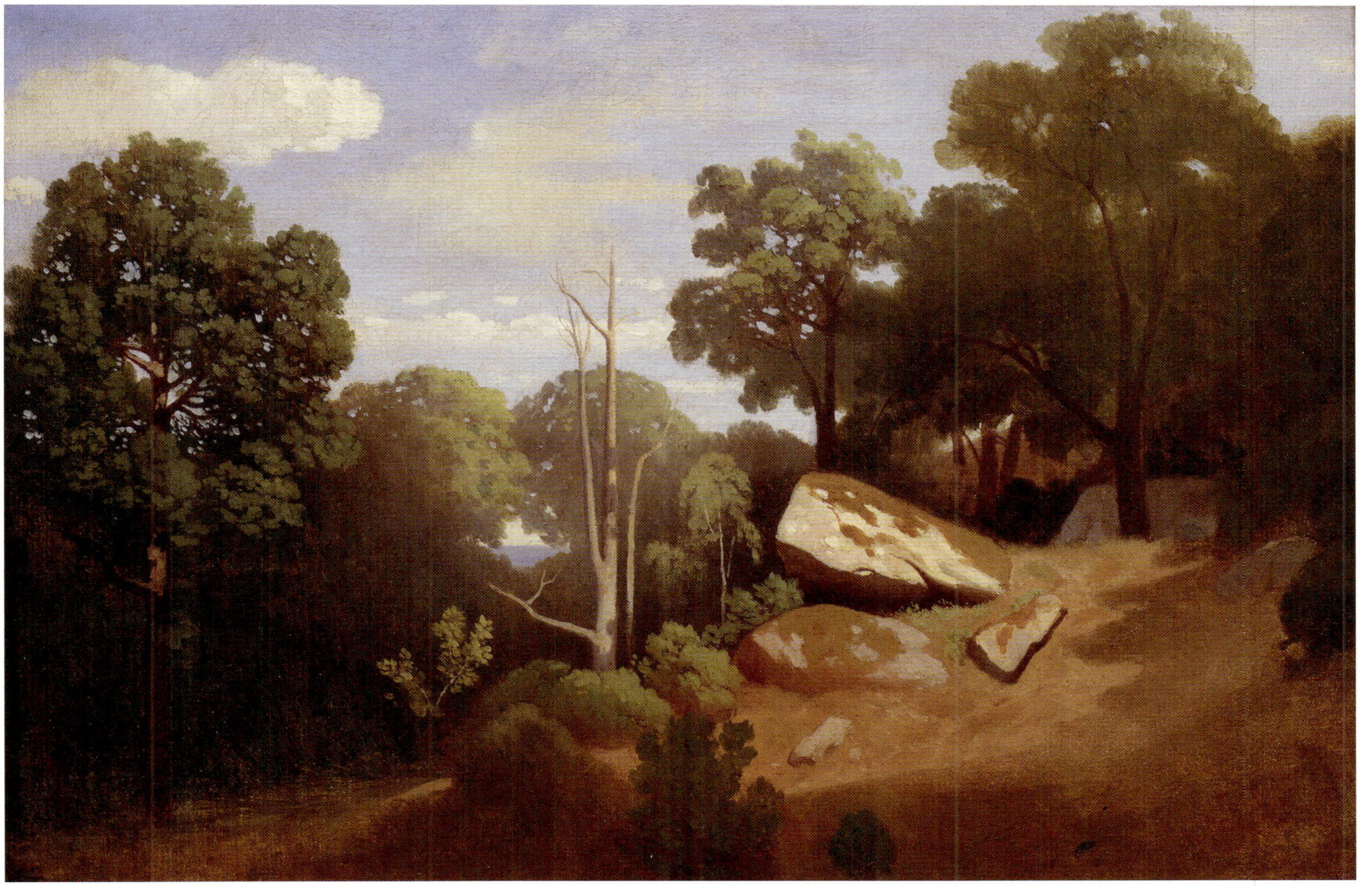

54

Théodore Claude Félix Caruelle d'Aligny

Rocks in the Forest of Fontainebleau, c. 1845, oil on canvas, 29.7 × 45.5 (11 11/16 × 17 15/16). Musée Départmental de l'Oise, Beauvais

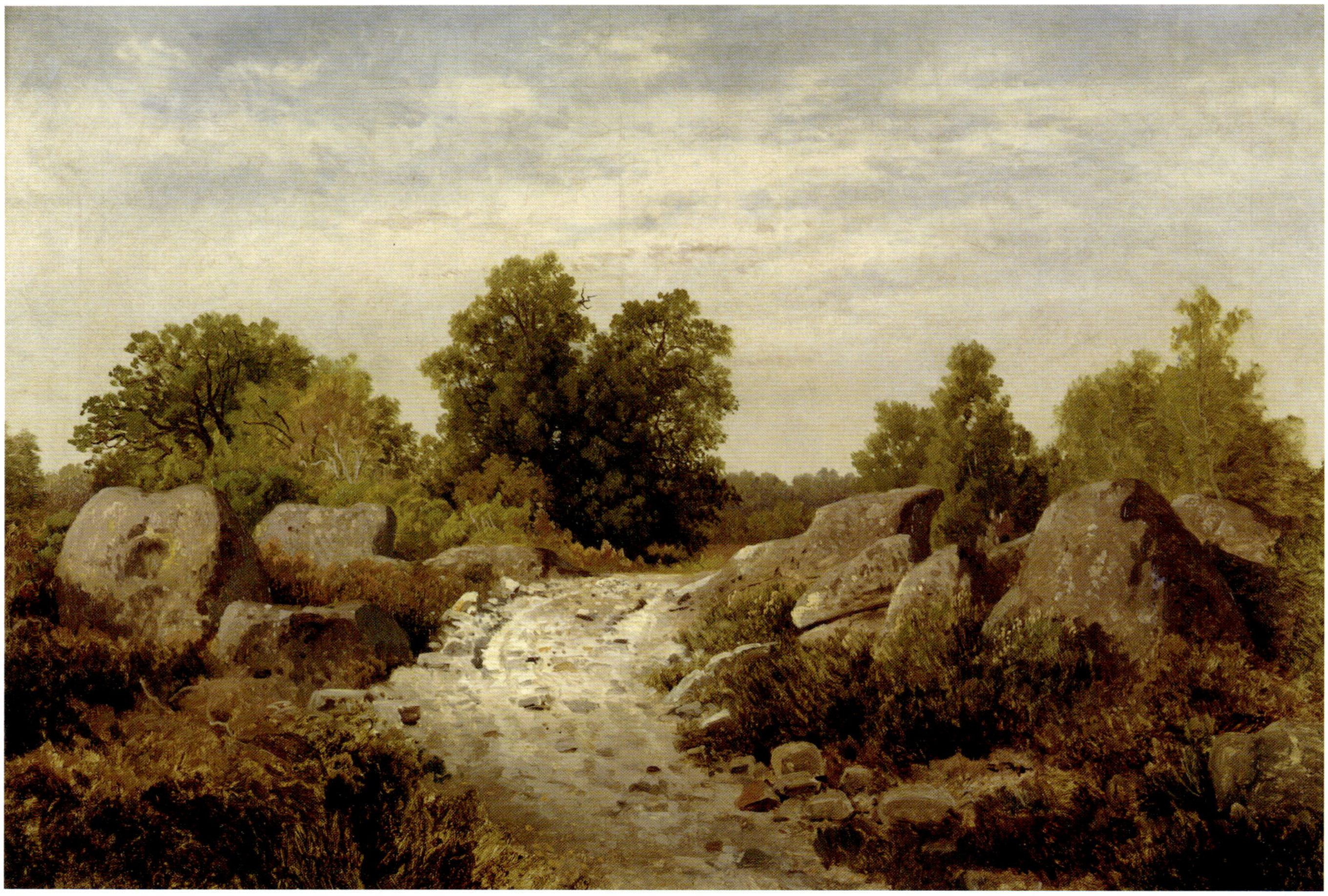

55

Georg Eduard Otto Saal

Path near Fontainebleau,
1858, oil on canvas,
46.5 × 68 (18 5/16 × 26 3/4).
Staatliche Kunsthalle
Karlsruhe

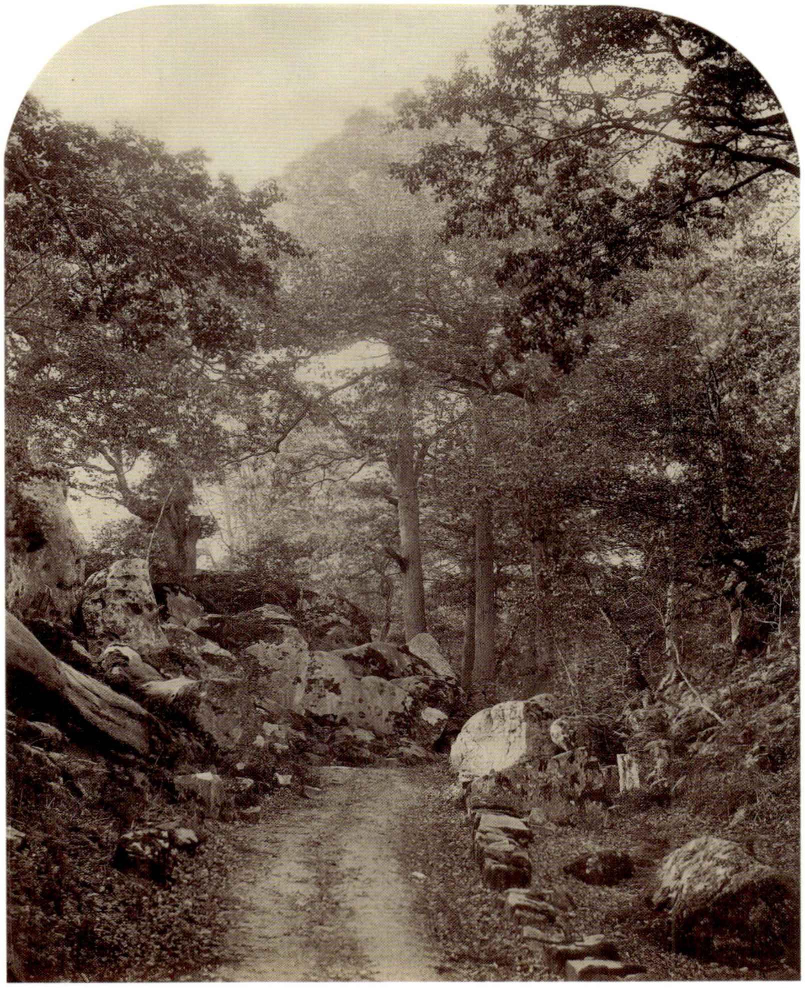

56

Alphonse Jeanrenaud

Fontainebleau, c. 1860s, albumen print, 32 × 26 (12 ⅝ × 10 ¼). National Gallery of Art, Washington, The Amy Rose Silverman Fund and Funds from an Anonymous Donor, 1999

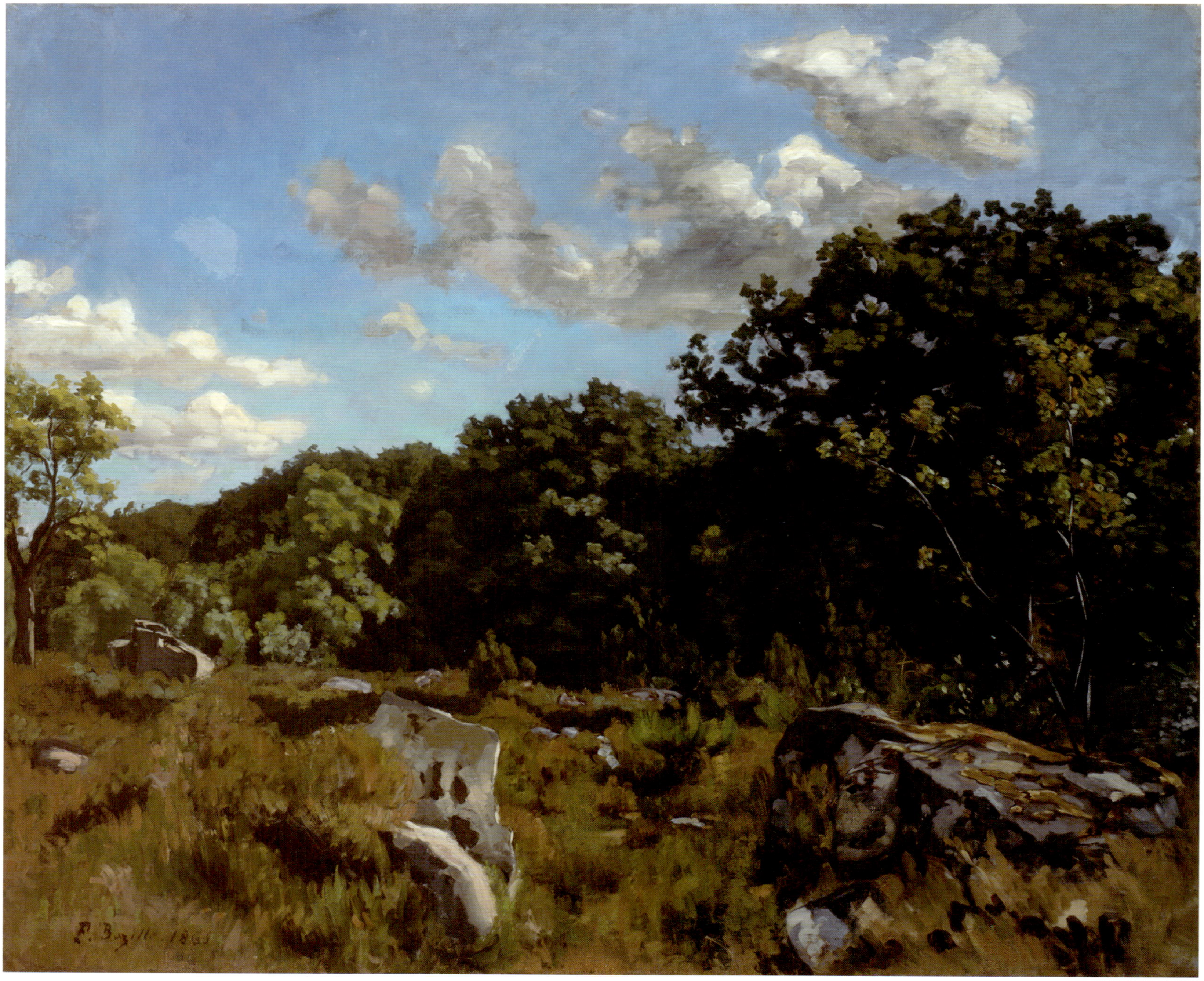

57

Frédéric Bazille

Landscape at Chailly,
1865, oil on canvas,
82 × 10.5 (32 5/16 × 4 1/8).
The Art Institute of
Chicago

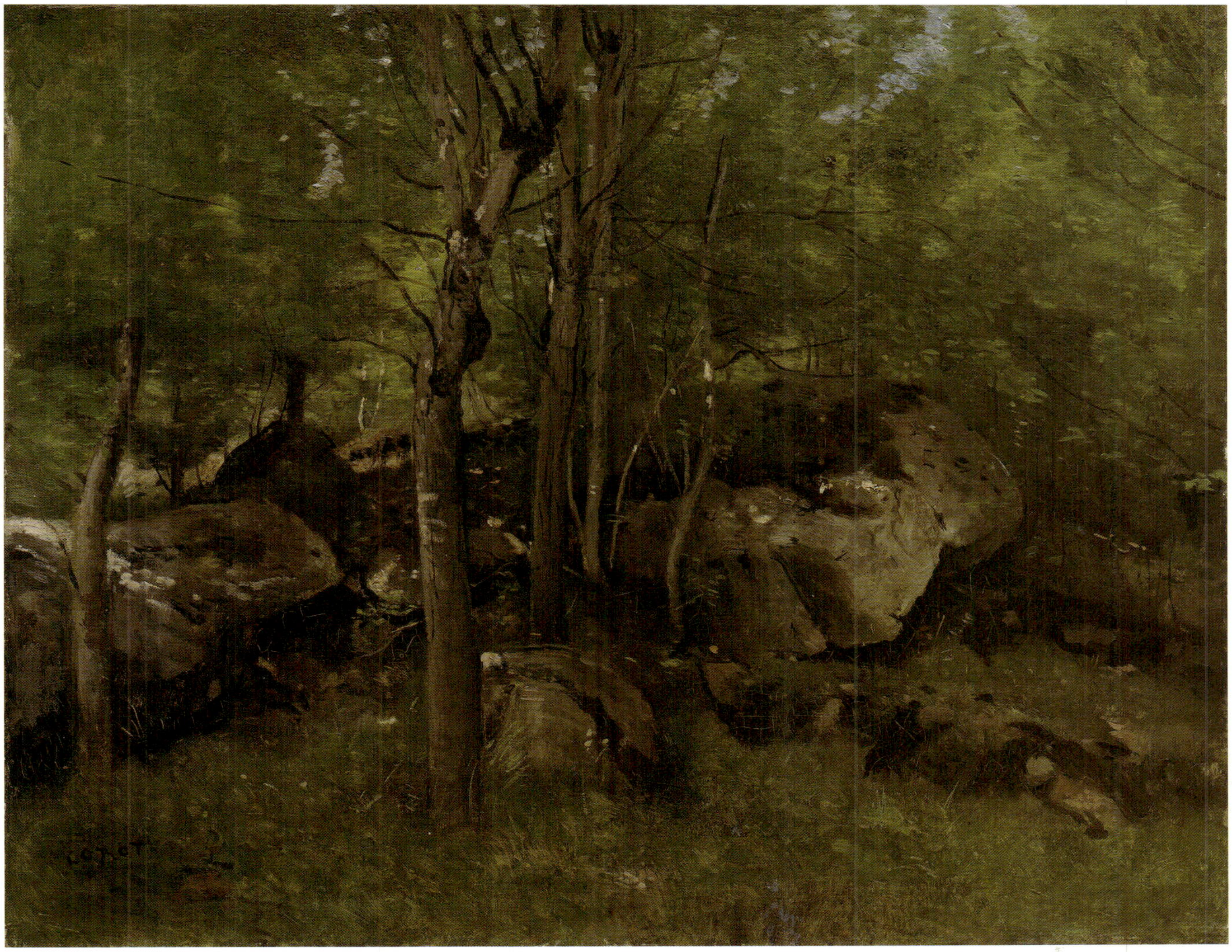

58

Jean-Baptiste-Camille Corot

Rocks in the Forest of Fontainebleau, 1860/1865, oil on canvas, 46 × 59 (18 ⅛ × 23 ¼). National Gallery of Art, Washington, Chester Dale Collection, 1963

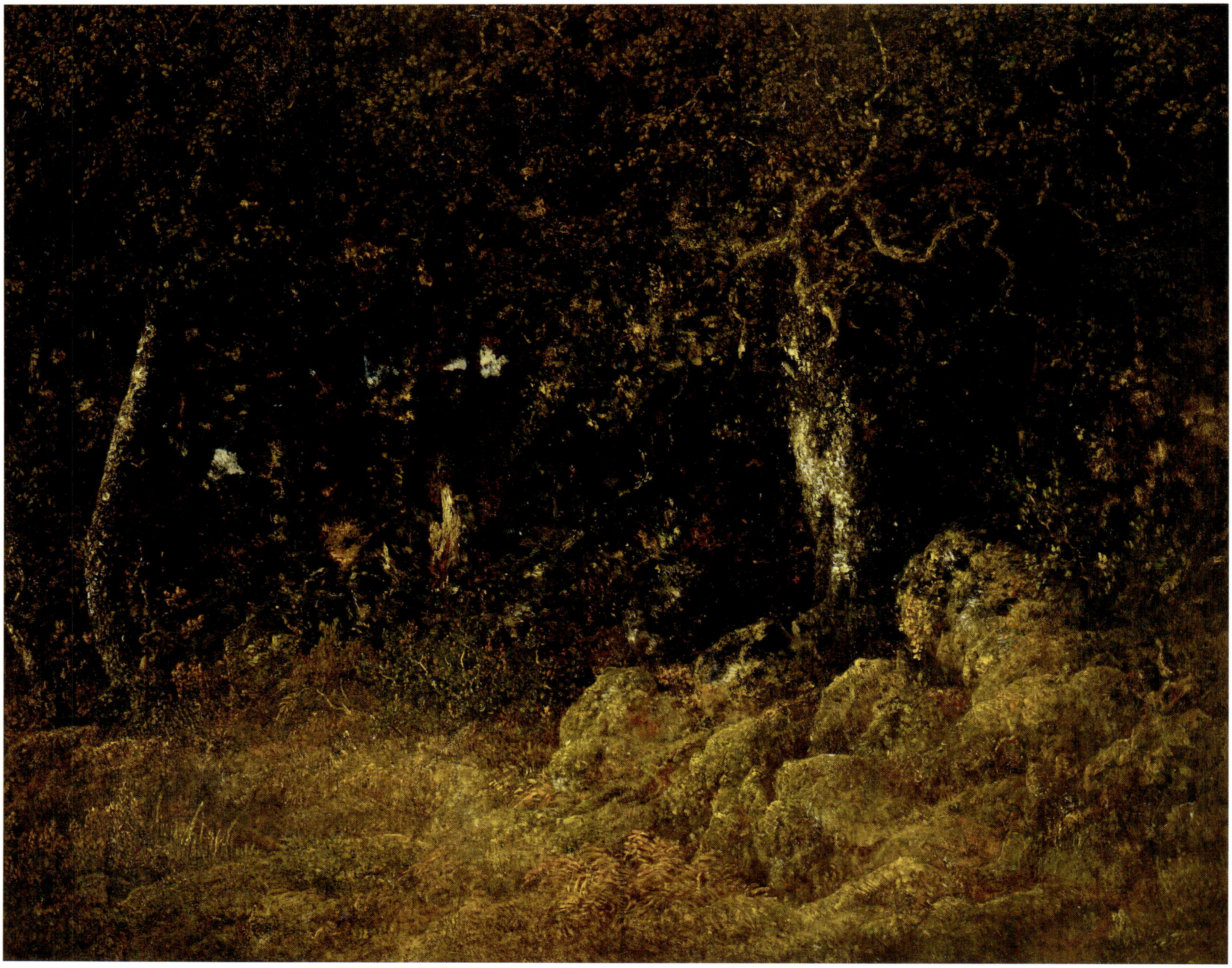

59

Théodore Rousseau

The Rock Oak (Forest of Fontainebleau), 1860, oil on panel, 88.9 × 116.8 (35 × 46). Private collection, New York

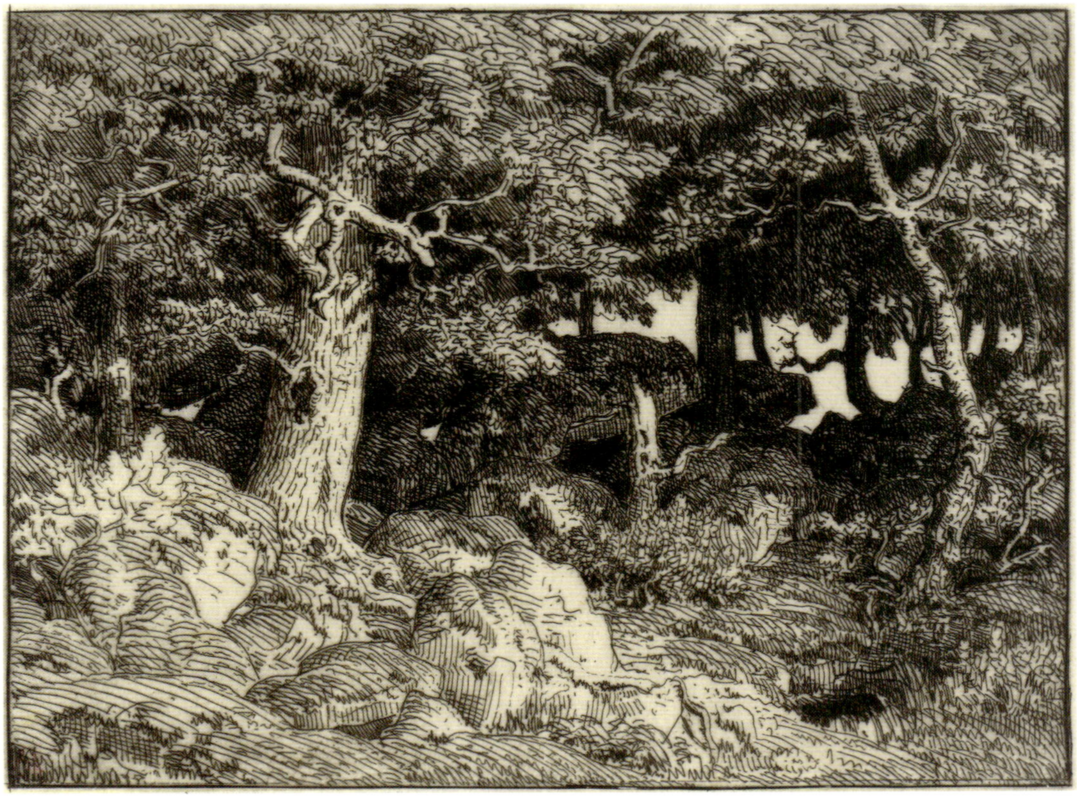

60

Théodore Rousseau

The Rock Oak (Forest of Fontainebleau), 1861, etching on Japan pelure, 12.8 × 16.87 (5 × 6 ⅝). National Gallery of Art, Washington, Rosenwald Collection, 1964

61

Jean-Baptiste-Camille Corot

Abandoned Quarry, Fontainebleau, c. 1850, oil on canvas, 29 × 43 (11 7⁄16 × 16 15⁄16). Van Gogh Museum, Amsterdam

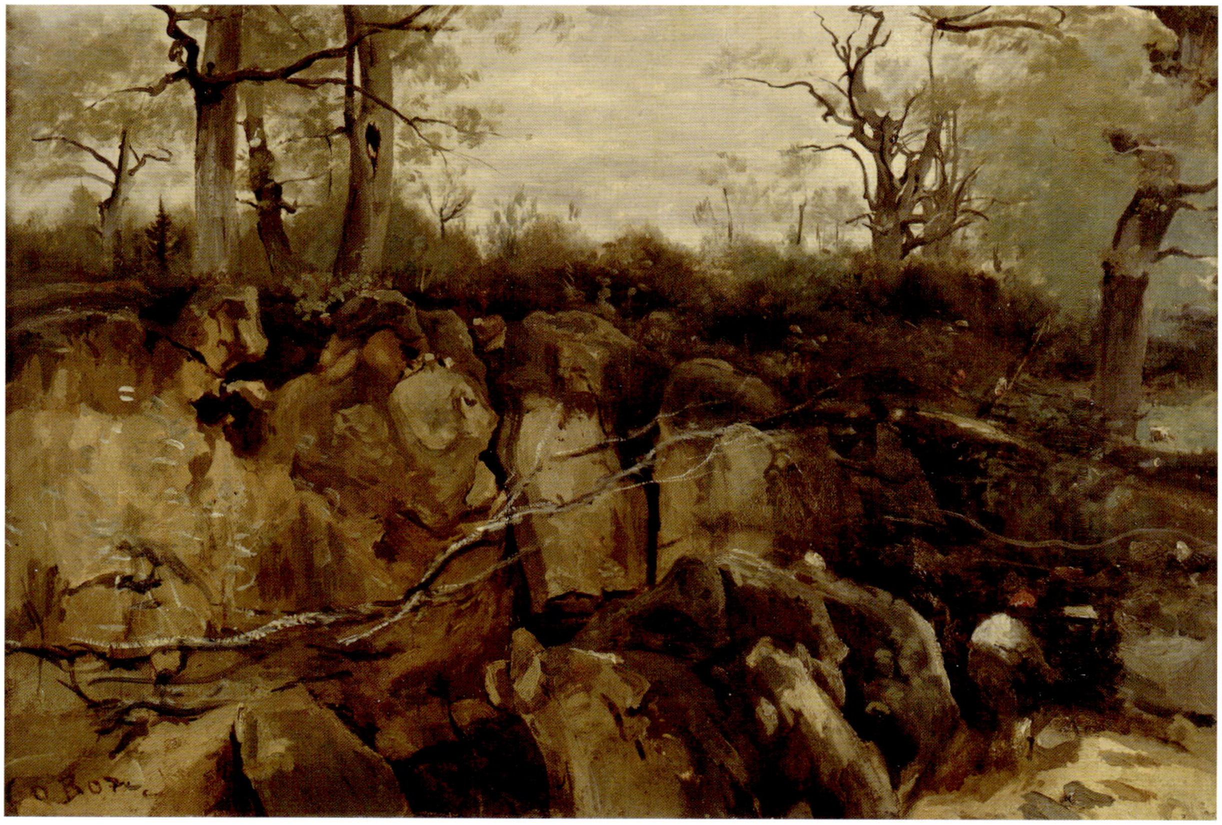

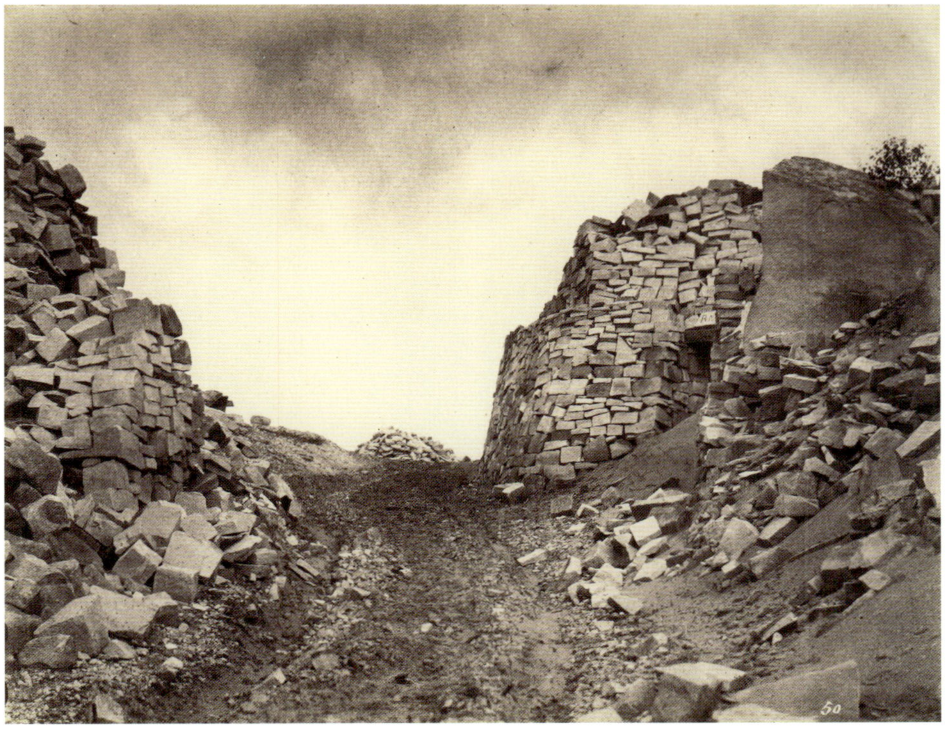

62

Eugène Cuvelier

Quarry at the Sands of Macherin, 1863, salted paper print from paper negative, 19.8 × 25.9 (7 13/16 × 10 3/16). Lent by The Metropolitan Museum of Art, Purchase, Harriette and Noel Levine Gift and Rogers Fund, 1996

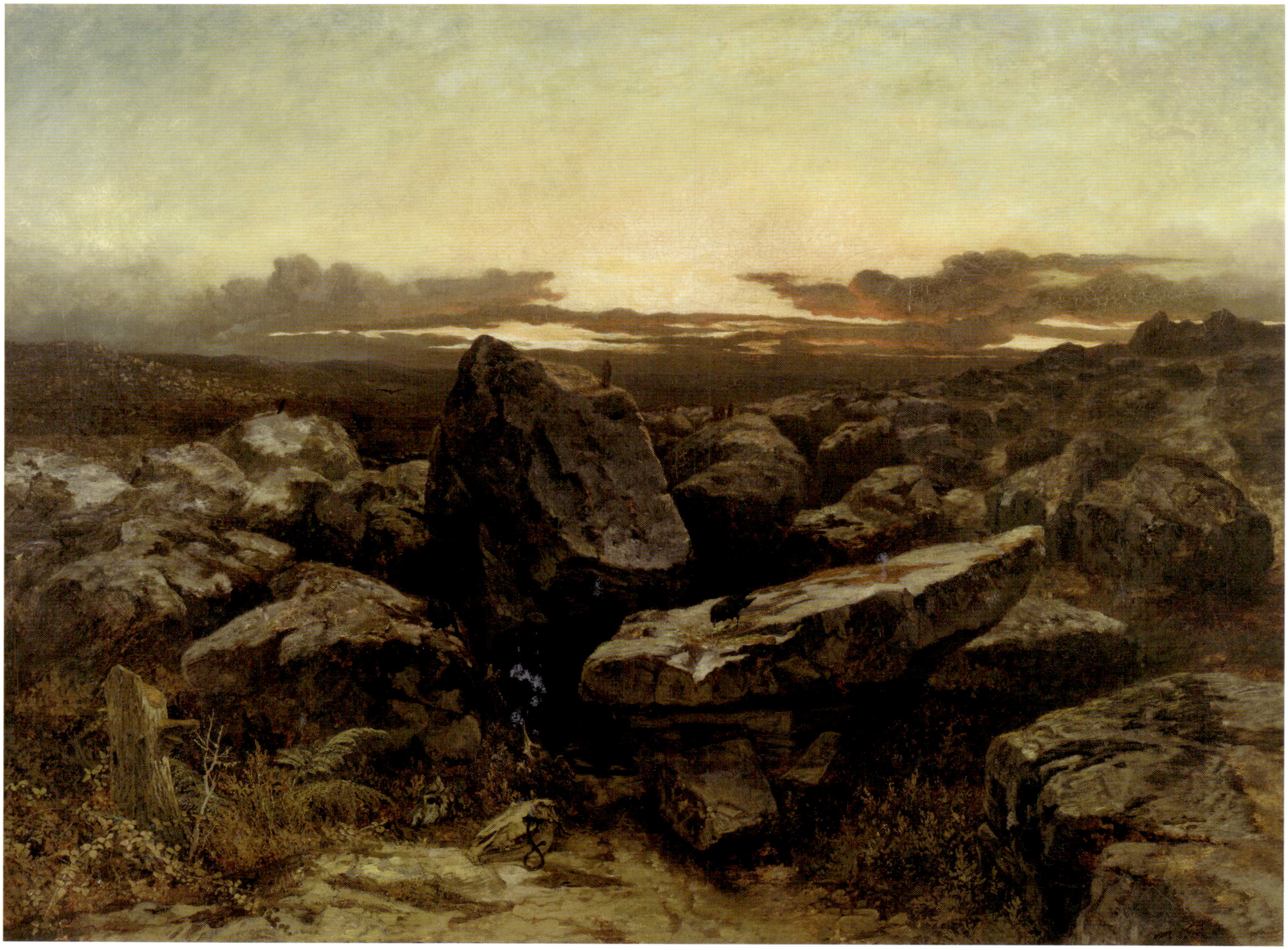

63

Martinus Antonius Kuytenbrouwer

The Gorges d'Apremont, 1848, oil on canvas, 94 × 129 (37 × 50 13/16). Museum Boijmans Van Beuningen, Rotterdam

64

Jacob Maris

Rocks near Fontainebleau, 1864, oil on canvas, 30 × 41 (11 13⁄16 × 16 1⁄8). Collection Willem Witsen/Loan Netherlands Institute for Cultural Heritage (ICN)

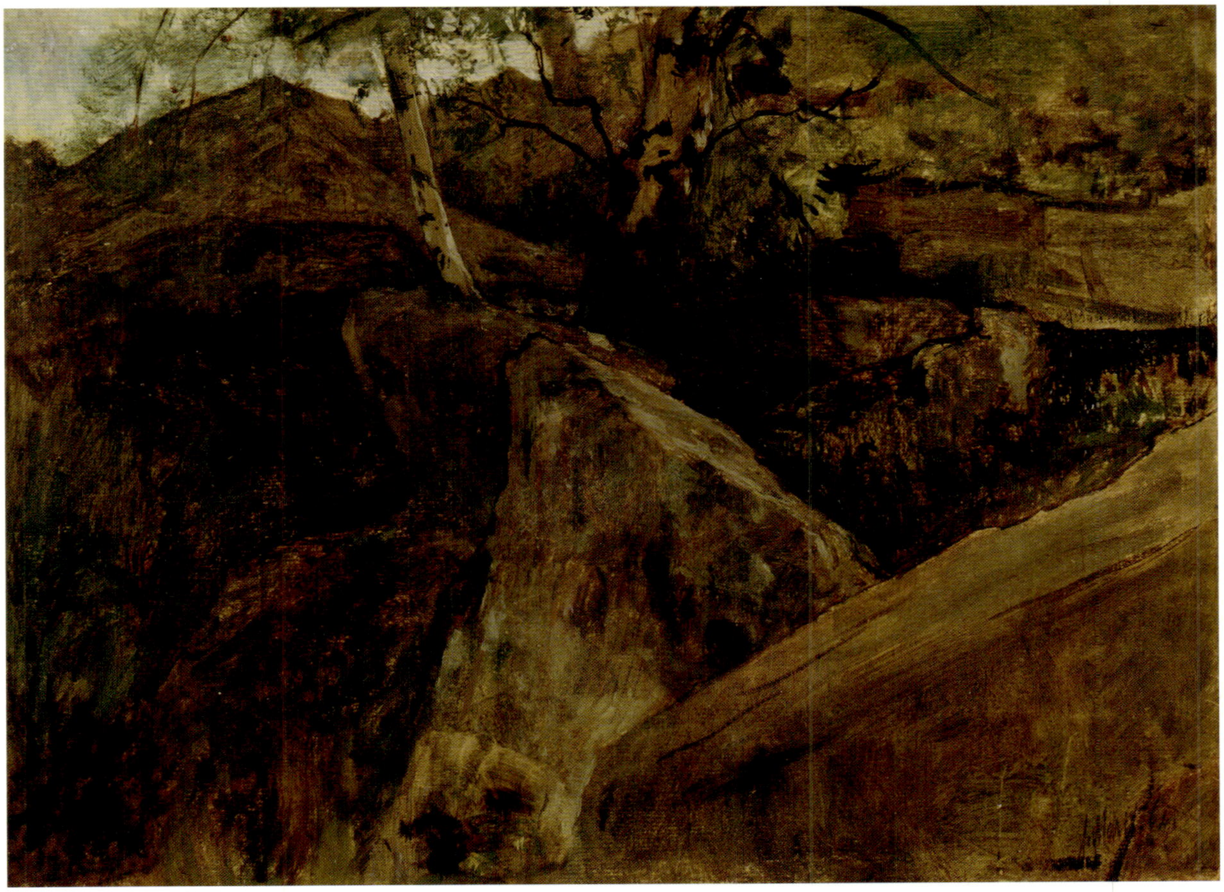

Village Life

In June 1849, Millet and his friend and fellow painter Jacque settled in the village of Barbizon. Upon their arrival, they discovered a modest rural society that depended on the cultivation of crops, primarily grains and vegetables as well as the prized *chasselas de Fontainebleau,* a muscadine grape native to Thomery that produced an exceptional table wine.[1] For Millet, who was drawn to scenes of rural labor, the daily life of the peasants going about their routines—farmers planting crops on the wide expanse of the plain of Chailly, shepherdesses tending their flocks, and laborers at rest—provided an endless source of inspiration (see pls. 75, 78, and 82–84). "The most joyful thing I know is the calm, the silence, that one enjoys either in the forests or cultivated lands," Millet wrote to his friend Sensier in 1851.[2]

The proximity of the Forest of Fontainebleau added a unique aspect to village life that was quite distinct from Millet's native Normandy. Just as the forest dominated the surrounding landscape, it likewise affected the daily rhythms of the local populace. Despite their proximity to it, the forest belonged not to the local inhabitants but to the French crown. Hunting game within Fontainebleau was not permitted, nor was the cutting of trees for personal use, because of their value as a source of income for the *liste civile* (pl. 72).[3] Furthermore, there were strict regulations (the so-called *droits d'usage*) regarding the use and exploitation of the forest by the residents of the neighboring villages. Chief among these was grazing rights. Historically, only cows and pigs could graze in the forest, though their numbers were limited (see pls. 31 and 102). According to the Forest Ordinance of 1669, a total of seventeen villages were accorded grazing rights in the Forest of Fontainebleau. Barbizon, Chailly, and Marlotte were among them and were permitted a total of 6,367 pigs and 12,117 cows within the forest precincts. Sheep and goats, in contrast, were forbidden entry entirely and were forced to graze on the edges of the forest and in the nearby plains (see pls. 71, 73, 81, and 85–88).[4]

The rules governing grazing access were strictly enforced and allowed for little change. Around late 1794 to early 1795, for example, a petition put forth by residents of Fontainebleau requesting permission for animals to graze in areas of the forest that were not planted was refused. It was deemed detrimental to the areas of the forest that were planted, since such areas would need to be traversed in order to reach desired grazing regions.[5] Local use rights were further limited by the Forest Code of 1827. Local forest guards were given full authority to dictate where, when, and how many cows could be pastured, and harsh penalties were threatened for proprietors who allowed sheep and goats to graze in the forest.[6]

In addition to grazing, wood gathering was another traditional privilege that was carefully controlled. Locals had long been permitted to collect brush and dead branches for use as firewood, provided the branches did not exceed six inches in circumference. By the early nineteenth century, this privilege had been curtailed, extending only to poor women, children, the elderly, or sick men and then only three days a week.[7] Only branches that had fallen and could be transported on the gatherer's back could be taken; animals and carts were forbidden to discourage abuse. Perhaps not surprisingly, the majority of criminal cases associated with the Forest of Fontainebleau involved illegal wood gathering rather than poaching, both of which were monitored by the rural guardsmen assigned to the forest (see pl. 70).[8] These tight controls would be loosened somewhat during the Second Empire, and by the 1870s, cutting instruments were allowed, as was the selling of fagots (bundles of dead wood).[9] Like so many aspects of the forest, these traditions were in a state of flux and were threatening to vanish even as artists captured them for posterity.

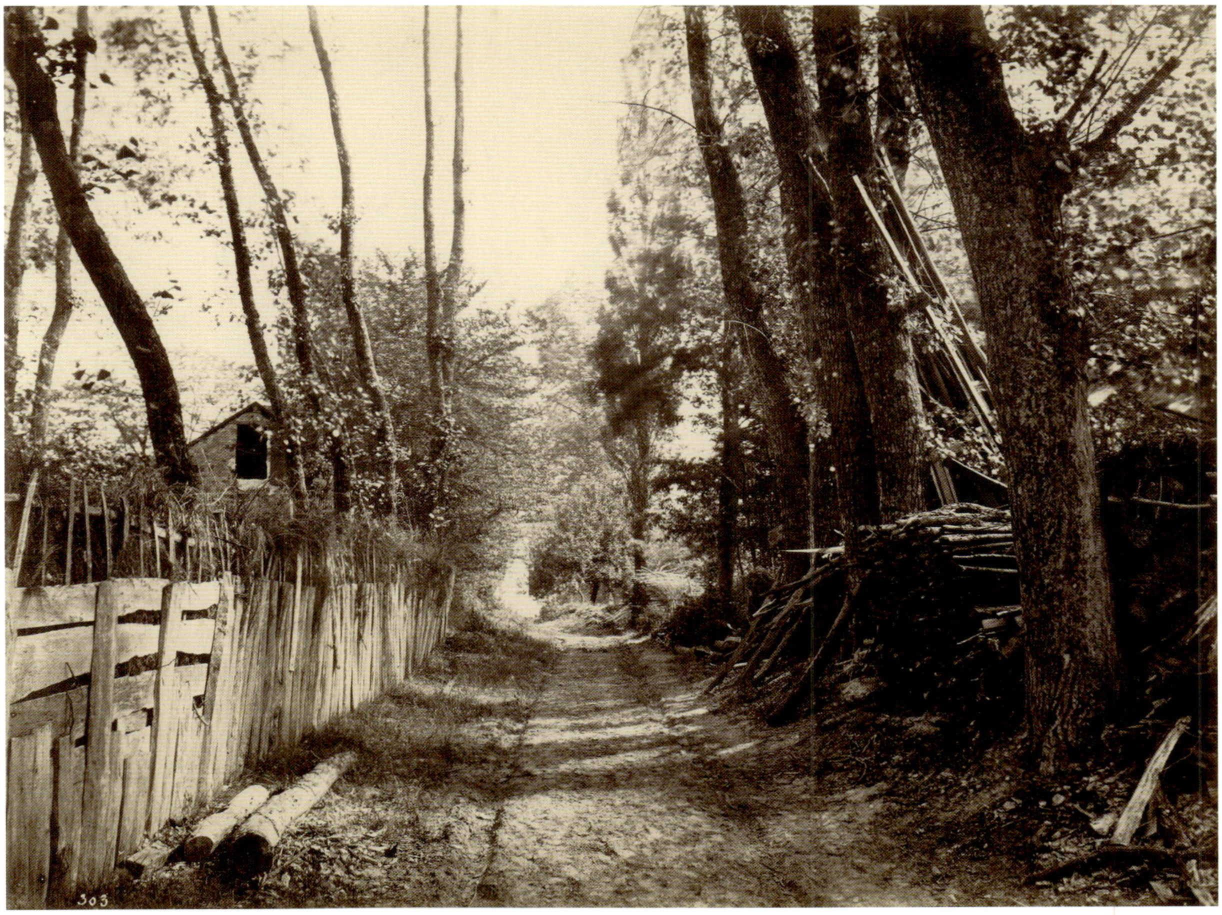

65

Eugène Cuvelier

Boundary of Barbizon, c. 1860s, albumen print from paper negative, 27.3 × 34 (10 ¾ × 13 ⅜). Museum of Fine Arts, Boston: Frederick Brown Fund

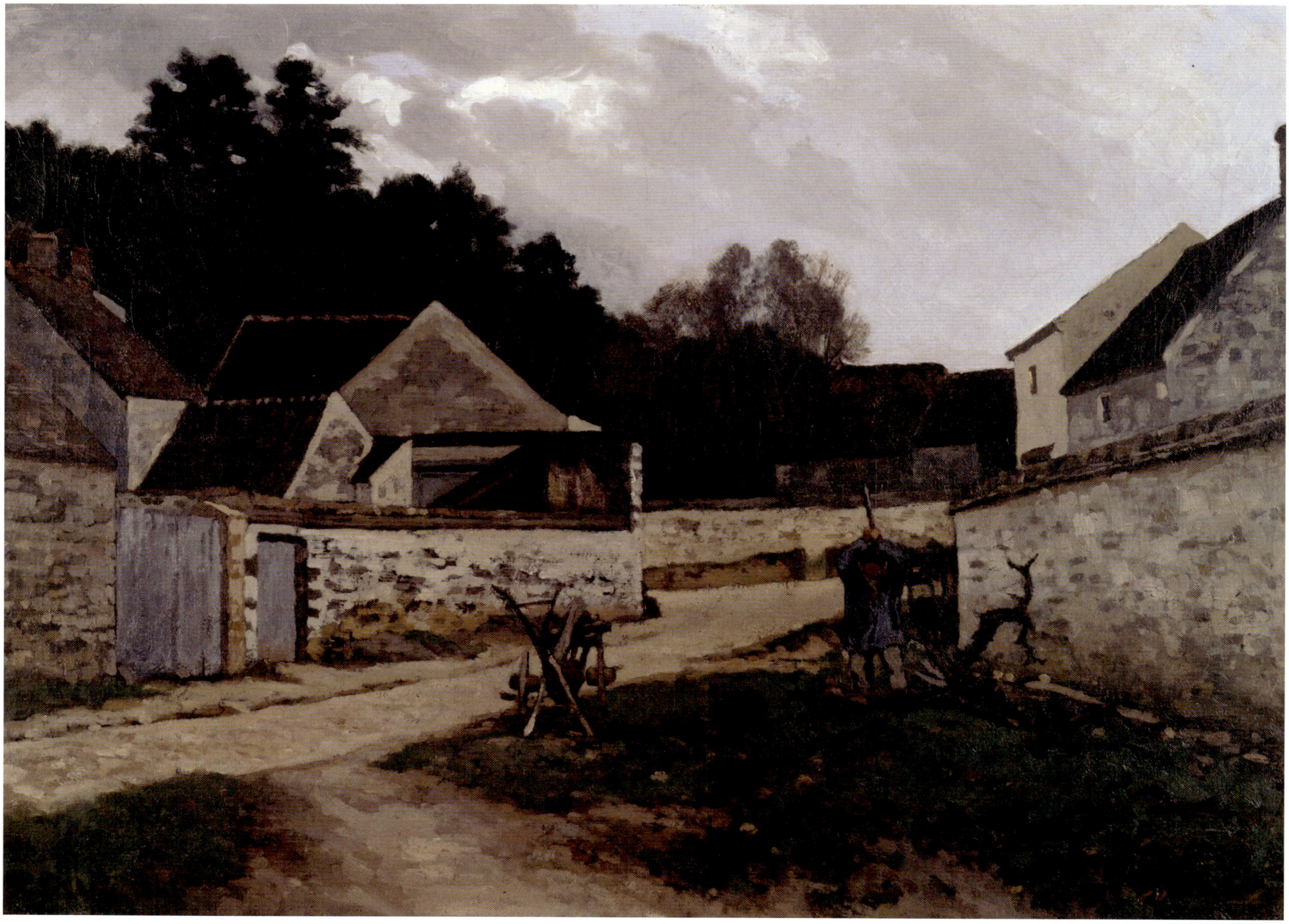

66

Alfred Sisley

Village Street in Marlotte,
1866, oil on canvas,
64.8 × 91.4 (25 ½ × 36).
Collection Albright-
Knox Art Gallery,
Buffalo, General
Purchase Funds, 1956

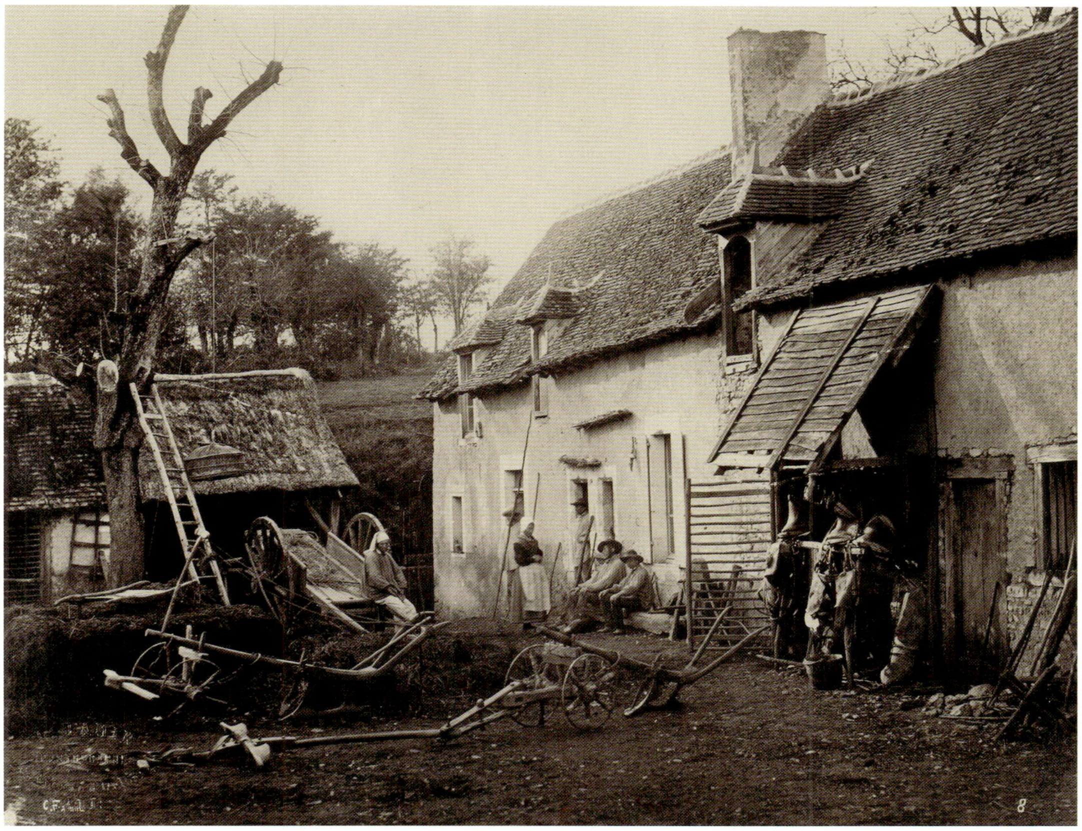

67

Constant Famin

Farm Workers, c. 1870, albumen print from collodion negative, 18.9 × 24.9 (7 $\frac{7}{16}$ × 9 $\frac{13}{16}$). Bibliothèque Nationale de France, Paris

68

Frédéric Bazille

Village Scene (Chailly), 1865, oil on canvas, 32.5 × 24 (12 13/16 × 9 7/16). Private collection

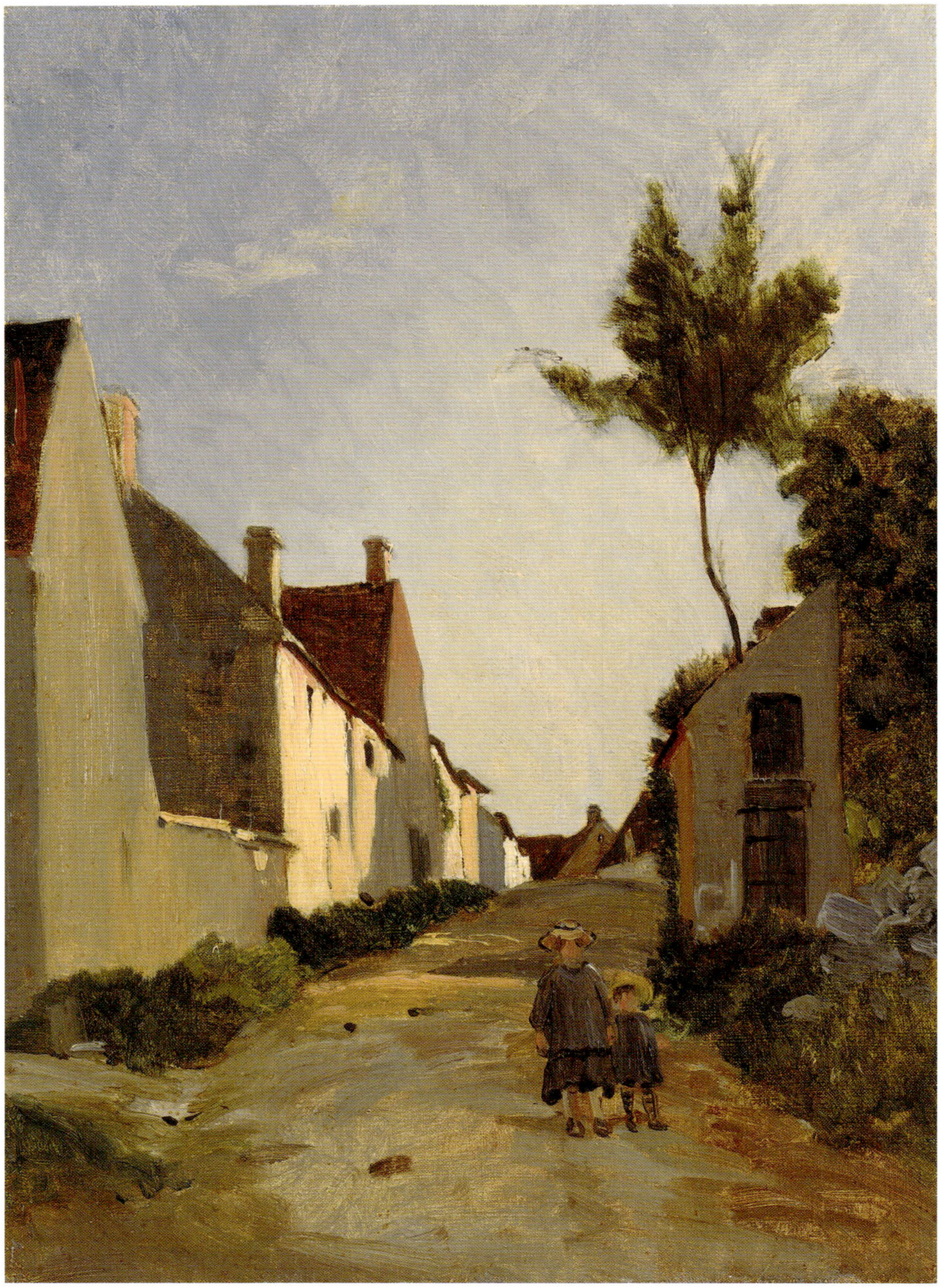

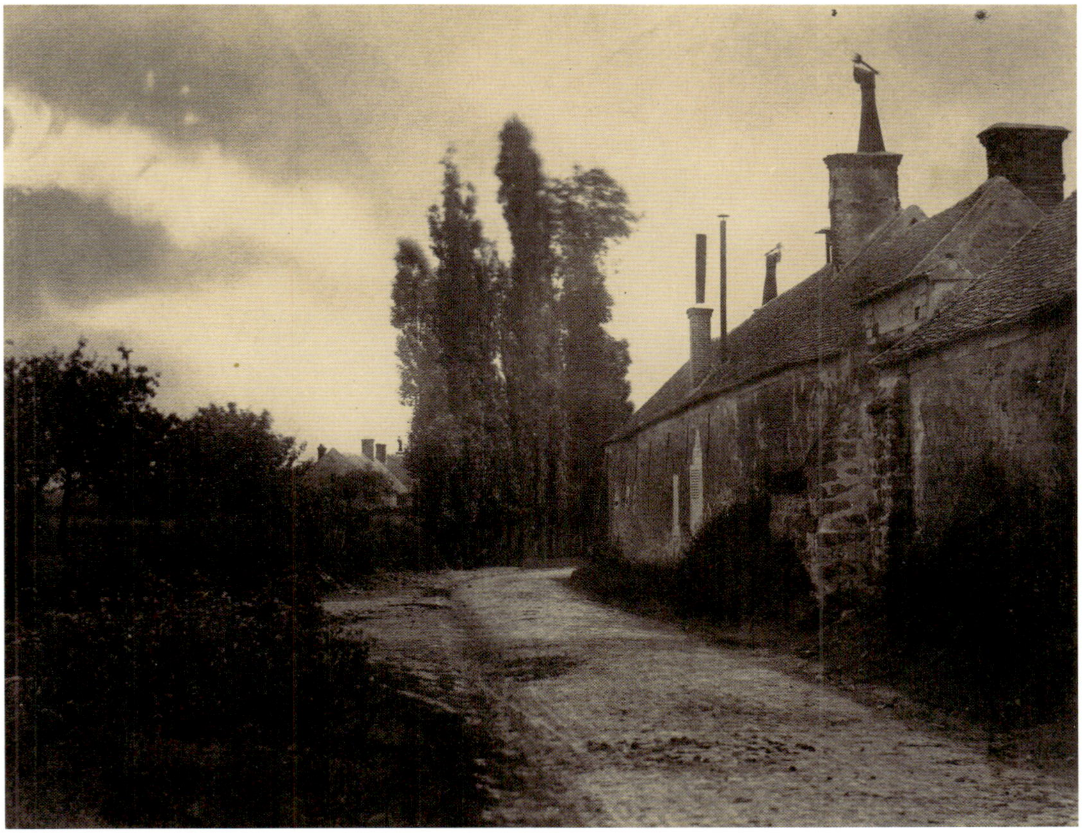

69

Eugène Cuvelier

Farm, Barbizon, early 1860s, salted paper print from paper negative, 18.1 × 26 (7 ⅛ × 10 ¼). Collection Tel Aviv Museum of Art

70

Alfred Sisley

Rural Guardsman in the Fontainebleau Forest, 1870, oil on canvas, 78 × 63.5 (30 11/16 × 25). Mr. and Mrs. Marsh Gibson

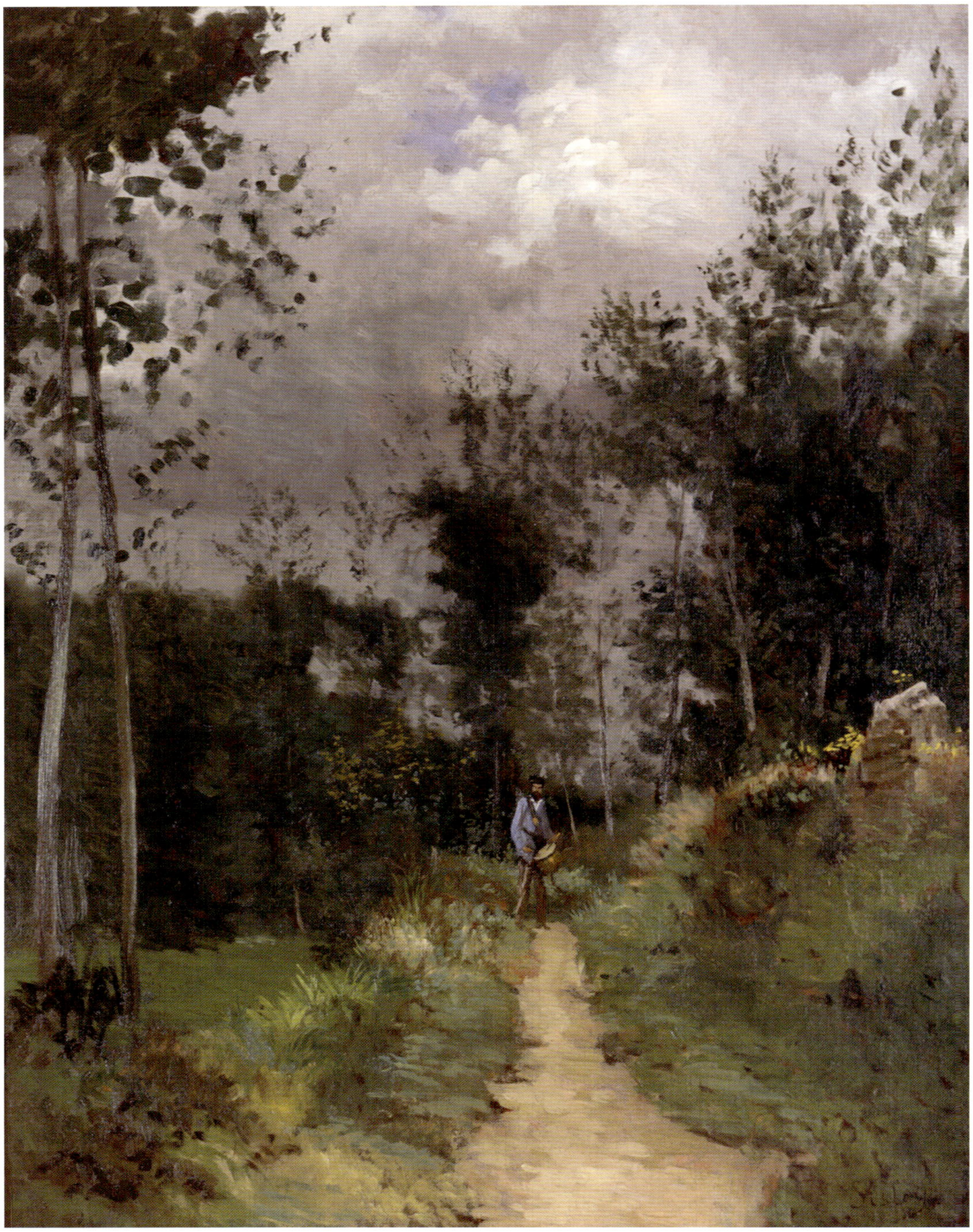

71

Charles-Emile Jacque

The Old Forest, 1860–1870, oil on wax-lined canvas, 83 × 67 (32 11/16 × 26 3/8). Brooklyn Museum, Bequest of Mrs. William A. Putnam

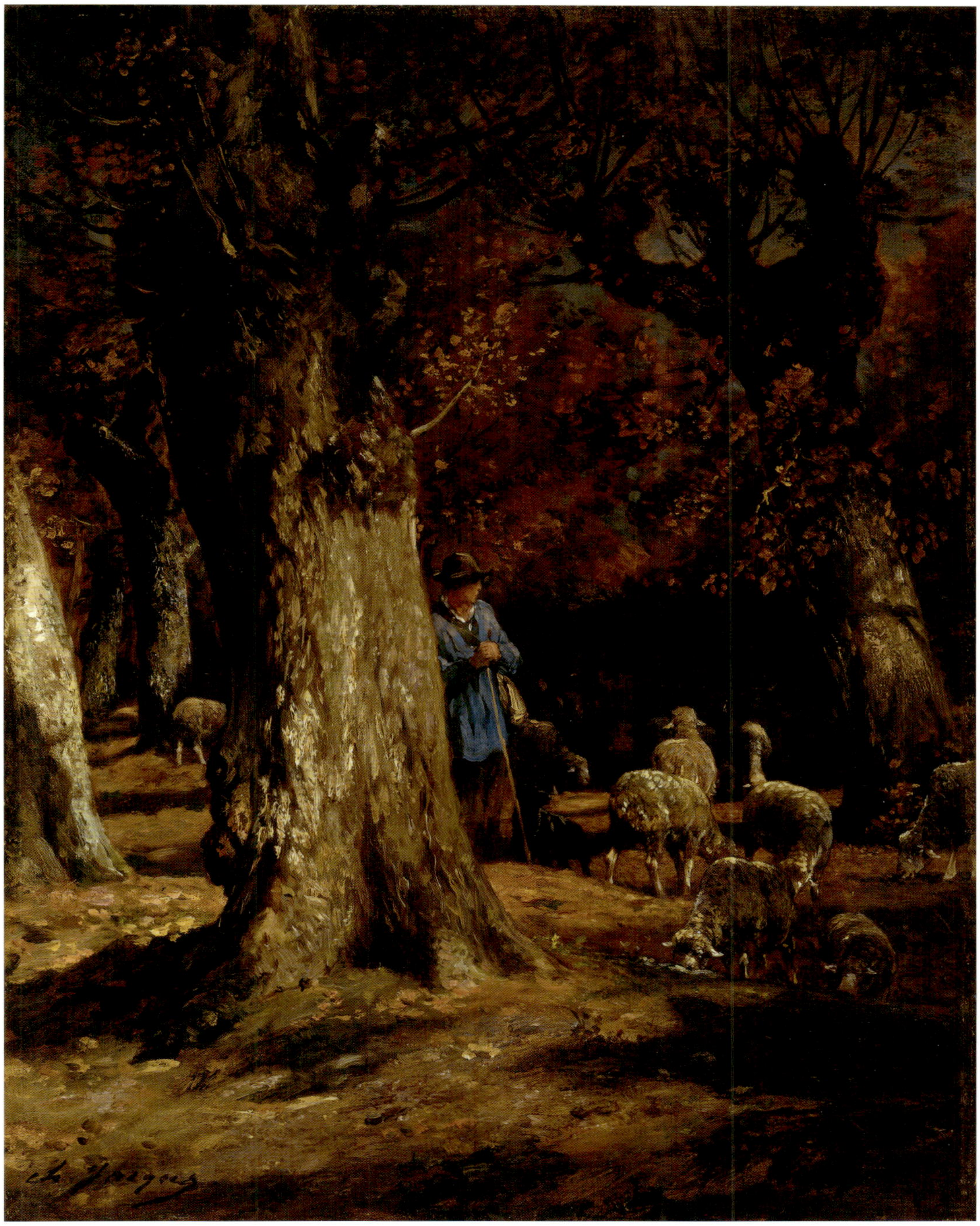

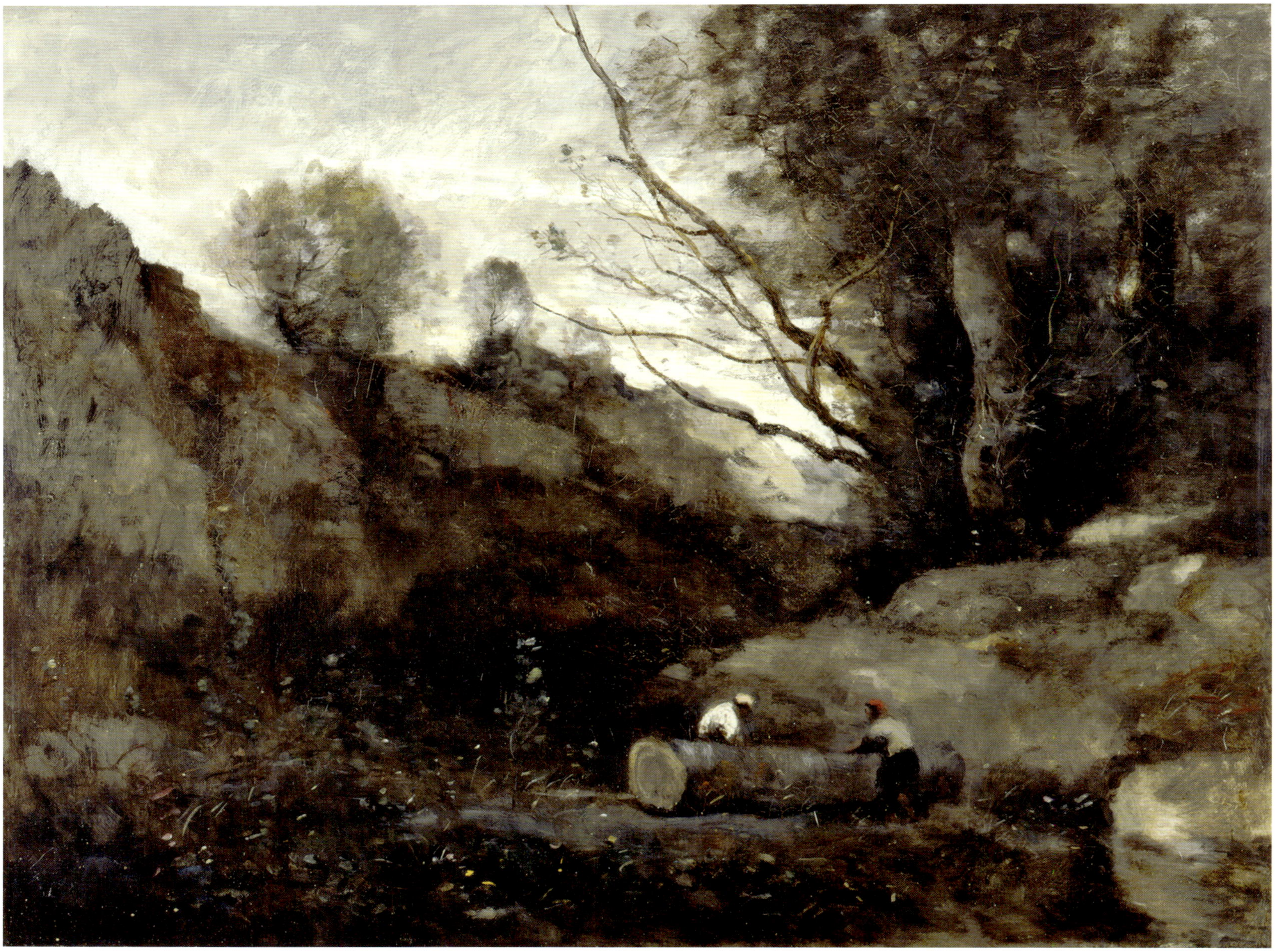

72

Jean-Baptiste-Camille Corot

Woodcutters in a Forest Valley, 1872, oil on canvas, 61 × 82 (24 × 32 5/16). Museum der Bildenden Künste, Leipzig

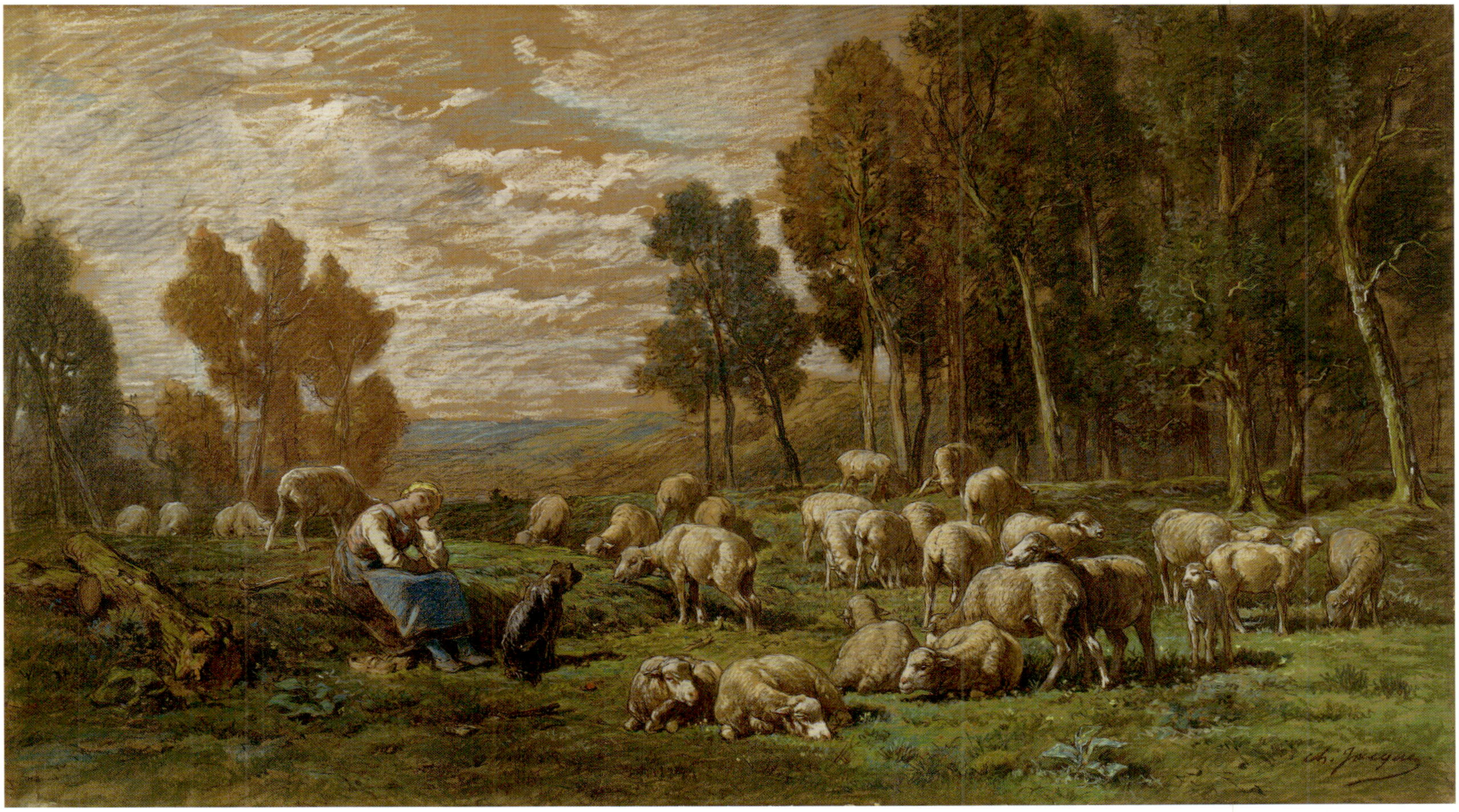

73

Charles-Emile Jacque

The Shepherdess, c. 1869, pastel on brown wove paper, 52.6 × 94.9 (20 11/16 × 37 3/8). National Gallery of Art, Washington, Gift of Mr. and Mrs. James T. Dyke, 1996

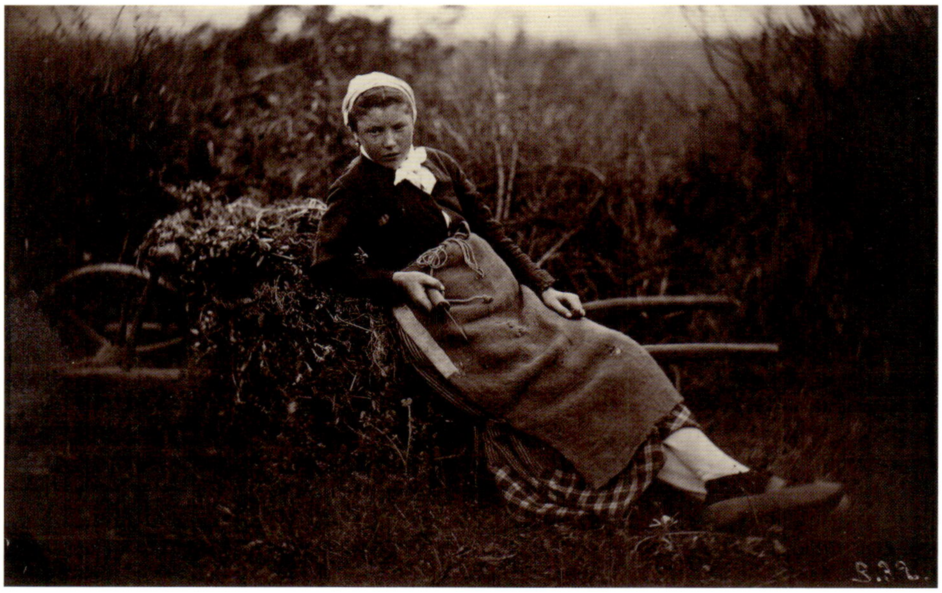

74

Auguste Giraudon's Artist

Peasant, c. 1870, albumen print from collodion negative, 10.9 × 17.1 (4 5/16 × 6 3/4). National Gallery of Art, Washington, The Horace W. Goldsmith Foundation through Robert and Joyce Menschel, 2002

75

Jean-François Millet

Noonday Rest, 1866, pastel and black conté crayon on paper, 29.2 × 41.9 (11 ½ × 16 ½). Museum of Fine Arts, Boston: Gift of Quincy Adams Shaw through Quincy Adams Shaw Jr. and Mrs. Marian Shaw Haughton

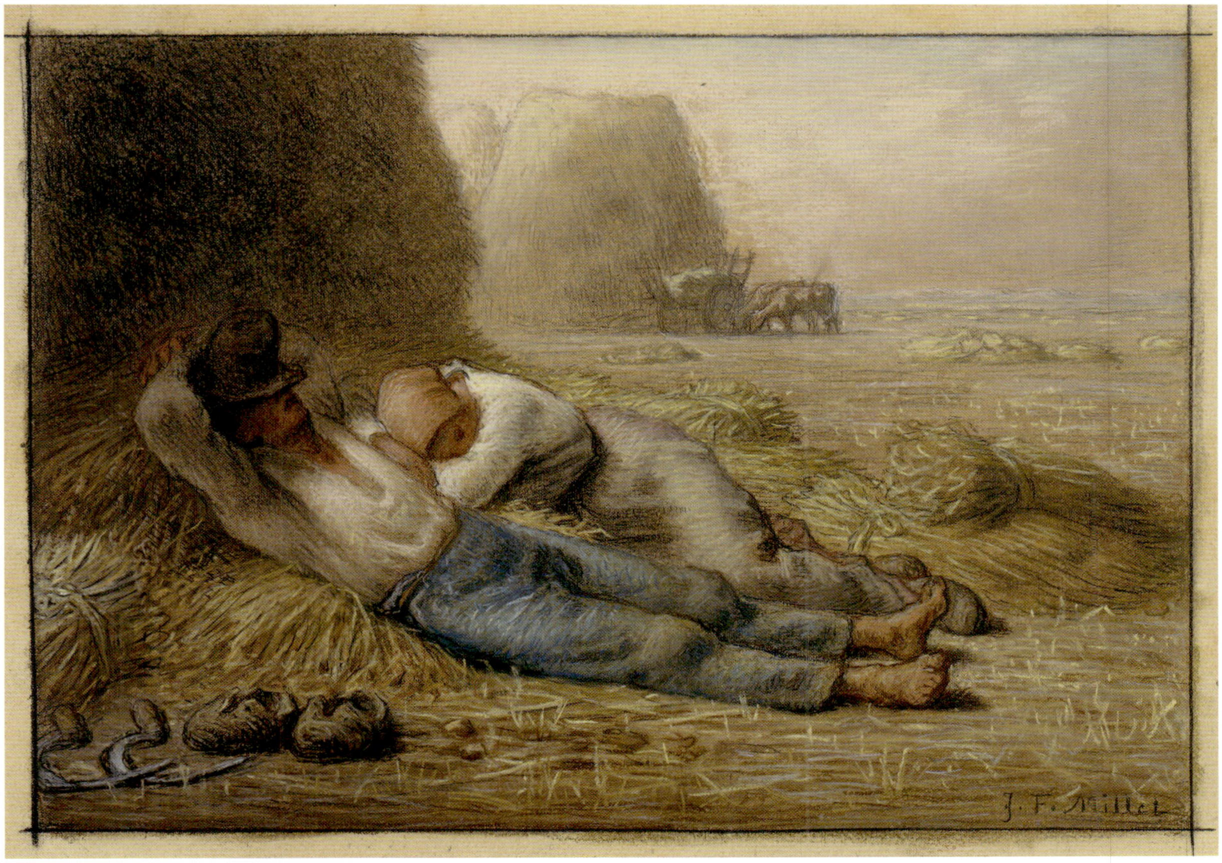

76

Auguste Giraudon's Artist

Two Young Peasant Women in the Hay, 1878, albumen print from collodion negative, 15.3 × 11.7 (6 × 4 ⅝). Musée d'Orsay, Paris; Gift of Marie-Thérèse and André Jammes, 1984

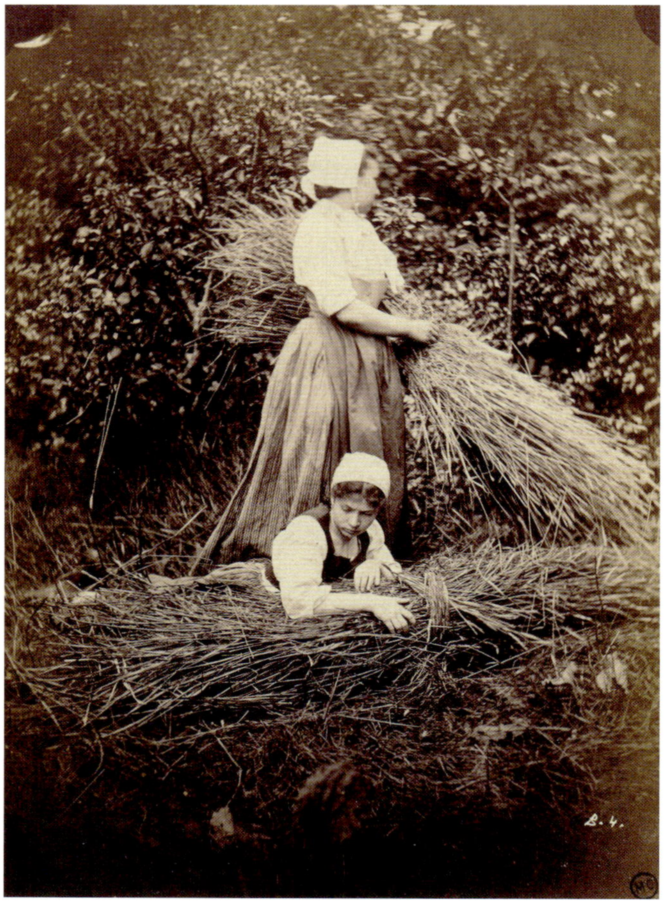

77

Auguste Giraudon's Artist

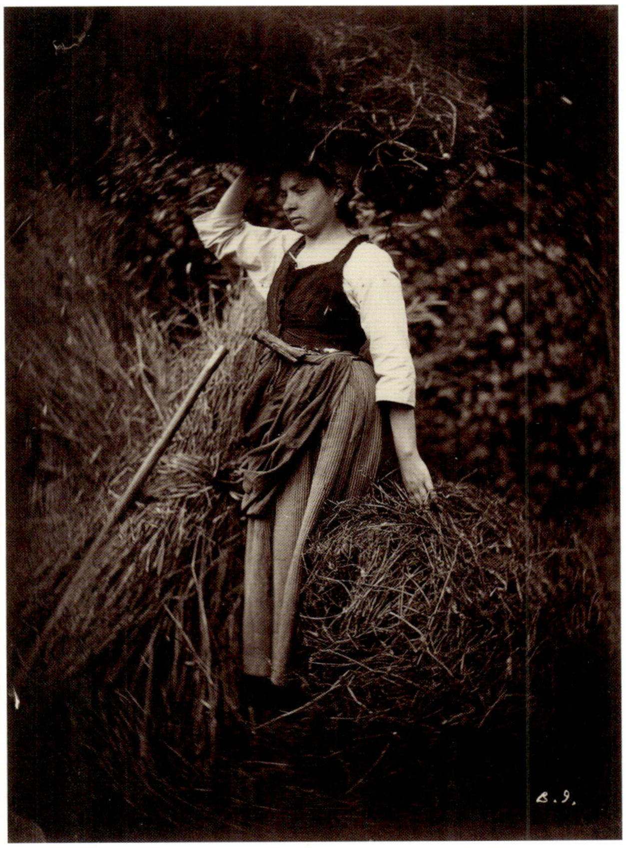

Peasant, c. 1870, albumen print from collodion negative, 17.1 × 12.6 (6 ¾ × 4 15/16). National Gallery of Art, Washington, The Horace W. Goldsmith Foundation through Robert and Joyce Menschel, 2002

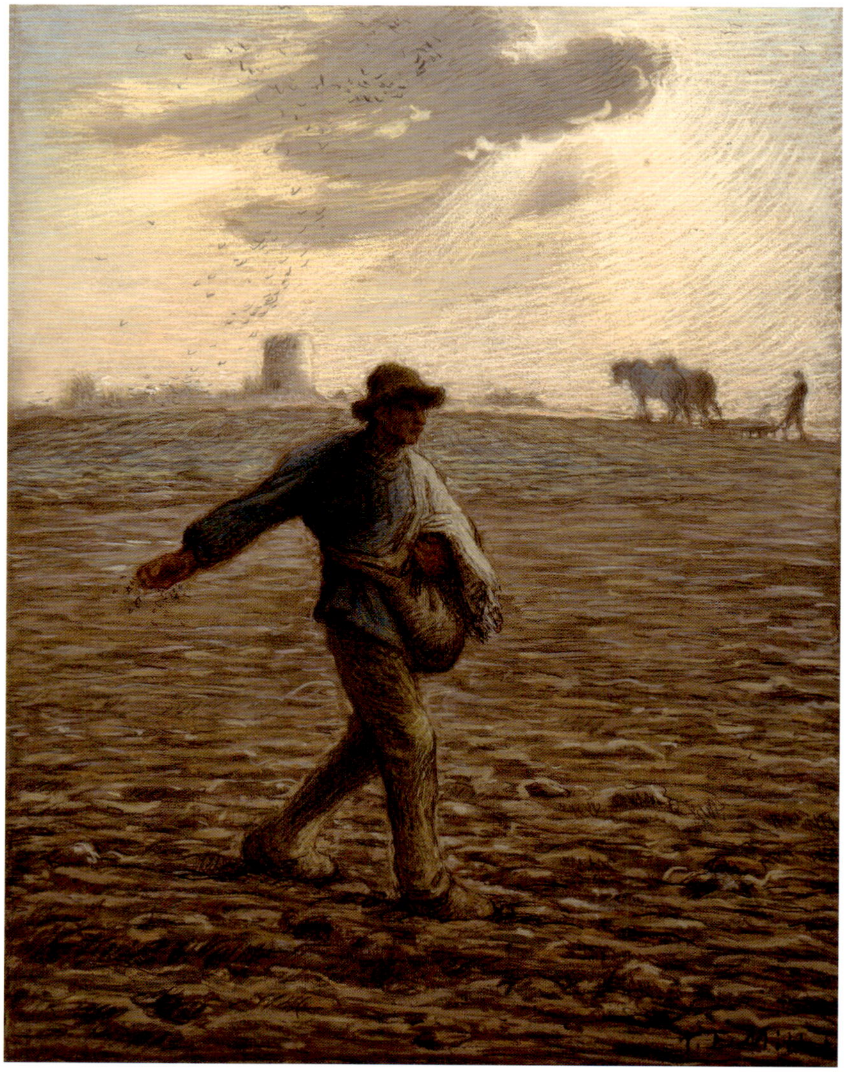

78

Jean-François Millet

The Sower, 1865–1866,
black conté crayon
and pastel on paper,
47.1 × 37.5 (18 9/16 × 14 3/4).
Sterling and Francine
Clark Art Institute,
Williamstown,
Gift of Mr. and Mrs.
Norman Hirschl

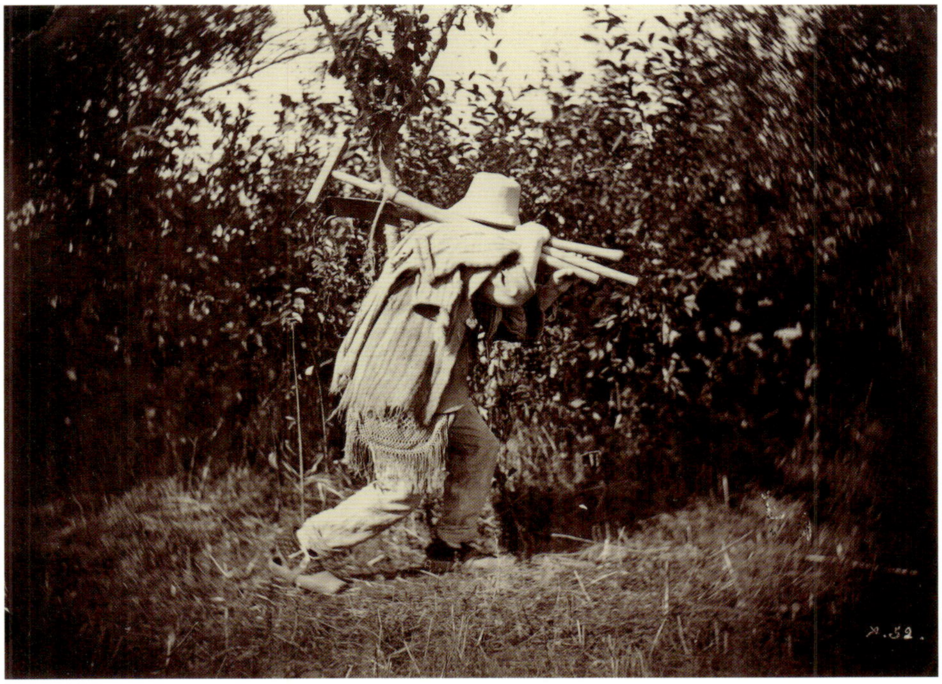

79

Auguste Giraudon's Artist

Peasant, c. 1870, albumen print from collodion negative, 12.2 × 16.9 (4 13/16 × 6 5/8). National Gallery of Art, Washington, The Horace W. Goldsmith Foundation through Robert and Joyce Menschel, 2002

80

Constant Famin

Two Young Peasants,
c. 1870, albumen print
from collodion negative,
17.1 × 12.5 (6 ¾ × 4 15/16).
Bibliothèque Nationale
de France, Paris

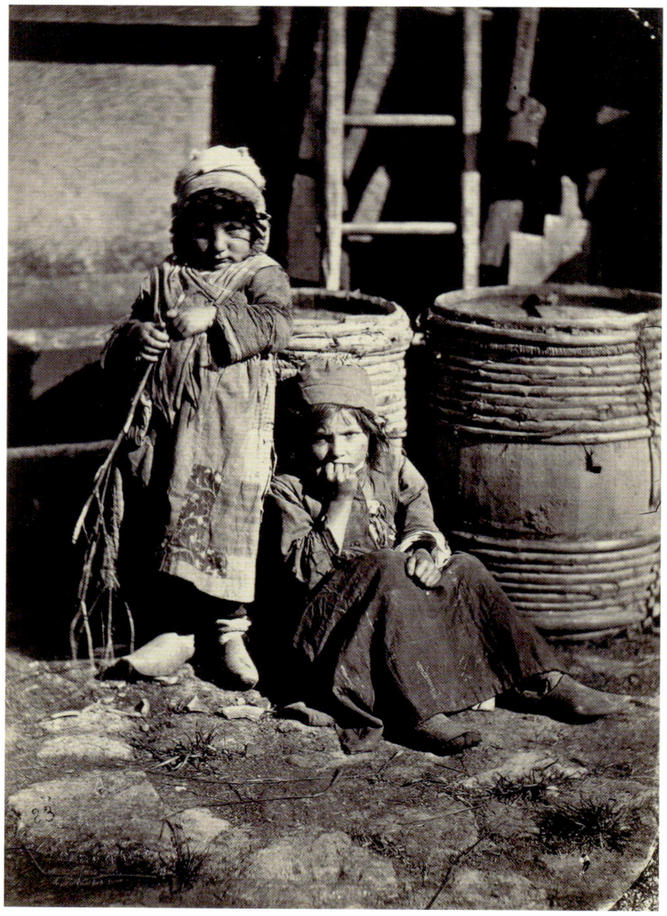

81

Jean-François Millet

Shepherdess Knitting, outside the Village of Barbizon, c. 1860–1862, pastel over black conté crayon on paper, 40 × 29 (15 3/4 × 11 7/16). Museum of Fine Arts, Boston: Gift of Quincy Adams Shaw through Quincy Adams Shaw Jr. and Mrs. Marian Shaw Haughton

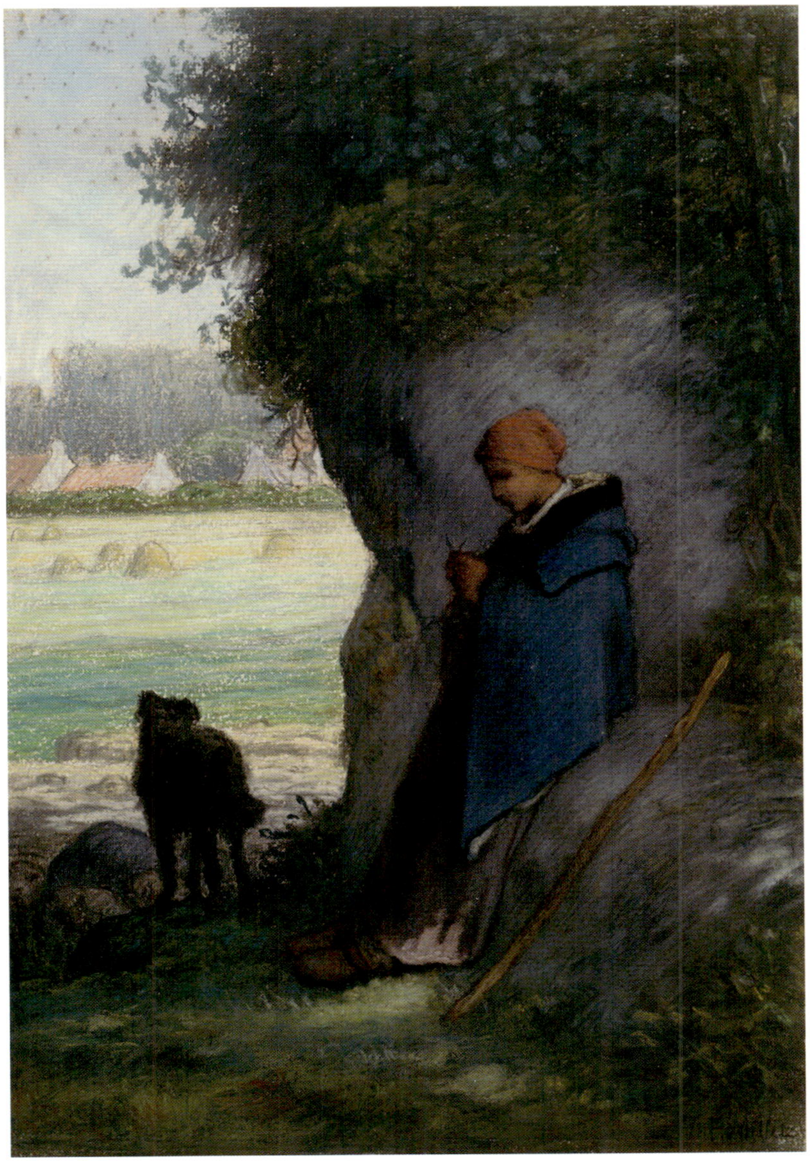

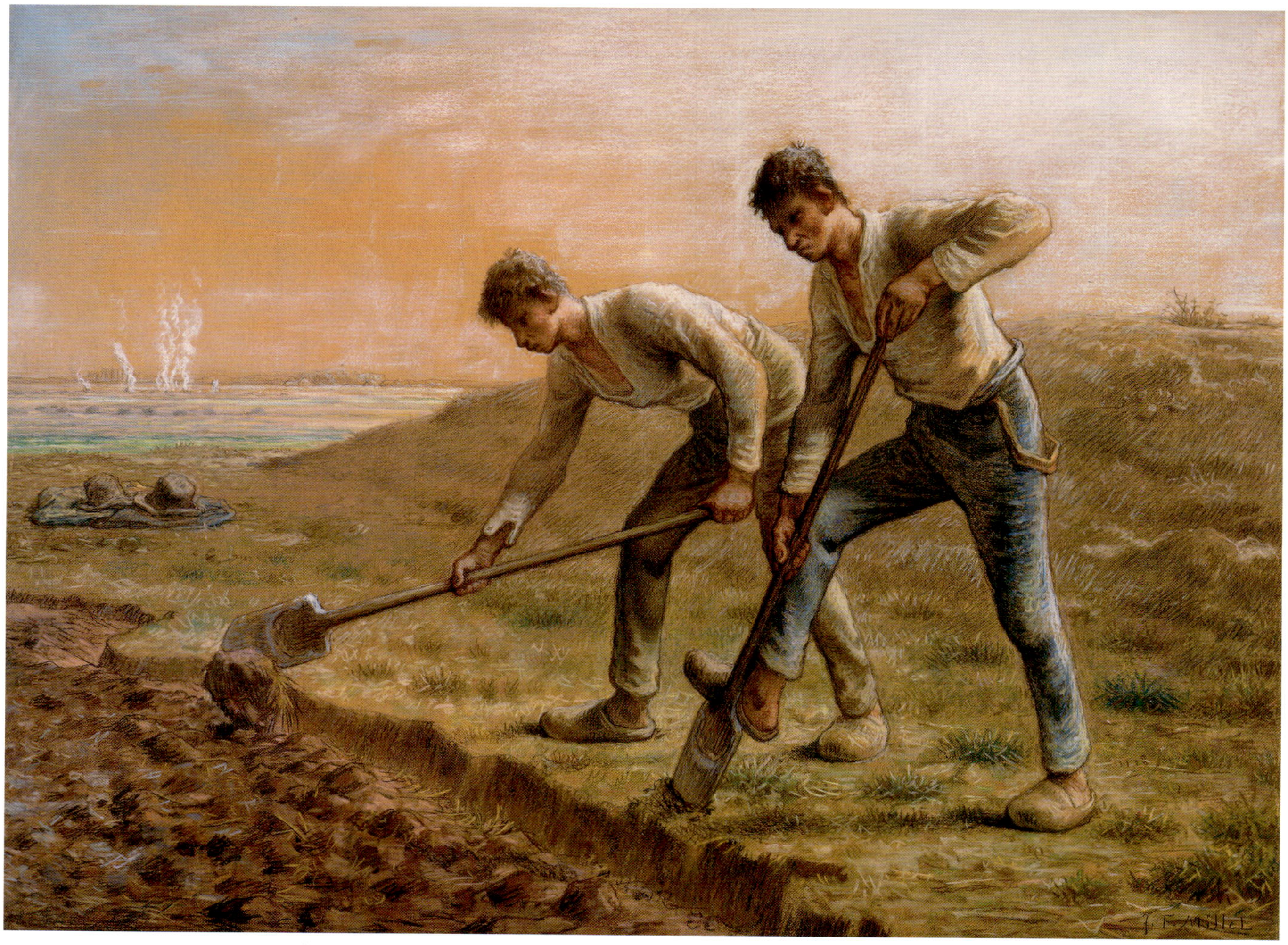

82

Jean-François Millet

Two Men Turning over the Soil, 1866, pastel and black conté crayon on paper, 69.9 × 94 (27 ½ × 37). Museum of Fine Arts, Boston: Gift of Quincy Adams Shaw through Quincy Adams Shaw Jr. and Mrs. Marian Shaw Haughton

83

Jean-François Millet

The Potato Harvest, 1854–1857, oil on canvas, 54 × 65.1 (21 ¼ × 25 ⅝). The Walters Art Museum, Baltimore

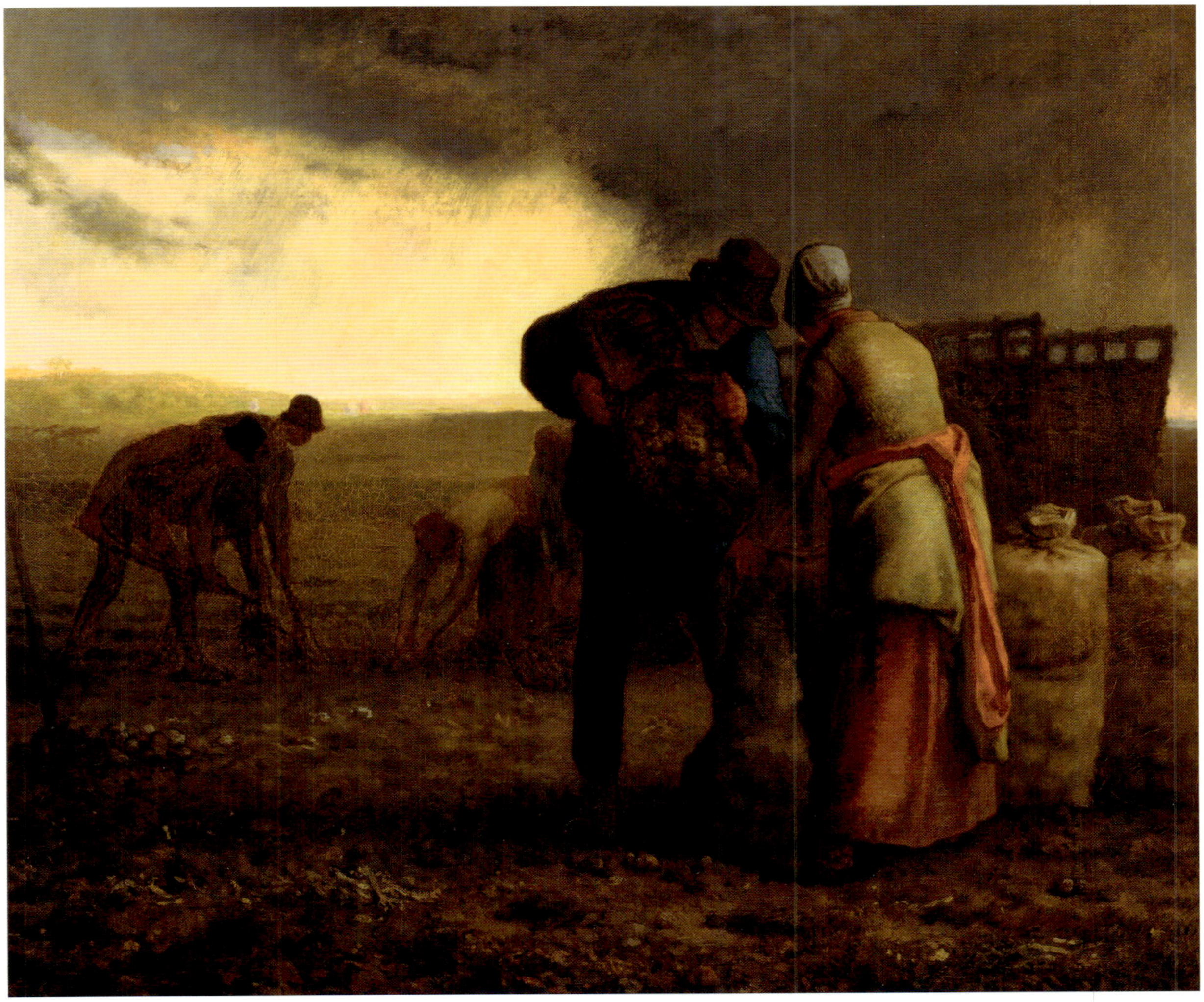

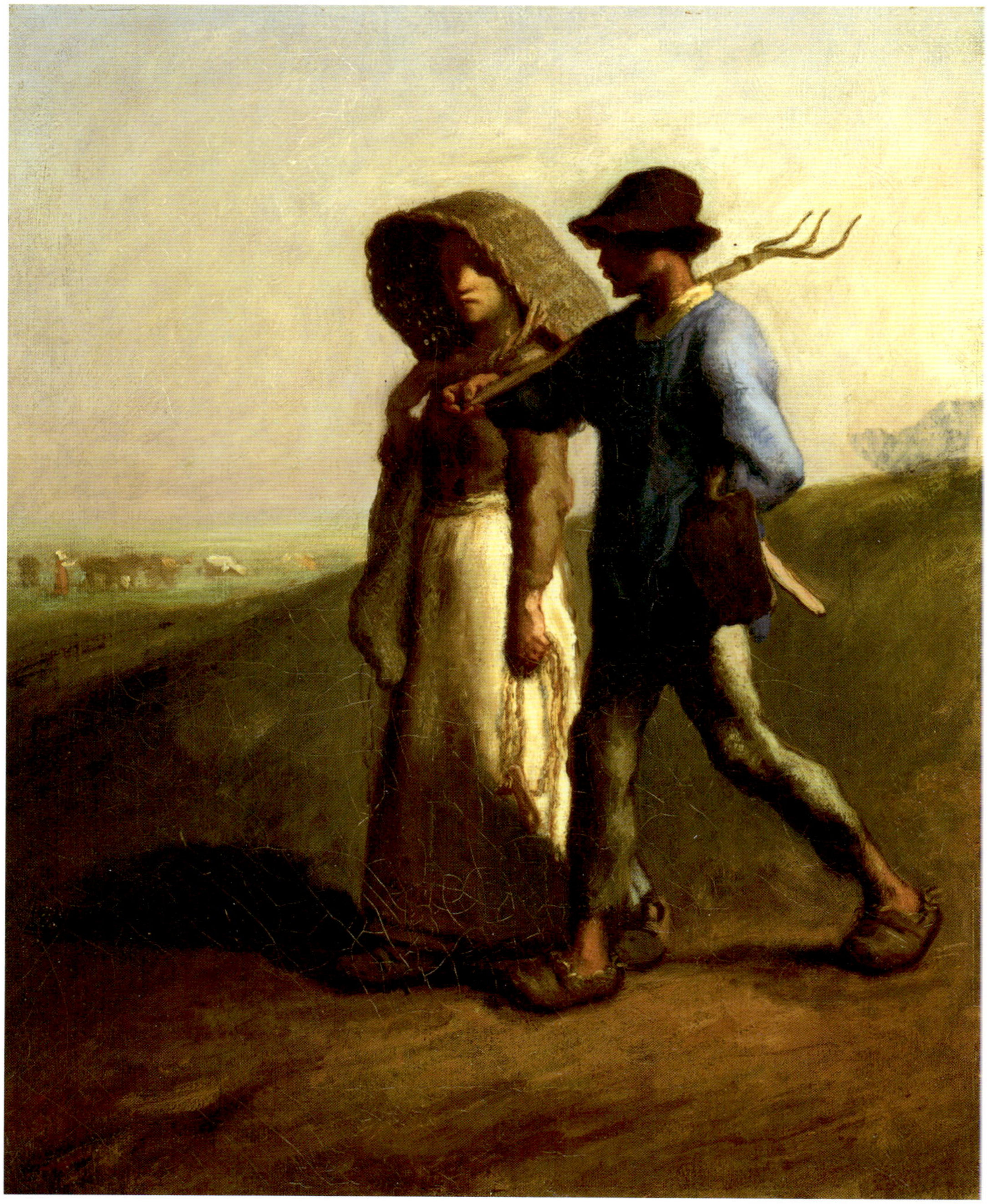

84

Jean-François Millet

Going to Work, 1851–1853, oil on canvas, 55.9 × 45.7 (22 × 18). Cincinnati Art Museum, Bequest of Mary M. Emery

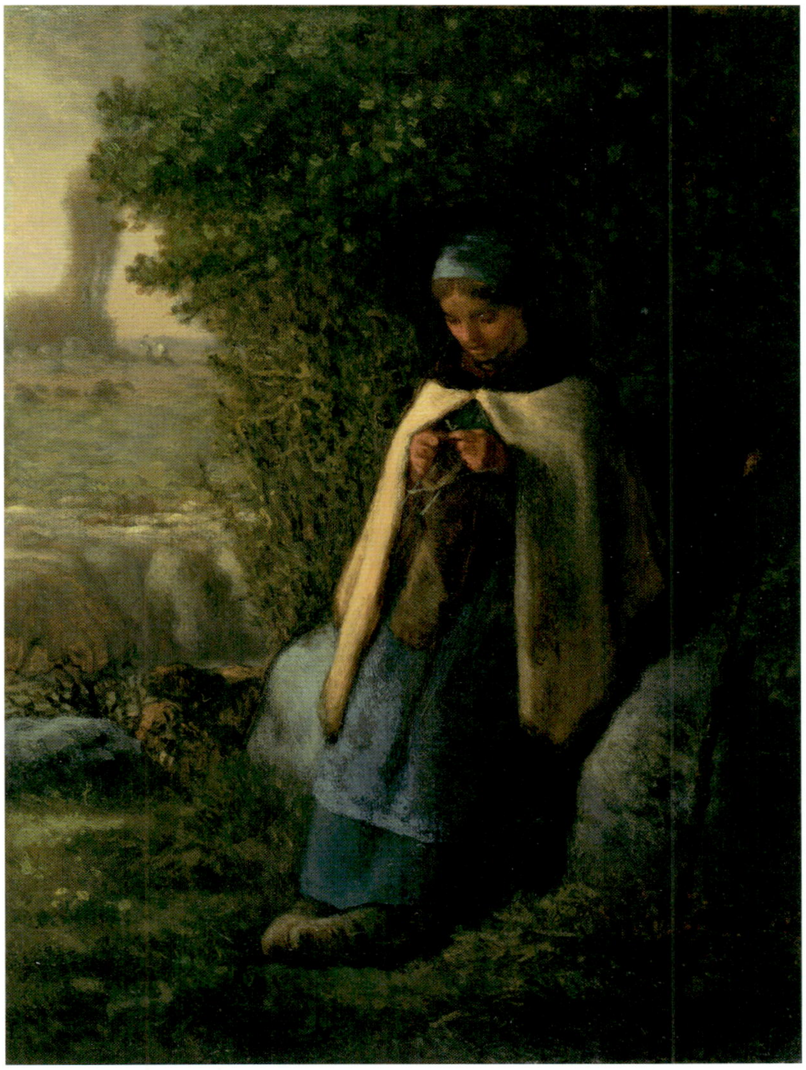

85

Jean-François Millet

Shepherdess Seated on a Rock (The Knitter), 1856, oil on canvas, 35.5 × 28 (14 × 11). Cincinnati Art Museum, Gift of Emilie L. Heine in memory of Mr. & Mrs. John Hauck

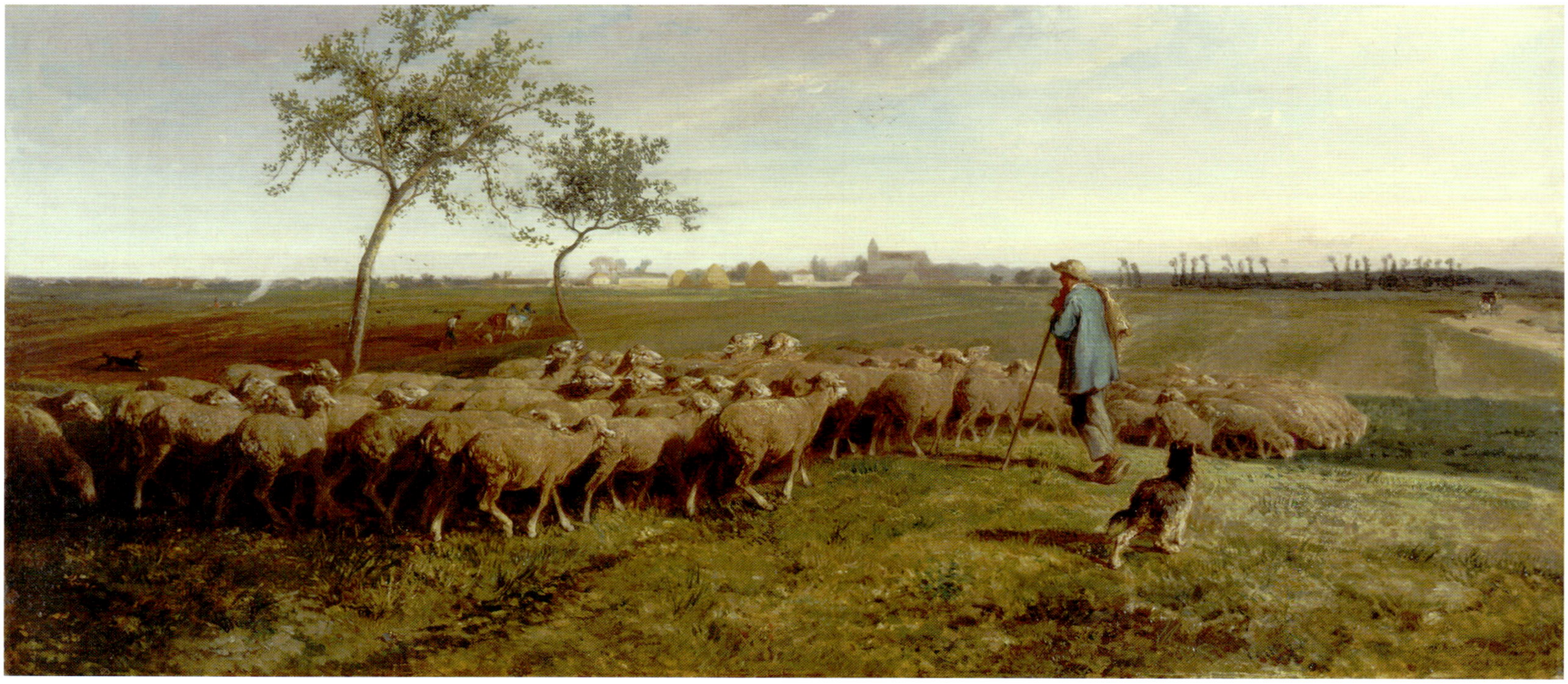

86

Charles-Emile Jacque

Flock of Sheep at the Edge of the Field, 1856, oil on canvas, 49.5 × 118 (19 ½ × 46 7/16). Museum der Bildenden Künste, Leipzig

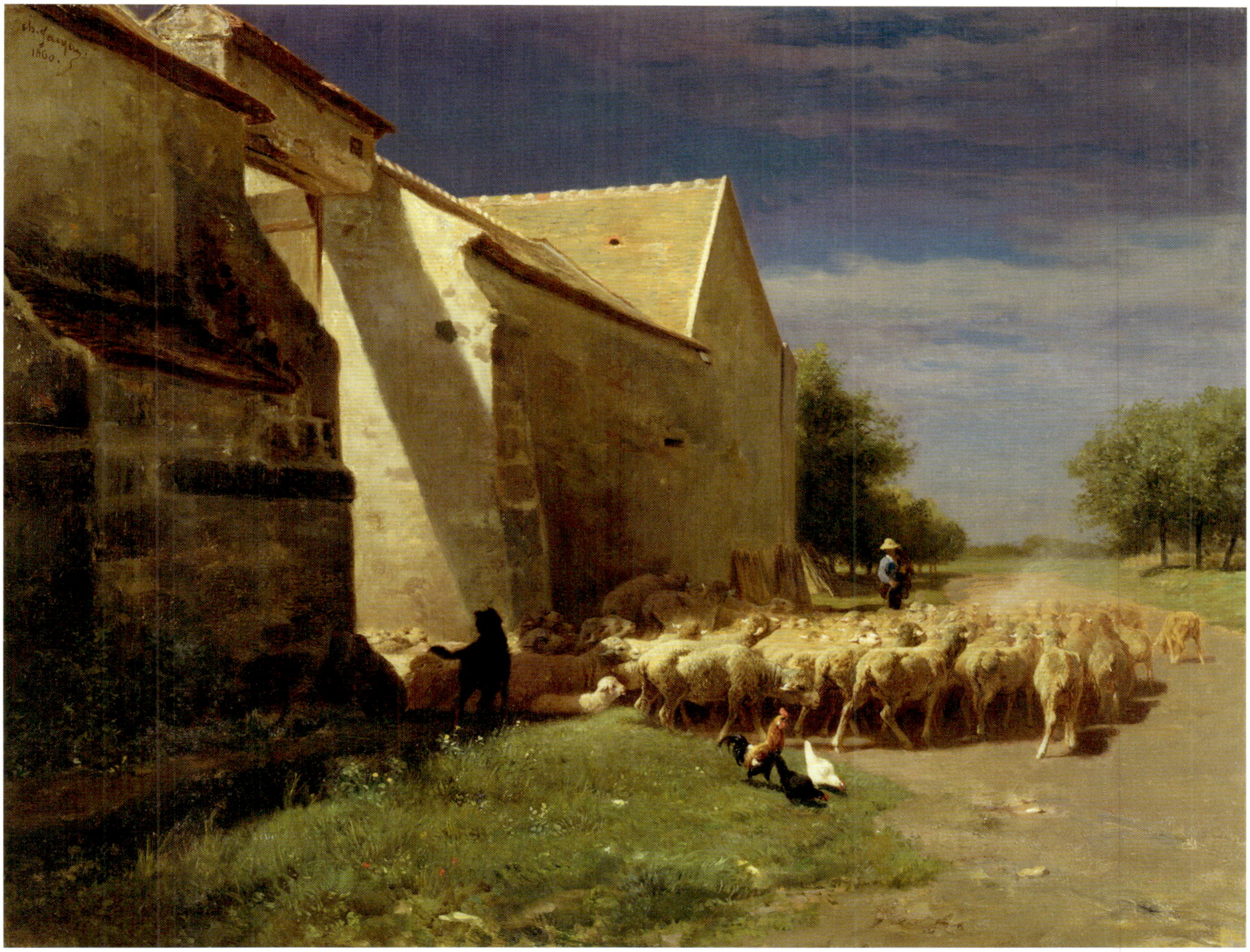

87

Charles-Emile Jacque

The Departure of the Flock,
1860, oil on canvas,
54.3 × 71.9 (21 3/8 × 28 5/16).
Philadelphia Museum
of Art, John G. Johnson
Collection, 1917

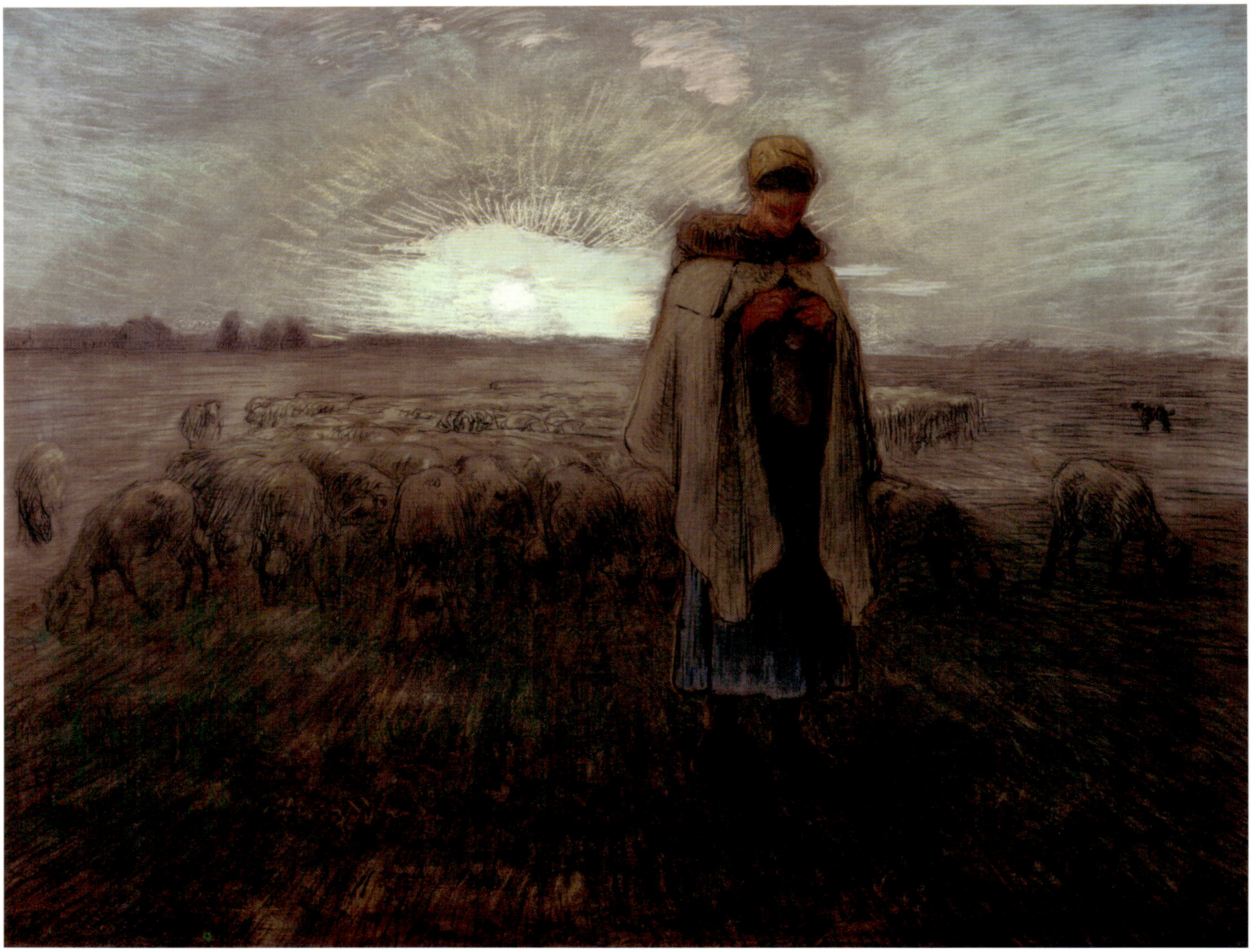

88

Jean-François Millet

The Shepherdess, 1870–1874, pastel and black conté crayon on gray paper, 68.8 × 93.3 (27 1/16 × 36 3/4). The Baltimore Museum of Art, The Helen and Abram Eisenberg Collection

89

Jean-François Millet

The Sheepfold, Moonlight, 1856–1860, oil on panel, 45.4 × 63.2 (17 ⅞ × 24 ⅞). The Walters Art Museum, Baltimore

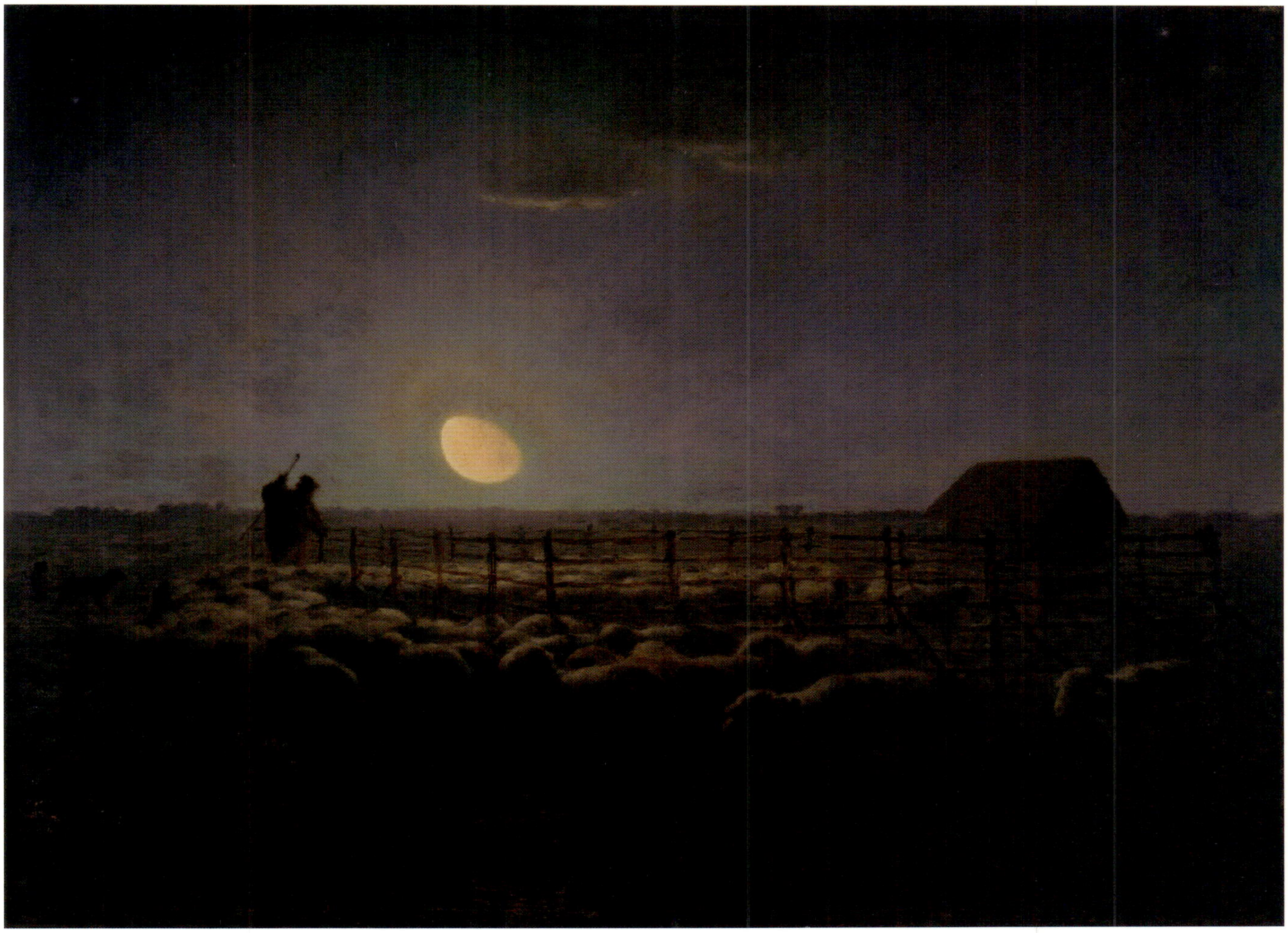

Nature and Observation

"The physiognomy of nature is even more ceaselessly variable than the physiognomy of man," wrote Thoré in 1844; nowhere was that philosophy more thoroughly tested than in the Forest of Fontainebleau.[1] Part of Fontainebleau's allure as a center for open-air painting is the diversity of its seasons, which are distinct and visually striking. Spring and summer have their charms, of course, but it was autumn that captured the artist's imagination. "Autumn is, perhaps, the most beautiful season in Fontainebleau, and certainly the most analogous to this place," a writer observed in 1812.[2] Rousseau and Diaz in particular were fascinated by the coloristic effects of autumnal foliage contrasted against overcast skies (see pls. 94 and 98). And the mournful inevitability of lush summer greenery as it fades with the onset of winter also made it a favorite subject of visiting artists.

By contrast, winter was the exclusive province of artists who resided in the environs of Fontainebleau on a more or less permanent basis. Within the microclimate of the forest, winters were often rigorous, deterring the casual visitor. An especially harsh winter in 1819–1820 killed some one million plants and trees in the forest, while the extreme cold and freezing rains of 1879–1880 proved equally destructive. Even in more temperate years, frosts would occur an average of 108 days out of the year, nearly double that found in the surrounding regions.[3] Rather than detracting from the forest's appeal, the harshness of the season only heightened it. Stripped of its foliage and the vibrant hues of summer and autumn, the forest presented a stark, monochromatic landscape that fascinated artists. Millet was especially enchanted by winter in the Forest of Fontainebleau. Shortly after his arrival in Barbizon, he informed Sensier that the desire to paint a winter landscape had become "an obsession," later writing that he had painted three sketches of snow, including one of Porte aux Vaches, one of his favorite motifs (pl. 92).[4]

Millet's correspondence made frequent reference to the meteorological conditions he observed during his treks through the forest. "We have fog effects perfectly superb, and the most fairy-like frost, beyond any imagination," he wrote in 1865, "The forest was wonderfully beautiful."[5] Millet was not alone in his interest. Contemporaries often remarked upon the mutability of the Forest of Fontainebleau and the quicksilver moods of its seasons. As Jules Michelet observed, "It [the forest] has the tendency to change within a single day. . . . You believe the heavy mass of its sandstone to be invariable, yet it changes aspect, color, even form, I dare say, hourly."[6] Thoré expressed this even more eloquently, admiring the harmony of "the charming veil of morning mist, with the magnificence of midday, with the vagaries of sunset, with the phantoms of night."[7]

It was this ever-changing atmosphere that artists strove to capture in the forest above all else. Sensier remarked that Rousseau "lived like an artist-Trappist monk," devoting himself to the study of his chosen motifs with the most painstaking observation.[8] Diaz was similarly attentive. "He thinks only of light," one critic remarked, "It is that which he pursues, that which is the inexhaustible subject of his work."[9] For the group of artists later considered part of the Barbizon School, this pursuit of nature at its most ephemeral was both their primary goal and their constant motivation. Painters and photographers alike embraced this principle, but none more so than Cuvelier. He was perhaps the most faithful observer of the myriad moods of the forest, rendering the place in snow, frost, storm, and fog with astonishing and unprecedented sensitivity (see pls. 90, 91, 96, and 99).

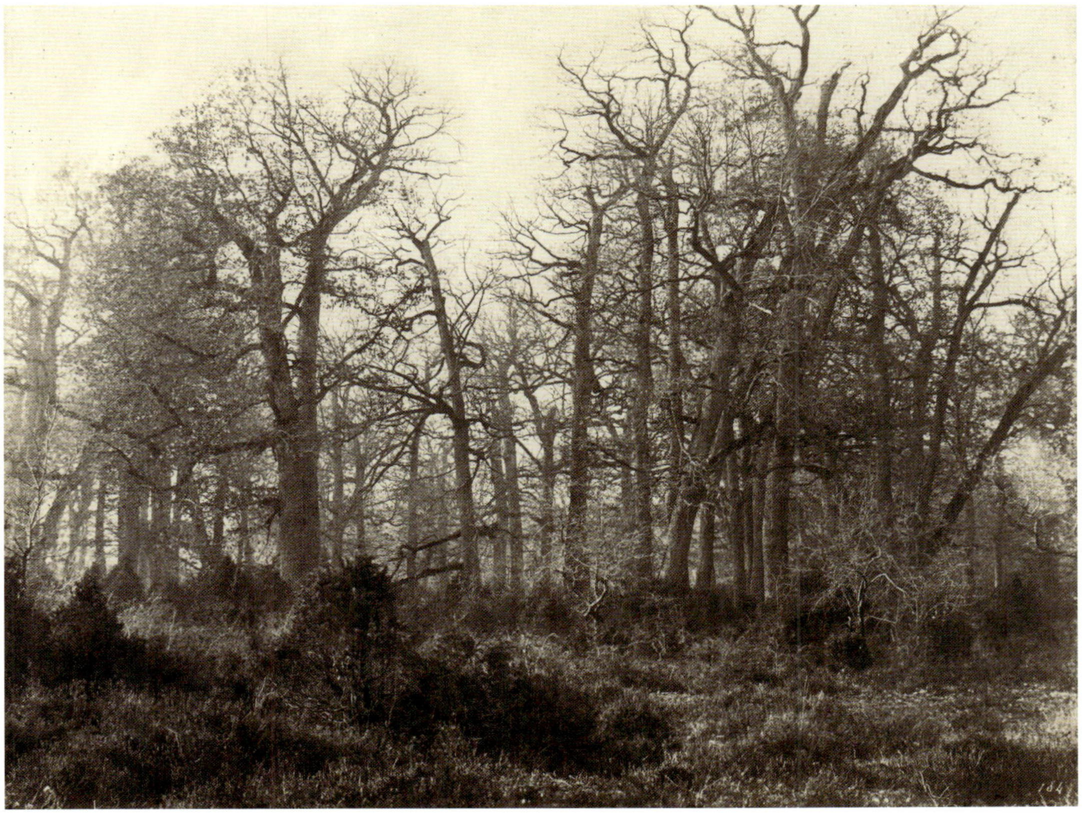

90

Eugène Cuvelier

Carrefour de l'Epine, early 1860s, salted paper print from paper negative, 19.3 × 25.7 (7 5/8 × 10 1/8). National Gallery of Art, Washington, Patrons' Permanent Fund, 1995

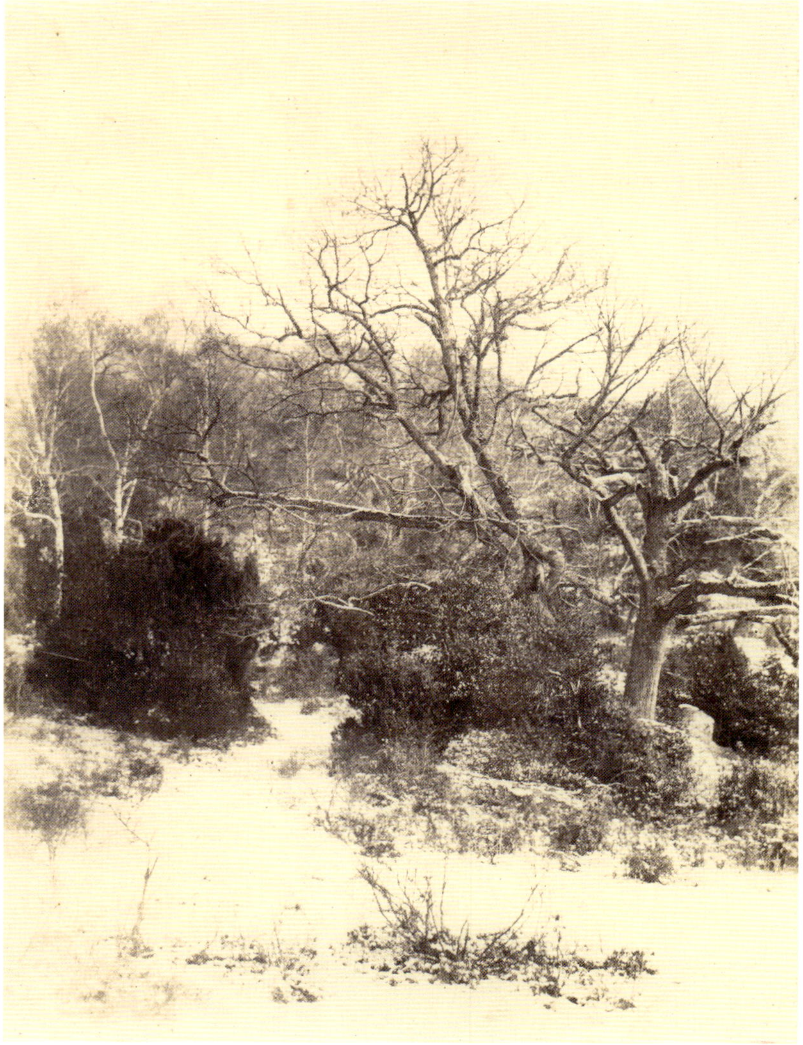

91

Eugène Cuvelier

Pathway in the Forest of Fontainebleau in the Snow, early 1860s, salted paper print from paper negative, 25.9 × 19.8 (10 3/16 × 7 13/16). Rolf Mayer Collection

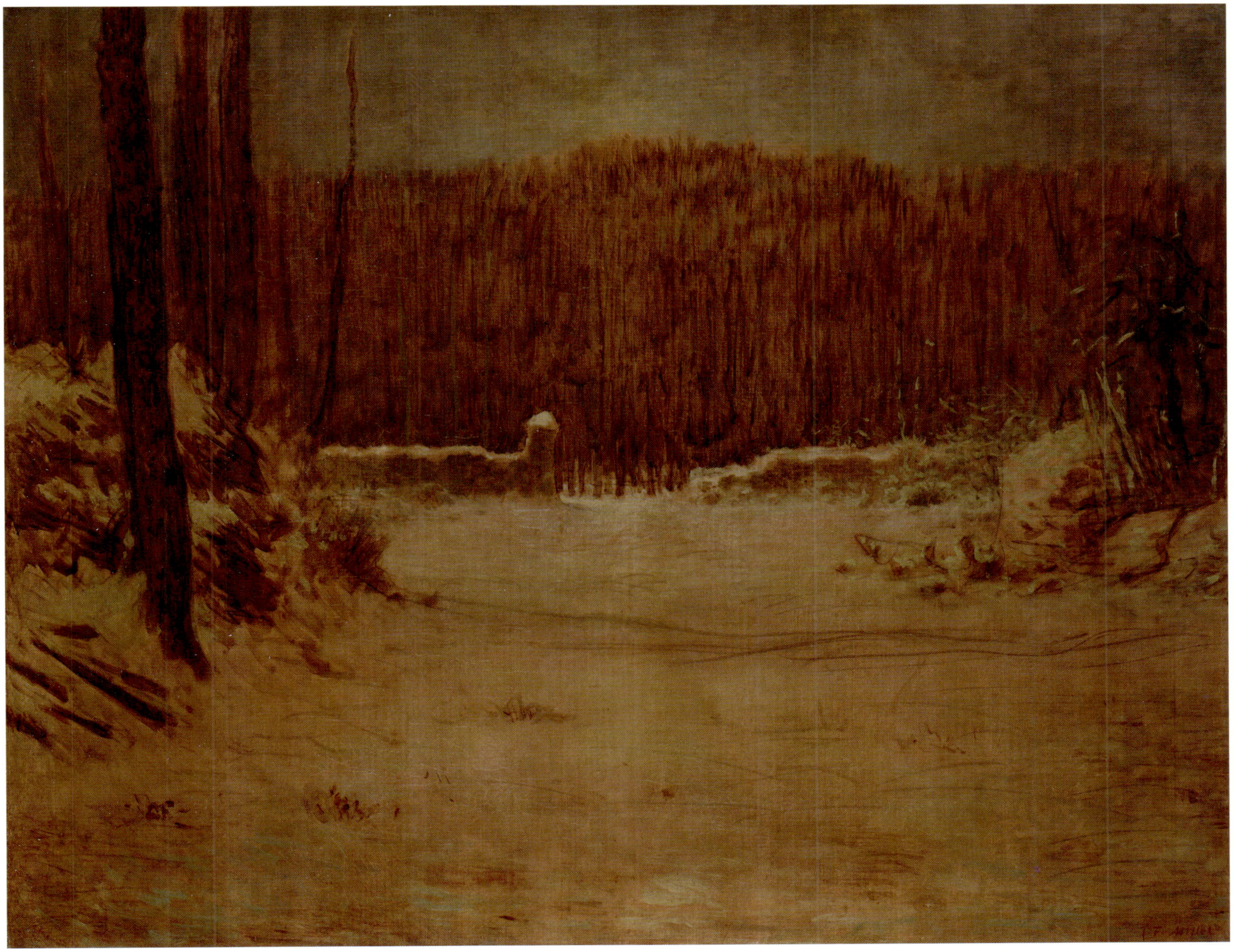

92

Jean-François Millet

Solitude, 1853, oil on canvas, 85.4 × 110.5 (33 ⅝ × 43 ½). Philadelphia Museum of Art, Purchased with the W. P. Wilstach Fund, 1906

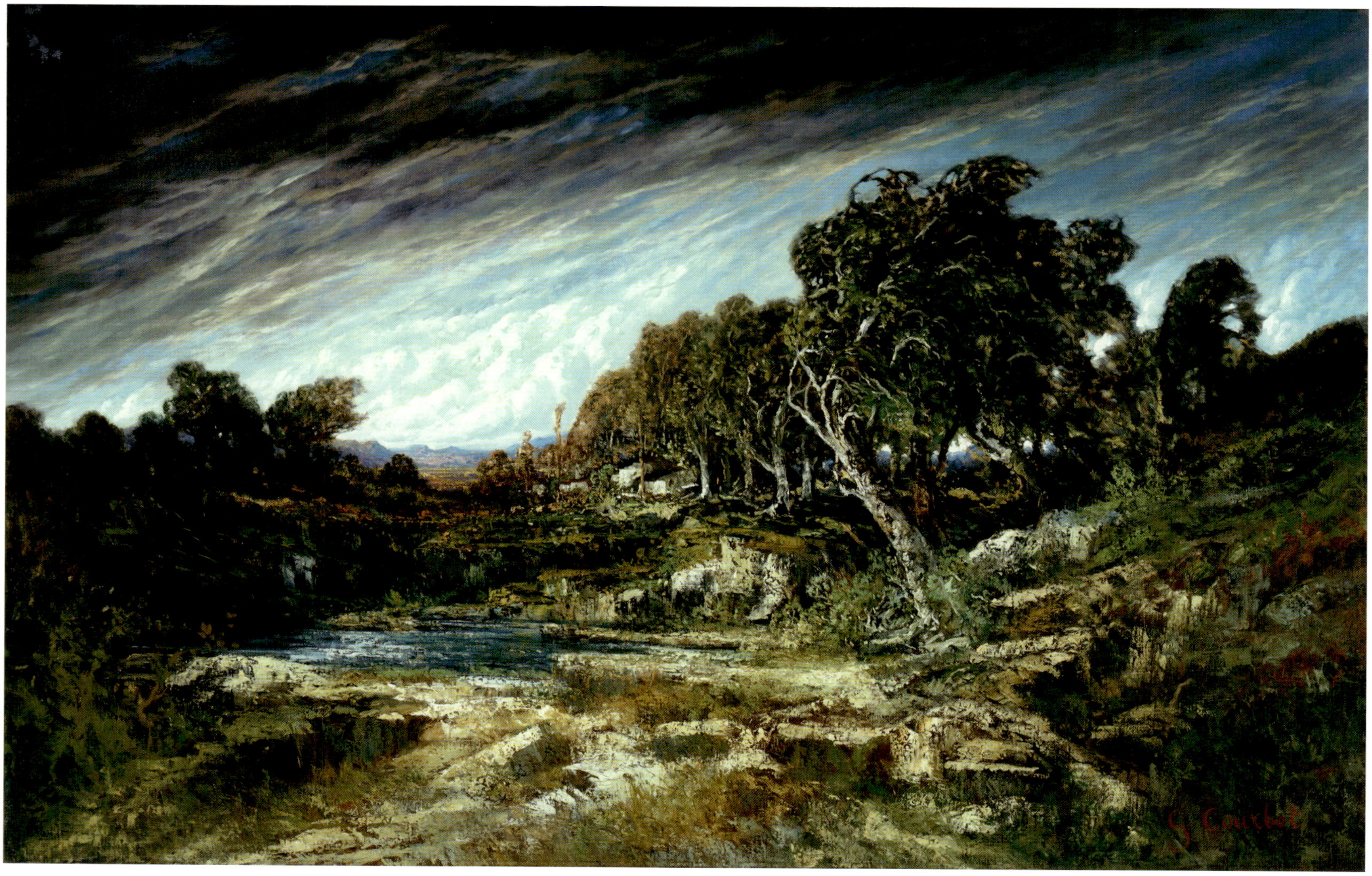

93

Gustave Courbet

The Gust of Wind,
c. 1865, oil on canvas,
143.5 × 228.5 (56 ½ × 89 15/16).
The Museum of Fine
Arts, Houston, Gift of
Caroline Wiess Law

94

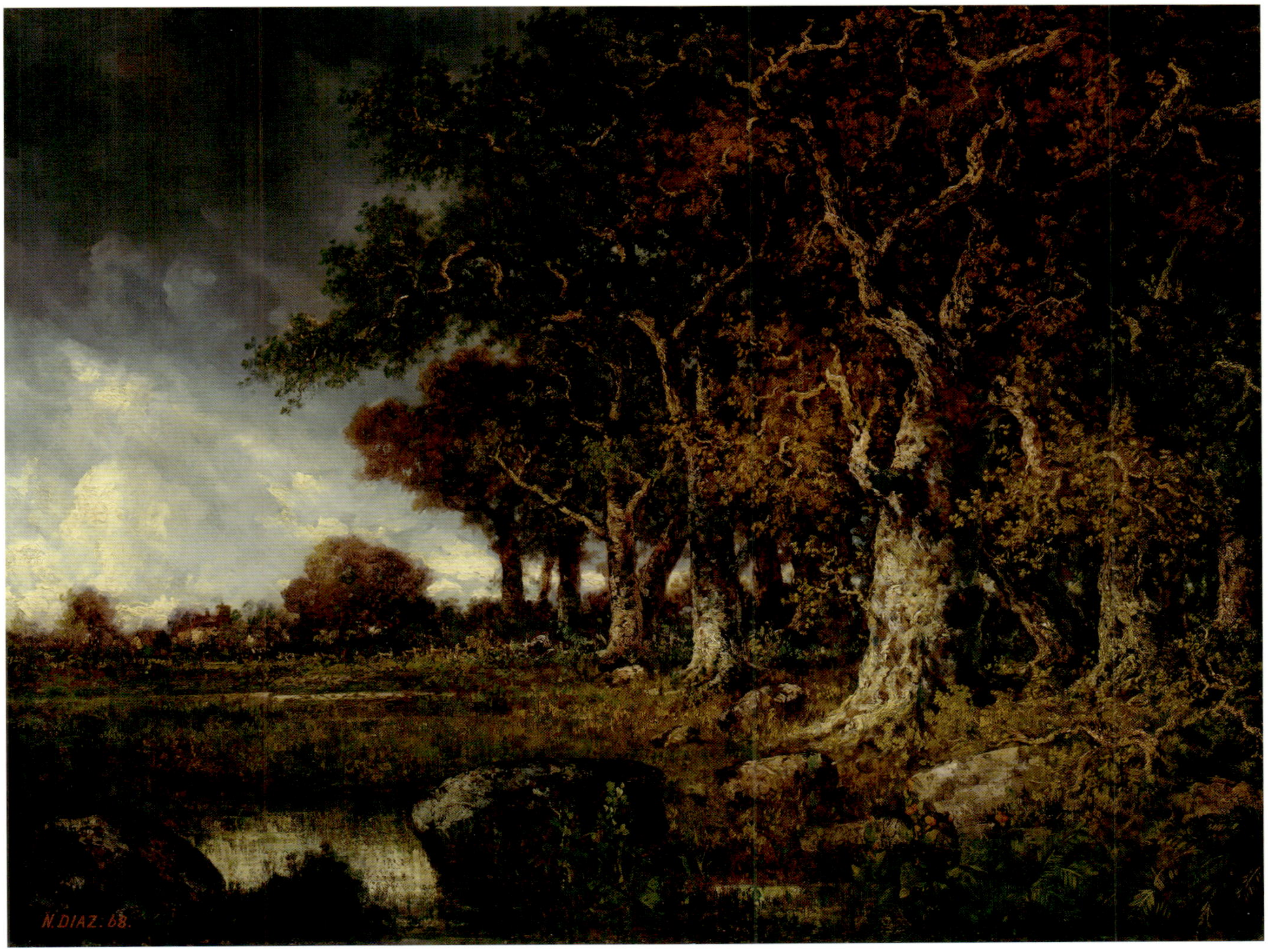

Narcisse-Virgile Diaz de la Peña

The Edge of the Forest at Les Monts-Girard, Fontainebleau, 1868, oil on canvas, 97.8 × 125.5 (38 ½ × 49 7/16). National Gallery of Art, Washington, Chester Dale Fund, 2000

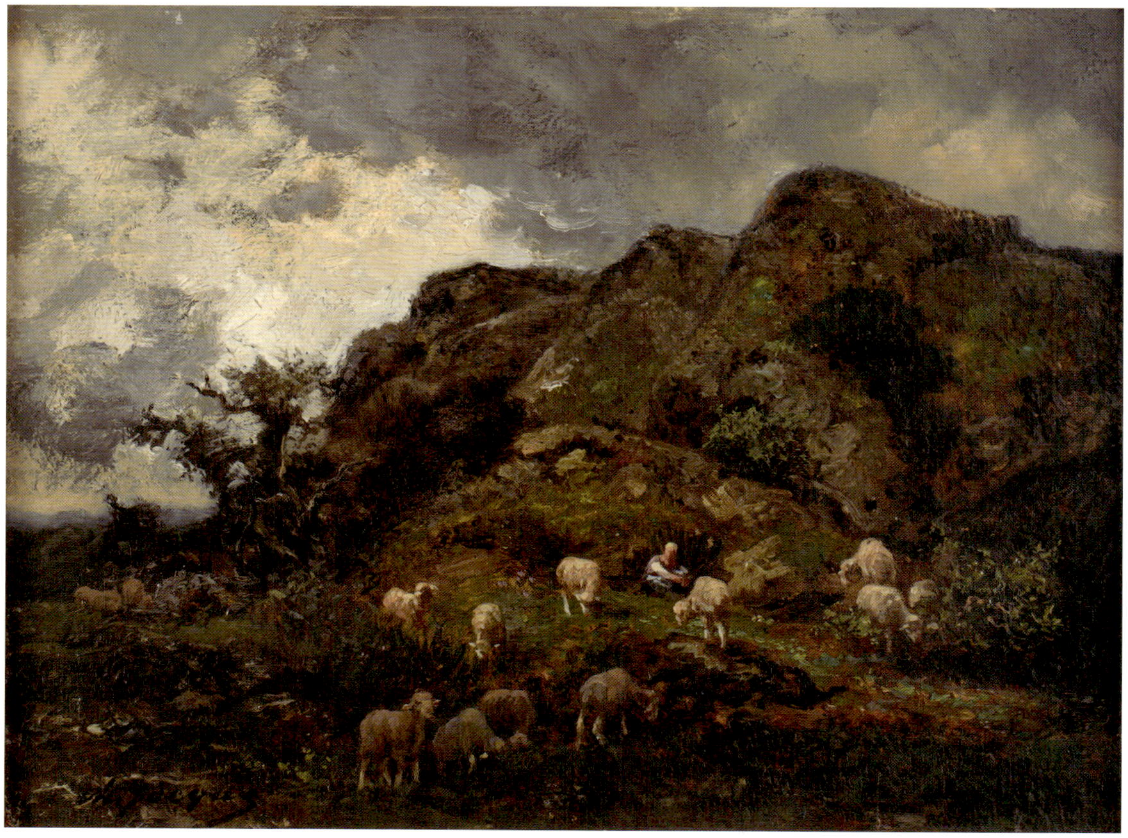

95

Charles-Emile Jacque

Shepherdess and Sheep,
c. 1870, oil on wood,
24 × 32.5 (9 7/16 × 12 13/16).
The City of Fontainebleau

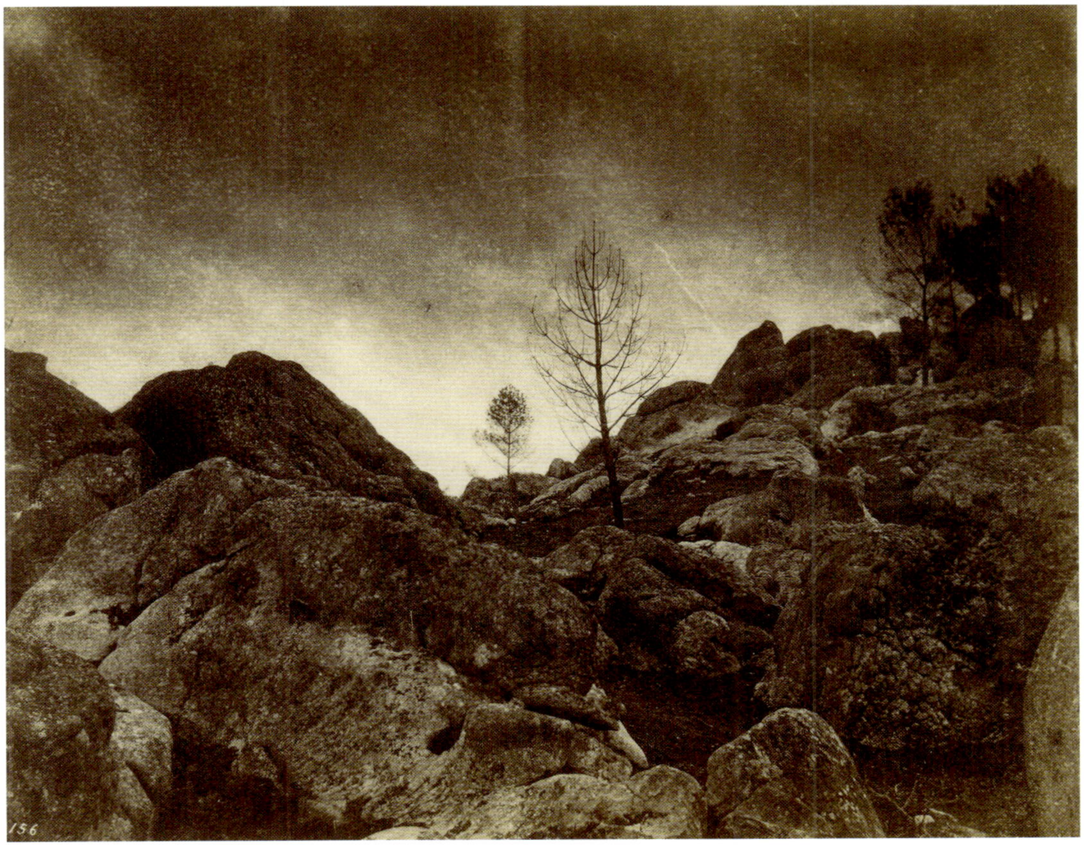

96

Eugène Cuvelier

Storm, Fontainebleau, 1860, albumen print from paper negative, 20 × 25.2 (7 ⅞ × 9 15/16). Musée d'Orsay, Paris; Gift of Jacques Foucart, 1980

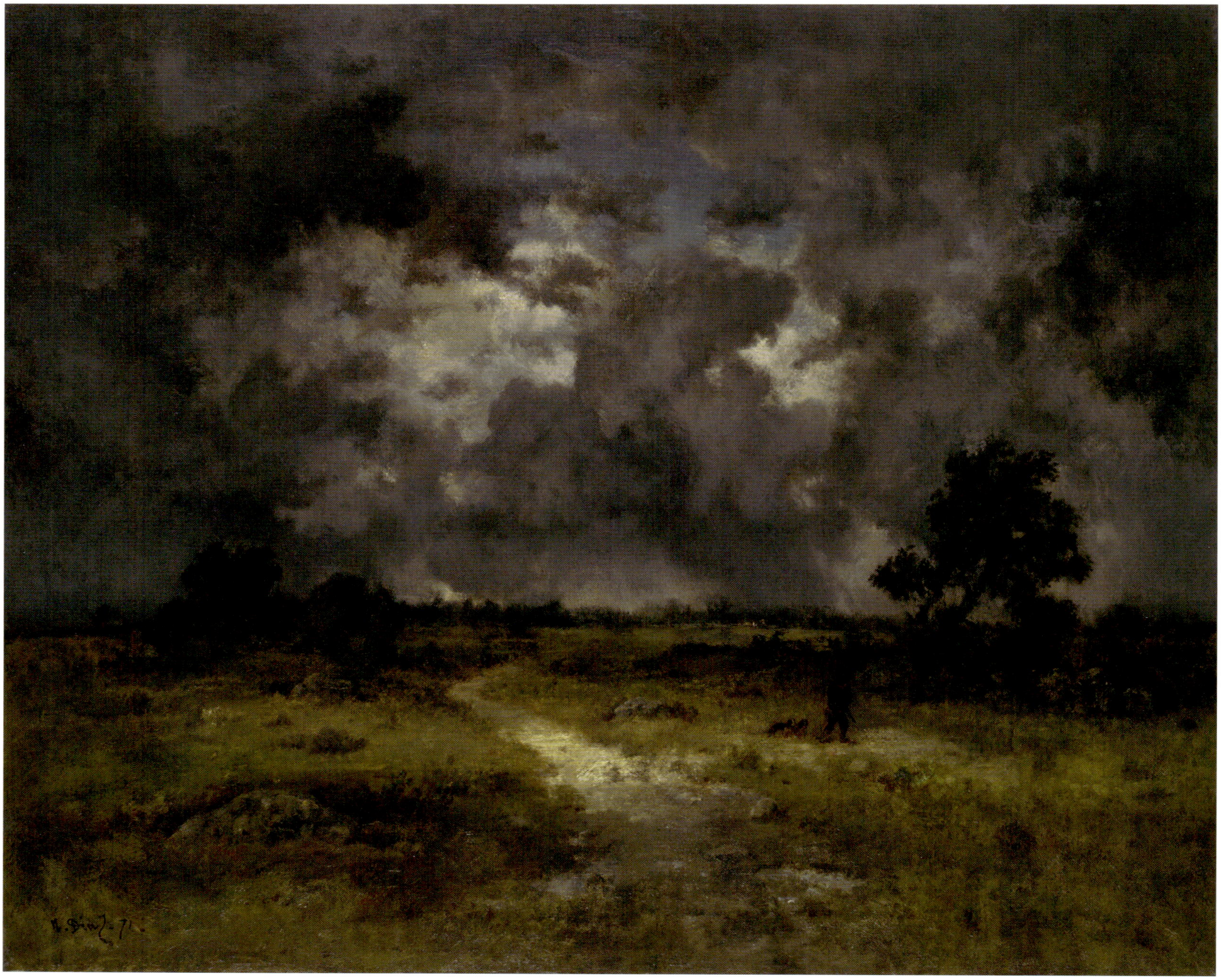

97

Narcisse-Virgile Diaz de la Peña

The Storm, 1871, oil on mahogany, 62.2 × 76.5 (24 ½ × 30 ⅛). The National Gallery, London, Salting Bequest, 1910

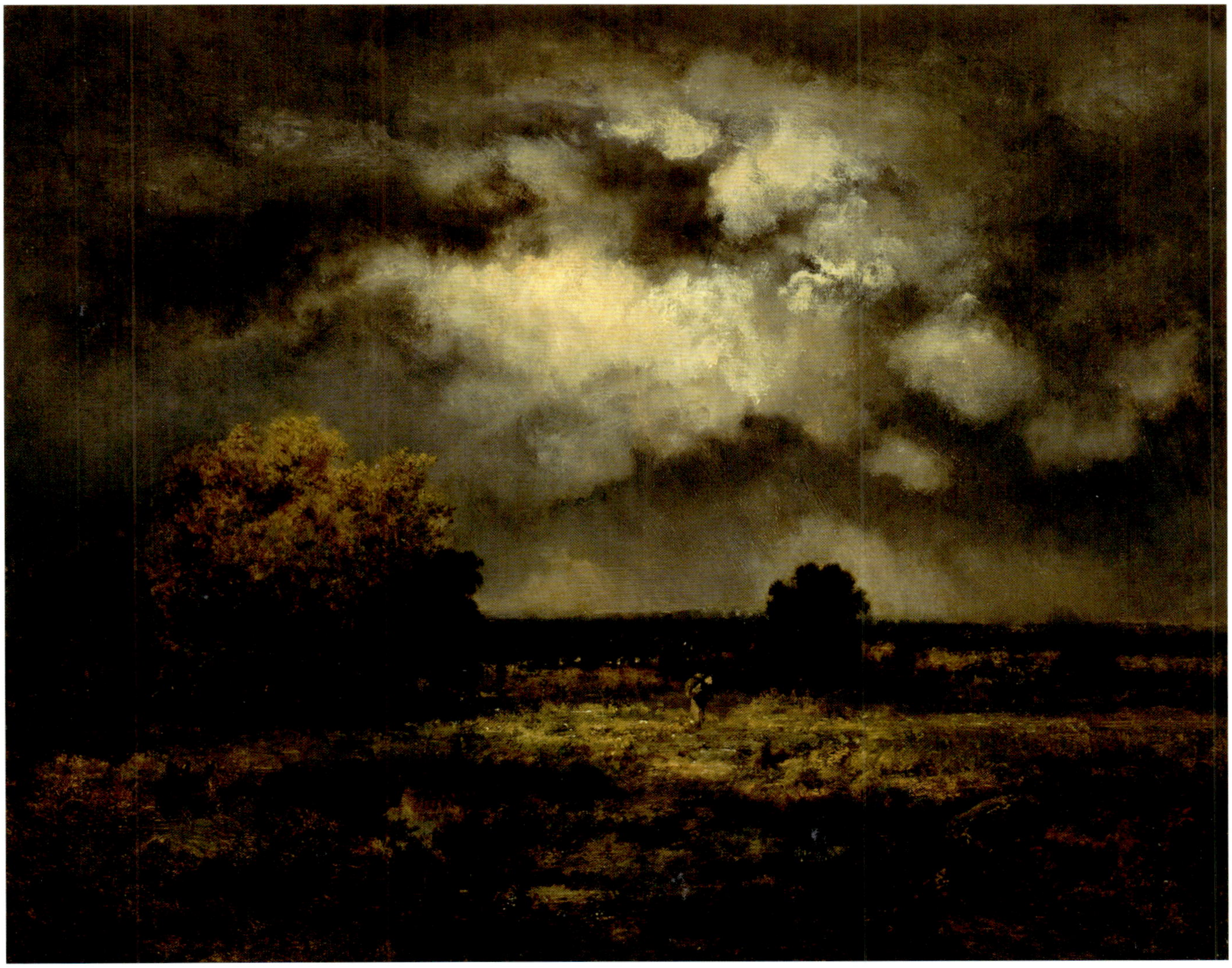

98

Narcisse-Virgile Diaz de la Peña

Stormy Landscape, 1872, oil on panel, 47.6 × 60 (18 ¾ × 23 ⅝). Los Angeles County Museum of Art, Gift of Mrs. Rowena Thom Rathbone, in memory of Mr. and Mrs. Erskine Pembroke Thom

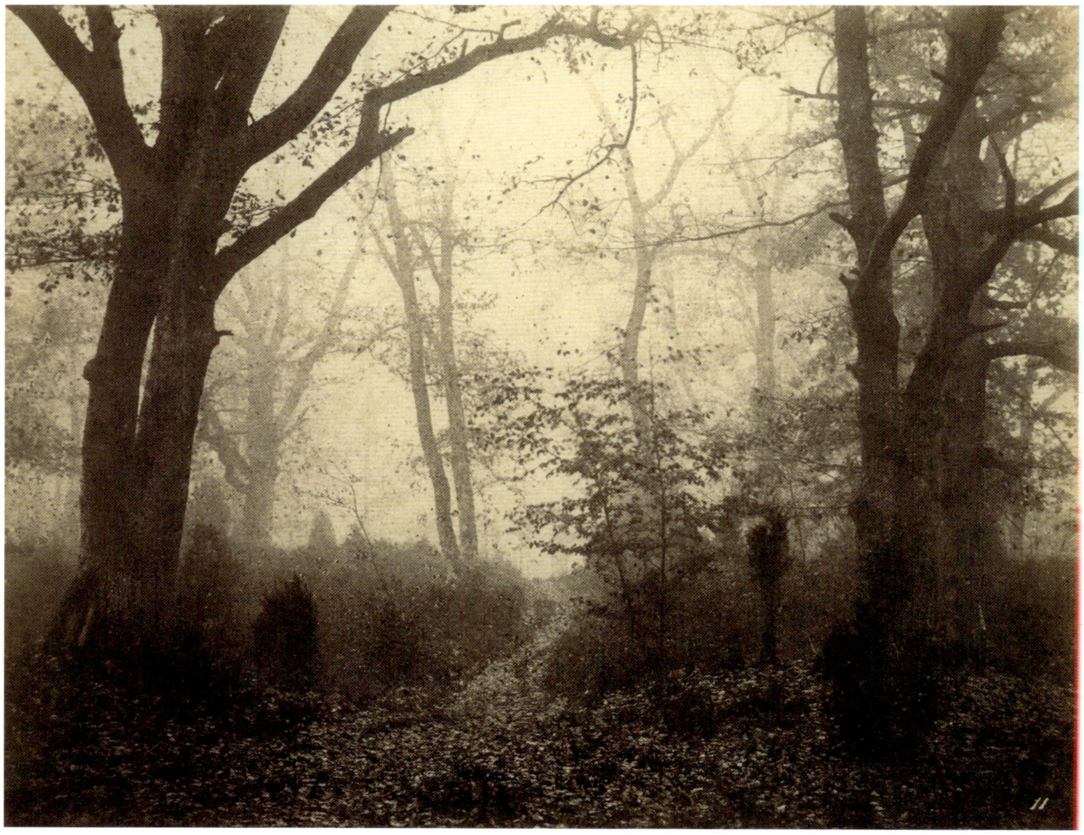

99

Eugène Cuvelier

The Forest of Fontainebleau, early 1860s, salted paper print from paper negative, 19.8 × 25.9 (7 13/16 × 10 3/16). Lent by The Metropolitan Museum of Art, Purchase, The Howard Gilman Foundation and Joyce and Robert Menschel Gifts, 1988

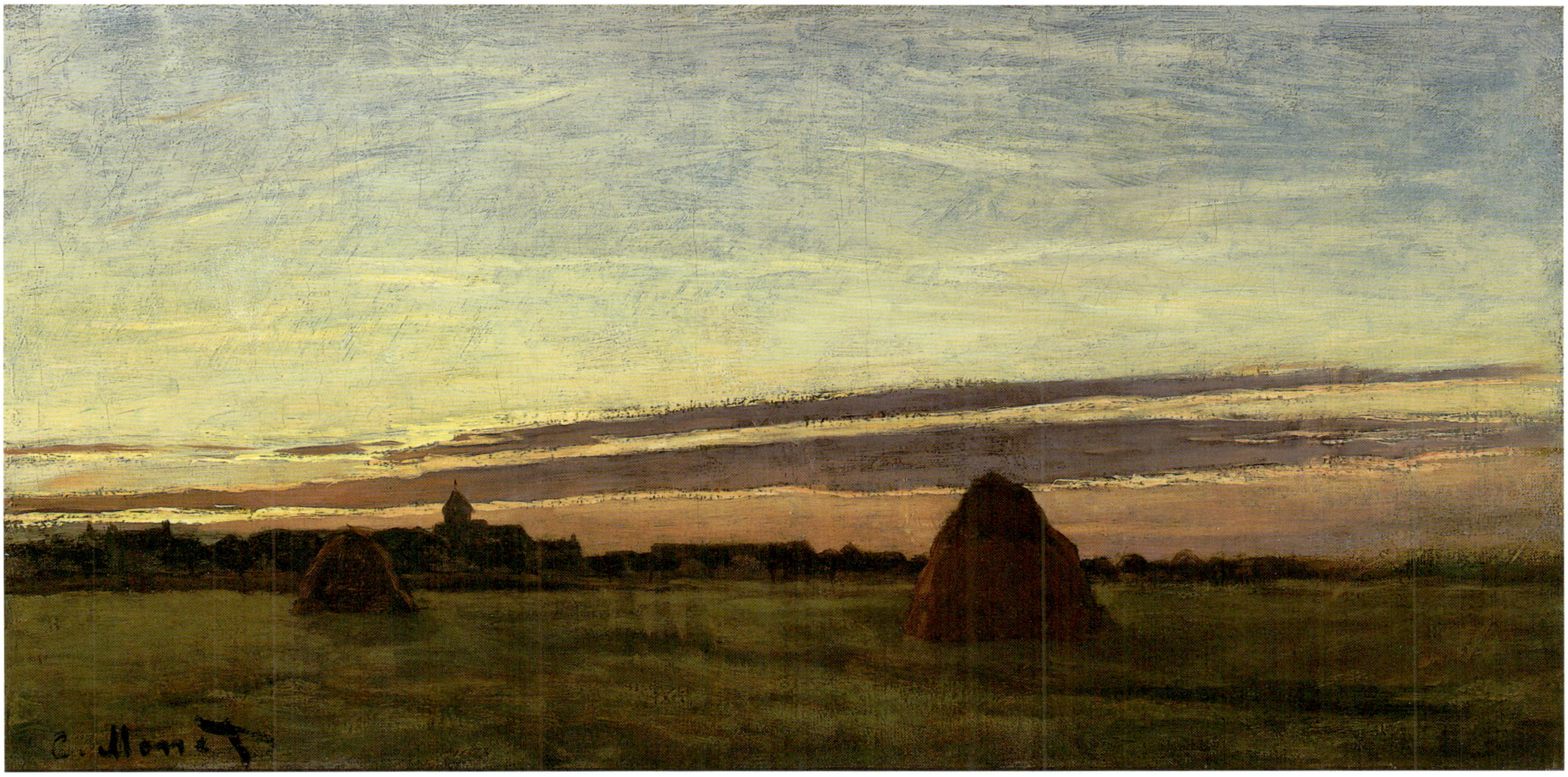

100

Claude Monet

Haystacks near Chailly, 1865, oil on canvas, 30 × 60 (11 13/16 × 23 5/8). San Diego Museum of Art, Museum purchase

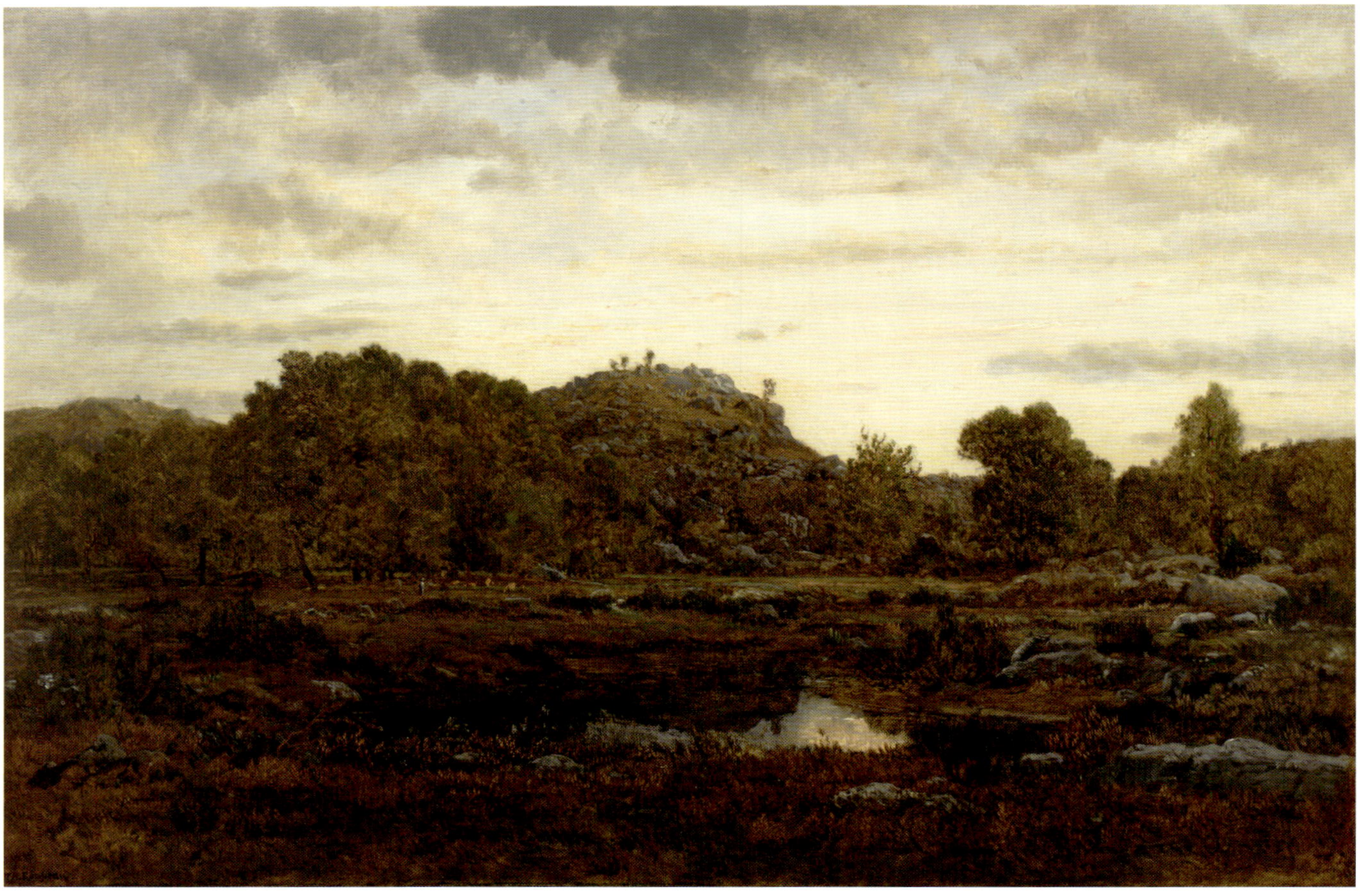

101

Théodore Rousseau

Gorges d'Apremont (Forest of Fontainebleau), 1857, oil on canvas, 64.8 × 100.3 (25 ½ × 39 ½). Middlebury College Museum of Art, Vermont; Gift of Mrs. Louis Alexander Turner, Princeton, New Jersey, in memory of her father, Frank Jewett Mather Jr.

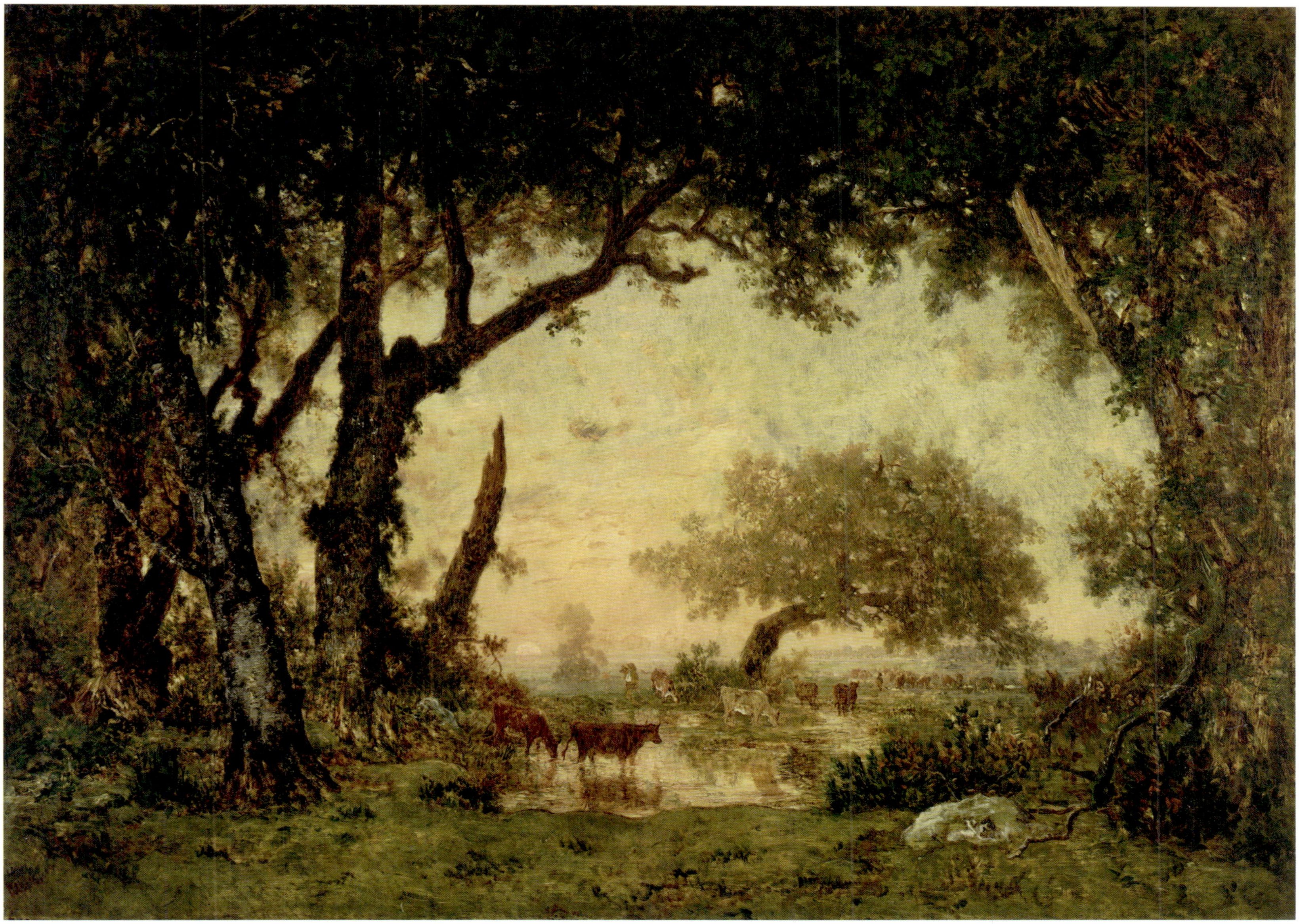

102

Théodore Rousseau

Edge of the Forest of Fontainebleau, Sunset, 1848–1850, oil on canvas, 142 × 198 (55 7/8 × 77 15/16). Musée du Louvre, Paris

NOT IN EXHIBITION

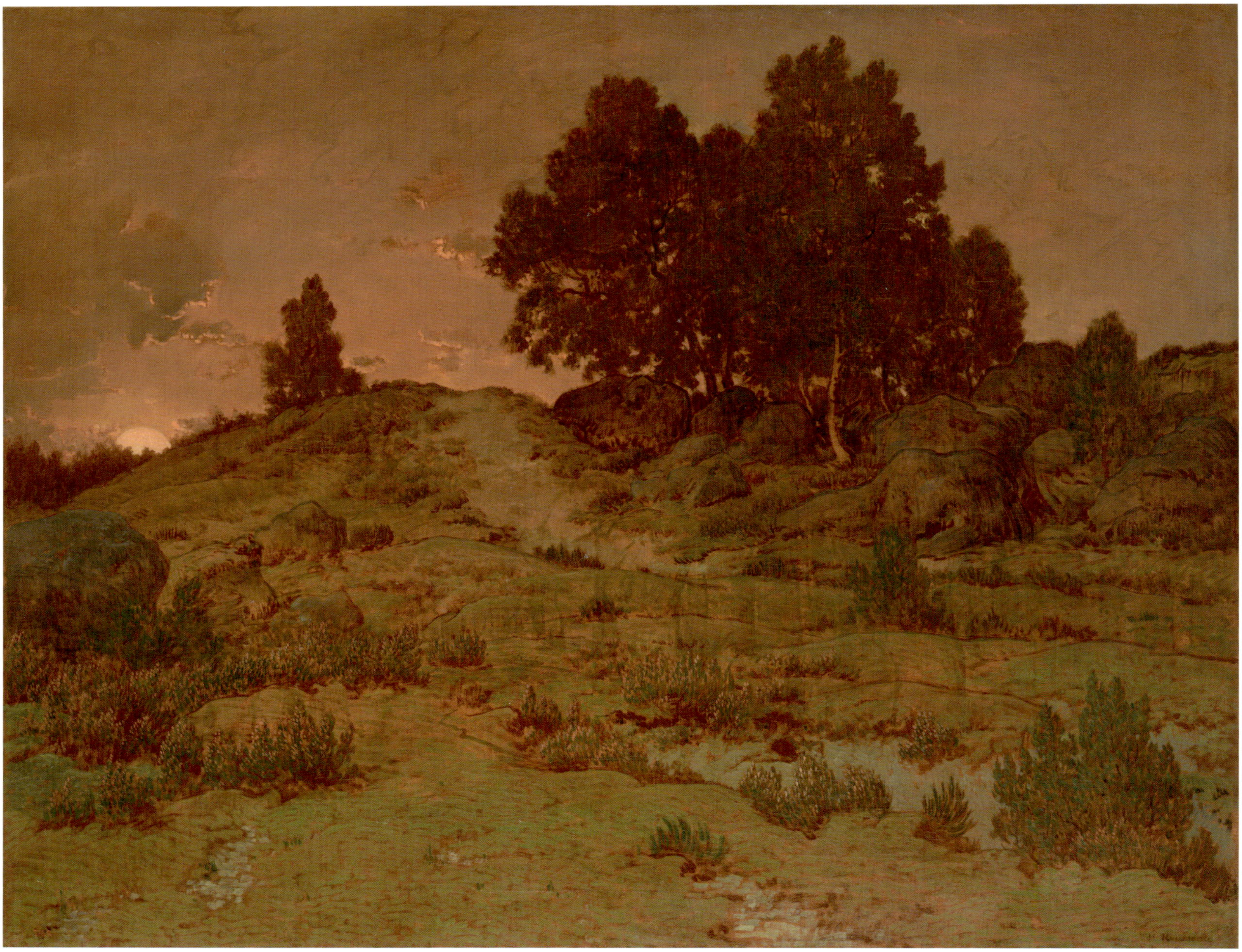

103

Théodore Rousseau

Sunset over the Sands of Jean de Paris, 1864, oil on canvas, 90.2 × 117.5 (35 ½ × 46 ¼). Wadsworth Atheneum Museum of Art, Hartford, Gift in honor of Helene and Mark Eisner, by exchange

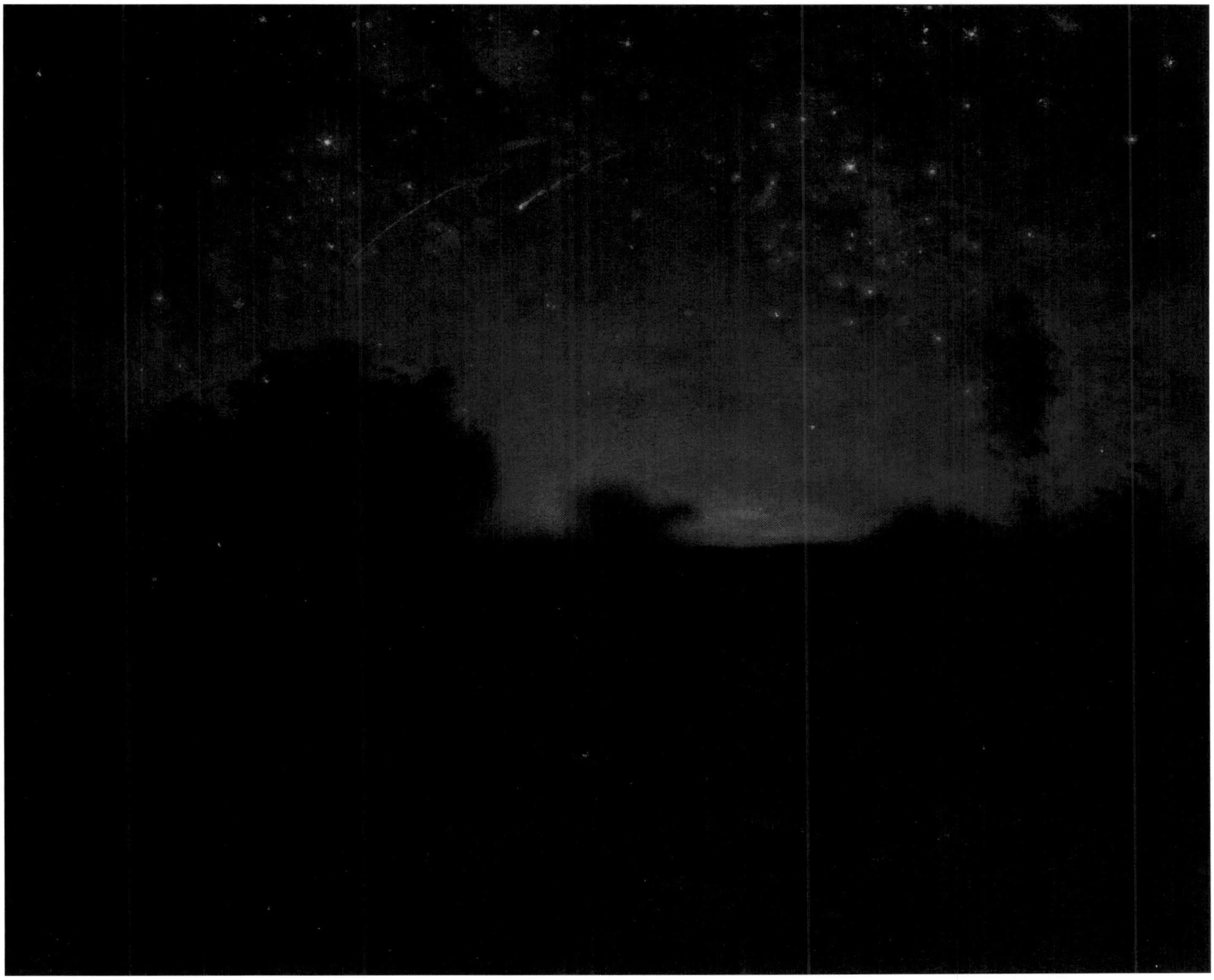

104

Jean-François Millet

Starry Night, c. 1855–1867, oil on canvas mounted on board, 65.4 × 81.3 (25 ¾ × 32). Yale University Art Gallery, New Haven, Leonard C. Hanna Jr., B.A. 1913, Fund

SIMON KELLY

The Mystery of the Forest *Paintings of Fontainebleau at the Salon*

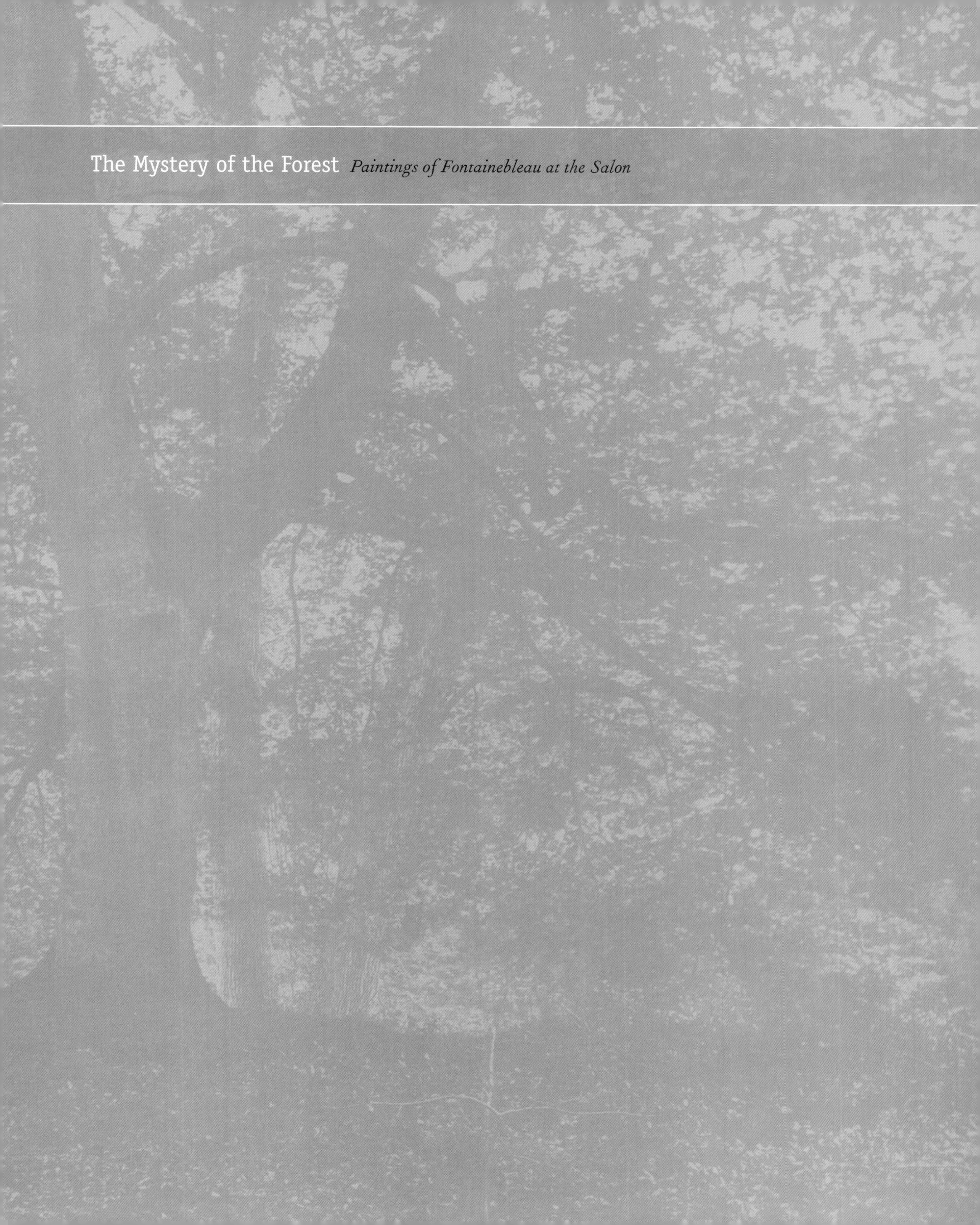

The Mystery of the Forest

Paintings of Fontainebleau at the Salon

Right Detail of pl. 30

In 1876, the artist and critic Frédéric Henriet affirmed, "The Forest of Fontainebleau is the true school of modern landscape."[1] His comment reflects the remarkable importance of the forest in the rise of nineteenth-century landscape painting. Over the course of the century, the greatest landscape painters of the age—including such diverse artists as Jean-Baptiste-Camille Corot, Théodore Rousseau, Jean-François Millet, and Claude Monet—intensively explored Fontainebleau, spending months and often years of study there and using motifs in the forest as a crucible for their avant-garde experiments. For these artists, views of the Forest of Fontainebleau were influential not only in their private studies but also in the ways in which they presented themselves publicly, particularly in their exhibition strategies. Their depictions appeared in dealer galleries, auction houses, and shows organized by artists' societies, but their work gained the greatest recognition from participation in the Paris Salon—the preeminent forum for the exhibition of paintings in nineteenth-century France.

Throughout the nineteenth century, landscape painting played an increasingly significant role in the history of Salon exhibitions, and by the 1860s, thirty percent of the works on display were landscapes.[2] Within this wider trend, scenes in the Forest of Fontainebleau were pivotal. Indeed, the number of Fontainebleau views on display increased steadily from nineteen in 1833, to forty-two in 1857, to seventy-seven in 1880.[3] A recent estimate suggests that around 1,800 paintings of the forest were exhibited at the Salon during the nineteenth century.[4] A review of titles in the Salon catalogues indicates that landscape artists explored the full geographical variety of the forest, including the Gorges d'Apremont, the old wood of the Bas-Bréau, the Plateau de Belle-Croix, and the villages of Barbizon and Marlotte.[5] At the same time, artists depicted the wide range of activities that took place in the forest, from the ancient practices of grazing cows and gathering fagots to the more recent practices of quarrying and commercial lumbering.

The July Monarchy

Views of the Forest of Fontainebleau first appeared at the Salon in 1781, but it was only during the early years of the July Monarchy (1830–1848) that the motif became increasingly popular.[6] In the early 1830s, the forest scenes by François-Edouard Bertin, Théodore Claude Félix Caruelle d'Aligny, and Jean-Baptiste-Camille Corot attracted the most interest. All three artists had traveled extensively in Italy, but they began to focus on the Forest of Fontainebleau, especially its rocks, to which they devoted as much attention as the hallowed sites of the Roman *campagna*. In 1831, Bertin exhibited a large-scale painting of a Fontainebleau quarry (Musée de Picardie, Amiens) to critical acclaim.[7] Two years later, Aligny also referenced quarrying in his *Sandstone Quarries of Mont Saint-Père* (Musée d'Art Roger-Quilliot, Clermont-Ferrand), which portrays a site four miles north of Fontainebleau. The composition is animated with resting workers who enjoy a meal of bread, pears, and wine, and it is distinguished by its sense of linearity and complex pattern-making. The critic Auguste Jal described it as "the imitation of nature by abstraction."[8]

For his part, Corot placed the forest at the heart of his exhibition strategy in the early 1830s, showing paintings on that theme at three consecutive Salons from 1831 to 1834. *Forest of Fontainebleau* (pl. 30), shown as *Une forêt* in 1834, was among those works, but perhaps even more notable was *View of the Forest of Fontainebleau* (fig. 1), which was exhibited at the Salon of 1833. The canvas measures 180 × 245 centimeters, and it signaled a new level of ambition in Corot's naturalism. The work reflects not only his diligent study in the forest but also his awareness of seventeenth-century Dutch art—the dead beech tree in the center is clearly borrowed from Jacob van Ruisdael—and it brought him his first serious critical praise. At a Salon particularly noteworthy for the new importance of naturalistic landscape, Charles Lenormant described Corot's work as the most "perfect" example on display.[9] Thereafter, Corot's studies in the forest would continue to

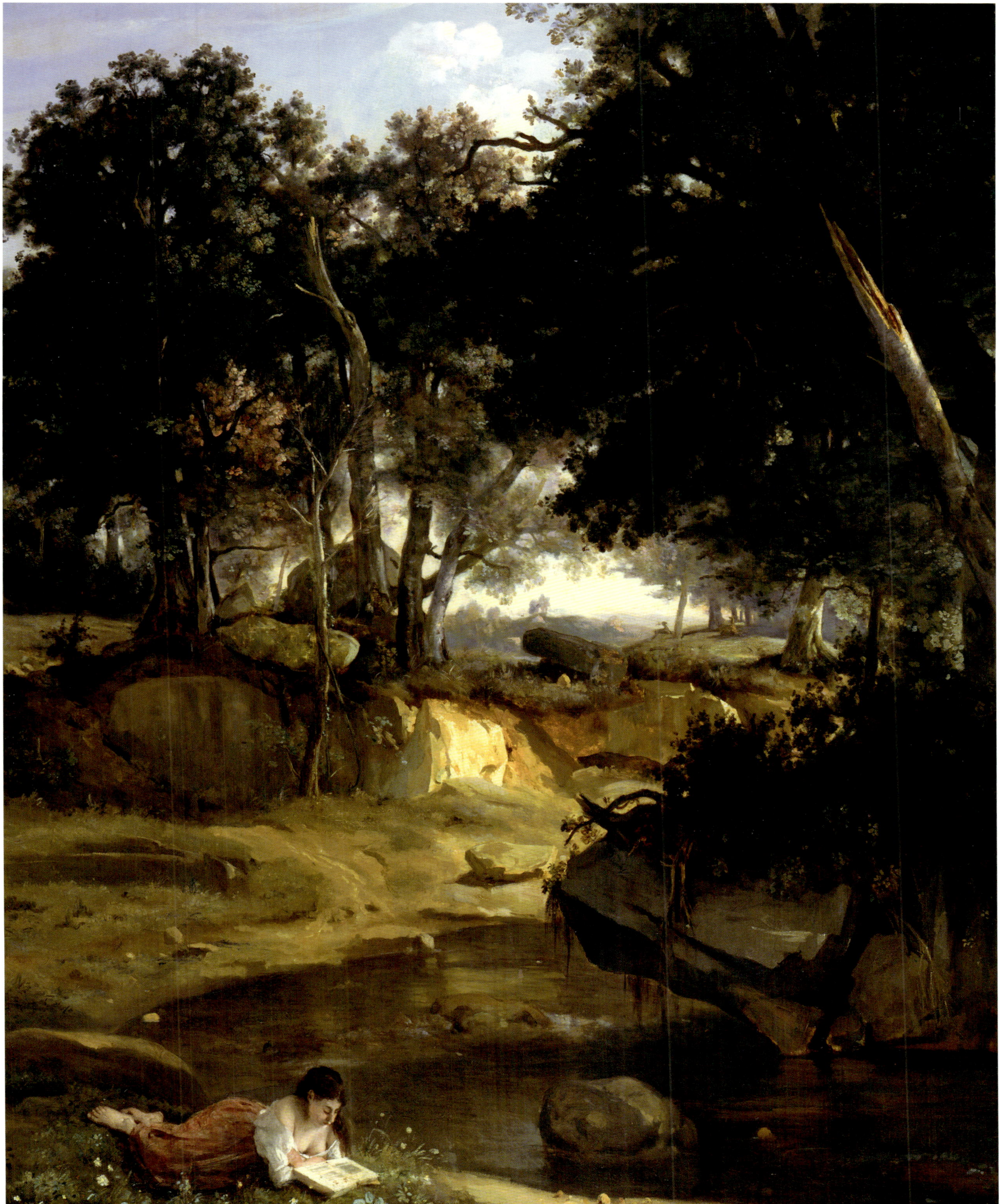

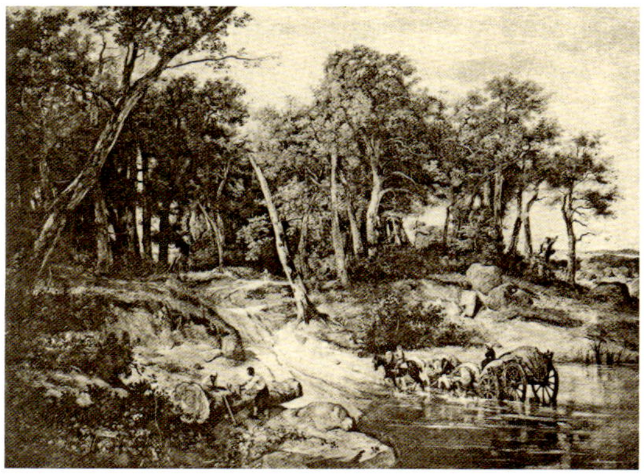

Fig. 1 Jean-Baptiste-Camille Corot, *View of the Forest of Fontainebleau,* 1832 (Salon of 1833), oil on canvas, 180 × 245 cm. Location unknown

underpin his historical landscapes such as *Hagar and the Angel* (Metropolitan Museum of Art, New York), presented at the Salon of 1835. He exhibited only one more naturalistic view of the forest: *The Forest of Fontainebleau,* which was shown in 1846 (pl. 31). This rendering of cows descending to a pool was inspired by an earlier oil study completed in the Gorges d'Apremont and is representative of his restrained tonal palette. The work was roundly criticized, however, for its lack of color. Félix Pyat, for example, assailed the artist for using the "dirt from his boots" as paint and noted, "nothing sparkles."[10] Others focused on his "unfinished" facture, remarking on the work's "naïve gaucherie."[11] The critical trope of "gaucherie" that surrounded Corot's work at this time might in fact be seen as a testament to his formal innovation and willingness to break away from the constraints of academic *fini.*[12] Corot experienced difficulties in finding private patronage throughout the 1840s, and this work would remain unsold until the end of his career, when he donated it to a benefit sale for the family of his pupil Auguste Anastasi, himself a dedicated painter of the forest.

By the 1840s, the representations of the forest that won the highest accolades were those of Narcisse-Virgile Diaz de la Peña and Constant Troyon. Diaz had studied in Fontainebleau since the late 1830s, and he first exhibited a forest view in 1837. From 1844 to 1848, he regularly exhibited such scenes and developed a particular specialty in depicting undergrowth *(sous-bois).* His principal critical apologist, Théophile Thoré, likened his richly colorful compositions to "a pile of precious stones."[13] Diaz' works were often reproduced in art magazines, and they enjoyed enthusiastic support from patrons who, as Thoré also noted, were so intoxicated by his hallucinogenic color that they ignored their prejudices about his lack of *fini.*[14] In 1848, Diaz showed *Pack of Hounds in the Forest of Fontainebleau* (fig. 2), with hunting dogs tumbling down a forest path in pursuit of prey. This work is characterized by its shimmering russet and orange impasto and use of the palette knife, as seen in the yellow foreground marks. The picture was praised by Clément de Ris as an "enchanting eruption of excited howls in an even more enchanting oasis, filled with rays of light, reflections, foliage, and greenery."[15] As with much of Diaz' work from this time, it demonstrates a compositional debt to the œuvre of his close friend Rousseau.[16]

Constant Troyon, although better known today as an animalier, also focused on landscapes in the 1840s. He was an important figure in the artistic community at the Auberge Ganne and exhibited a series of large and ambitious paintings of the forest to considerable acclaim. In 1846, the radical critic Charles Blanc noted, "M. Troyon represents at the Louvre what is most vigorous and solid in the modern execution of landscape."[17] Troyon's exhibited views in this decade culminated with his *Forest of Fontainebleau* (fig. 3), shown at the Salon of 1848. It depicts woodcutters in a large clearing surrounded

Fig. 2 Narcisse-Virgile Diaz de la Peña, *Pack of Hounds in the Forest of Fontainebleau,* 1848 (Salon of 1848), oil on canvas, 103 × 82 cm. Ordrupgaard Museum, Copenhagen

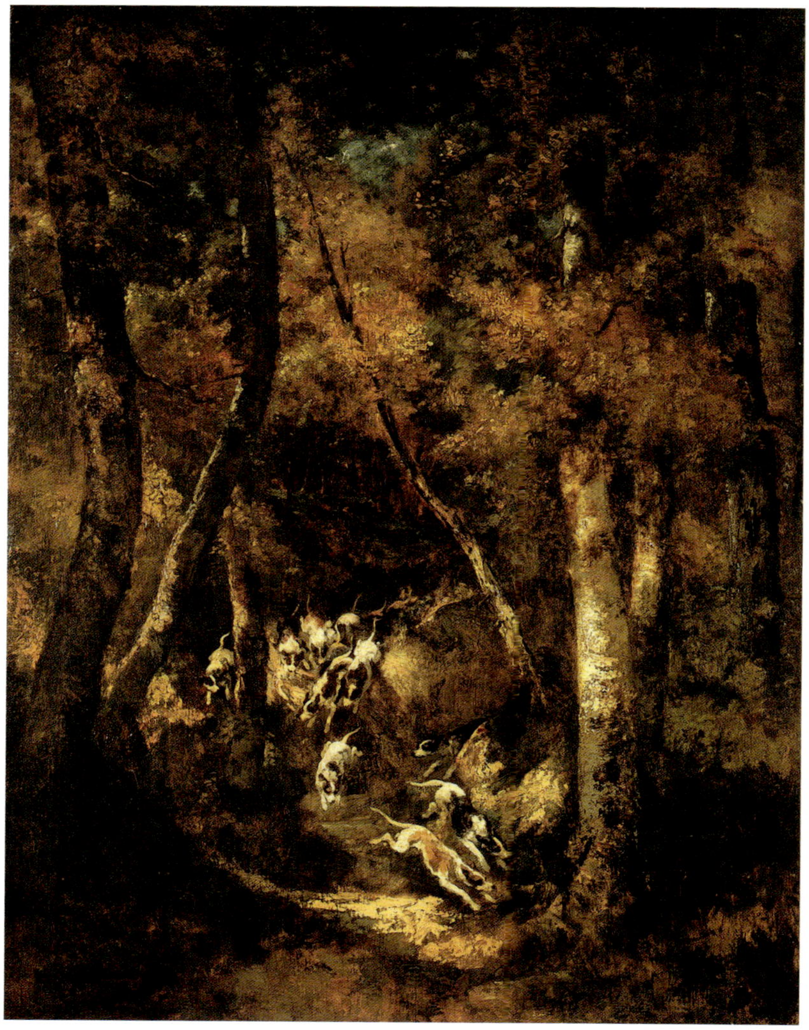

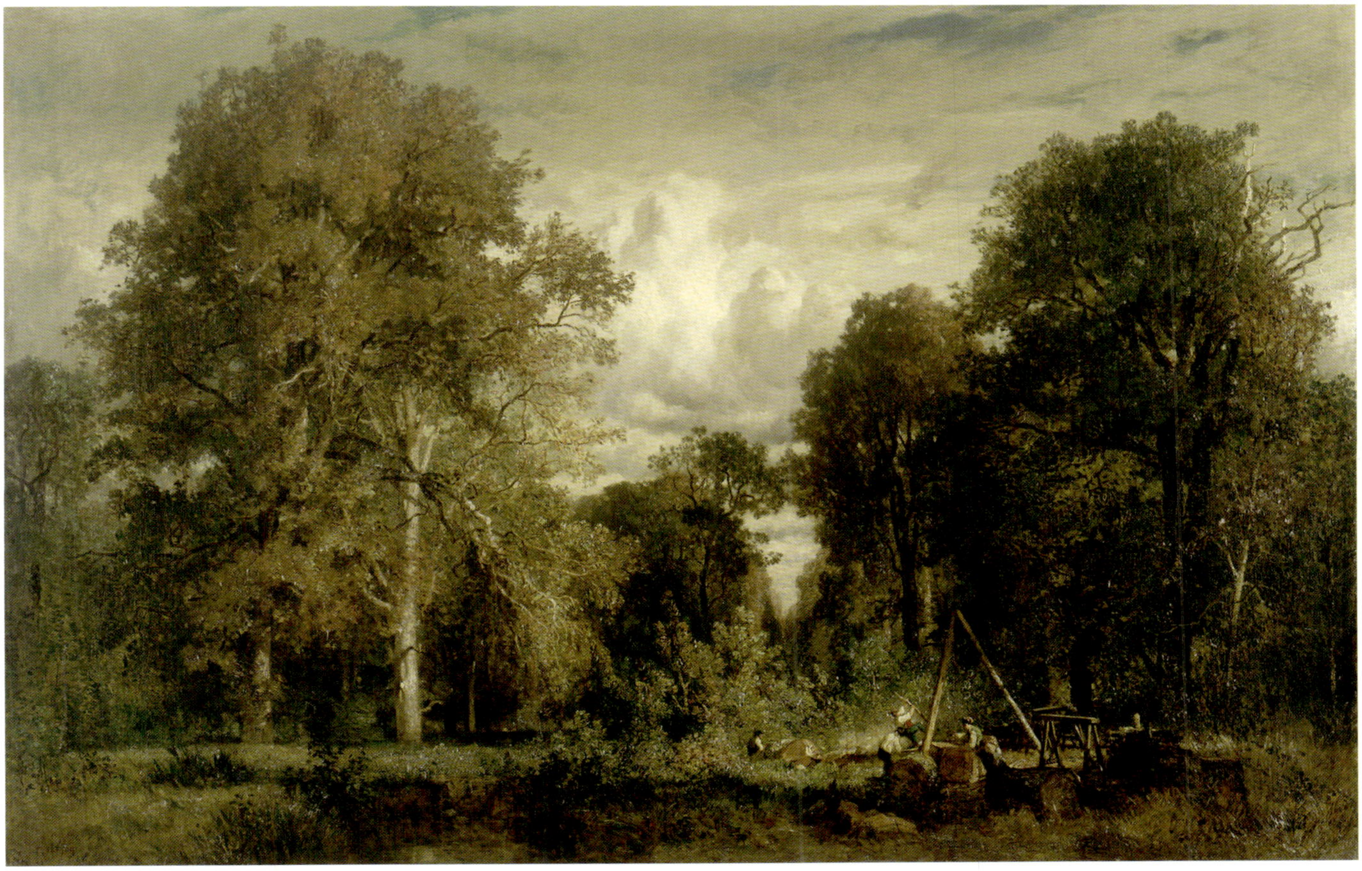

Fig. 3 Constant Troyon, *Forest of Fontainebleau*, 1848 (Salon of 1848), oil on canvas, 145 × 227 cm. Musée des Beaux-Arts, Lille

by grand oak trees, lifting an enormous log in order to place it on trellises, presumably so that it could be cut into smaller pieces. The painting is distinguished by its rich, virtuoso brushwork and complex variety of greens (from emerald to viridian), offset by the touches of red and blue in the workmen's clothing. Like Diaz, Troyon was recognized as a colorist—for Théophile Gautier, he was a "colorist to his very core"—and this canvas, which won him a first-class medal at the Salon,[18] was acquired by the state, perhaps reflecting the enthusiasm of Charles Blanc, the new director of beaux-arts in the Second Republic, for the artist's work.[19]

Théodore Rousseau: "The Ruisdael of the Forest of Fontainebleau"

Théodore Rousseau was perhaps the greatest and most diligent painter of scenes in the Forest of Fontainebleau. After suffering refusals of his work during the July Monarchy, he returned to the Salon in the Second Republic, and during the 1850s and 1860s, he was the artist who most consistently represented the forest at the Salon.[20] In 1850 he had an ambitious exhibition in which six of the seven works on display were paintings of Fontainebleau. His compositions were also placed in sought-after locations, and they soon sparked rather intense controversy in the press. Gautier wrote, "The painter who catches the eye and attracts the most heated debate is M. Théodore Rousseau. . . . he has this precious gift of ruffling the feathers of the bourgeoisie and even quite a few painters."[21] The largest picture in the exhibition was *Edge of the Forest of Fontainebleau, Sunset* (pl. 102).[22] Rousseau here evoked a world far from the recent political upheavals in Paris, suggesting pastoral sentiment through the staffage of a cowherd blowing his horn, a figure in blue reclining to the left of the pool, and the demi-orb of the distant setting sun. For all its pastoral allusions, critics were shocked by the work's lack of finish. Gabriel de Ferry compared the rugged, vigorous brushwork of the tree trunks to a "frottis" (or scumble) and noted that the painting remained "in the state of an ébauche."[23] François Sabatier-Ungher described the artist's "whipped facture."[24] Others denounced his thinly painted foreground or his "negligence" in treating pools of water like "islands of syrup."[25] Gautier summed up an ambivalence that many people experienced between suspicion of Rousseau's technique and admiration of his keen understanding of

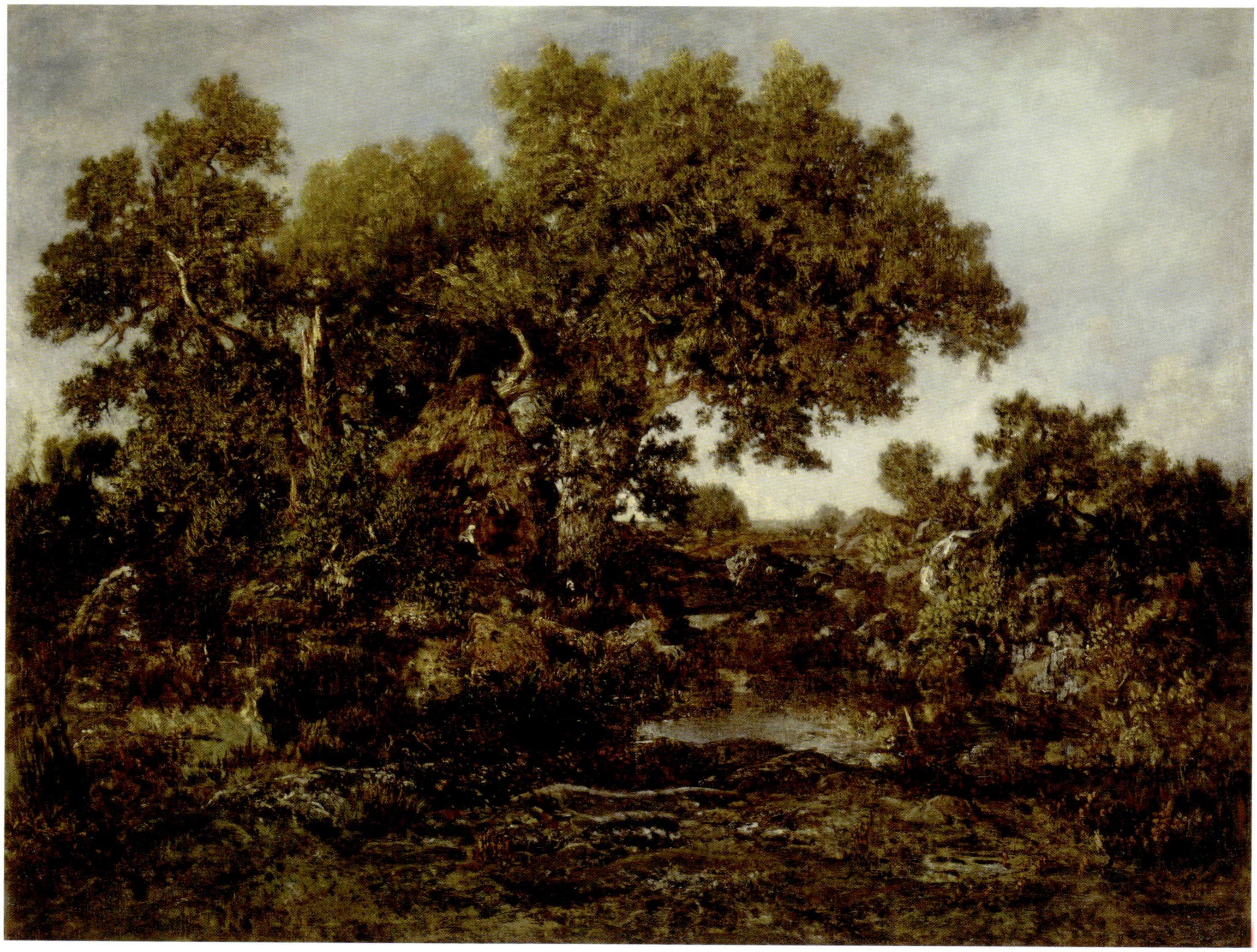

Fig. 4 Théodore Rousseau, *The Plain of Belle-Croix (Forest of Fontainebleau),* 1848–1850 (Salon of 1850–1851), oil on canvas, 90 × 117 cm. Musée du Louvre, Paris

nature: "Certainly, there are at the Salon, twenty landscapists who draw and paint better than M. Rousseau; but no one makes the sap run through the trunks, the grass, the mosses as he does.... we admit it freely, his execution is sometimes slack, sometimes violent, careless like a sketch or brutally excessive; but this supreme quality of plant life consumes everything."[26]

Rousseau also displayed *The Plain of Belle-Croix (Forest of Fontainebleau)* (fig. 4), which can be identified as the work better known as *The Charcoal-Burner's Hut*.[27] He often depicted this ancient plain, some two and one-half miles to the east of Barbizon, and described this work in a letter to a potential patron: "The size is four and one-half feet including the frame and the purely rustic composition presents a completely different character to that which you asked for... the fertile abundance is there nonetheless and, in terms of detail, in the middle ground, a group of old oaks shelters a rustic hut and, in the foreground, two cows drink at a pond surrounded by terrain where heather, broom and gorse grow profusely."[28]

The two cows to which Rousseau referred are roughly defined just to the left of the pond and almost merge with the surrounding landscape. He also animated the scene with a tiny figure wearing a white bonnet and sitting in front of the hut. In seeking a sense of "fertile abundance," he built up the surface with delicate flecks of paint (while also scratching out paint with the tip of his brush handle) and compared his unorthodox working procedures on his canvas to "the work of nature," where alluvial deposits gradually build up on the surface of a landscape.[29] Rousseau, indeed, arguably sought to mimic the textures of nature in his complex surfaces. The critic Paul Mantz, in an echo of Gautier's commentary, recorded the words of a bystander who imagined that he could see in Rousseau's work "the grass growing and hear the sap running through the branches."[30] Sabatier-Ungher noted that the hut was so well integrated into the landscape that "it seemed a natural product of the earth or, at the very least, a bird's nest."[31] Alexandre du Pays saw similarities between the unorthodox techniques of Rousseau and Corot in that both were willing to subvert established conventions of academic finish; he alluded to the "ruggedness" of Rousseau's facture and the "naïveté" of Corot's execution.[32]

Many critics attacked the "unfinished" foregrounds of Rousseau's Salon works, accusing him of "charlatanism" in exhibiting shoddily produced paintings, but it is possible that he was experimenting with a pictorial means of representing the very act of looking.[33] His decision to leave his foregrounds ill-defined mimics the way in which blurred foreground vision offsets a carefully defined image in the distance. The critic Prosper Haussard indeed noted that his approach was "intentional" and reflected a "system."[34]

Following the Salon of 1850–1851, Rousseau continued to show views of the forest, but he shifted his exhibition strategy toward the display of more highly finished and, as a result, less incendiary works. It appears that he had planned to exhibit his majestic *Winter Forest* (Metropolitan Museum of Art, New York)—arguably his greatest representation of the forest— in the early 1850s, but for unclear reasons, he did not realize this goal.[35] Instead, he displayed more modestly scaled depictions of the forest on a regular basis throughout the decade. Seven of the thirteen works in his retrospective at the Exposition Universelle of 1855 constituted views of the Forest of Fontainebleau. These ranged from ancient sites threatened by commercial deforestation (such as the Lisière des Monts-Girard) to recently cultivated fields.

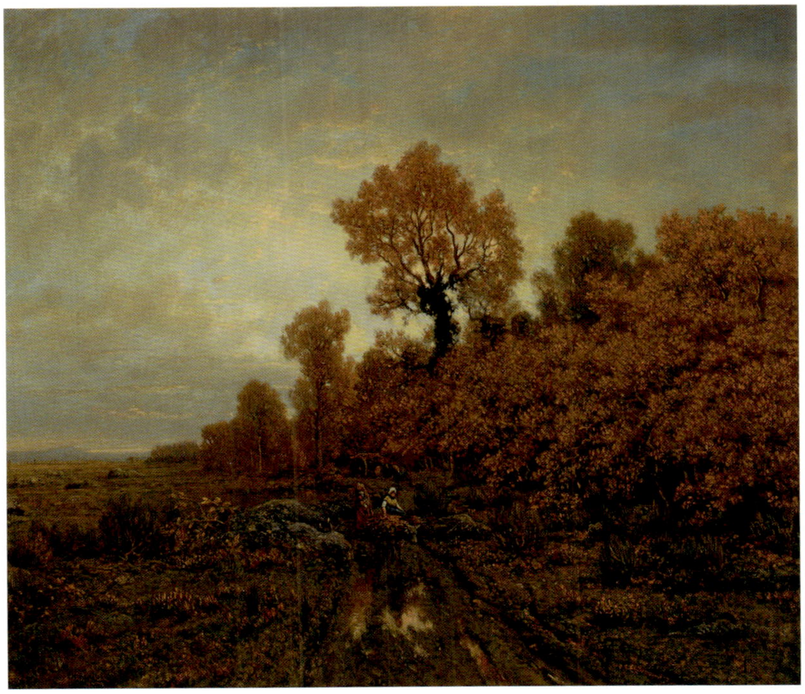

Fig. 5 Théodore Rousseau, *Edge of the Wood, Plain of Barbizon*, 1859 (Salon of 1859), oil on canvas, 54.7 × 65.3 cm. Museum of Fine Arts, Boston, Bequest of Mrs. David P. Kimball

At the Salon of 1859, three of Rousseau's five works on display featured Fontainebleau, and he was subsequently dubbed the "Ruisdael of the Forest of Fontainebleau" by the critic Mathilde Stevens.[36] Most prominent among his submissions was the grand *Gorges d'Apremont (Forest of Fontainebleau)* (pl. 101), a rendering of the rocky plain that was well known for its sense of desolation.[37] Rousseau wrote that his aim was to evoke the "general character of solitude" as well as the "various kinds of vegetation" and "their stages of triumph over the barrenness of the soil."[38] At the same Salon, Rousseau showed *Edge of the Wood, Plain of Barbizon*, which can now be identified as the canvas currently in Boston (fig. 5). Rousseau generally painted his staffage engaged in traditional activities such as grazing and fagot gathering, rather than the more modern signs of tourism or logging in the forest. Here, two women, one of whom rides on a donkey, transport fagots along a path soaked from a recent rainfall. The painting is perhaps particularly notable for Rousseau's structuring of space through chiaroscuro as he silhouettes the meticulously detailed forms of the trees against a luminous sky of clouds tinged with pink. The young avant-garde critic Zacharie Astruc praised this work at length and used an established critical trope in inviting the spectator to "take a walk" in the picture where he might "inhale fully these powerful rustic odors."[39]

During the 1860s, Rousseau regularly showed Fontainebleau scenes at the Salon. His public pronouncements during this decade also highlighted the metaphysical sentiment underpinning these works. In 1864, he contributed an autograph letter and accompanying sketch to the album, *L'Autographe au Salon de 1864 et dans les ateliers*. Here, he affirmed his belief in an all-encompassing "tout" beneath natural appearances and noted that when viewing a beautiful sunset "one's spirit will be lost in the grandiose." He went on to compare the profiled forms of a laborer or fagot-gatherer to "the spirits of the earth."[40] His meditative approach to the forest was also evident in *The Rock Oak (Forest of Fontainebleau)*, exhibited at the Salon of 1861 (pl. 59). In that painting, Rousseau depicted a solitary oak tree that had grown up among rocks and dense vegetation. In describing this work, he alluded to his "taste for the old forests," and as in his other Salon exhibits of the time, he conspicuously screened out the signs

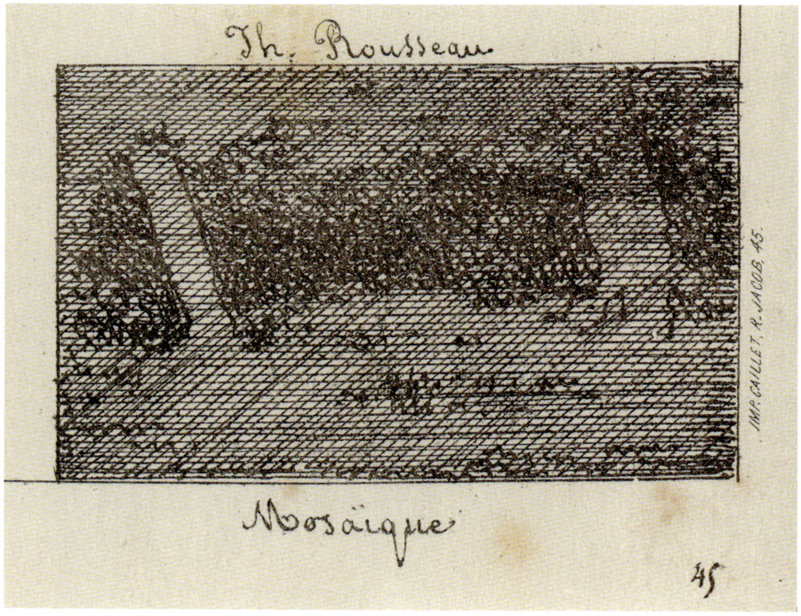

Fig. 6 Galletti, "Mosaïque," from *L'Album caricatural,* Salon of 1861 (Paris, 1861)

of expanding tourism in the forest.[41] He employed a complex palette with a range of greens offset by accents of color, such as the red berries of a holly bush or a pink, coral-like shrub. His use of meticulous, uniform flecks of paint—so characteristic of his late work and in marked contrast to his earlier gestural handling—confused most critics. The caricaturist Galletti, in a reference to Rousseau's uniformity of touch, produced a cartoon of the picture as a "mosaic" in *L'Album caricatural* (fig. 6). And Olivier Merson compared Rousseau's repetitive facture to "a tapestry with tiny stitches."[42] Rousseau's old friend Théophile Thoré, who had recently returned from exile, was more responsive, noting that the work was "very mysterious and very powerful" and would benefit from being exhibited in a room on its own—almost like an altarpiece—rather than in the impersonal rows of works at the Salon.[43]

Jean-François Millet

Another of Rousseau's close friends, Jean-François Millet, regularly presented views of the Forest of Fontainebleau at the Salon from 1853 to 1870.[44] While the trees of the forest fascinated Rousseau, Millet focused on the open plains surrounding the forest, particularly the expansive plain of Chailly.[45] His correspondence reveals his sensitivity to light effects, in particular the twilight hour when he often took walks on the plain. In 1852, for example, he wrote of one such walk with Rousseau when the two men saw "the tiny star shining... after such a splendid sunset, and the silhouette [of a figure] walking so solemnly over the heights."[46] The following year, he showed *Shepherd, Evening Effect* at the Salon

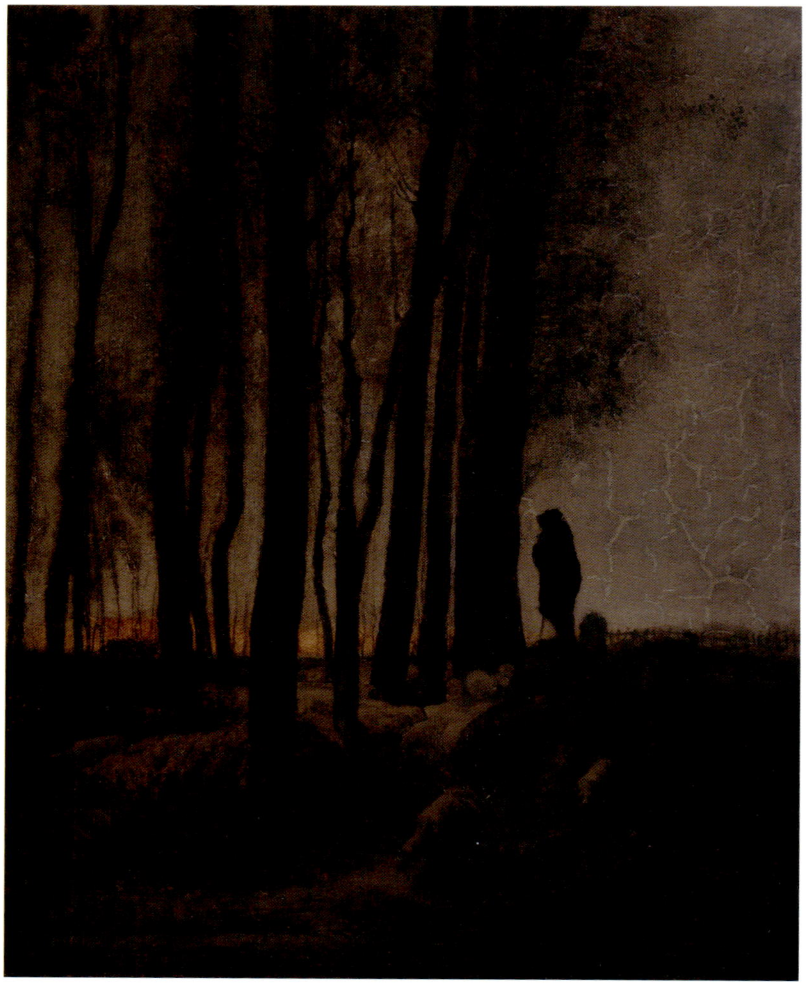

Fig. 7 Jean-François Millet, *Shepherd, Evening Effect,* 1853 (Salon of 1853), oil on canvas, 60.0 × 49.5 cm. Museum of Fine Arts, Boston, Gift of Quincy Adams Shaw through Quincy Adams Shaw Jr. and Marian Shaw Haughton

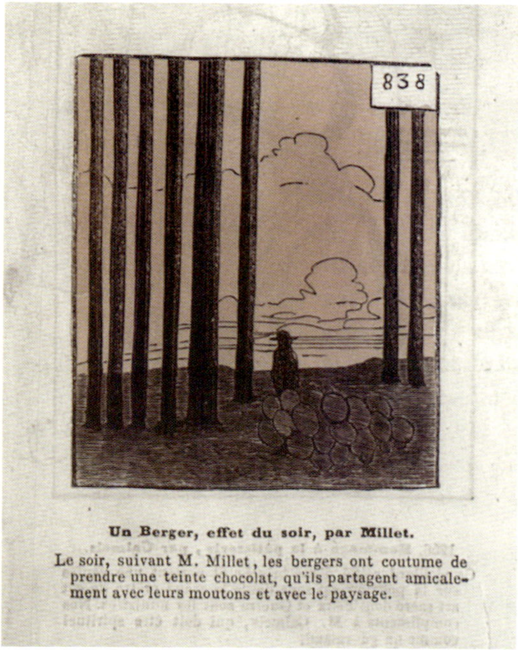

Fig. 8 Charles-Albert d'Arnoux Bertall, Caricature of Millet, *Shepherd, Evening Effect,* from "Le Salon dépeint et dessiné par Bertall," *Le journal pour rire,* 16 July 1853

(fig. 7). The painting portrays a solitary, silhouetted shepherd who looks out from a rock between a copse of bare trees and a sheepfold, while the orange light of the setting sun illuminates the horizon.

Millet is known to have used bitumen in his paint, and Bertall caricatured the darkness of the work with the accompanying caption: "In the evening, according to M. Millet, shepherds customarily turn a chocolate color which they share in friendly fashion with their sheep and the landscape" (fig. 8).

In the years thereafter, Millet exhibited a series of politically charged compositions showing workers toiling on the Chailly plain. The group culminated with *Man with a Hoe*, which Millet presented at the Salon of 1863 with a clear awareness that the painting would incite impassioned debate (fig. 9).[47] The work depicts an exhausted laborer leaning on his hoe after he has broken up the surrounding clay ground, which is covered with weeds, brambles, and stones; piles of steaming manure are visible in the distance. The conservative critic Paul de Saint-Victor attacked the "ugliness" of Millet's figure and ridiculed his propensity for portraying "cretins."[48] The more sympathetic Jules Castagnary saw the poignancy of the worker, whom he likened to a "lamentable Christ of eternal labor," an allusion to the crown of thorns in the tangled shrubbery at the left of the composition.[49] Millet himself defended his painting from accusations of "ugliness" and affirmed his aim to represent accurately both the harshness of the peasant's toil and the delicate beauty in nature, including, as here, the "haloes of dandelions."[50]

In the late 1860s, Millet shifted to more explicit landscape treatments of the forest and exhibited two daringly minimalist views of the plain of Chailly in winter.[51] From his early years in Barbizon, Millet's correspondence had indicated his deep affinity for the desolation and emptiness of winter.[52] *Winter* (Oesterreichische Galerie Belvedere, Vienna) appeared at the Salon of 1867 and received some praise, but it was overshadowed by Millet's larger retrospective

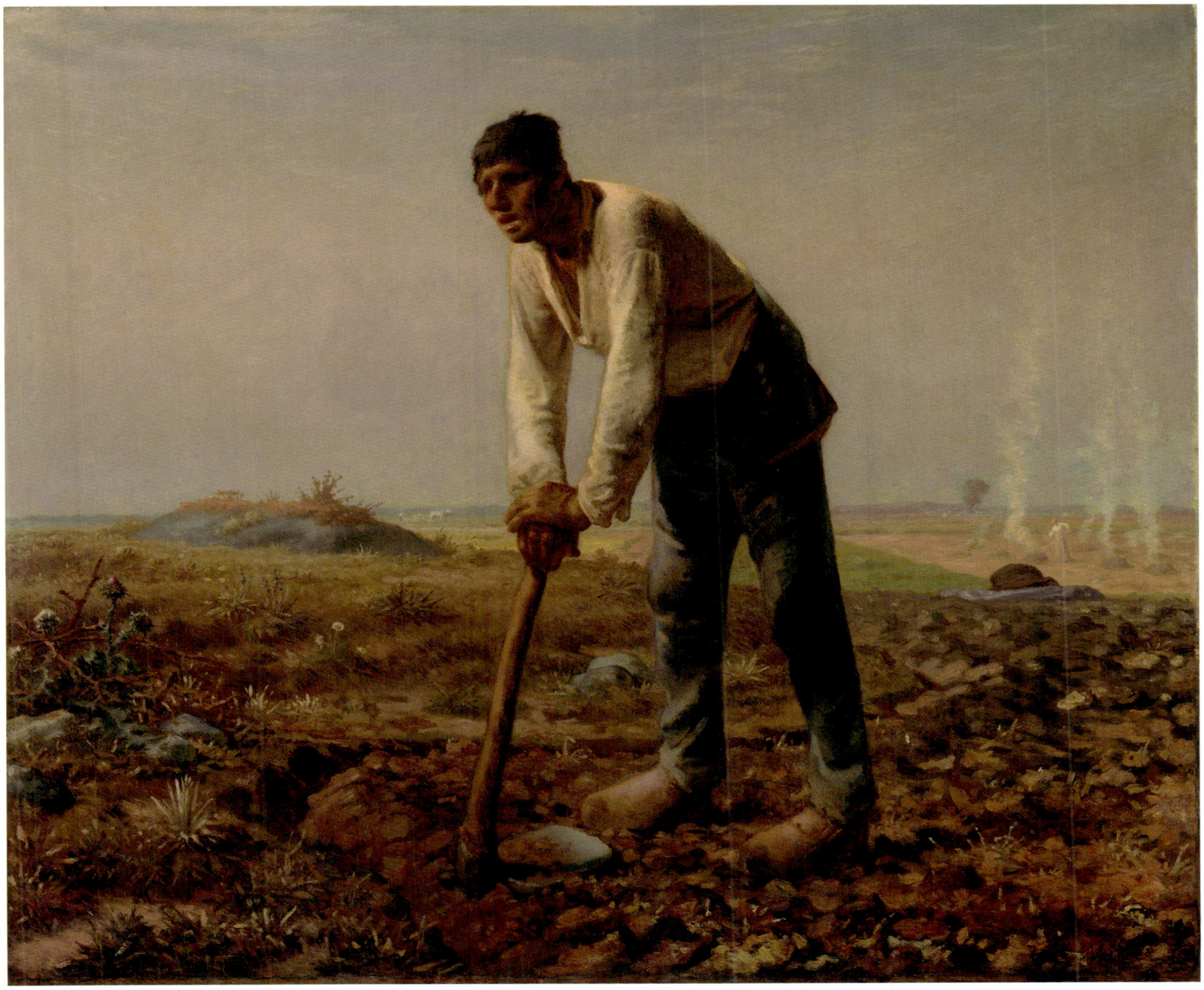

Fig. 9 Jean-François Millet, *Man with a Hoe*, 1863 (Salon of 1863), oil on canvas, 80 × 99 cm. The J. Paul Getty Museum, Los Angeles

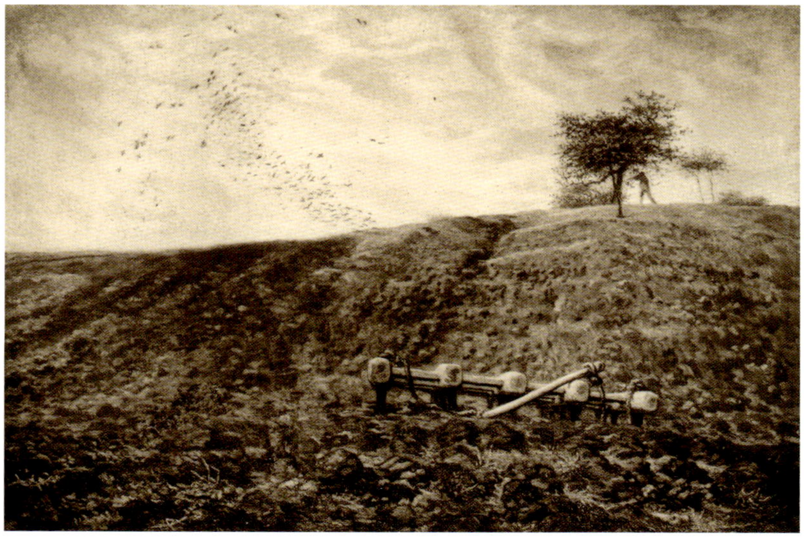

Fig. 10 Jean-François Millet, *November*, 1870 (Salon of 1870), oil on canvas, 92 × 140 cm. Location unknown

at the Exposition Universelle. Nonetheless, the critic Edmond About called it "an absolutely masterly work which would not be out of place in any display at the Louvre."[53] Three years later, Millet showed a larger and bolder winter scene entitled *November* (fig. 10). In this painting, distinguished by its high horizon, Millet focused on an expanse of earth recently tilled by a harrow, while in the distance he included the bare silhouettes of apple trees and a man firing a rifle in an attempt to scare off a flock of crows. The composition was celebrated for the radical way in which Millet had managed to give a sense of poetry to such an ostensibly banal and non-picturesque motif. Alfred Sensier, the artist's future biographer, declared: "This landscape is vast and solemn, and M. Millet has known how to bring out from this fragment of earth, banal as anything, the terrible cry of nature."[54] The young critic Théodore Duret, a future supporter of the impressionists, praised Millet for treating a subject that "the eyes of artists had never yet been lowered to see" and noted of this landscape as well as Millet's genre painting *La Baratteuse* (Yamagata Museum of Art, Japan): "it seems to me that, not only at the Salon of this year but that in the whole modern school, there is nothing greater than these two Millets."[55]

The Impressionists and the Future

As is well known, the young impressionists worked intensively in the Forest of Fontainebleau during the mid-1860s. Auguste Renoir and Frédéric Bazille did not show forest views at the Salon, but both Alfred Sisley and Claude Monet did exhibit Fontainebleau paintings on a single occasion, the Salon of 1866. Sisley's monumental painting of a copse of chestnut trees (see Aurisch essay, fig. 8) has recently been identified as representing Fontainebleau; although probably intended for exhibition in the Salon of 1865, it never in fact appeared.[56] The following year, Sisley showed two complementary scenes of rural life in the village of Marlotte to the south of the forest where he had worked regularly in the early 1860s. One depicts a group of women departing the village to collect fagots (see Aurisch essay, fig. 9), and the other, *Village Street in Marlotte* (pl. 66), shows a woodcutter raising his axe to chop a gnarled tree branch. In his portrayal of the buildings in these works, Sisley created a complex, architectonic pattern of interlocking shapes characteristic of a new kind of "realist" landscape that emerged in the mid-1860s. Such geometrical pattern-making may also reflect his awareness of Corot's early Italian plein-air sketches. Yet Sisley's work was largely overlooked by the critics.[57]

Claude Monet was the most ambitious of the young "realists." He had originally planned to show *Le Déjeuner sur l'herbe*, an enormous image of modern life in the forest, at the Salon of 1866. Ultimately, however, he did not submit it and instead showed *Forest of Fontainebleau* (fig. 11), a view of the well-known Pavé de Chailly, the principal road traversing the forest. Monet produced several unpopulated scenes of the road, but this is exceptional in its depiction of a team of white and brown horses pulling a cart loaded with two felled trees—a reference to the contemporary theme of logging.[58] The sharp receding lines of the path pull the viewer's gaze into the distance but are also offset by the flat patterns of light and shade on the tree foliage (a reflection of Monet's awareness of Japanese prints). Although his other exhibition piece, a portrait of *Camille*, attracted more critical attention,[59] Monet considered the work a "success," and Thoré observed, "Monet has also produced his landscape, a superb 'ébauche' ... an evening effect with the sun illuminating the large trees. When you are a true painter, you can do whatever you want."[60] As the young critic Emile

Zola also noted, the objective "realist" aesthetic of Monet contrasted with that of the "hardened romantic" Rousseau, whose forest paintings were imbued with a sense of the metaphysical.[61]

By the 1870s, views of the forest were being shown at the Salon in ever-increasing numbers; but they no longer included major examples of avant-garde painting. During the previous four decades, such works had been crucial to innovative landscape production. For Rousseau and Millet in particular, representations of the forest had been at the center of their exhibition strategies. Although the foremost painters of Fontainebleau often ignored signs of modern life, such as the rise of tourism, they did demonstrate their "modernity" through highly gestural brushwork, unconventional compositions, and a preference for nonpicturesque motifs. The critical discourse surrounding their work — their "gaucherie," "naïveté," or "rudesse" — can itself be seen as a sign of their modernist credentials. While French painters explored the wide geographical range of their country in their Salon pictures, including views of plains, rivers, and the sea, their particular focus on the Forest of Fontainebleau ensured that it emerged as arguably *the* principal motif in the evolution of modern landscape painting.

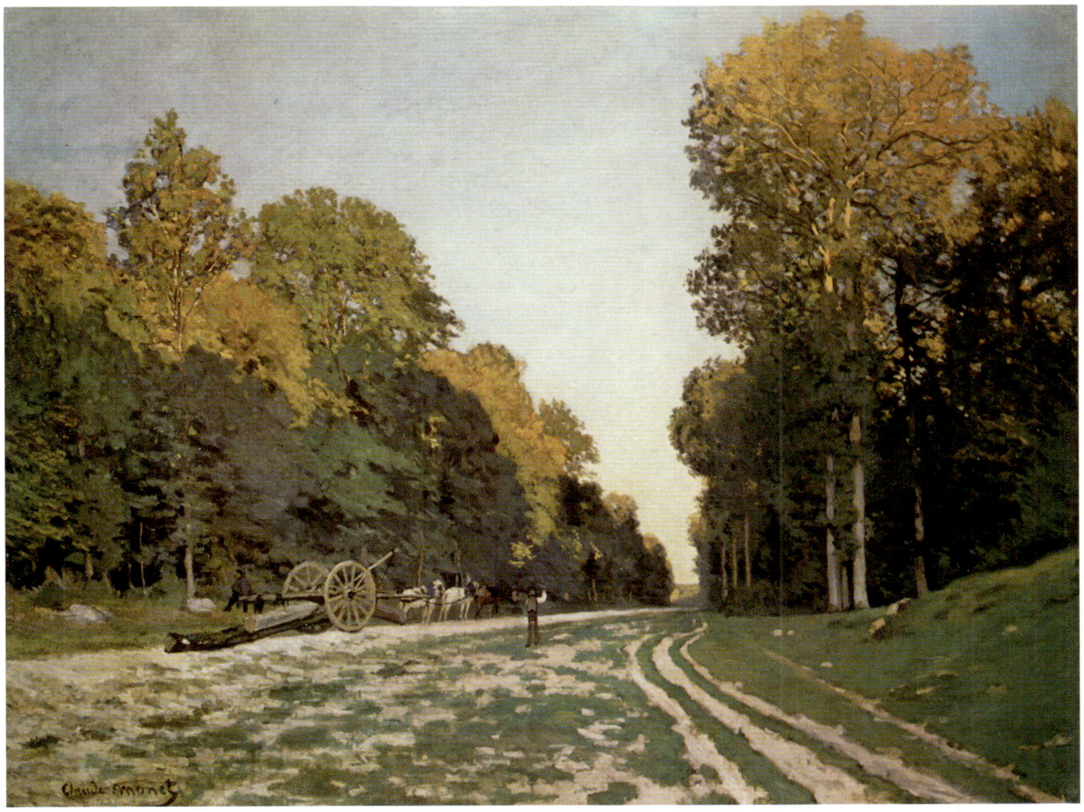

Fig. 11 Claude Monet, *Forest of Fontainebleau,* 1864 (Salon of 1866), oil on canvas, 98 × 130 cm. Private collection

SARAH KENNEL

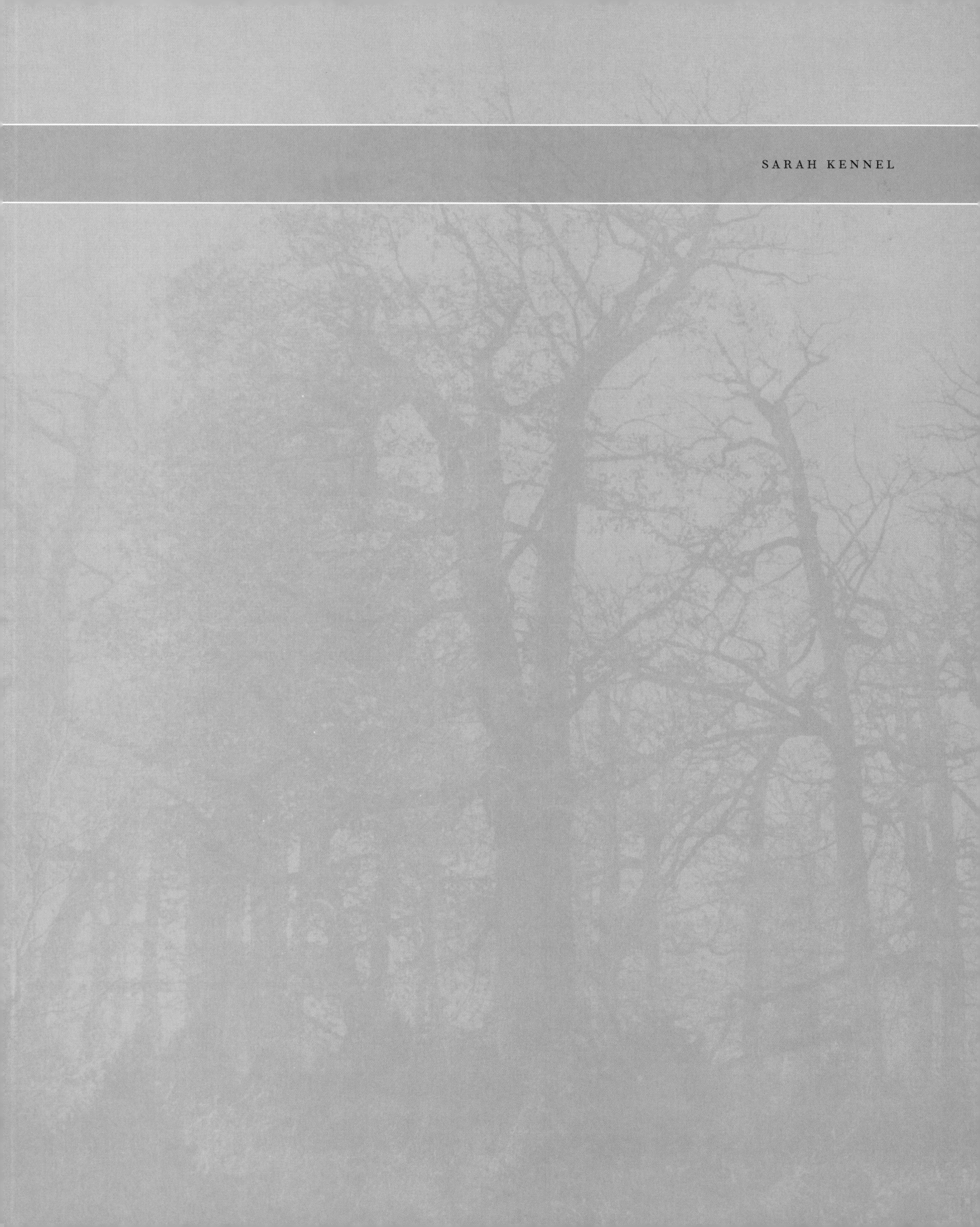

An Infinite Museum *Photography in the Forest of Fontainebleau*

An Infinite Museum

Photography in the Forest of Fontainebleau

Right Detail of pl. 48

Beginning in the late 1840s, photographers armed with cameras and tripods, rather than paint boxes and parasols, joined the ranks of landscape painters who made seasonal pilgrimages to the Forest of Fontainebleau to practice their craft *en plein air.* For photographers as for painters, the rich variety of pictorial motifs, the relative accessibility of Fontainebleau, and the pleasures of companionship and collegiality that often accompanied the trips made the forest a prime site for pictorial experimentation. While the increasingly important role of landscape in both painting and photography at midcentury fostered a vibrant dialogue between the two media, the Forest of Fontainebleau offered photographers specific physical conditions and conceptual challenges that helped to define and transform the practice of nineteenth-century French landscape photography.

Among the earliest photographs of the forest is a half-plate daguerreotype made in the 1840s that shows several large oaks dominating a level field enlivened by scrubby bushes, patches of raw earth, and a few scattered rocks (pl. 4). Skillfully composed and executed, it is the only known daguerreotype of the forest, though daguerreotypes of the Château of Fontainebleau from the same period do survive. The exact site of this scene is unknown, but it was likely made on the edge of the forest, perhaps near Barbizon or the Pavé de Chailly, since it would have been difficult to haul the necessary equipment up the often steep and rocky paths leading to the inner recesses of the forest. Although traveling daguerreotype kits existed at the time, even a relatively compact version like the one designed by Baron Séguir in 1839—the year that photography was officially introduced in France—weighed a not inconsiderable thirty-five pounds.[1] Moreover, the daguerreotype process itself was difficult to execute far from a studio. The polished copper plate first had to be exposed to iodine fumes, then after exposure in the camera, it was developed over mercury heated to seventy-five degrees centigrade. Although a few French photographers were experimenting with less cumbersome paper negatives, that process remained in its infancy until the late 1840s.[2]

Photography in the Forest of Fontainebleau began to flourish in earnest in 1849. The year is significant for several reasons: it witnessed the opening of the rail line from Paris to Fontainebleau (enabling easy access to the forest) as well as the resurgence of a cholera epidemic in Paris over the summer, which prompted many artists to flee the city in search of a healthier climate. Among those who sojourned in Barbizon during this time were Charles-Emile Jacque, Jean-François Millet, and the painter-turned-photographer Gustave Le Gray, who made his first photographs of the forest that year.[3] More broadly, two related developments in the late 1840s would transform mid-nineteenth-century French photography: the popularization of the paper negative process and the emergence of landscape as an increasingly important genre within French photographic theory and practice. As a result, photography in the Forest of Fontainebleau flourished.

Paper and Trees

With the dissemination of the paper negative process in France after 1847, photographers were able to work en plein air unburdened by all but the most basic necessities: camera, sensitized sheets of paper that acted as negatives, and folding tripod. The introduction of the collodion negative process in 1851 also proved a boon to voyaging photographers. The process, which entailed coating a glass plate with collodion and immersing it in a solution of silver nitrate before exposing it in the camera, was still bulkier and less convenient than using paper negatives, because it required on-the-spot preparation of the plates. In contrast, paper negatives could be prepared and stored in a lightproof container for several weeks in advance of their use. Once exposed in the camera, the paper negatives were again kept in a lightproof container until they were either printed out in sunlight or developed out with chemicals, a process that was usually executed within a day or two. The process thus allowed photographers to range more freely into spaces that had previously been inaccessible to the large wagons necessary for transporting heavy photographic equipment. Nöel-Marie-Paymal Lerebours enthu-

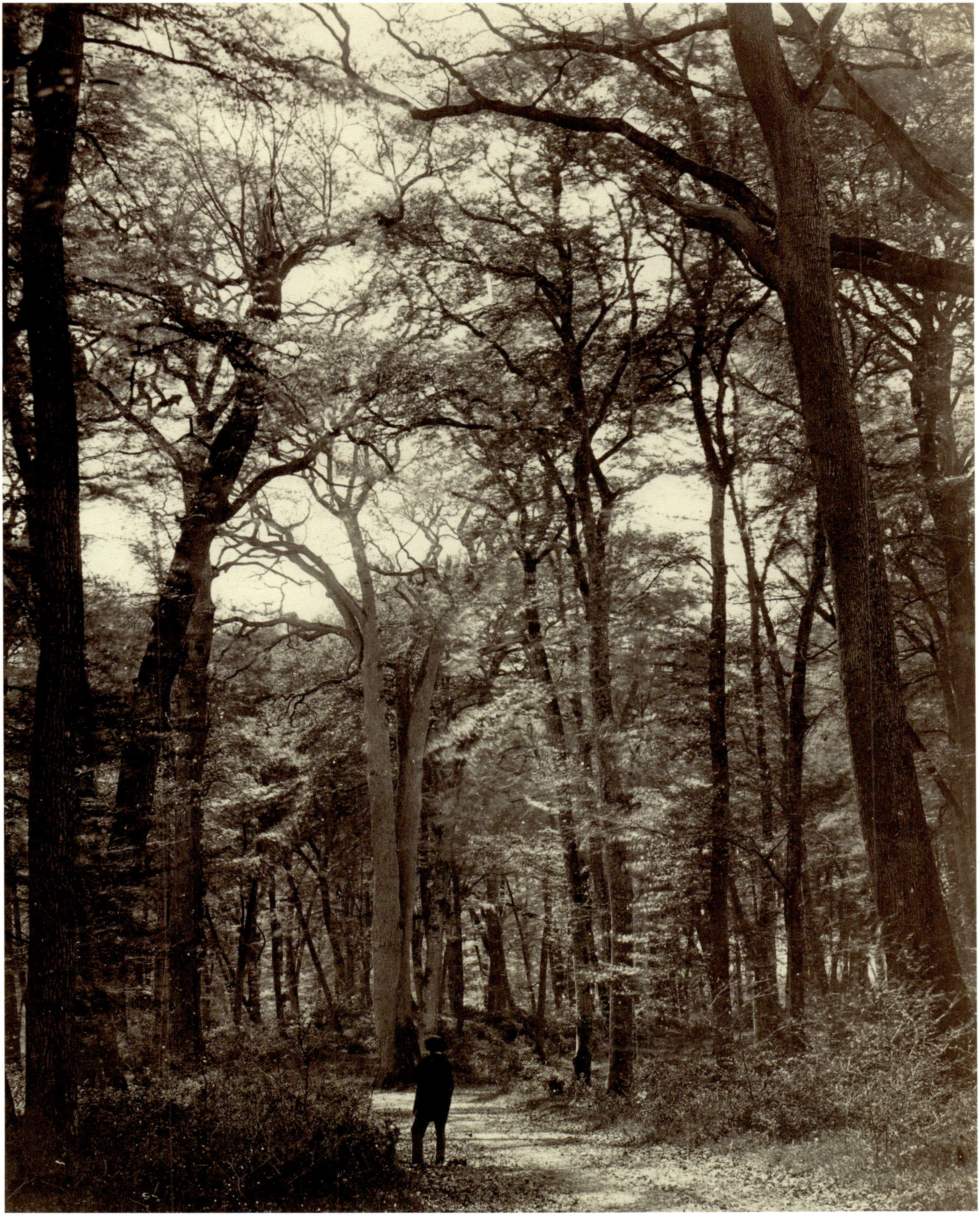

siastically captured the sense of liberation provided by the new process, writing in 1852: "Today one leaves Paris with a camera, tripod, twenty-five or thirty sheets of prepared paper in a cardboard box, *nothing more*!... Prepare your paper one or two days before the trip, and develop the images when you wish, as soon as you get back or even the next day."[4]

If the paper negative process proved convenient for travel, it also offered a new and intriguing set of aesthetic qualities and technical possibilities. Whereas daguerreotypes and prints made from glass negatives are characterized by a high degree of sharp detail, salted paper prints made from paper negatives (the most common form of print made from paper negatives) possess a soft, velvety appearance. This is, in part, because the silver image is absorbed within the paper fibers, rather than resting in a binder on the surface of the print. Salted paper prints also offer a rich and subtle tonal range that both captures detail and suggests broad harmonies of light and dark that are especially suited to the description of landscape. Moreover, paper negatives and the prints made from them, whether salted paper or albumen, were amenable to chemical and manual manipulations that allowed the photographer to modulate the final appearance of the print. For these reasons, paper photography began to accrue a specific aesthetic identity in the 1850s, one that was—in distinct opposition to the daguerreotype—increasingly associated with artistic subjectivity rather than scientific objectivity.[5] According to the critic Francis Wey, with the introduction of paper photography, "the camera had risen to the level of the intelligence which combines effects, simplifies execution, interprets nature, and adds the expression of sentiment and physiognomy to the reproduction of planes and lines."[6]

Among the first French photographers to perfect the paper negative process was the inveterate technical experimenter, Gustave Le Gray. A painter who had begun photographing in 1847, Le Gray developed the waxed-paper negative process around 1849. Although waxing negatives after exposure was not uncommon, Le Gray discovered that waxing the negative before sensitization both decreased exposure time and increased registration of detail. These improvements enabled him to capture moving objects like rustling leaves and to convey the delicate details of dense foliage, which was particularly difficult to record, since early photographic emulsions were relatively insensitive to green. Indeed, even with the sped-up exposure time of the waxed-paper negative, Le Gray noted, "one might need twenty minutes for photographing forest trees."[7]

No doubt Le Gray's *Study of Trees and Pathways*, likely made during his first journey to the Forest of Fontainebleau in 1849, required a lengthy exposure (pl. 22). The photograph, which records almost the full extent of the graceful upward sweep of trees in an otherwise flat clearing, reveals a space that is at once expansive and sheltering. A strong golden light bathes the tall trees, creating a lattice-like pattern of highlights and dark shadows that filter through the slender trunks. A dazzling beam of light caresses the length of a tree at left, drawing the eye to a signpost attached just below the place where the trunk issues forth its myriad branches. Like the photograph, the sign is a marker of human intervention in the forest, an inscription that shapes and guides the visitor's experience of the landscape.

Le Gray's other early works made in the forest nod toward human presence there, including the quiet scene of a modest pathway threading between slender, light-dappled trees. To the right, barely visible amidst bountiful foliage and saplings, stands a small camera on a tripod (fig. 1). As Sylvie Aubenas has noted, the camera likely indicates the presence of a companion, probably the American-born photographer John Beasley Greene, who studied with Le Gray and may have worked with him in the forest around 1852.[8] The photograph by Greene of a dense network of trees, also made in the forest, bears a strong kinship to his teacher's work in terms of both composition and deep, rich tonal range (pl. 23).

Le Gray made several other photographs in the Bas-Bréau, an area immediately east of Barbizon that was famous for its old-growth oaks and that, following a petition by the painter Rousseau in 1852, became the first "artistic preserve" in the forest and thus was protected from clear-cutting.[9] Certainly Le Gray, who continued to pursue his painting career in the early 1850s even as his photographic practice flourished, would have seen Rousseau's *Edge of the Forest*—which won a medal at the Salon of 1849—or the six Fontainebleau paintings by Rousseau at the Salon of 1850 that, according to Théophile Gautier, caught "the eye," attracted "the most debate," and ruffled "the feathers of the bourgeoisie and even quite a few painters."[10] Le Gray attempted to show nine salted paper prints made from paper negatives, including two Fontainebleau views, at the Salon of 1850.[11] The photographs were accepted at first but subsequently rejected by the jury, which

Fig. 1 Gustave Le Gray, *Bas-Bréau, Forest of Fontainebleau*, 1849–1852, albumen print from waxed paper negative, 29.7 × 37.6 cm. The J. Paul Getty Museum, Los Angeles

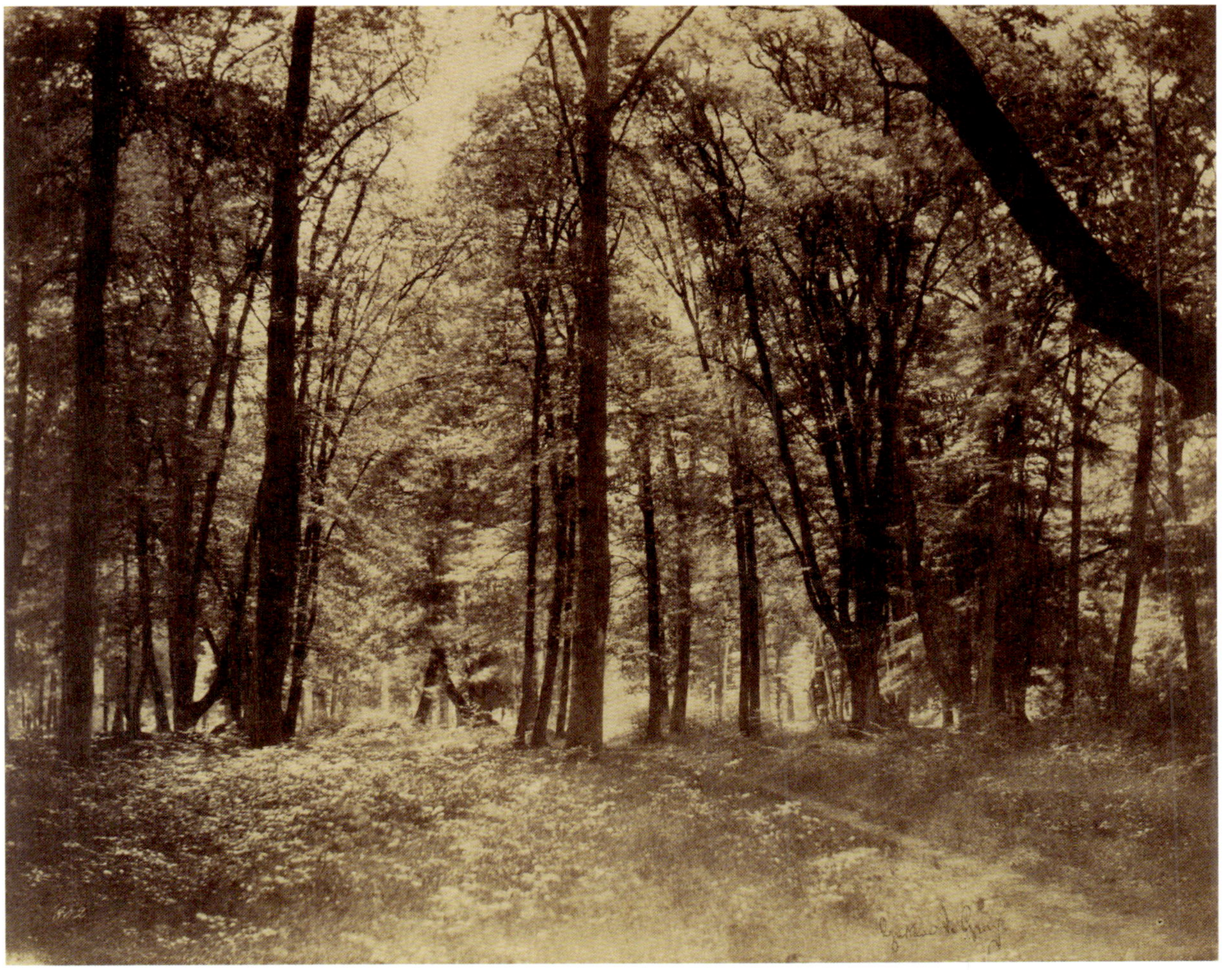

was unsure how to classify the objects that had been made with a camera but that looked, to eyes unfamiliar with the new paper process, like lithographs.[12]

By late 1853, both Le Gray's reputation as a photographer and the use of the paper negative in France had blossomed. In his article "A Visit to M. Le Gray's Studio," Marc-Antoine Gaudin singled out Le Gray's "delicious forest views" that possessed a harmony of tone while revealing "an infinity of details."[13] Several months later, *La Lumière*, France's leading photographic journal, published an article by Paul Nibelle designed to stimulate as well as account for photographers' growing interest in the forest. After the obligatory description of the Château of Fontainebleau, Nibelle turned his attention to the forest, "an infinite museum" that reflected in the very diversity of its landscape the political history of France — tranquil and picturesque in some places, dramatic and "tormented" in others.[14]

The enterprising and equally imaginative Claude-François Denecourt also associated the forest with the nation by naming its oldest and most impressive trees after great national figures, including Charlemagne, Pharamond, and Sully. As Kimberly Jones has noted, the unique combination of practical information, fulsome description, and imagined historical narratives offered up by Denecourt, who began publishing guidebooks to the forest in 1839, not only enabled visitors to traverse the forest "with ease and pleasure" but also mediated their experience in very specific ways by creating itineraries, singling out viewing points, and gracing nearly every element in the forest with a name culled from history, literature, art, or Denecourt's own fanciful imagination.[15]

Beech trees, along with old-growth oaks, were particularly favored by Denecourt who even tabulated the ratio of beech to oak trees in a listing of the "most remarkable century-old trees."[16] They were also a favorite motif for both painters and photographers, including Le Gray. In his magnificent *Beech Tree, Forest of Fontainebleau*, Le Gray marshals the resources of his craft to express the chthonic grandeur of a landscape that Denecourt had described as if arranged by some

"Diluvian upheaval" (pl. 36).[17] Here, Le Gray positioned his camera at the base of a mature beech tree, its exposed roots blasted by light and straining upward, tearing away from the earth below. The extreme depth of field and the tight, direct composition that crops the tree midway sacrifice spare elegance in favor of raw power. Le Gray, who was at this time working with both paper and collodion negatives, likely chose the latter process in this instance because the sharpness and clarity provided by the combination of glass negative and albumen print would emphasize the dazzling luminosity and unexpected boldness of the subject.

By focusing on the violent separation of the tree from the earth, Le Gray may also have been obliquely referencing contemporary debates over the management of the forest, in particular the issue of clear-cutting. At that moment, the Forest of Fontainebleau was at the heart of emerging debates over ecological and forestry practices. Already in 1839, the year of Denecourt's first guidebook for the forest, an article entitled "The Forest of Fontainebleau: Destructions," which was published in the journal *L'Artiste*, attacked forest officials for degrading the natural wonders of a "sacred oasis in the midst of the pious invasions of a destructive and improvident civilization."[18] In 1852, Rousseau petitioned the emperor Napoleon III to protect the forest from further devastation, citing the tragic destruction of the old trees, "which for artists are the source from which they derive their inspiration, their joy, and their future, and which are for all visitors venerable souvenirs of past ages."[19]

Le Gray made several other striking photographs of individual trees, such as a giant hollow oak with branches that furl outward, forming a delicate, twisting canopy that echoes the cropping of the print (pl. 39). Evocative and sophisticated, this stately portrait of a venerable tree also signals the place of photography in the forest, for visible in the background at left stands the carriage that Le Gray used to transport his equipment. Although Le Gray did not identify the tree, it may very well be the poetically named La Reine Blanche (Snow White), a hollow oak that was beloved by artists not only for its dramatic spray of branches but also for its large cavity, which evidently provided convenient storage for painting equipment, studies, and other necessary gear.[20]

Noting both Le Gray's fascination with individual trees and his evident desire to adhere closely to Denecourt's circuits, Eugenia Parry Janis has suggested that Le Gray "may have envisioned a public for his pictures, which was none other than Denecourt's own."[21] But of course Le Gray also had other audiences in mind, in particular the "chaotically emerging field" of French photographers, critics, and patrons.[22] For Le Gray and other photographers, the forest—and especially the ways in which light played across and through its dense interior and variegated topography—offered a new set of visual possibilities that resonated with the aims of those who sought to define photography as an art of selection and pictorial intelligence. The challenges of photographing in the forest, notably determining an exposure that captured details within thick foliage without overexposing the sky, encouraged photographers to refine their technical skills and artistic sensibilities.[23] As photography critic and collector of Barbizon painting Paul Périer wrote in 1855, "Nothing is more suited to the resources and limits of our art than the interiors of forests, the adorable lacework of boughs, trunks, and trifles, where nature betrays her exquisite coquetry even in her extreme dishevelment."[24] That the forest was understood to be an inherently "photographic" subject may in part account for the efflorescence of photographers working there in the 1850s and 1860s, among them Olympe Aguado, Paul Berthier, Eugène Cuvelier, Constant Famin, Paul Gaillard, André Giroux, Alphonse Jeanrenaud, Charles Marville, and Charles Nègre.[25] But the draw of the forest was also indebted to the critical and commercial success of Barbizon landscape painting and the important role it played in the evolving discourse of art photography in France.

Barbizon Painting and the Rise of Landscape Photography in the 1850s

By the 1850s, landscape was one of the most discussed, practiced, and theorized genres within both French painting and photography. The publication of Pierre-Henri de Valenciennes' treatise *Eléments de perspective pratique, à l'usage des artistes* (1800)—which advocated plein-air painting (and mentioned the forests of France as rich sites for outdoor sketching)—signaled the beginning of a gradual shift in the practice of landscape painting in France from an idealized, pastoral vision of nature to one based on close observation and naturalistic depiction.[26] Although relegated to the bottom rungs of the French Academy's hierarchy of genres, by the 1840s naturalist, *sur le motif* landscape painting dominated at both the Salon and in the marketplace. By 1852 the painters Corot, Diaz, Rousseau, and Troyon, once symbols of an anti-academic movement, had been awarded the cross of the Légion d'honneur.

While the aesthetics of Barbizon painting inflected the work of many photographers, especially those who had originally been trained as painters, they also complemented a growing desire within the photographic community in France to define photography as an art based on the sensitive and selective rendering of material reality. To this end, the depiction of the landscape became the primary ground for the elaboration of new photographic ideals. Particularly within the elite circles of the Société Française de Photographie (founded in 1854), landscape photography was especially esteemed, for it signaled both a desirable distance from commercial concerns (generally associated with portraiture) and a knowing engagement with contemporary artistic practice.[27]

Certain landscapes were, however, more expressive of these new ideals than others. In an article on photography at the Exposition Universelle of 1855, Paul Périer, vice president of the newly formed Société Française de Photographie, described the evolution of taste in landscape from the domesticated and manicured to the rustic and disheveled. Instead of "flower beds and trellises," he wrote, photographers now turned toward "forests, fields, great clouds, and vast horizons."[28] The shift in taste, in other words, complemented (if it did not wholly mirror) the evolution of landscape painting in France away from the classicizing, pastoral mode toward more naturalistic, homegrown landscapes, particularly as explored in Barbizon painting.

It is no coincidence that the valorization of landscape photography in France emerged at the precise moment when Paris was being dramatically transformed by the vast upheavals and dislocations of Baron Georges-Eugène Haussmann's plans to modernize the city. As Nicholas Green has argued, the embrace of *natura naturans*, or "natural nature," in both painting and photography is inextricable from this history of rapid urban growth.[29] For Périer, nature served as the regenerative balm that soothed the pain of this urban chaos: "While the sight of cities and society choked with people seems designed to revive all these wounds, the harmonious and rich silence of nature and the intimacy of its many marvels elevate the soul to heights that make it immune to petty miseries."[30]

Périer's romanticized vision of nature as the "other" to culture was a common trope in the literature concerning Fontainebleau, and it fueled a fascination with the forest as a place where one meandered alone, accompanied solely by one's thoughts, a day's rations, and perhaps some sketching materials. Just as Senancour's novel *Obermann* dramatized the figure of the lone wanderer lost in poetic reverie amidst the forest, photographers incorporated this motif in their art in different ways. Marville, who first began to photograph in the early 1850s, executed a number of landscape studies for the Lille-based publisher Blanquart-Evrard, including a rustic portrayal of a man relaxing under a chestnut tree that suggests the protective, generative force of nature (fig. 2). By contrast, Famin, a professional photographer who specialized in landscape and animal studies, explored the awesome grandeur of the forest in a photograph that shows a diminutive, black-clad figure contemplating a pathway through the giant trees that Flaubert described as "astonishingly tall, like patriarchs or emperors" (pl. 48).

Fig. 2 Charles Marville, *Man Lying beneath a Chestnut Tree*, 1850–1853, salted paper print (Blanquart-Evrard process) from paper negative, 20.9 × 16.2 cm. Metropolitan Museum of Art, Harris Brisbane Dick Fund, 1946

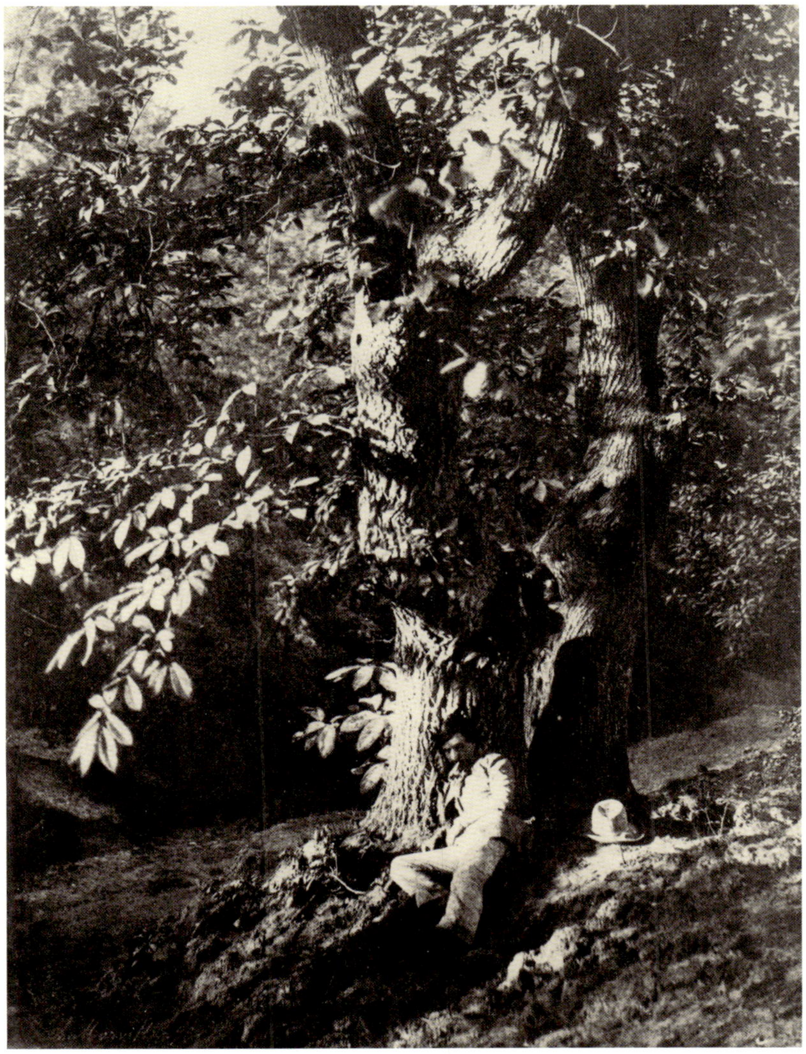

In one of Famin's most romantic images, a man grasping a walking stick pauses to behold the still waters of one of the forest's beloved marshes, the Mare aux Fées (pl. 32).[31] The figure is Théophile-Narcisse Chauvel, a landscape painter, etcher, and avid collector of photographs, many of them studies made in the forest by Famin, Charles Bodmer, Marville, Achille Quinet, and others.[32] The scope of Chauvel's activities as an artist, tourist, and patron of photography testifies to the manifold interactions between the different media that flourished in the forest.

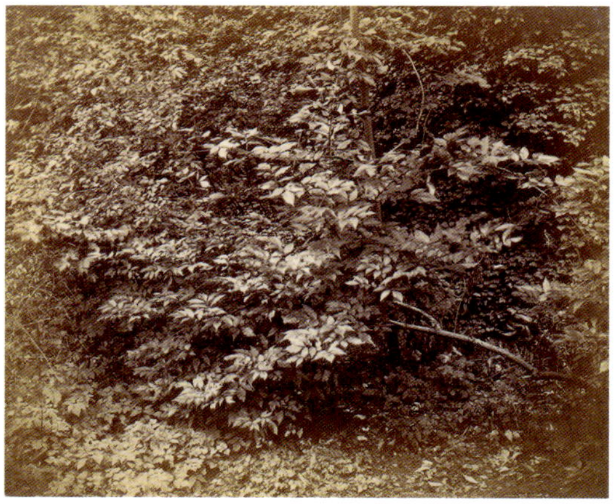

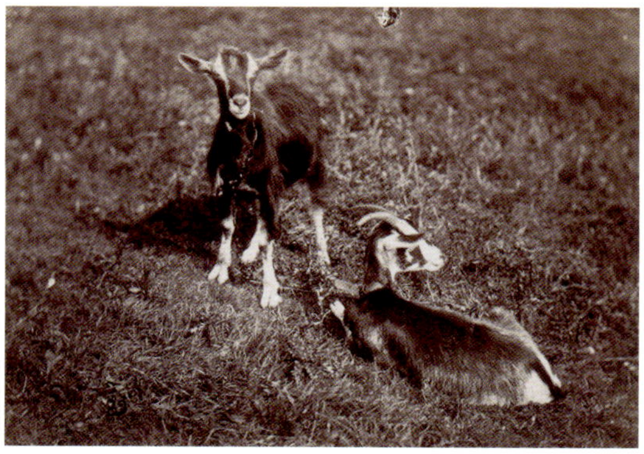

Fig. 3 Unknown photographer, *Leaf Study*, 1876, albumen print, 20.2 × 26 cm. Musée d'Orsay, Paris

Fig. 4 Attributed to Constant Famin, *Two Goats*, 1880, albumen print, 9.6 × 13.9 cm. Musée d'Orsay, Paris

Colleagues and Collaborators

For a number of artists working in the forest, painting and photography were corollary practices. André Giroux—the brother of Alphonse-Gustave Giroux and a silent partner in his brother's firm, Giroux et cie., which manufactured daguerreotype cameras starting in 1839—is primarily known for his landscape paintings, though more recently his photographic work has gained attention.[33] Despite his early contact with photography, Giroux did not practice the medium until about 1853, when he began to make harmoniously composed landscapes described by one critic as "ready-made small paintings" in which "nature seems to have posed for him, and taken it upon itself to compose these charming studies."[34] Using his skills as a painter, Giroux often obtained striking effects through retouching both negative and print, a fact that did not escape Ernst Lacan, who noted in *La Lumière*:

> **M. Giroux is a talented painter. If one did not know this, it would be easy to guess it by examining his photographic landscapes. . . . Numerous incidents of retouching have sharpened and firmed up the often indistinct outline of the trees, with their leaves that tremble at the slightest breath of wind. . . . The works are thus both drawings and photographic prints, so they have a special character about them. . . . In the final analysis, this is the important point, and the artist must be permitted to employ all the means at his disposal to depict the appearance of nature with all possible truth and charm.**[35]

"Painterly" in terms of production as well as composition, Giroux's picturesque landscapes frequently evoked references to the work of Barbizon artists; Lacan, for example, compared his work to that of Jules Dupré and Rousseau.

Such comparisons between landscape photography and Barbizon painting were commonplace. To a critic writing in 1857, one of Le Gray's photographs of "a tree splendidly illuminated in the foreground" seemed to have been "painted by Diaz in one of his greatest moments."[36] Writing of a chestnut tree photographed by Henri Le Secq, Périer claimed it could "astonish Rousseau himself, Dupré, and Diaz, and remind them of the great days of Barbizon."[37] Other photographers garnered similar praise, including Alphonse Jeanrenaud, whose delicate rendering of a rock-strewn, curving pathway seems to invite the viewer to follow the trail into the forest (pl. 56). Using the term *paysagiste*, a label generally reserved for painters, Lacan praised Jeanrenaud's work as possessing "to a high degree a feeling for nature which constitutes true landscapists."[38]

Just as many photographers had been trained as painters and were acutely aware of the currents of contemporary landscape painting, some of the leading landscape painters in France, including Corot, Millet, and Courbet, collected photography, especially in the form of the photographic study called the *étude d'après nature* (study from life, or nature study).[39] Ranging from rustic landscape studies and seemingly unadorned, highly descriptive renderings of flora to more prosaic subjects—such as farm animals who refused to hold still for the long poses required by painters—these photographic corollaries to the plein-air sketch at once drew upon and complemented the shift in Barbizon painting from compositions created with a distinct point of view toward landscapes that treated each element of nature, from ground to sky, with equal attention (figs. 3 and 4).

Accessibility was partly the key to the étude's popularity, many of which were published by Blanquart-Evrard in two albums titled *Photographic Studies* and *Studies and Landscapes* (1853–1854). The photographs were often unsigned, and many were given simple titles (landscape, river scene, forest, tree) that downplayed specific geographical identity to create visual typologies of nature that drew upon both picturesque and topographic conventions (fig. 5). Far from mere raw material for artists, these studies, Lacan argued in *La Lumière*, actually helped educate viewers to see and better understand the new schools of landscape painting so that "even the least artistic eye will perfectly understand Th[éodore] Rousseau, by studying the beautiful *Forest* of Mr. Le Secq."[40]

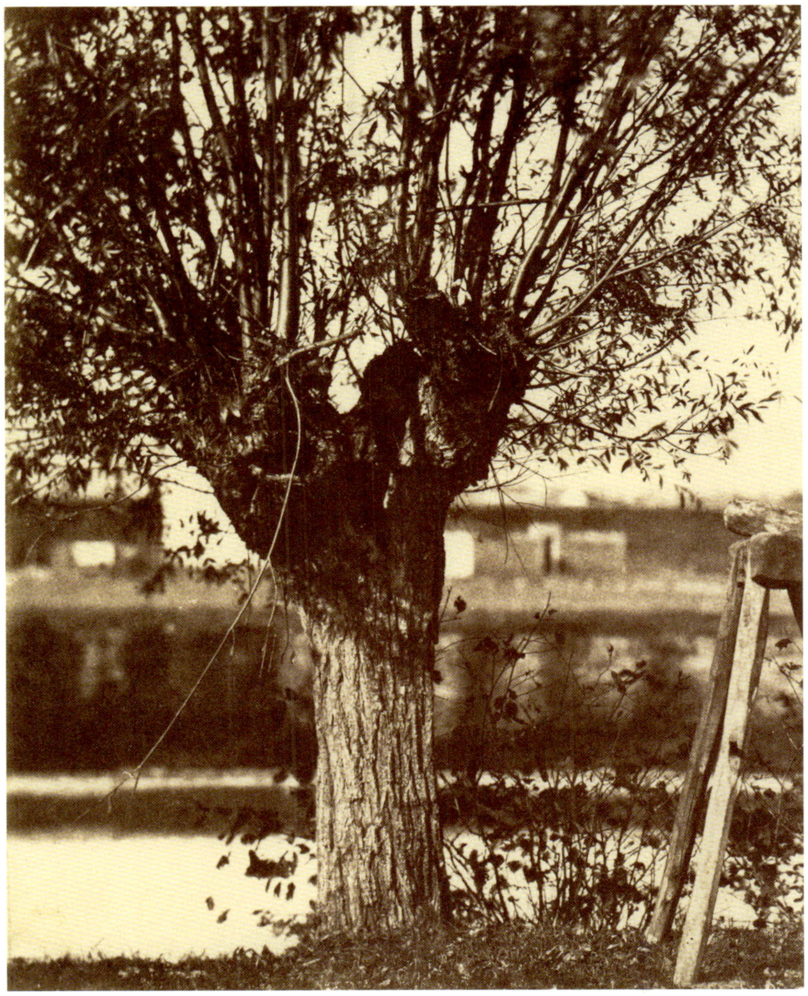

Fig. 5 Louis Désire Blanquart-Evrard, publisher, *Tree*, 1853, salted paper print, 21.3 × 17.3 cm. The J. Paul Getty Museum, Los Angeles

Although Blanquart-Evrard ceased publishing in 1855, the vogue for photographic nature studies continued in the 1860s and 1870s. Not all focused on landscape per se; an extraordinary series made in Barbizon by "Giraudon's artist"—a painter commissioned by the publisher Giraudon to make photographs of peasants—depicts women, children, and occasionally men posing with their tools and resting against bales of hay or engaging in agricultural activity.[41] Combining immediacy and artifice to great effect, the photographs attest to the cultural and artistic fascination with the figure of the peasant in nineteenth-century French art. In particular, the subtly eroticized representations of young peasant women in passive, nonthreatening poses present the countryside as feminine and welcoming, a trope that was common in late-nineteenth-century literature concerning rural subjects (see pls. 74, 76, 77, and 79).[42] As carefully composed as any pastel by Millet, the prints were sold to painters both in Barbizon (Chauvel, for example, purchased pl. 76) and in Paris, where Giraudon's business was located.

The most direct exchange between painters and photographers in and around the Forest of Fontainebleau took the form of the *cliché-verre* (literally "glass negative," though the term also refers to the print made from the negative). Essentially a hybrid of photography and printmaking, the cliché-verre process involves coating a glass plate with an opaque substance (usually collodion, smoke, or printer's ink), using a needle to scratch a design into that matrix, and contact printing the plate (which acts as a negative) onto sensitized paper.[43] William Henry Fox Talbot first conceived the process in the 1830s, but Adalbert Cuvelier, a merchant, landscape painter, and amateur photographer, independently rediscovered it with the painters Constant Dutilleux and Léandre Grandguillaume in 1853. The trio formed the center of an important circle of landscape artists working in Arras during the 1850s.[44] In April 1853, Cuvelier and Dutilleux introduced the technique to Corot who executed sixty-six clichés-verre over the next two decades, refining and exploring the medium's potential in a variety of ways. Characterized by remarkably free and open handling, most of Corot's clichés-verre are rapidly sketched landscapes occasionally enlivened with the presence of small figures, as in *The Hermit's Woods*, a "souvenir" of Italy that may have been inspired by his work in the Forest of Fontainebleau (fig. 6). Drawn to the fluidity and relative freedom of the technique, Corot left the task of printing from the negative to his colleagues in Arras, including Adalbert Cuvelier, Dutilleux, Grandguillaume, and the photographer and lithographer Charles Desavary.

While Arras was the center of cliché-verre production, the technique was practiced by other artists working in the forest, including Daubigny, Dutilleux, Jacque, Millet, Rousseau, and the little-known Adolphe-André Wacquez, an engraver and landscape painter who exhibited Fontainebleau subjects at the Salon. Wacquez' mastery of the cliché-verre process is ably demonstrated in *The Bodmer Oak at Bas-Bréau*, a remarkable rendering of the oak named for the painter Karl Bodmer (pl. 44). The agitated handling and the fantastic, tentacle-like branches that fill the entire frame of the work beg comparison not only with Rousseau's lively etching *The Rock Oak (Forest of Fontainebleau)* and Claude Monet's *Bodmer Oak, Fontainebleau Forest* (1865) but also to the photographs of Adalbert Cuvelier's son Eugène, in particular his magnificent *Beech Tree near Bodmer Oak*, which was made in nearly the same spot in the forest during the early 1860s (pls. 42, 43, and 60).

Eugène Cuvelier had in fact experimented with the cliché-verre process in Arras, where he worked alongside his father. In the early 1850s, Adalbert photographed with great sensitivity and technical proficiency views of Arras, rustic farm scenes, and contemplative portraits of acquaintances and workers, such as a burly blacksmith perched on a barrel (fig. 7).[45] For Eugène as for Adalbert, photography and painting were contiguous practices. In Arras, Eugène studied with the landscape painters Dutilleux and Xavier Dourlens, and in 1856 and 1857, he made several trips to the Forest of Fontainebleau where he registered as a painter at the Auberge Ganne.[46]

The trips to Barbizon may have had another inspiration, for on 7 March 1859, with Corot, Millet, and Rousseau in attendance, Eugène Cuvelier married the innkeeper's daughter, Louise Ganne. It was after this move to Barbizon and through his daily contact with the forest that Cuvelier's extraordinary talent as a photographer emerged. Over the next decade, he sustained a passionate engagement with the forest, photographing its diverse topography in all seasons, primarily for his own pleasure.[47] The resulting body of work forms a visually stunning, historically sensitive interpretation of the forest. Made at a crucial moment in Fontainebleau's history, Cuvelier's photographs build a portrait of the forest not simply as a beautiful escape or series of natural wonders but also as a complex, aggregate ecology shaped by the interplay of environmental, cultural, economic, and artistic forces.

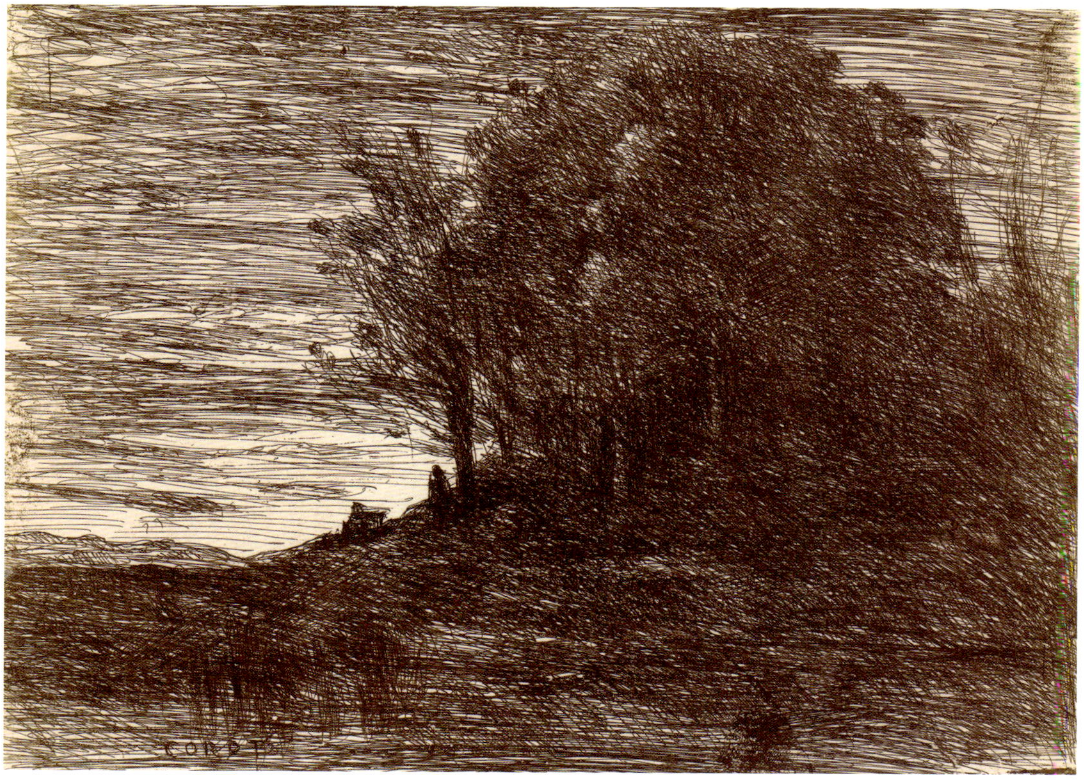

Fig. 6 Jean-Baptiste-Camille Corot, *The Hermit's Woods*, or *The Banks of Lake Trasimène*, 1858, salted paper print from cliché-verre negative, 16.4 × 23 cm. National Gallery of Art, Washington, Gift of Dan and Mary Solomon and Patrons' Permanent Fund, 2006

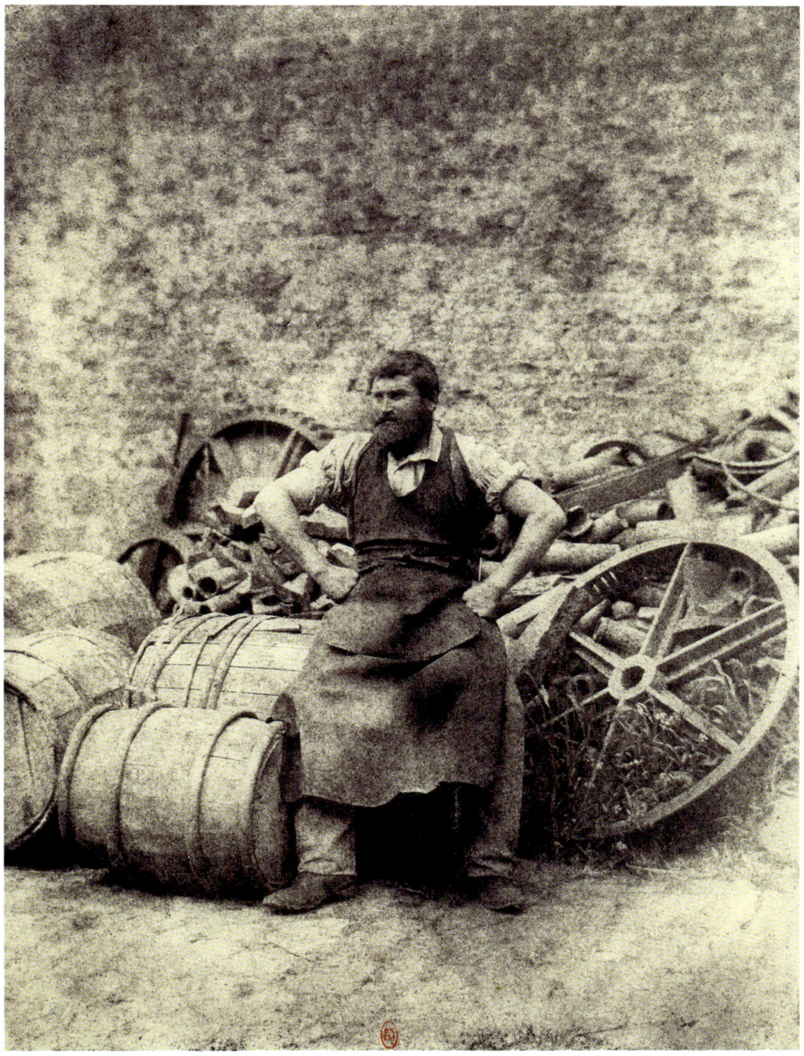

Fig. 7 Adalbert Cuvelier, *Blacksmith*, c. 1852, salted paper print from paper negative, 28 × 22 cm. Bibliothèque Nationale de France

Eugène Cuvelier: Fontainebleau's "Inside Man"

Cuvelier's marriage to Louise Ganne in 1859 placed him in the very center of artistic activity in Barbizon. The Auberge Ganne was the preferred rendezvous for artists wishing to work in Fontainebleau, and it was an easy walk to many of the *délices de la forêt* (delights of the forest) promoted and packaged by Denecourt. For Cuvelier, as for other artists working in the forest, particular sites were especially beckoning. The nearby Bas-Bréau, with its magnificent old-growth oaks and beech trees, the dramatic rock formations of the Gorges d'Apremont, and the "savage" deserts of the Macherin appear frequently in his oeuvre. Visually complex, these sites were also accessible, thanks in part to Denecourt's system of painted blue arrows that guided visitors to the most popular sites along the three hundred kilometers of trails he established through the forest. Although a decree by Napoleon III protected many of these sites from logging, they were not safe from the ravages of tourism—to the great distress of Rousseau and others who felt that Fontainebleau was being transformed, tamed, mapped, modified, and commercialized by an ever-increasing influx of visitors, Sunday painters, and, increasingly, professional photographers like Alfred Briquet, Famin, Quinet, and others.[48]

Unlike those photographers, Cuvelier neither published nor sold his work commercially. Although he participated in several exhibitions of the Société Française de Photographie (and became a member in 1855), he assumed the identity of a cultivated amateur for whom photography was a passionate avocation.[49] He maintained especially close ties with the Barbizon painters, including Rousseau and Millet. The latter greatly admired Cuvelier's photography, writing to Rousseau in 1861, "you must have seen Eugène Cuvelier: he showed me a few very beautiful photographs, some taken in his region and others in the forest. They are taken with taste and in the most beautiful places, all destined to disappear."[50]

Cuvelier was thus at once an insider who lived in Barbizon and knew the forest (and its most famous painters) intimately and an outsider who worked on the margins of photographic practice in the 1860s. Moreover, as a well-to-do provincial, his orientation was neither fully metropolitan (which is to say, Parisian), nor was it rural or working class. This complex regional, class, and artistic identity shaped his photographic work in subtle ways. In contrast to the painters and photographers who lived in Paris and worked in the forest during spring, summer, or fall for a week or two, Cuvelier lived in Barbizon and photographed the forest year-round, often venturing out in inclement weather. He was especially intrigued by the possibilities of rendering the changeable effects of weather and light, as evidenced by his moody, mysterious photograph of a storm (pl. 96). In other works, such as the lacy and delicate *Pathway in the Forest of Fontainebleau in the Snow* (pl. 91), Cuvelier rose admirably to the challenge of photographing bright snow scenes, a favorite—if also vexing—subject for photographers, since an exposure that was long enough to register detail in dark areas, such as foliage, usually meant that the snowy elements turned a blank, undifferentiated white. Cuvelier's use of the paper negative and salted paper print processes also enabled him to render with great sensitivity and

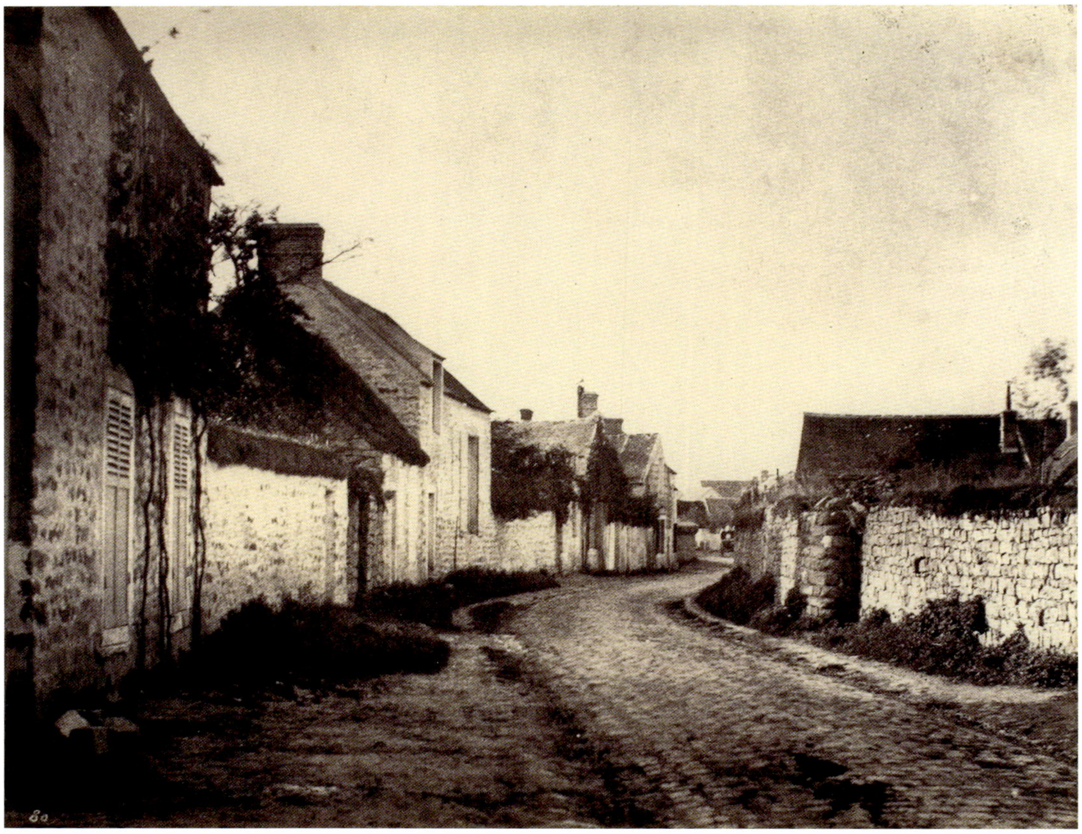

Fig. 8 Eugène Cuvelier, *Barbizon*, c. 1863, salted paper print from paper negative, 20.32 × 25.94 cm. Prentice and Paul Sack Photographic Trust of the San Francisco Museum of Modern Art

subtlety the ephemeral effects of changing light, such as the diaphanous mist that blankets the leaf-covered interior in *The Forest of Fontainebleau* (pl. 99). In many of his photographs, Cuvelier exploited the salted paper print's tendency to render soft, delicate, and nearly *sfumato* tones of violet and gray that could convey equally the quiet illumination of a fog-suffused dawn or the cool, waning light of approaching dusk.

By the early 1860s, when Cuvelier was photographing the forest, the paper negative process had been almost wholly superseded by the more rapid collodion negative process, which yielded sharply defined prints with high-keyed detail. While he used collodion negatives when the occasion demanded it, his continued allegiance to the paper negative is unusual. In part, this may have been a practical decision, for he could prepare his negatives at home and thus traipse through the forest relatively unburdened. But it was also a deliberate aesthetic choice, one that hearkened back to the first generation of French photographers who worked with the paper negative. Further, his use of the technique signaled a departure from commercial photographers, who generally favored the collodion negative process.

Like other artists working in the Forest of Fontainebleau, Cuvelier occasionally photographed its renowned oaks, including the Bodmer and the Clovis. Yet he just as often avoided the highlights of the tourist circuits in order to explore the captivating visual dimensions of the forest and, in particular, the action of light across its tangled, patchwork surfaces. In the glorious *Beech Tree near Bodmer Oak*, for example, Cuvelier ignored the famous oak nearby, choosing instead to render with exquisite sensitivity the way light filtered through the beech's immense yet ethereally delicate skein of branches and leaves (pl. 42).

The strange topography of the many marshes in the forest also fascinated Cuvelier, whose *Belle-Croix* evokes the biological density of a primordial, swampy landscape where tree roots, "interlaced on the ground like veins," sink into a shimmering, mirrored surface (pl. 33).[51] By slightly overexposing the negative to create high contrast between light and dark masses, Cuvelier achieved a nearly hallucinatory wealth of detail that confuses boundaries between trees and water, ground and sky. The point of view is equally extraordinary, for the viewer is positioned amidst glistening puddles and riotous tree roots.

Cuvelier was particularly attentive to the processes of growth and destruction — both organic and man-made — in the forest. The somber, regal beauty of barren trees in *Carrefour de l'Epine* records the seasonal change that denuded the famous oak trees of their leaves in what was one of the most contested sites in the forest (pl. 90). While the proponents of clear-cutting and logging feared that the oaks were too old to reseed and believed that setting aside the Bas-Bréau and other old-growth areas would result in their imminent destruction, Rousseau, a supporter of protecting the forest at all costs, preferred that these "reminders of druidic times... be left to die tranquilly in peace."[52]

Although Cuvelier photographed the town of Barbizon, it seems he did not make images of its inhabitants, with the exception of a few portraits of his fellow artists. Unlike Famin's rustic, anecdotal photographs of farmers and village life (pls. 67 and 80), Cuvelier's photographs of Barbizon explore its everyday, banal aspects, including long, rutted roads, deserted streets, simple houses, and wooden gates opening onto uninhabited courtyards (fig. 8). Cuvelier was especially intrigued by roads that marked the boundary between forest and town, such as the long-furrowed path on the edge of Barbizon that was braced on one side by a ramshackle wood fence and on the other by piles of felled trees, possibly gathered for construction or firewood (pl. 65).

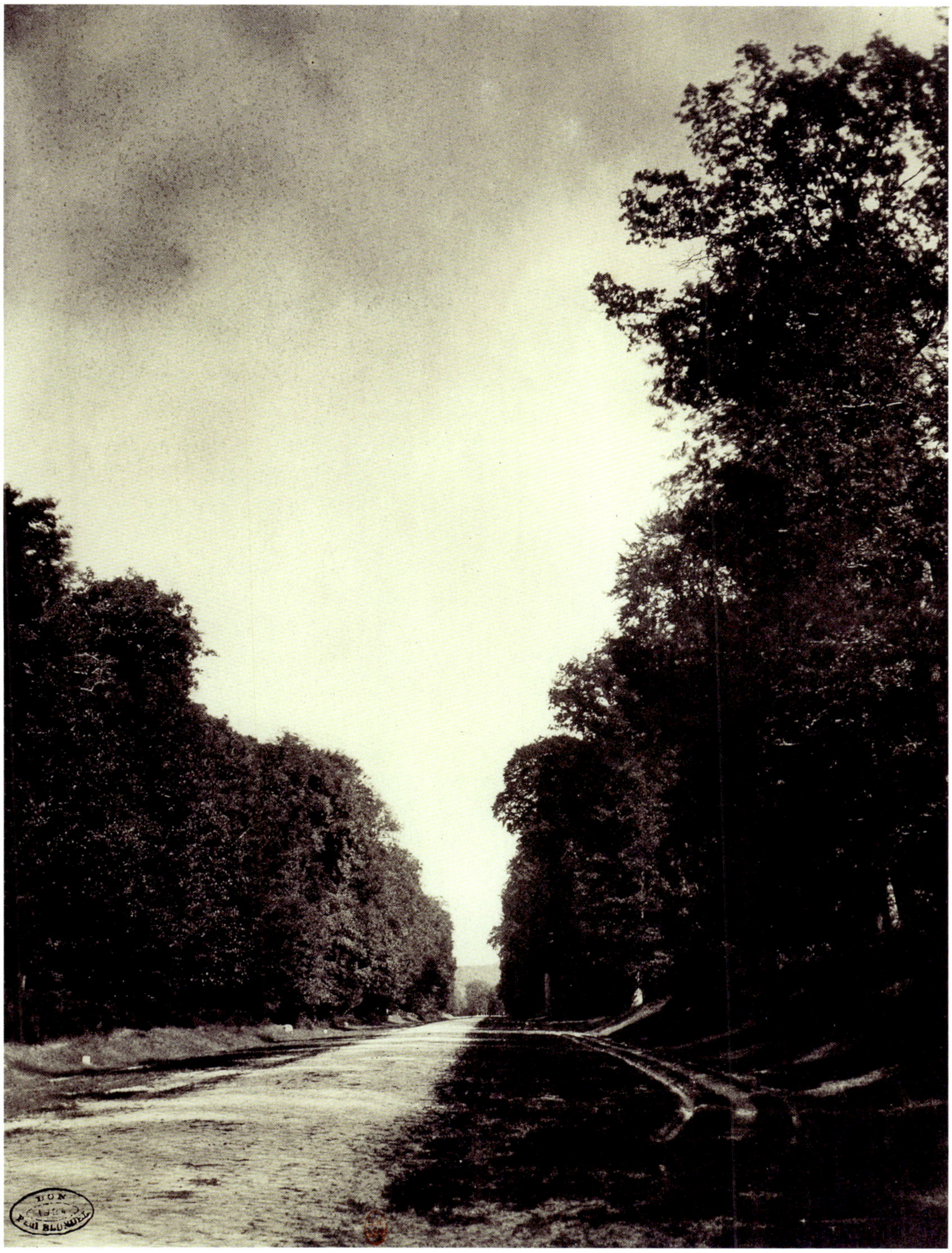

Fig. 9 Eugène Cuvelier, *The Pavé de Chailly*, c. 1863, salted paper print from paper negative, 26.9 × 20.7 cm. Bibliothèque Nationale de France

Like Le Gray before him, Cuvelier used several angles to explore the striking contrast of colossal trees flanking the long, flat, seemingly endless Pavé de Chailly, the most important road traversing the forest and the direct route to and from Paris (fig. 9). The road was an important motif for painters as well, including Corot, Rousseau, and Monet, whose *Pavé de Chailly*, painted from nearly the same vantage point as that of Cuvelier's photograph, is similarly constructed out of veering orthogonals and bold contrasts between shadows and highlights (pl. 13).[53]

The paved road, which was the symbolic connection between Paris and the town of Chailly, also encoded the political economy of the forest. The paving stones themselves had come from quarries in the forest, and the road also served as the primary route for the transport of many tons of paving stones to Paris, where they were laid down by the millions along Haussmann's broad new boulevards.[54] The "prodigious consumption" of paving stones in Paris and, more generally, the toll of the quarries on the forest was frequently lamented by artists, writers, and many visitors who sought refuge from city life in the forest; one author noted that in addition to the noise from excavations and the vehicles carrying stones, it was only a matter of time before the exploitation of the quarries resulted in "the total and definitive destruction of the rocks" that gave the forest its "very strange and picturesque character."[55]

The desolation and barrenness described in the preceding lament is evoked in Cuvelier's stark photograph of the quarry at Macherin (pl. 62). Here, a narrow, curving pathway flanked by haphazard piles of sandstone blocks slopes upward, leading the viewer's eye to a dramatic, unexpected void. Cuvelier's sensitivities to the political economy of the forest are also manifested in other photographs that record the destructive effects of logging—one of the most important and contested industries there.

Though Cuvelier was keenly aware of human intervention in the forest, figures rarely appear in his work. A notable exception is the photograph of a solitary figure looking out over the vast, rocky Gorges de Franchard (pl. 9). The jumbled rocks of Franchard were, of course, one of the most visited sites in the forest, their antediluvian chaos extolled by Denecourt who saw "everywhere traces of a flood... the image of breathtaking disorder."[56] The motif of figures amidst the tumult of those primordial rocks was a common one; Corot's *An Artist Passing through a Chaos of Rocks at Fontainebleau*, for example (see Jones essay, fig. 1), epitomizes the romantic image of man—here, the artist—immersed in nature. In Cuvelier's *Franchard*, the figure standing on the rocks and looking out upon the barren landscape appears less as a symbol of romantic unity with nature and more as a self-reflexive cipher for the photographer (or tourist) as viewer, at a slight remove from the landscape he studies. Cuvelier thematized attentive observation again in the brooding, melancholic photograph of two men atop boulders, surveying damage caused by a recent fire (fig. 10). Like the photographer himself, these men bear witness to the lifecycle of the forest.

Although shaped by tourism and, more broadly, the fascination with landscape representation during the mid-nineteenth century, Cuvelier's photographs refuse metropolitan fantasies of rural life and a *natura naturans*—or a return to a primal, unspoiled, prelapsarian nature—in favor of a sustained inquiry into the complex visual and ecological identity of the forest. If Cuvelier's photographic practice was partly driven by the desire to reclaim the forest from tourism and its regimes of representation, the body of work he produced rendered the forest at once more transparent and more complex. He neither wholly shunned the well-trodden sites nor portrayed the forest as a pristine space untouched by human invention. Rather, he photographed its complex ecosystem through the eyes of a passionate yet steadfast observer. "Taken with taste and in the most beautiful places," Cuvelier's photographs of the Forest of Fontainebleau form a richly evocative, composite portrait of a place that was, in the words of Millet, "destined to disappear."

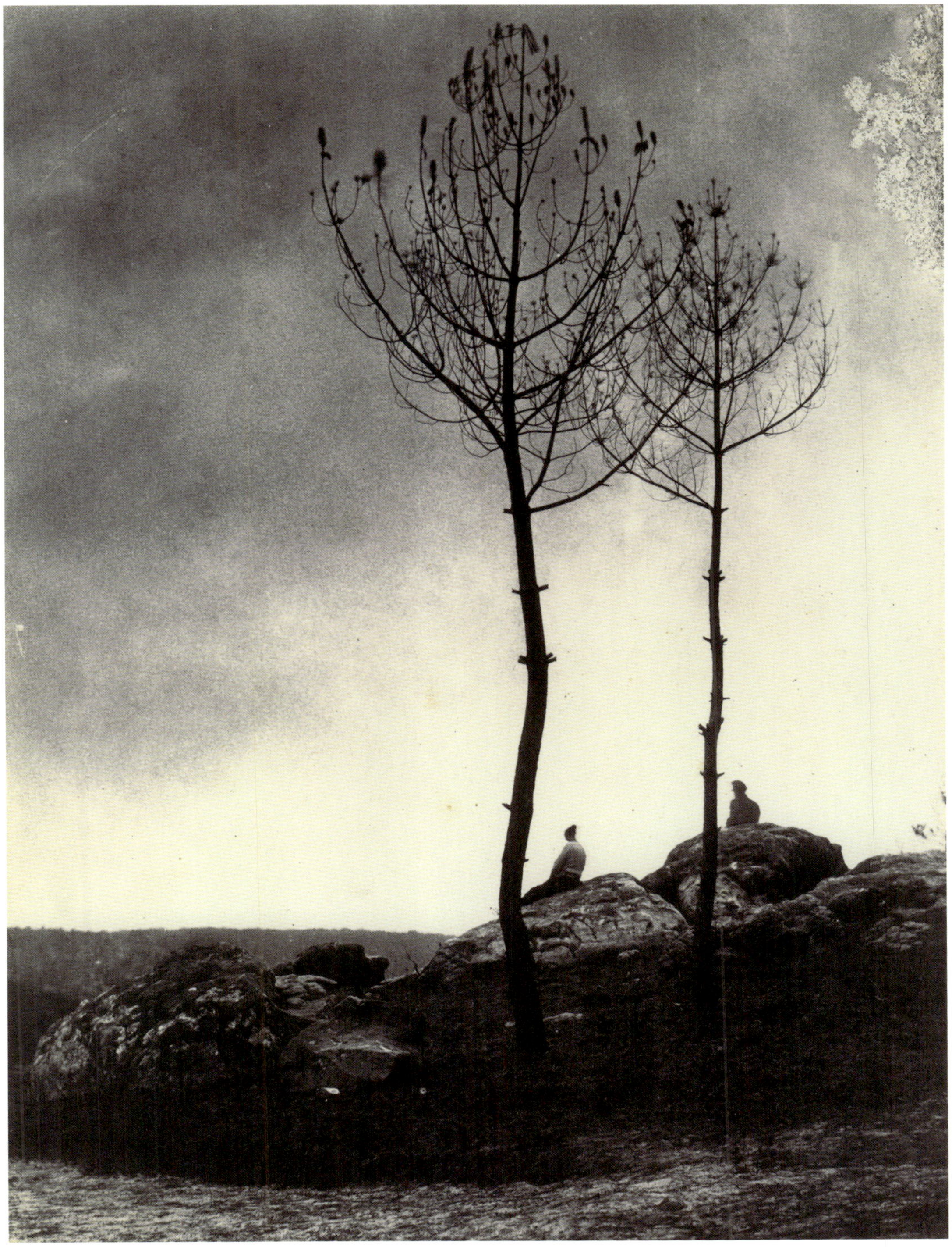

Fig. 10 Eugène Cuvelier, *Near the Cavern, after the Fire,* early 1860s, salted paper print from paper negative, 26 × 19.8 cm. Metropolitan Museum of Art, The Herbert and Nannette Rothschild Memorial Fund Gift, in memory of Judith Rothschild, 1996

HELGA AURISCH

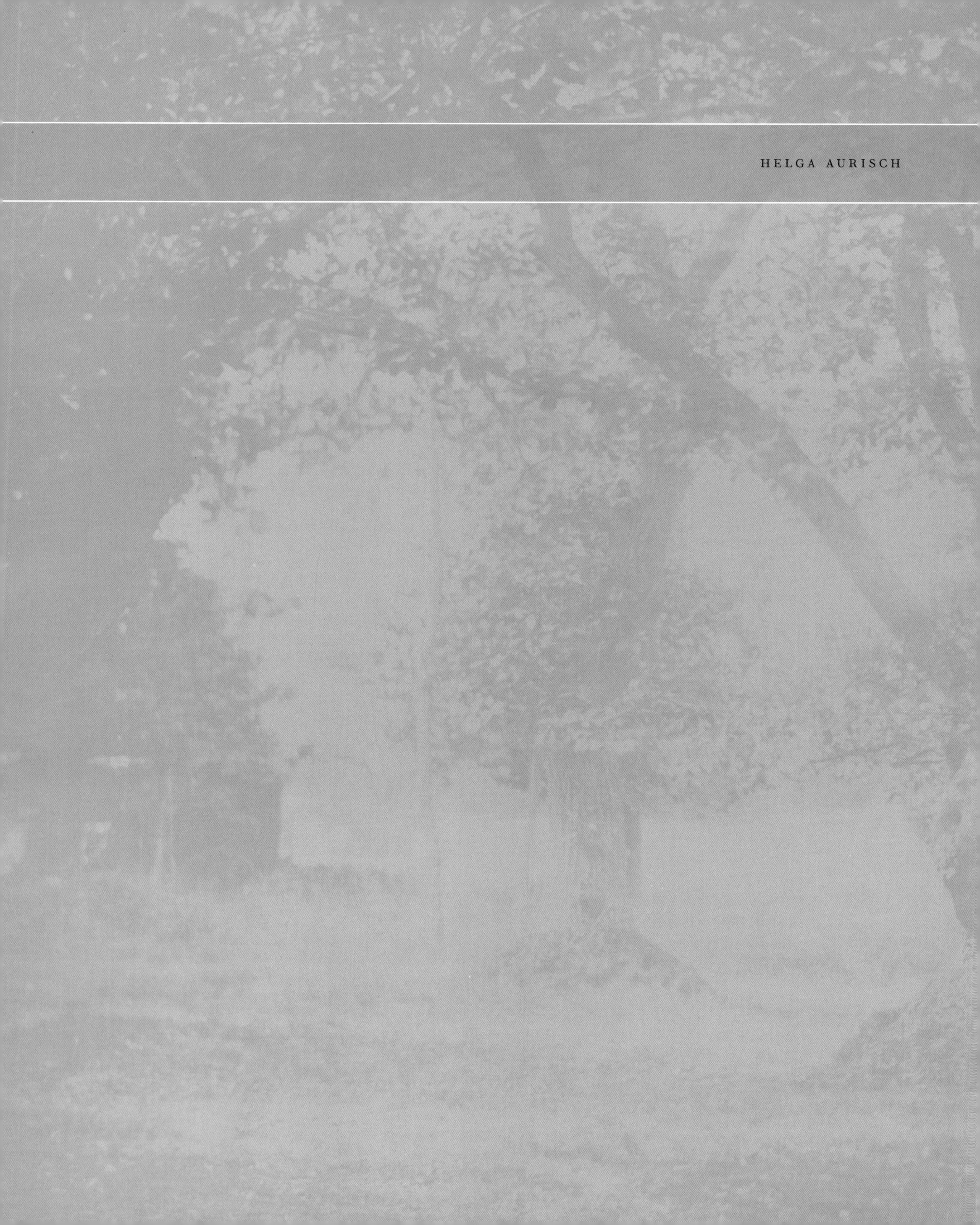

The Impressionists at Fontainebleau

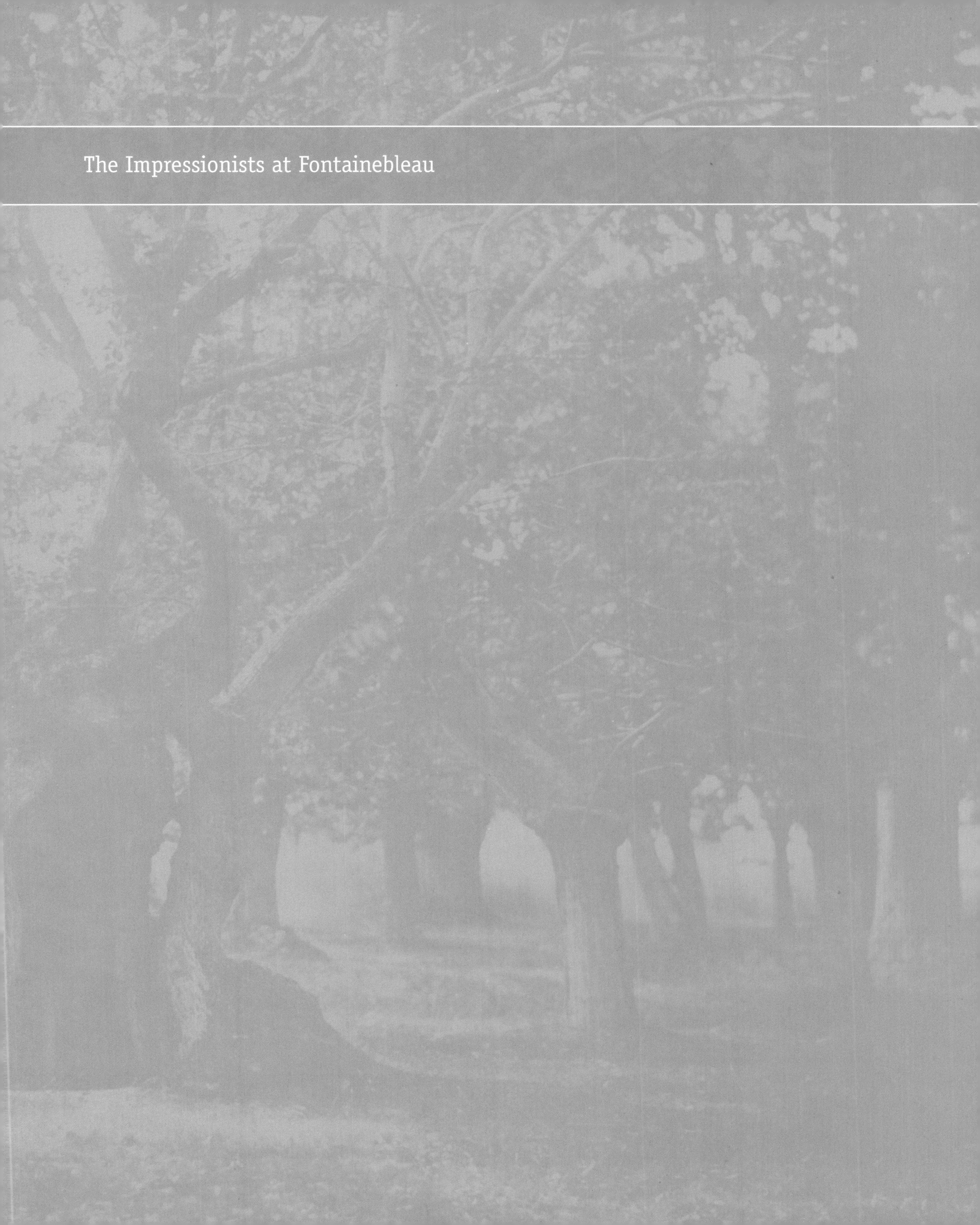

The Impressionists at Fontainebleau

Right Detail of pl. 68

The last group of artists to seek out the Forest of Fontainebleau as their "natural studio" was a handful of young students who had met at the studio of Charles Gleyre: Frédéric Bazille, Claude Monet, Auguste Renoir, and Alfred Sisley. They came individually and in groups, spending many spring and summer months throughout the 1860s living and working in the villages of Chailly, Barbizon, or Marlotte. They sketched and painted, modeled for one another, and discovered anew the manifold beauties of this already well-established crucible of French landscape painting. Although much research has been devoted to each of these artists and numerous scholars have reiterated their respective relationships with the painters of the Barbizon School, no systematic comparison of the works created by the impressionist painters in the Forest of Fontainebleau has been undertaken to date.[1] Yet it is a particularly gratifying effort, for it was here and during these years that these young artists, some taking their first tentative steps in landscape painting, began to develop their individual styles. Conscious of the achievements of their elders and often influenced by them, they went on to new experiments, laying the foundations for the style that would be known as impressionism.

Frédéric Bazille

According to the register of the Auberge Ganne, the popular artists' hostelry in Barbizon, Alfred Sisley was the first of this group to make his way to the Forest of Fontainebleau in 1861, but unfortunately there are no artistic records of his early foray into the forest.[2] In fact, it is Bazille's small oil sketch *Study of Trees* of 1863 (private collection) that is the first of the series of works by the impressionists in the forest. In this work, massive boulders dominate the foreground, while the barren branches of a group of trees spread across the canvas like a filigree screen. The dark earth tones and black branches are set off by a light blue sky enlivened with cottony clouds. The composition is somewhat awkwardly weighted toward the left, and the foreground seems disproportionately heavy. These discrepancies of scale and unevenness of execution attest to an as yet unskilled hand, and indeed it is one of Bazille's first attempts in oil.

After joining Gleyre's studio immediately upon his arrival in Paris in November 1862, Bazille was required to limit himself to drawing for the first few months. As late as March 1863 he wrote, "I have not touched paint yet," but just a few weeks later he took this decisive step during his first sojourn in the Forest of Fontainebleau.[3] He may have been following Gleyre's advice to "paint outside the studio," which has often been interpreted as an encouragement to work out of doors.[4] He had joined Monet, Renoir, and Sisley as they made their way to Chailly in April. From there, Bazille wrote to his parents that he was working on some tree studies, a statement seen as confirmation for a secure dating of *Study of Trees*. Although the sketch is in many respects a modest work, it is symptomatic of the plein-air practice that the young impressionists followed from their earliest visits to the forest, inspired no doubt by their precursors Jean-Baptiste-Camille Corot, Narcisse-Virgile Diaz de la Peña, and Théodore Rousseau. Bazille wrote further that he was working on six or seven paintings during his first visit, gratefully mentioning the help he received from the much more experienced Monet.[5] None of these works seems to have survived, although Dianne Pitman argues that *Forest of Fontainebleau* (pl. 16) dates from this visit.[6] This quiet scene includes a large tree on the left, spreading its branches toward the center of the composition, while a small path leads the eye into the middle distance where a group of trees and bushes establishes the horizon line. The warm rays of sunlight falling between the trees enliven the masses of variegated green foliage, whereas the light blue summer sky emphasizes the feeling of serenity arising from the woods.

Although Monet undoubtedly offered technical advice at this early stage in Bazille's career, it is Gustave Courbet whose style Bazille emulates in *Forest of Fontainebleau*. Bazille had met the older painter in 1863 and as a youth in Montpellier had

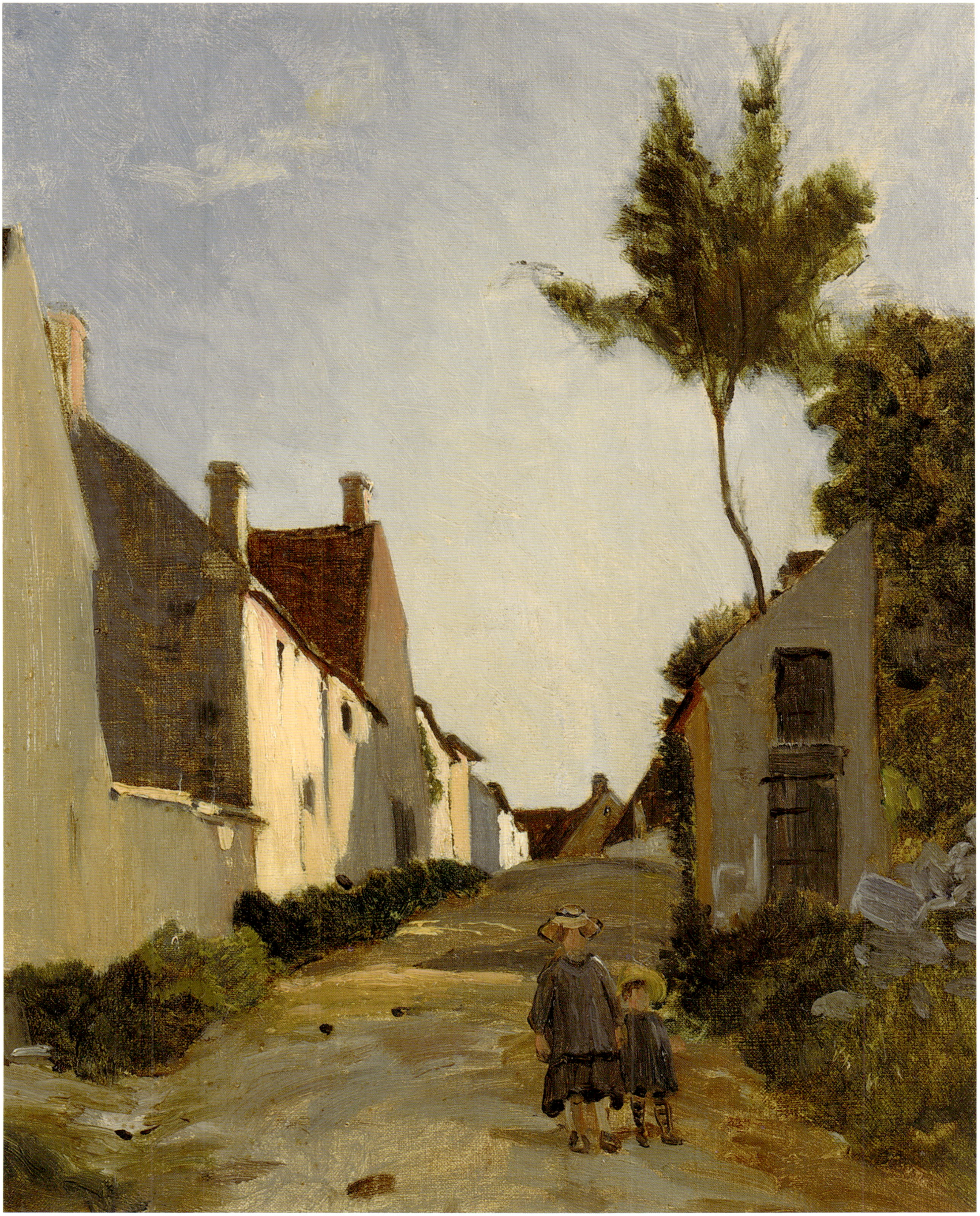

known Courbet's oeuvre through the collection of the latter's patron Alfred Bruyas.[7] It is above all the direct approach to the subject and the heavy impasto that Bazille learned from Courbet.[8] He still lacked Courbet's dexterity and audacity, but his attempt at characterizing the foliage of each tree with differentiated brushstrokes and his use of alternating passages of light and shade in a solidly composed overall view nonetheless reveal a keen understanding of Courbet's work. The difference between this painting and the earlier sketch is indeed so remarkable that François Daulte and Michel Schulman date the canvas as part of Bazille's output from the late summer of 1865.[9] Much supports this later date, especially the fact that Bazille, having abandoned his study of medicine in 1864, was able to devote himself exclusively to painting.

Bazille's final visit to the Forest of Fontainebleau in 1865 was brief but extraordinarily productive. Monet had already arrived in Chailly in May and had asked Bazille to join him there. Although possible, there is no record of a spring visit to Fontainebleau by Bazille,[10] who was very busy with a commission and seems to have remained in Paris until August, when he finally responded to his friend's ever more anxious entreaties.[11] Monet was feeling increasingly desperate, because he was depending on Bazille to be a model for his ambitious *Déjeuner sur l'herbe* (figs. 1–3; pl. 10). Bazille, although quite willing to help, never understood the urgency Monet felt regarding the completion of this painting. As he himself enjoyed the luxury of his father's financial support, he never had to live by his art. He may also have been naturally more inclined to indolence than the driven and industrious Monet. Indeed, perhaps it was Monet's influence that prompted Bazille to work so assiduously that summer. It is astonishing that within a mere fortnight he was able to paint not only *Forest of Fontainebleau* but also *Landscape at Chailly* and *Valley in the Forest of Fontainebleau* as well as *Village Scene (Chailly)* and *The Improvised Field Hospital* and at the same time serve as a model for numerous figures in Monet's *Déjeuner sur l'herbe*.[12]

There are noticeable stylistic differences among these works, a typical phenomenon for a relatively inexperienced young artist seeking his way. As noted above, Bazille's great admiration for Courbet dominates his *Forest of Fontainebleau*, but a reference to Théodore Rousseau's russet tonality is also apparent.[13] Bazille's *Landscape at Chailly* (pl. 57), on the other hand, is remarkably close to the work of Diaz, especially *The Rocks of the Belle Epine, Barbizon* (pl. 51), which was completed almost twenty years earlier. The stark contrast of the intensely blue sky and russet foreground with the impressive boulders is similarly handled in both compositions.

While those canvases document Bazille's attentive study of the older styles, his *Valley in the Forest of Fontainebleau* (private collection) is noteworthy for its forward-looking, impressionist technique. The central motif of a group of trees, along with the entire landscape, is defined with a nervous, flickering brushwork that is far removed from other works he had painted that year. Yet another difference in style and approach can be seen in his charming plein-air study *Village Scene (Chailly)* (pl. 68). Picturesque villages at the edge of the forest had long been popular subjects, but Bazille did not depict the humble laboring peasants of Jean-François Millet. Only Jules Hereau's *Monsieur Lafontaine Visits Barbizon* from September 1859 (pl. 11) offers an earlier example of an informal village scene created in a comparably sketchy manner. Hereau captured Monsieur Lafontaine humorously perched on his small donkey, while Bazille portrayed two small children with sensitivity but completely without pathos. The simplified forms of the cottages in Bazille's work recall Corot's paintings of Italian villages, such as his *View of Volterra* from 1834 (Musée du Louvre, Paris), but the fluidity of Bazille's brushwork points decidedly toward his more impressionist production.

Bazille's most original work from his sojourns in the forest, however, is not a landscape, but an interior. In *The Improvised Field Hospital* (pl. 7), he depicted his friend Monet laid up in bed with an injured leg.[14] The composition is carefully constructed, with the canopied bed viewed from an angle and the bedding meticulously detailed. Bazille quite obviously delighted in rendering the many textures and patterns of the bed, carpet, and wallpaper, yet he focused on his suffering friend. As a former student of medicine, Bazille had conceived the ingenious contraption of the suspended water barrel and was clearly proud to capture it on canvas. Like Renoir's *Inn of Mother Anthony* (pl. 6), discussed below, this anecdotal scene gives us a glimpse of the everyday companionship enjoyed by these young artists working at Fontainebleau. Sadly, it is also the last of Bazille's paintings from the forest. In the few short years before his tragic death during the Franco-Prussian War in 1870, he did not return to the place where he not only had painted his first plein-air oil sketch but also had made enormous progress as a landscapist.

Claude Monet

Monet was undoubtedly the driving spirit behind the nascent impressionists' first trip to the Forest of Fontainebleau in 1863. The works of the Barbizon painters, especially those by Corot, Charles-François Daubigny, and Constant Troyon, had immediately impressed him when he saw them as a nineteen-year-old student during his first visit to the Paris Salon in 1859. He sought out Troyon for advice but refused to take his recommendation to enter the studio of Thomas Couture and apply himself to life-study classes. He opted instead for the much more liberal Académie Suisse, where Corot and Courbet had studied. His admiration for those artists not only continued but also soon extended to other Barbizon painters, including Decamps, Rousseau, Dupré, and Millet.[15] It had not abated when, upon his return from military service, he joined the studio of Charles Gleyre in late 1862. In order to follow in the footsteps of his idols, Monet urged his fellow students Bazille, Renoir, and Sisley to go to Fontainebleau at the earliest opportunity, the Easter holiday in April 1863.

The group's first trip to the Forest of Fontainebleau had the greatest impact on Monet. When the other artists dutifully returned to their studies in Paris after the Easter break, Monet, who was quite taken by the infinite charm of Chailly, stayed on until late May. Fontainebleau was the place where Monet, who had been raised on the rugged Normandy coast, first encountered the forest as a subject. Unfortunately, none of his works from this first campaign (assumed to have been "exploratory sketches") have survived, nor is there any record of Monet or his friends returning to Fontainebleau again in 1863. With the closing of Gleyre's studio in May 1864, however, they all returned in June of that year. Monet, the most eager to return, preceded the others in April.[16]

Monet's *Woodbearers in the Forest* of 1864 (Museum of Fine Arts, Boston) is one of his earliest extant paintings of a Fontainebleau subject.[17] Two small figures carrying heavy bundles of wood are advancing from the edge of the forest across a wide expanse of grass. Although Millet, who had made these poor wood gatherers the focus of several works, undoubtedly influenced Monet's choice of motif, for Monet the figures are incidental to the landscape.[18] While Monet rendered the foreground with broad brushstrokes, he used short flickering strokes for the vibrant golden foliage of the trees. The open brushwork gives this painting the appearance of a sketch, an impression that is contradicted by its firm X-shaped composition.[19] George Shackelford pointed to the painting's stylistic affinity with the works of Courbet, particularly his *Stream in the Forest*.[20] Yet despite a similar tonality, Monet achieved a lightness of touch that is unlike Courbet's and is already characteristic of his own later style.

Two further canvases from 1864, *Forest of Fontainebleau* (see Kelly essay, fig. 11) and *Road in the Forest* (private collection, Japan), are characterized by comparable open brushwork.[21] The same tree-lined road is the subject of both compositions and leads the eye deep into the background. The foreground in both instances is painted very summarily, making it appear out of focus. Virginia Spate argues that Monet could have learned this device either from Eugène Boudin, who used it in his small-scale works, or possibly even from the Japanese prints that Monet claimed to have discovered in the 1850s.[22] Like many works by the Barbizon painters—most notably those by Corot, Rousseau, or Millet—the larger and more finished *Forest of Fontainebleau* includes a small scene of people laboring in the forest. Men loading lumber onto a horse-drawn wagon was no doubt a common occurrence in nineteenth-century Fontainebleau, but their inclusion in Monet's landscape may be an allusion to the growing concerns about deforestation. Many of the Barbizon artists, Rousseau in particular, had vehemently petitioned against this practice for some time.[23] Monet submitted this painting to the Salon of 1866, where much to his delight it was accepted together with *Camille*, or *The Woman in a Green Dress* (Kunsthalle, Bremen).[24] His joy was not complete, however, for the work he had planned to submit—his intended chef d'oeuvre *Déjeuner sur l'herbe*—remained unfinished.

With the large-scale *Déjeuner*, Monet aspired to go beyond anything ever painted in the Forest of Fontainebleau, striving to outdo past masters as well as contemporaries. In this work—known today by virtue of an oil sketch at the Pushkin Museum, Moscow (fig. 1), a detail sketch at the National Gallery of Art in Washington (pl. 10), and two large fragments of the final version (figs. 2 and 3)—a dozen life-sized figures and one elegant

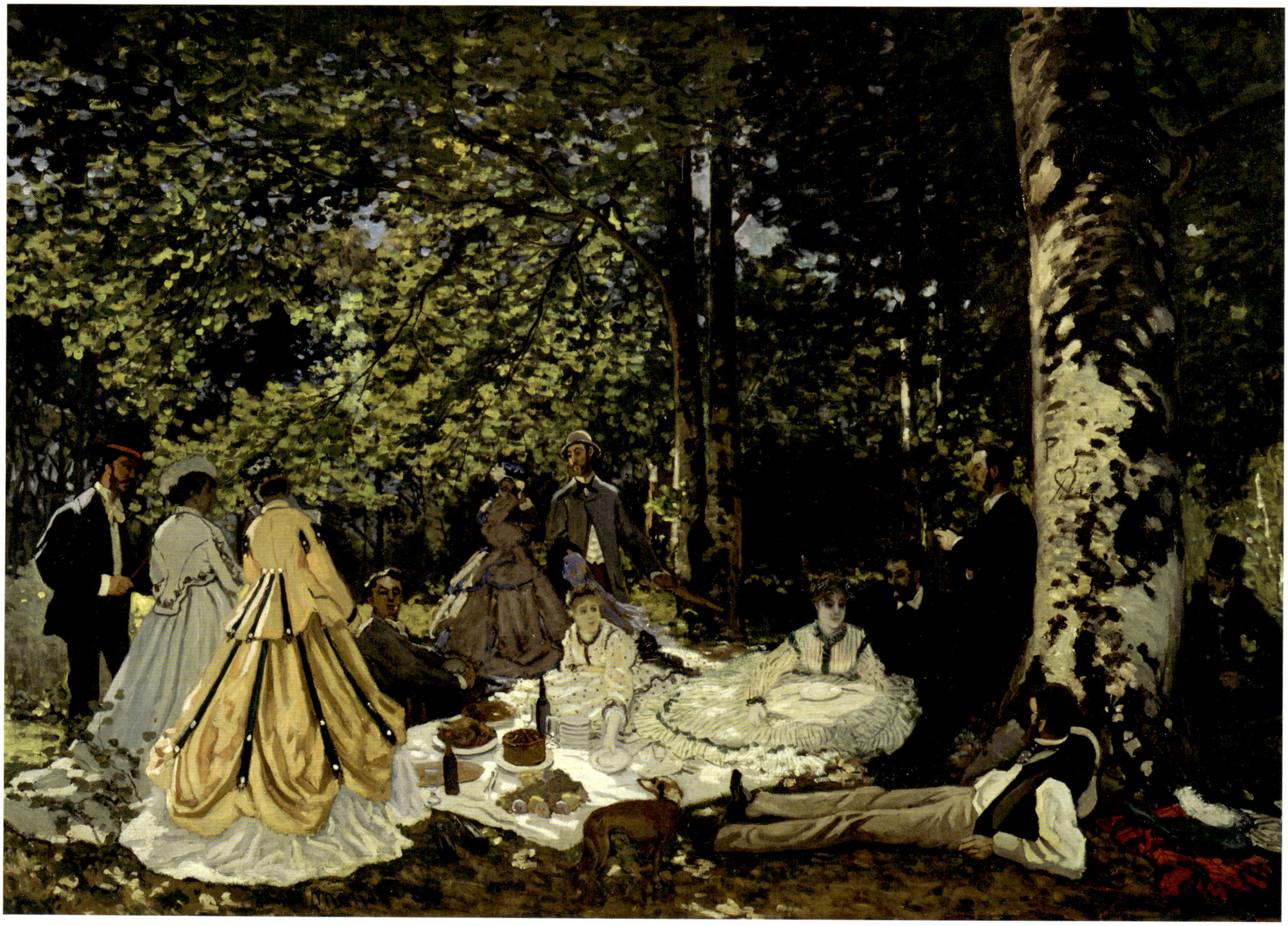

Fig. 1 Claude Monet, *Le Déjeuner sur l'herbe*, 1865, oil on canvas, 130 × 181 cm. The State Pushkin Museum of Fine Arts, Moscow

dog are gathered around a white tablecloth placed on the ground and laid with tempting delicacies. The young people are recognizable as bourgeois Parisians by their stylish clothes, which were typical of the tourists making their way to the Forest of Fontainebleau in increasing numbers thanks to the convenient railway connection. They are, in fact, Monet's friends and colleagues, including Camille Doncieux (his future wife) and the exceptionally tall Bazille. The identities of the others are speculative: Albert Lambon des Pilitères, Sisley, Courbet, and two young women known only as Gabrielle and Eugénie may be represented here.[25] Monet's primary concern was not the individual portraits but the integration of a casual group of everyday visitors into the forest setting, with its magnificent sun-dappled foliage and deep shadows.

There is no doubt that Edouard Manet's daring and scandalous *Déjeuner sur l'herbe* of 1863 (Musée d'Orsay, Paris) served as the direct inspiration for Monet's undertaking.[26] Monet chose a canvas five times larger than Manet's, with the clear intention of making his rival's creation seem insignificant. Monet's simpler, less provocative theme, on the other hand, was meant to be seen as totally modern in comparison to "the disquieting artificiality of Manet's world."[27] Monet also challenged Courbet's most famous work, *Burial at Ornans* of 1849–1850 (Musée d'Orsay, Paris), which was the first large-scale painting to elevate a moment of daily life to dimensions reserved until then for important events of ancient history.

From the outset, Monet must have decided to set this scene in the Forest of Fontainebleau, and many of his paintings executed there throughout the summer and fall of 1865, notably the magnificent *Bodmer Oak, Fontainebleau Forest* (pl. 43), must be seen as preparatory works. In this true tour de force of a shimmering forest interior, Monet concentrated fully on the effects of sunlight falling through the trees, allowing it to penetrate every part of the composition, thereby essentially solving the mise-en-scène of his intended masterpiece. In scope of vision and brilliance of execution, *The Bodmer Oak* goes beyond other preparatory works, such as *The Path in the Forest* (Fondation Rau pour le Tiers Monde, Zurich), *Fontainebleau Forest* (pl. 47), or the single tree study *An Oak at Bas-Bréau, The Bodmer Oak* (private collection).

The setting Monet chose for his *Déjeuner*, the road leading from Chailly to the Forest of Fontainebleau, was the site he found most fascinating from his first visits. It is probable, but undocumented, that he sketched it during his first stay at Chailly in 1863. He painted the scene twice in 1864 and twice more in 1865. Although virtually identical in prospect, *Le Pavé de Chailly* (fig. 4), distinguished by its golden luminosity, is considered a sketch for the larger *Route to Chailly* (pl. 13).[28] A row of trees on the left casts dense shadows across the path and presents a curious pattern on part of the sun-drenched foreground, where a stand of beeches anchors the composition on the right. A deep blue sky dotted with white summer clouds extends over the path and leads the eye into the background. This view, as documented by a black chalk drawing at the National Gallery of Art in Washington, was Monet's original choice for the setting of his

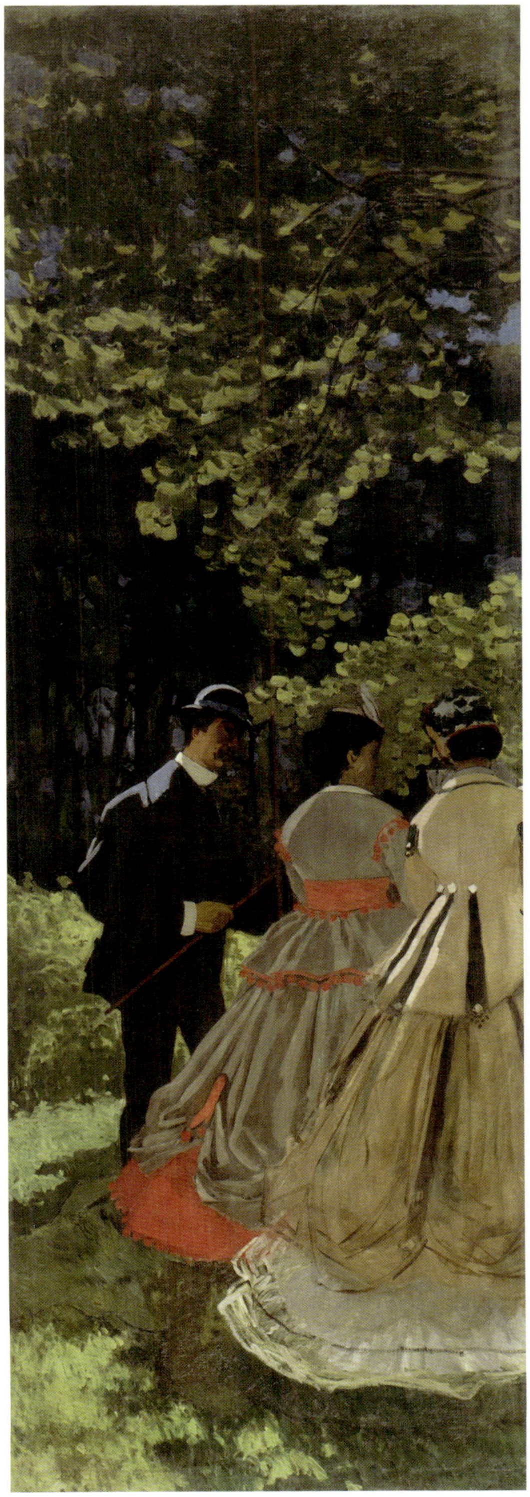

Fig. 2 Claude Monet, *Le Déjeuner sur l'herbe*, left fragment, 1865/1866, oil on canvas, 418 × 150 cm. Musée d'Orsay, Paris

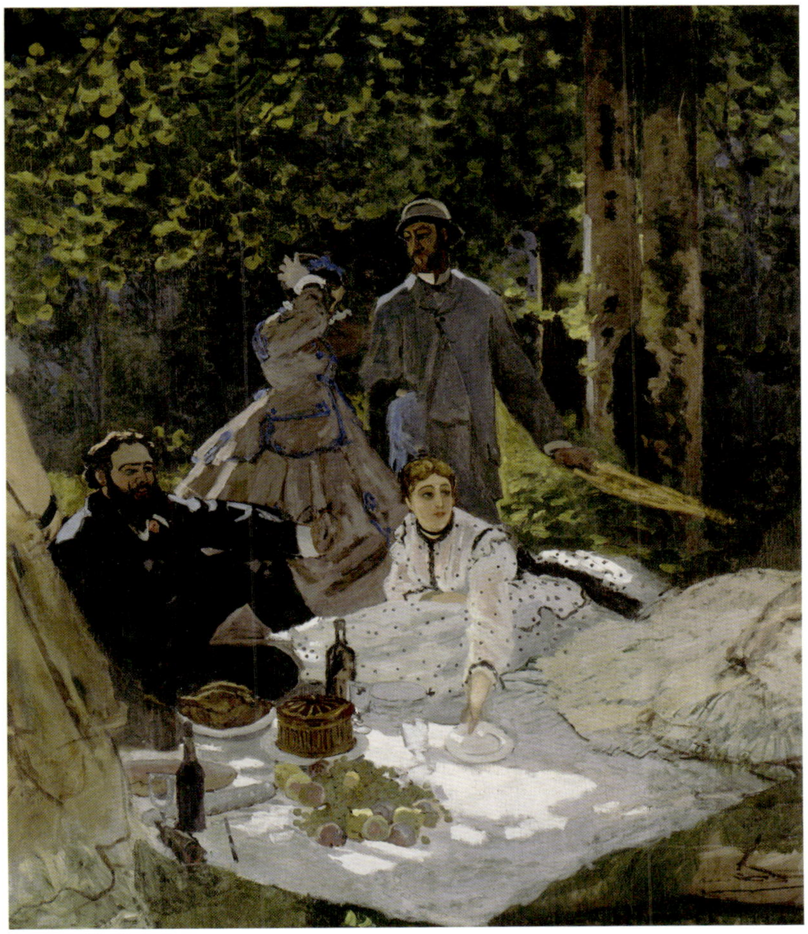

Fig. 3 Claude Monet, *Le Déjeuner sur l'herbe*, central fragment, 1865/1866, oil on canvas, 248 × 217 cm. Musée d'Orsay, Paris

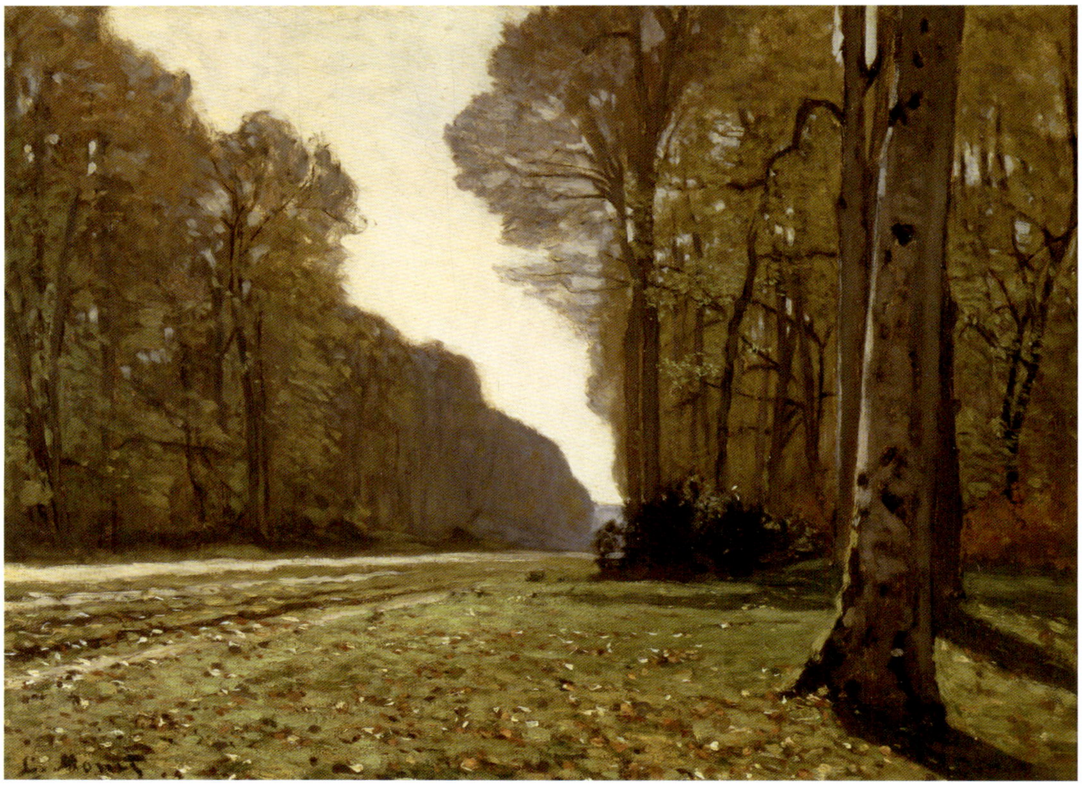

Fig. 4 Claude Monet, *Le Pavé de Chailly*, c. 1865, oil on canvas, 42 × 59 cm. Musée d'Orsay, Paris

Déjeuner. Monet was not the first to make this road his subject; it was a popular location with a long pictorial history. Corot and Rousseau had already chosen to portray this picturesque and easily accessible site during the 1820s, with Louis Français, Alexandre Decamps, and Ferdinand Chaigneau following suit over the course of the next decades. And both Gustave Le Gray and Eugène Cuvelier photographed the scene repeatedly between 1849 and 1863 (see pls. 12 and 14).[29]

Monet had to overcome a series of challenges in the creation of *Déjeuner*. Above all, it was extraordinarily ambitious to attempt a composition of twelve life-size figures without having had much training or experience in figure painting. Ironically, "as a 'recent escapee' from the studio of Suisse and Gleyre," one who had purposely eschewed the tedious "academies" or figure studies, Monet now found that he lacked the skills necessary for tackling large figural compositions. In order to achieve a cohesive group and place it "naturally" in an outdoor setting, he made numerous drawings and sketches—far more than for any other single work. Although quite a number of drawings and pastels by Monet exist for various projects, it was so unusual for him to make multiple preparatory sketches for a particular work that he even had to beg Bazille to bring paper and pencils to Chailly that he had forgotten in Paris.[30] A rough pencil sketch at the Musée Marmottan Monet shows only a general layout, but the chalk drawing at the National Gallery in Washington is already close to the oil sketch (fig. 1). Portraying the figures under the gloriously lit, spreading branches of the trees, however, required Monet to change his viewpoint. Instead of looking down the path, he turned the composition to the right by 90 degrees to face a stand of beeches from a point in the middle of the road.

In an attempt to make his work look modern, Monet took a great deal of trouble in rendering the fashionable attire of his picnickers. A drawing from 1865 of the female figure on the left (Family of Richard S. Davis) shows how meticulously he worked out the intricate black embroidery of the dress. He then carefully transferred that image to the large oil sketch, *Bazille and Camille (Study for "Le Déjeuner sur l'herbe")* (pl. 10). This study—with its fresh tonality, open brushwork, and subtle play of light and shade over the figures and throughout the background—has all the hallmarks of having been done *en plein air*. Fortunately, this section of the final painting has been saved (fig. 2), giving us an opportunity to ponder Monet's creative process. The passages of light and shadow in the landscape and on the figures remain the same in the final version, yet the figures are turned at slightly different angles. In place of the embroidered dress Monet depicted an ensemble with red in the trim and underskirt to add a flash of brilliant color, yet he struggled with details of other dresses (see figs. 2 and 3).[31]

Both the oil sketch from the Pushkin Museum and the final version of *Déjeuner* were unquestionably painted in the studio. The sheer size of the latter would have prohibited any attempt to paint it out of doors. Indeed, during the fall and winter of 1865–1866, Monet worked intensively on the painting in the spacious studio he shared with Bazille, but he eventually abandoned it for a variety of reasons. Although his friends, including Courbet, admired the work, he simply could not surmount the technical difficulties, particularly those he encountered with the figures.[32] He was not able to realize an essentially traditional academic painting on this scale, constructed in the studio from plein-air sketches, adopting the new style of painting with its emphasis on immediacy and directly observed subjects.

Monet's *Déjeuner sur l'herbe* held special importance for the artist. Although he was known to have destroyed canvases that displeased him, he kept this unfinished work for many years. He had left it as security with a landlord in 1878 but bought it back six years later. By then the edges of the huge canvas had become moldy, and he subsequently cut it apart. But instead of discarding the fragments, he kept them for the rest of his life.[33] Clearly, they represented more to him than an early failure. Perhaps they reminded him of a special summer in the Forest of Fontainebleau, filled with friends, youthful abandon, incredible artistic energy, and the hope of great achievements, perhaps even of a turning point in his career.

Monet's *Haystacks near Chailly* (pl. 100) is diminutive in scale compared to his *Déjeuner sur l'herbe* but has great significance in its choice of subject. In it Monet captured the striated sky at sunrise with its golden and orange hues extending over the fields around the village of Chailly, which is silhouetted in the background. For the first time, the ponderous forms of haystacks (or grain stacks) make their appearance in Monet's oeuvre, predating his iconic series paintings on this motif by more than twenty-five years. Furthermore, the artist's fascination with this time of day presages his famous *Impression, Sunrise* (1872), the painting that would give the impressionist movement its name.

Auguste Renoir

Auguste Renoir, unlike Bazille, Monet, and Sisley, whom he knew from the studio of Charles Gleyre, studied simultaneously at the Ecole des Beaux-Arts. His professors there, who were steeped in the rigorous academic tradition of the school, did not encourage their students to work out of doors. Thus the impetus to do so must have originated from his friends at Gleyre's, whom he joined on their first trip to Fontainebleau in the spring of 1863.[34] Although none of Renoir's efforts from this initial journey into the forest survives, a momentous encounter with Diaz is reported to have taken place that summer. Diaz, finding Renoir at work in a forest clearing, encouraged him to lighten his palette, a criticism the younger artist took to heart.[35] During the summer of 1864, Renoir returned to Fontainebleau and stayed in Marlotte, where for the next few years he was the frequent guest of his friend and colleague Jules Le Coeur.[36] He and Sisley were in Marlotte together in 1865, and Renoir's earliest extant painting from the forest, *Clearing in the Woods* (pl. 28), dates from that year. The only pure landscape by Renoir with a Fontainebleau subject, the work has a remarkable affinity with Sisley's *Avenue of Chestnut Trees at La Celle-Saint-Cloud* (see fig. 8), which should correctly be titled *Edge of the Forest of Fontainebleau* (see below).[37] The foregrounds in both works are rocky expanses, typical of Fontainebleau topography. Magnificent chestnut trees are the focal point in each case, seen from a greater distance in Sisley's work and closer up and more differentiated in Renoir's rendition. Kermit Champa has previously noted the similarities of their compositional layouts, giving rise to the speculation that the artists may have painted the works side by side.[38]

Although a quarter of Renoir's output consists of landscape paintings, he always saw himself primarily as a figure painter. Indeed, as he put it, painting landscapes was "useful for the painter of figures. In the open air you are inspired to use colours that would have been unimaginable in the attenuated lighting of the studio."[39] This is exactly what we find in *La Mare aux Fées*, also known as *Outing in a Rowboat* (private collection), which was probably completed in the summer of 1865 and was exhibited in the spring of 1866 in Pau.[40] Although comparatively modest in scale, *Outing in a Rowboat* comes closest to Monet's ambitious *Déjeuner sur l'herbe* in its depiction of a group of young merrymakers in

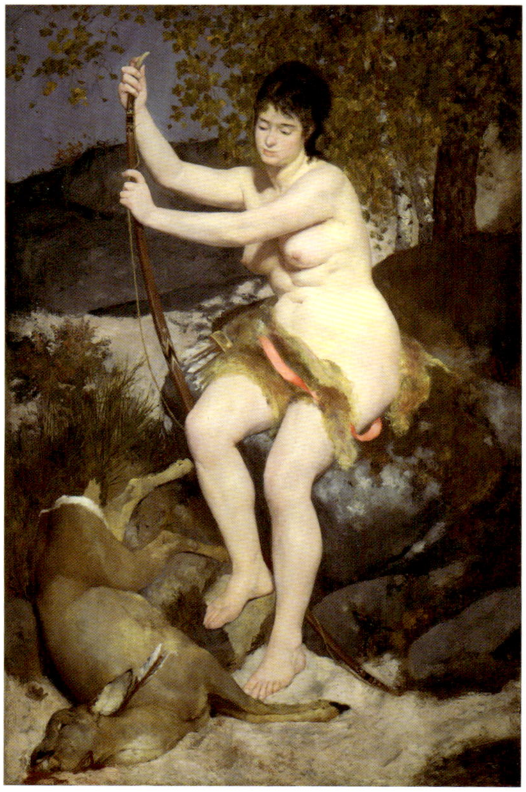

Fig. 5 Auguste Renoir, *Diana*, 1867, oil on canvas, 199.5 × 129.5 cm. National Gallery of Art, Washington, Chester Dale Collection, 1963

the forest. With its heather, limpid pools, large trees, and verdant bushes, the Mare aux Fées was one of the most popular destinations in the Forest of Fontainebleau. Renoir, like Monet, clearly characterized his figures as tourists, in their city finery and sports dress, including the striped tricot and straw hats of the boaters, which would reappear in many subsequent impressionist paintings of regattas and other water sports. Stylistically, Renoir remained very dependent on Courbet at this date, especially in his handling of the landscape elements. Yet his work already shows an interest in light and reflection—still rather awkwardly rendered here—that will be of prime importance for the development of impressionism.

After a long walking tour through the forest with Le Coeur and Sisley in February 1866, Renoir painted *The Inn of Mother Anthony* (pl. 6) at Marlotte. Many years later, he told Ambrose Vollard, "It is one of my pictures that I remember with most pleasure. It is not that I find the painting itself particularly exciting, but it does remind me of good old Mother Antony [*sic*] and her inn in Marlotte. That was a real village inn!"[41] Renoir identified the artists gathered around the table as Sisley (in profile) and Jules Le Coeur (standing), with himself probably shown between them.[42] It is symptomatic for Renoir's career as a portraitist and figurative painter that his most memorable work from the Forest of Fontainebleau is a group portrait set in an interior. No landscapes by Renoir seem to have survived from this walking trip through the forest, but this painting, more than any other, conjures up the spirit of the artists' colonies in the Forest of Fontainebleau as they must have existed for many years at Marlotte, Chailly, and Barbizon. The scene hints at the camaraderie, exchange of ideas, rivalries, and high spirits of these young men, who worked all day in their natural "studio" and enjoyed each other's company during meals and convivial evenings.

Fig. 6 Auguste Renoir, *Lise*, 1867, oil on canvas, 184 × 115 cm. Museum Folkwang, Essen

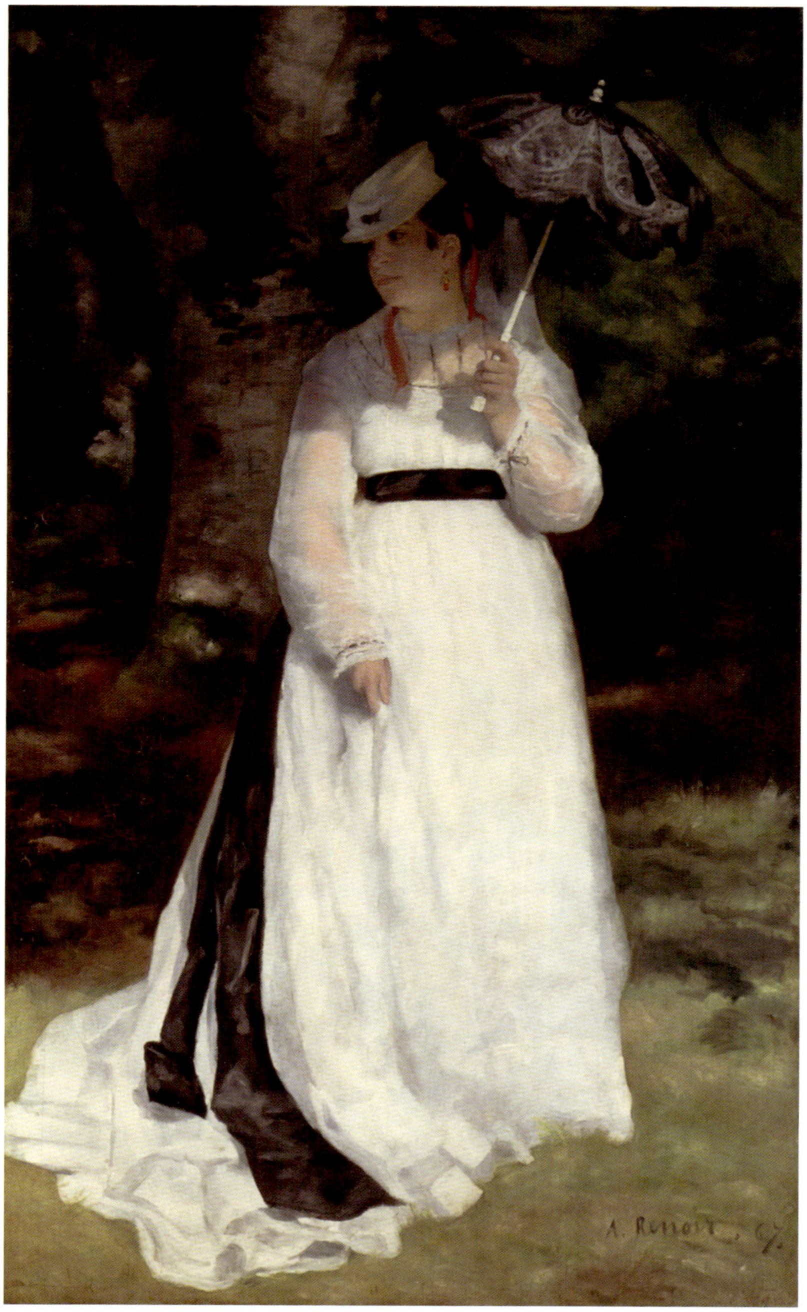

Renoir's *Jules Le Coeur and His Dogs Walking in the Forest of Fontainebleau* (Museu de Arte de São Paulo Assis Chateaubriand, São Paulo) portrays his friend and host setting out for an excursion into the forest. Although Renoir was in Marlotte in July 1866, the warm reds and golden browns that dominate the foliage and forest floor suggest that this was painted in autumn. According to Colin Bailey, two preparatory studies were made *en plein air*, whereas the final work was painted both before the motif and in the studio.[43] The theme recalls the many landscapes with hunters by Courbet, whose palette knife technique Renoir was also emulating at this time.

Both Courbet's stylistic manner and his choice of subject similarly informed Renoir's *Diana* of 1867 (fig. 5). Although the figure—his mistress Lise Tréhot, thinly disguised as the Roman goddess of the hunt—was painted in the studio, the landscape setting is the Forest of Fontainebleau.[44] The Salon jury of 1867 rejected the work as improper, but Renoir succeeded the following year with *Lise* (fig. 6), his final painting in the Forest of Fontainebleau. Obviously inspired by Monet's *Déjeuner sur l'herbe*, Renoir here tried his hand at painting a life-size figure out of doors.[45] Thanks to his academic training in figure painting and the much less ambitious scope of the work, Renoir was able to complete the painting and submit it to the Salon of 1868. Like Monet, Renoir consciously strove for modernity, depicting the young woman in the latest fashion: a high-waisted white dress with a train that puddles at her feet and a black sash that echoes the black lace of her diminutive parasol. The interplay of light and shade in this work is particularly refined, with the summarily painted trees of the background and the model's head steeped in shadow, while the brilliantly white dress and the grassy foreground are bathed in sunshine. The painting was exhibited at the Salon of 1868 and gained the artist mixed reviews in the press.[46]

Alfred Sisley

Alfred Sisley was the first of the impressionists to venture into the Forest of Fontainebleau, and he was the last to leave. In 1861, while still a student in Gleyre's studio, he went to Barbizon, staying at the Auberge Ganne, and after many repeat visits over the course of his lifetime, he spent his last years living on the southern outskirts of the forest at Moret-sur-Loing. Unfortunately, because of the destruction of his studio during the Franco-Prussian War, only a limited number of his works survive from between 1860 and 1870.[47] One of his earliest images of the forest is an oil sketch entitled *The Painter Claude Monet in the Forest of Fontainebleau* (fig. 7). A wonderful document of his fellow artist working directly before the motif, it is itself a plein-air painting. The relatively small figure of Monet—wearing his characteristic wide-brimmed hat and painter's smock—is shown sitting in front of a canvas propped on a portable easel, while a second, much smaller seated figure is depicted at the foot of the large boulder in the center of the composition. The sketchily rendered landscape almost engulfs both figures. From the beginning, capturing other painters at work *sur le motif* had been a frequently recurring subject of Barbizon paintings, including Auguste-Xavier Leprince's *Painters at Rest, Fontainebleau*, from about 1824 (pl. 3) and Augustin Enfantin's *An Artist Painting in the Forest of Fontainebleau* from about 1825 (pl. 1). Sisley's version of the subject distinguishes itself with its very open brushwork.

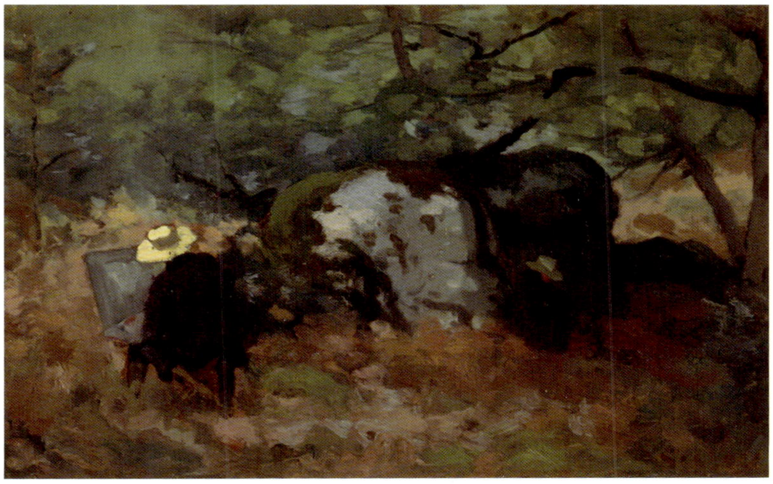

Fig. 7 Alfred Sisley, *The Painter Claude Monet in the Forest of Fontainebleau*, c. 1865, oil on canvas, 36 × 55 cm. Saarland Museum, Saarbrücken

Undoubtedly inspired by Monet's monumental *Déjeuner sur l'herbe*, Sisley undertook a very large painting in 1865 that was probably intended for the Salon. Thanks to recently published research by Chantal Georgel, it can now be recognized as a landscape from the Forest of Fontainebleau. Though its current title is misleading, *Avenue of Chestnut Trees at La Celle-Saint-Cloud* (fig. 8) was sold directly by Sisley to Jean-Baptiste Faure as *Edge of the Forest of Fontainebleau*, and the site's identity is further confirmed by markings on the stretcher and by a 1903 publication.[48] The wide expanse of rocks in the foreground is painted in the muscular manner of Courbet, while the solid mass of trees under a bright blue sky is reminiscent of early plein-air sketches by Corot such as *Oak Trees at Bas-Bréau* from 1832–1833. The motif of the forest's edge also supports the attribution to paintings from Fontainebleau: both Bazille and Monet chose this setting for important paintings in 1865: *Forest of Fontainebleau* (pl. 16) and *Le Déjeuner sur l'herbe* (pl. 10; figs. 1–3), respectively. A later work called *Avenue of Chestnut Trees near La Celle-Saint-Cloud* (pl. 20) may also represent Fontainebleau. Its composition is particularly close to Monet's *Path in a Forest* of 1865, though its compact brushwork and monochromatic green tonality diverge from Monet's flickering shades of gold and light green and point to Courbet.[49]

Sisley started two village scenes during his stay in Marlotte in 1865, *Women Going to the Woods: Landscape* (fig. 9) and *Village Street in Marlotte* (pl. 66), and finished them by the spring of 1866 in time to be shown at the Salon. As in so many of his paintings, the influences of both Corot and Courbet can be detected here. Sisley, with his "sense of design that is almost prismatic in its tautness," followed Corot's reduction of architectural elements, but his vigorous brushwork and darker palette recall Courbet.[50] The insistence on a highly articulated surface texture, as in the treatment of the cottage walls, is typical of Sisley. The two scenes, clearly conceived as pendants, differentiate the chores performed by men and women and define the villagers' dependence on the bounty of the forest.[51] Not yet truly impressionist works, they provide the first hint of Sisley's later interest in repeating the same motif under different atmospheric conditions (his series on the church at Moret-sur-Loing follows the example of Monet's series on Rouen Cathedral).

Sisley's paintings underwent remarkable stylistic change in the five years between his completion of these village scenes and his creation of the *Rural Guardsman in the Fontainebleau Forest* (pl. 70). Nothing of the robust brushwork or darker palette

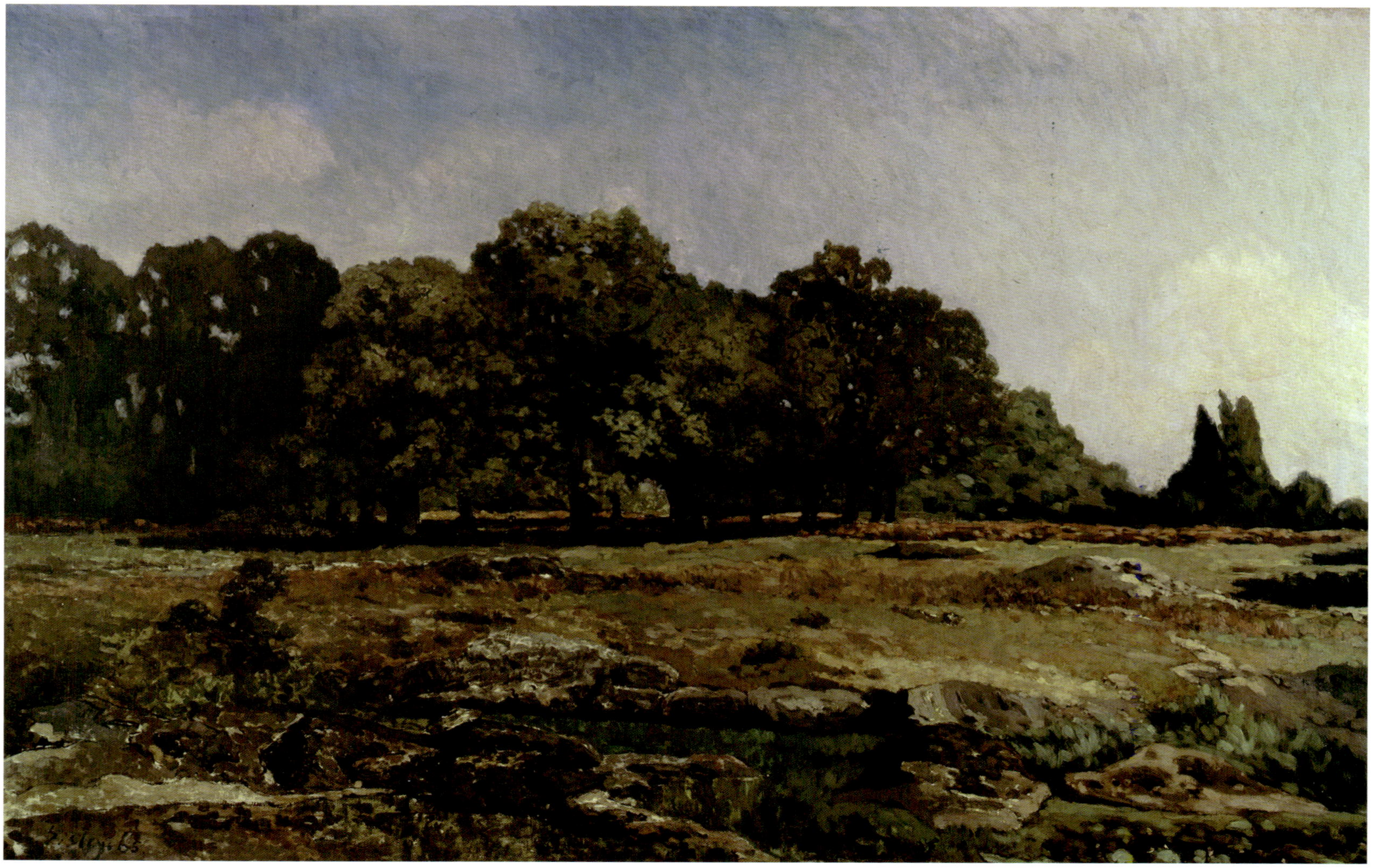

Fig. 8 Alfred Sisley, *Avenue of Chestnut Trees at La Celle-Saint-Cloud,* 1867, oil on canvas, 129 × 208 cm. Musée du Petit Palais, Paris

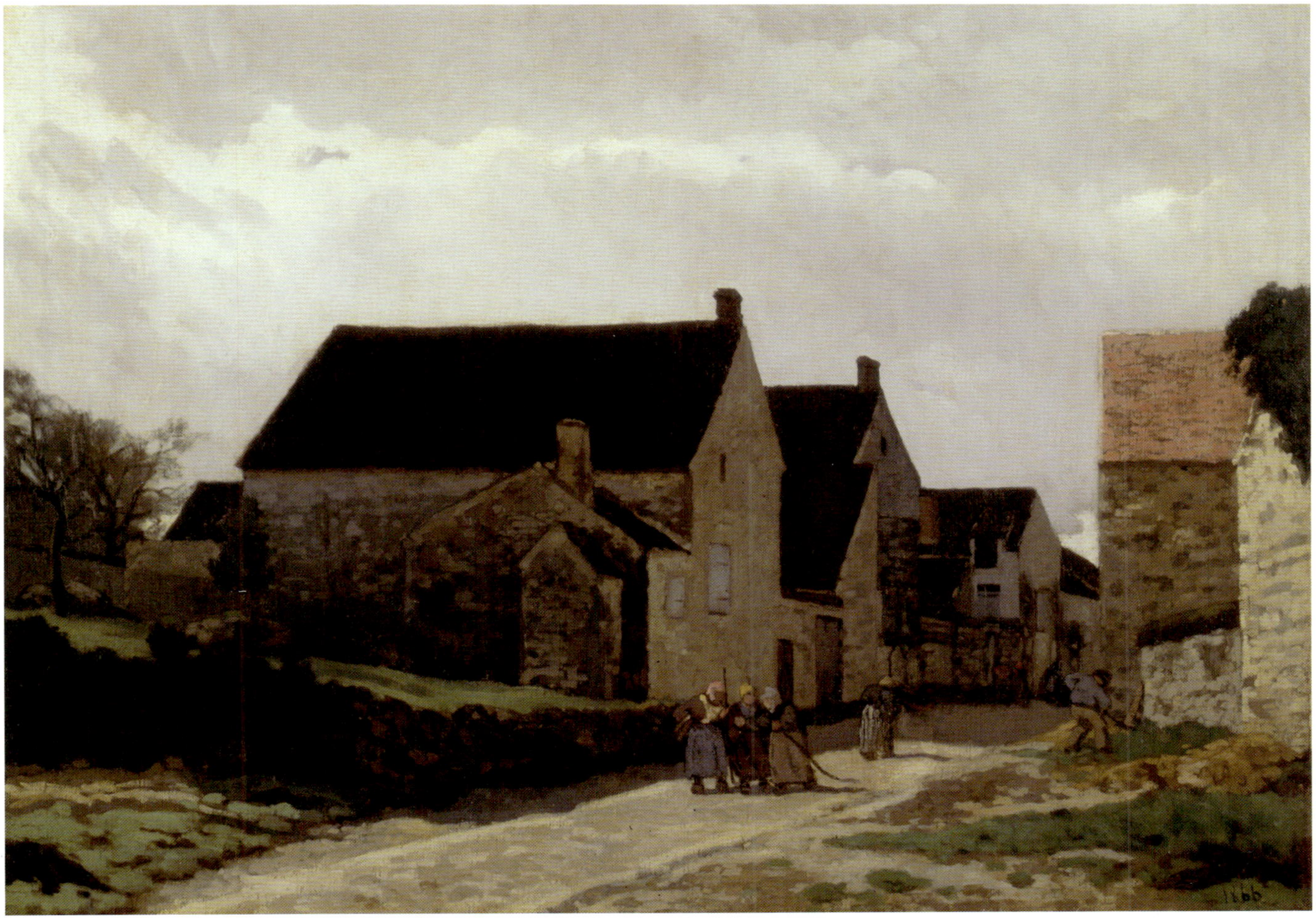

Fig. 9 Alfred Sisley, *Women Going to the Woods: Landscape,* 1866, oil on canvas, 65 × 92 cm. Bridgestone Museum of Art, Ishibashi Foundation, Tokyo

of Courbet remains. Instead, the delicate foliage of the slender trees seems to rustle in the breeze, with individual leaves freely sketched in loose daubs of paint. The same lightness of touch characterizes the grassy borders of the narrow path that winds its way gently up, interrupted only by the tall figure of the guardsman with his drum, placed at the very center of the composition. Sisley's preference for painting directly on canvas, his open brushwork, and the light tonality give this work all the hallmarks of an impressionist painting.

"Every picture shows a spot with which the artist has fallen in love," Sisley once wrote to a friend, expressing a sentiment that seems applicable to every work by the future impressionists that was painted in the Forest of Fontainebleau.[52] Inspired by the works of the previous generation of masters to seek out the forest, they made huge strides in their personal development—from their first hesitant plein-air sketches to their most ambitious masterpieces—and together succeeded in moving French landscape painting a significant step closer to impressionism.

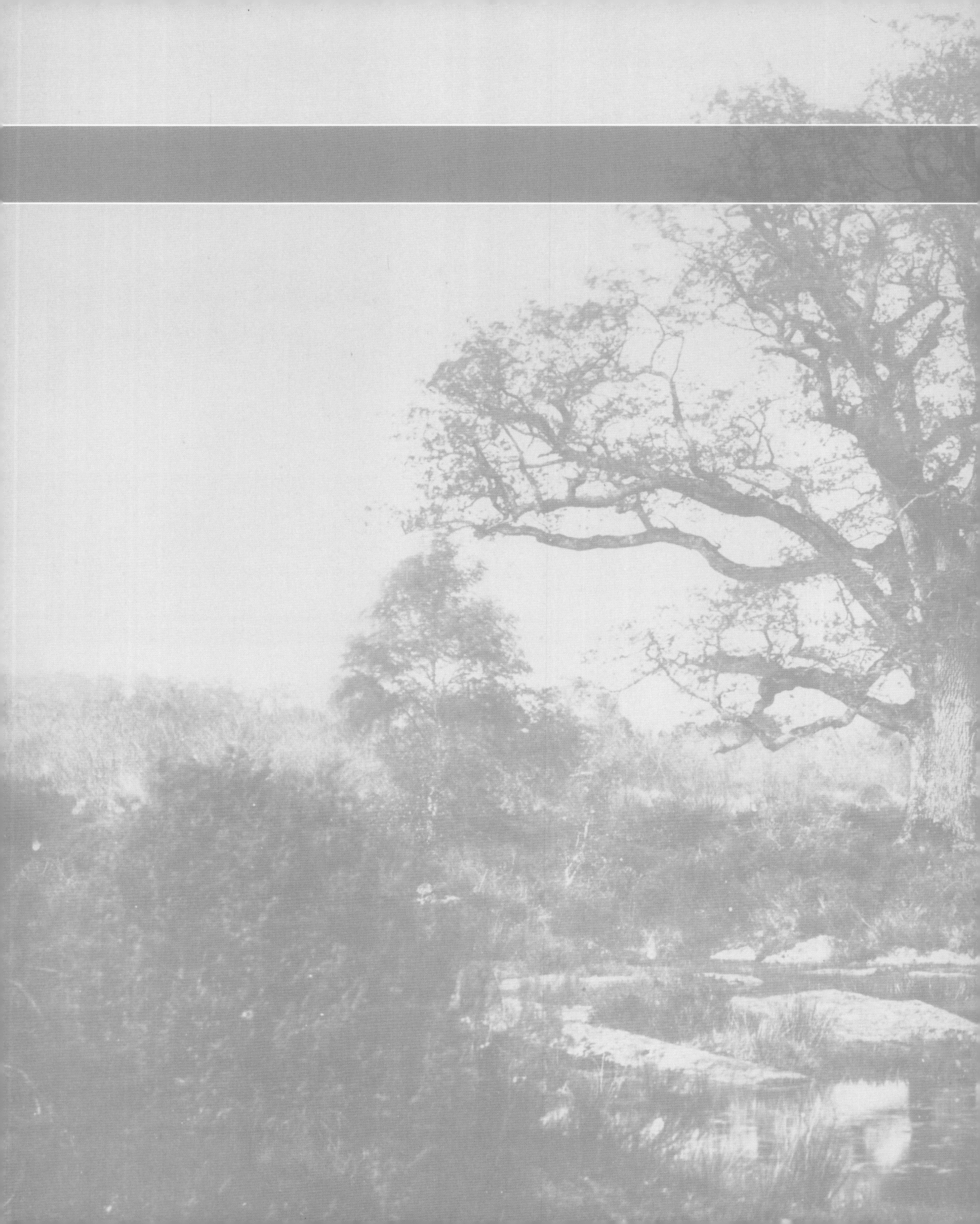

Chronology, Notes, Bibliography, Index, Photography Credits

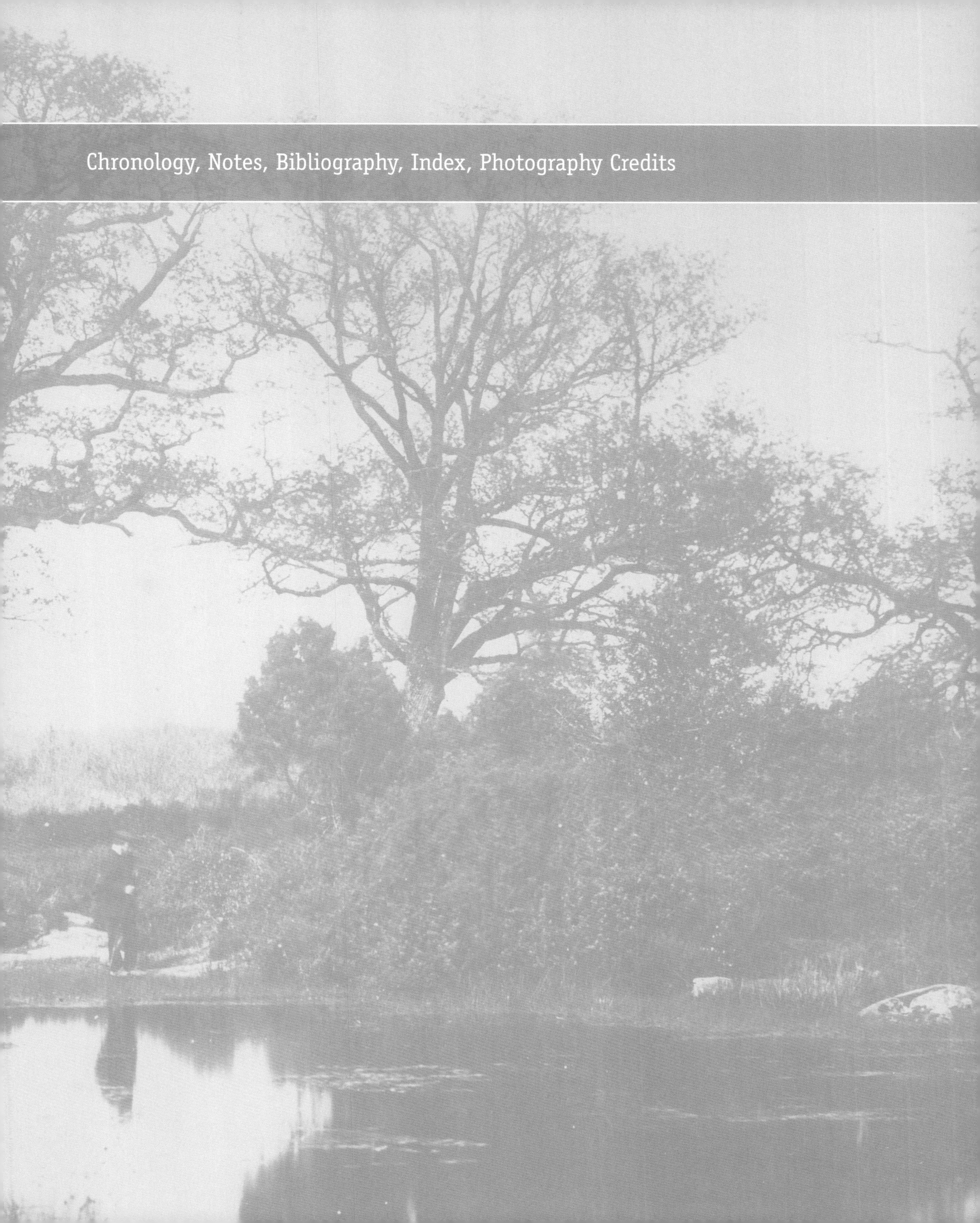

Chronology

1731

Abbé Guibert's *Description historique des château, bourg, et forest* [sic] *de Fontainebleau* is published.

1781

Jean-François Hue exhibits *View Taken in the Forest of Fontainebleau* (no. 212) at the Paris Salon. He is the first artist to show a view of the forest at the Salon.

1783

Jean-Joseph Bidauld and Jean-François Le Gillon are working in Fontainebleau.

1786

Pine trees are first introduced into the forest. They are the primary species planted in the forest during the nineteenth century.

1789

The French Revolution begins.

1790

23 OCTOBER: By official decree of the National Assembly, Bois-des-Seigneurs is seized from the church and reintegrated into the Forest of Fontainebleau. Declared a *bien national*, the fully restored forest is entered into the *liste civile* along with the Bois de Boulogne, the Bois de Vincennes, the Bois de Sénart, and various palaces.

1791

Three paintings of the Forest of Fontainebleau are shown at the Paris Salon: Le Gillon's *View of the Forest of Fontainebleau, Several Figures and Animals near a Fountain* (no. 8), Lazare Bruandet's *View Taken in the Forest of Fontainebleau* (no. 157), and Louis Gadbois' *View and Site near Fontainebleau* (no. 374).

1804

Etienne Pivert de Senancour's novel *Obermann* is published.

18 MAY: Napoleon Bonaparte declares himself Emperor Napoleon I. The First Empire begins.

1805

Jean-Jacques Paulet's *Observations sur la vipère de Fontainebleau, et sur les moyens de remédier à sa morsure* is published.

René-Richard Castel's poem "La forêt de Fontainebleau. Poème" is published.

1806

François-Hippolyte Paillet's *Description physique de la forêt de Fontainebleau* is published.

1814

The French Restoration begins.

1820

Charles Rémard's *Le guide du voyageur à Fontainebleau* is published. It is the first true guidebook of the forest.

1821

Stamati Bulgari, a student of Jacques-Louis David, is working in Fontainebleau.

1822

SPRING: Jean-Baptiste-Camille Corot is believed to have made his first studies in the forest under the direction of Achille-Etna Michallon.

OCTOBER: Corot visits Fontainebleau on the advice of Jean-Victor Bertin.

1823

Discovery in the forest of a rock containing what are believed to be fossilized human remains. They are later disproved.

1824

The Auberge Ganne opens in Barbizon.

George Sand makes her first visit to the forest.

JUNE: Auguste-Xavier Leprince is working in the Franchard region of Fontainebleau.

1825

Jacques-Raymond Brascassat is believed to have been in Fontainebleau.

SEPTEMBER: Leprince is in Chailly. His brother Robert-Léopold Leprince is working at Bas-Bréau.

SEPTEMBER: Corot leaves for Italy where he remains until 1828. He encounters a number of landscape artists there, including Théodore Claude Félix Caruelle d'Aligny, François-Edouard Bertin, Brascassat, Augustin Enfantin, and André Giroux, all of whom work in Fontainebleau.

1827

16 OCTOBER: Enfantin dies.

1828

Alexandre Desgoffe begins working in Fontainebleau.

Aligny is working in Marlotte and Bas-Bréau.

Bertin makes his first sojourn in Fontainebleau and makes subsequent visits in 1829, 1832, 1839, 1842, 1843, and 1865.

Théodore Rousseau passes through Fontainebleau and stops to sketch the Pavé de Chailly.

23 SEPTEMBER: The artist Richard Parkes Bonington dies.

1829

Aligny is working around Bourron.

Production of paving stones reaches its peak, with 2.9 million stones shipped from Fontainebleau to Paris.

SPRING: Corot is in Fontainebleau.

1830

Aligny is in Fontainebleau.

1831

Corot exhibits his first Fontainebleau work, *View Taken in the Forest of Fontainebleau* (no. 400), at the Salon. His friend Bertin exhibits his first Fontainebleau work, *View Taken in the Forest of Fontainebleau* (no. 3111). The latter was subsequently acquired for the Musée du Luxembourg.

SPRING – SUMMER: Brascassat is in Fontainebleau along with Aligny. He returns the following year as a guest at the Auberge Ganne.

JULY: Corot sojourns at Chailly and in Fontainebleau.

1832

Claude-François Denecourt, an employee of the department of war administration, is transferred from Versailles to Fontainebleau. He is dismissed from his job soon after.

1833

At the Salon, Aligny exhibits *View Taken from the Sandstone Quarries of Mont Saint-Péré, Forest of Fontainebleau* (no. 18); Brascassat exhibits *View Taken in the Forest of Fontainebleau; Landscape and Animals* (no. 283); Jules Coignet exhibits *Interior of the Forest of Fontainebleau* along with two other forest scenes (nos. 423, 425, 427); Corot exhibits *View of the Forest of Fontainebleau* (no. 468); and Leprince exhibits *View Taken in the Environs of Fontainebleau* (no. 1572). Corot receives the second-class medal.

A new edition of Senancour's *Obermann* is published with a preface by Charles Augustin Sainte-Beuve.

AUGUST: Alfred de Musset and George Sand spend nine days in Fontainebleau.

NOVEMBER 1833 – FEBRUARY 1834: Rousseau stays at the Auberge de Mère Lemoine in Chailly.

1834

Corot exhibits the Fontainebleau work *Forest of Fontainebleau* at the Salon (no. 371; pl. 30).

E. Jamin's *Fontainebleau, ou notice historique et descriptive sur cette résidence royale* is published (a second edition is published in 1838). It includes a chapter on the forest as well as a map.

AUTUMN: Corot returns from Italy and spends six weeks in Fontainebleau.

NOVEMBER: François-René de Chateaubriand spends five days in Fontainebleau, sending letters to Madame Récamier from this "délicieux désert." He returned to the forest again in May 1843.

1835

An article devoted to Fontainebleau appears in *Le magasin pittoresque*. It is republished in 1846.

1836

Jean-Baptiste-Alexis Durand's poem "La forêt de Fontainebleau" is published.

Musset's novel *La confession d'un enfant du siècle* is published. It recounts his love affair with George Sand and includes a fictional account of a nocturnal visit they made to Franchard. Sand evokes the same episode in her novel *Elle et lui* (1859).

Narcisse-Virgile Diaz de la Peña begins to frequent Fontainebleau.

AUTUMN: Rousseau stays at the Auberge Ganne.

1837

Diaz exhibits *View Taken in the Gorges d'Apremont* at the Salon (no. 352).

George Sand makes two trips to Fontainebleau, one with the actor Pierre Bocage (summer), the second with her son Maurice (August).

Jamin's *Quatre promenades dans la forêt de Fontainebleau, ou description physique et topographique de cette forêt royale* is published.

Rousseau begins to visit Fontainebleau regularly.

APRIL: Stendhal is in Fontainebleau.

OCTOBER: Aligny is in Barbizon.

1838

Stendhal's novel *Mémoires d'un touriste* is published.

FEBRUARY: Brascassat is in Fontainebleau once more.

1839

Denecourt's earliest guidebooks, *Camp de Fontainebleau, Sa position topographique et l'itinéraire des promenades y conduisant* and *Guide du voyageur dans la forêt de Fontainebleau ou Choix des promenades les plus pittoresques*, are published.

"La forêt de Barbizon — Dévastations" is published in *L'Artiste*. The article laments the recent deforestation in Fontainebleau.

19 AUGUST: Louis-Jacques-Mandé Daguerre's invention of the daguerreotype is publicly announced in Paris.

1840

Antoine-Laurent Castellan's two-volume *Fontainebleau. Etudes pittoresques et historiques sur ce château ...* is published posthumously. Although ostensibly devoted to the château, it includes fifteen plates depicting the forest.

Denecourt begins to publish a number of lithographic albums featuring Fontainebleau as well as other scenic locales in the outskirts of Paris.

A new edition of Senancour's *Obermann* is published with a preface by George Sand.

SUMMER: Brascassat is in Fontainebleau.

SEPTEMBER: Aligny is working in Fontainebleau.

20 SEPTEMBER: The Paris-Corbeil line is inaugurated.

1841

FEBRUARY: William Henry Fox Talbot patents the calotype (paper negative) process.

1842

Denecourt creates his first sentier at Mont Chauvet.

John Ruskin is in Fontainebleau.

JULY – OCTOBER: Aligny is working in the forest around Bourron, the Mare aux Fées, and the Gorges aux Loups.

1843

Charles-François Daubigny and Constant Troyon are in Barbizon.

1845

AUTUMN: Corot is in Fontainebleau.

SEPTEMBER: Aligny is in Fontainebleau.

8 NOVEMBER: The article "Résidences royales. Fontainebleau — La forêt" is published in *L'Illustration*.

1846

Corot exhibits *The Forest of Fontainebleau* at the Salon (no. 422; pl. 31).

1847

Louis Désiré Blanquart-Evrard publishes the procedure for the paper negative process in France, making the process widely available for the first time.

SUMMER: Rousseau rents a house in Barbizon that will become his permanent residence.

NOVEMBER: Théophile Thoré visits Fontainebleau in the company of Rousseau. His account of this visit, "Par monts et par bois," is published in *Le Constitutionnel*.

1848

24 FEBRUARY: King Louis-Philippe abdicates the French throne, and the Second Republic is proclaimed. Louis-Napoleon Bonaparte is later elected president.

28 AUGUST: Charles Marville visits the Forest of Fontainebleau for the first time.

1849

The American expatriate artist William Perkins Babcock moves to Barbizon.

Karl Bodmer arrives in Fontainebleau.

JUNE: Charles-Emile Jacque and Jean-François Millet settle in Barbizon.

17 AUGUST: The Paris-Tonnerre rail line is inaugurated and includes a stop at Avon.

SEPTEMBER – OCTOBER: Gustave Le Gray makes salted paper prints from paper negatives in Fontainebleau, possibly in the company of the photographer Charles Nègre, who visits Barbizon in October.

1850

Bodmer exhibits three Fontainebleau works, all entitled *Forest Interior* (nos. 268–270), at the Salon. The first is acquired by the French state for the Musée du Luxembourg. Rousseau also exhibits a major group of Fontainebleau subjects at the Salon (pl. 102).

The brothers Edmond and Jules de Goncourt are in Fontainebleau.

Henry Murger discovers Marlotte and will eventually take up residence there.

SUMMER: *Trains de plaisir* between Paris and Fontainebleau are introduced.

AUGUST – SEPTEMBER: Aligny is working in the forest at Gorges aux Loups.

1851

Durand's *Indicateur. Quatre promenades historiques et pittoresques dans la forêt de Fontainebleau* is published.

Frederick Archer publishes the collodion negative process.

NOVEMBER: Aligny purchases a house at Marlotte.

2 DECEMBER: President Bonaparte stages a coup d'état and proclaims himself Emperor Napoleon III. The Second Empire begins.

1852

The Fontaine Sanguinède is created.

Le Gray returns to Fontainebleau, possibly in the company of John Beasley Greene.

Murger settles in Marlotte.

Rousseau submits a petition to Emperor Napoleon III requesting that a portion of the forest be protected from future exploitation.

AUTUMN OR EARLY 1853: Babcock takes William Morris Hunt to Barbizon to meet Millet whose work he admires. Hunt purchases *The Sheep Shearers* (Museum of Fine Arts, Boston) and commissions a number of unfinished paintings. A strong friendship develops between Millet and Hunt, who becomes an important patron for Millet.

1853

Previously attributed to the French state, the forest is made part of the *liste civile* and is placed under the authority of Napoleon III.

Rosa Bonheur visits Barbizon.

JANUARY – MARCH: Murger's novel *Scènes de campagne; Adeline Protat* is published in installments in *Revue des deux mondes* and in novel form the following year. It features a landscape painter who works in Fontainebleau.

APRIL: Adalbert Cuvelier, Constant Dutilleux, and Léandre Grandguillaume teach Corot the cliché-verre process.

APRIL – JUNE: George Sand's *La filleule* is published in installments in *Le Siècle* and subsequently in novel form. It is set partially in Fontainebleau.

8 – 12 OCTOBER: Corot resides at the Hôtel de la Sirène in Fontainebleau and works in the forest.

23 NOVEMBER: Emperor Napoleon III and Empress Eugénie inaugurate the Fort l'Empereur (later renamed Tour Denecourt). Constructed in 1851, it collapses in 1878 and is later rebuilt.

24 DECEMBER: Albert de la Fizelière's article "Les auberges illustrées" is published in *L'Illustration*.

1854

Charles Marville photographs Corot and Diaz in Fontainebleau.

OCTOBER: Aligny is working in the forest at Gorges aux Loups.

1855

Denecourt's *Fontainebleau. Paysages, légendes, souvenirs, fantasies; Hommage à C. F. Denecourt* is published. It includes contributions from a number of prominent contemporary writers and poets.

Le Gray's views of the forest are exhibited at the Société Française de Photographie (SFP), Paris.

APRIL: Matthew Arnold's poem inspired by *Obermann*, "Stanzas from the Grande Chartreuse," is published in *Fraser's Magazine*.

1856

Adolphe Joanne's first edition of *Fontainebleau. Son palais, ses jardins, sa forêt* is published.

La Reine Blanche, one of the famed trees of the forest, is destroyed in a fire.

20 – 23 MARCH: George Sand makes her final trip to Fontainebleau.

JUNE/JULY: Hippolyte Taine, who made annual visits to the forest, spends three weeks in Fontainebleau.

SEPTEMBER: Eugène Cuvelier arrives in Fontainebleau and signs into the registry of the Auberge Ganne on 15 September as "Artist." Other entries in the registry include his visits on 15–30 September 1857 and 5 July 1858.

1857

Millet exhibits *The Gleaners* at the Salon (no. 1936).

Taine's *Notes sur Paris. Vie et opinions de M. Frédéric Thomas Graindorge* is published. It includes a description of the Forest of Fontainebleau.

SUMMER: Jules Michelet is in Fontainebleau.

JULY: Jules Breton is working in Fontainebleau. He stays in Marlotte at the Auberge de la Mère Anthony.

1858

The Americans John William Casilear and Christopher Pearce Cranch are working in Fontainebleau.

Michelet's book *L'Insecte* is published. The foreword, written in Fontainebleau the previous year, contains lavish descriptions of the forest.

SEPTEMBER – OCTOBER: Georg Eduard Otto Saal is staying at the Auberge Ganne.

1859

Antoine-Louis Barye settles in Barbizon at 26 Grande Rue.

Bonheur settles in the Château de By in Thoméry, a village on the eastern edge of the forest.

Champfleury's novel *Les amis de la nature* is published. One of the characters, Gorenflot, bears an unflattering resemblance to Denecourt, who threatens a lawsuit against Champfleury.

George Sand's *Elle et lui* is published. It includes a fictional account of a nocturnal visit she made to Franchard in the company of Musset. Musset had evoked the same episode in his novel *La confession d'un enfant du siècle* (1836).

Murger's novel *Le sabot rouge* is published. It is set in the environs of the Forest of Fontainebleau.

MARCH 7: Eugène Cuvelier marries Louise, the daughter of François Ganne, proprietor of the Auberge Ganne. Corot acts as best man; Millet and Rousseau provide the decorations.

APRIL: Paul Gaillard and Alfred Louviot exhibit photographs of the forest at the SFP.

NOVEMBER: Corot is in Fontainebleau.

1860

AUGUST 22: The painter Alexandre Decamps dies as a result of a riding accident. An engraved stone block marks the site of his accident near Cuvier-Chatillon.

1861

Alfred Sisley makes his first visit to Fontainebleau and stays at the Auberge Ganne.

Rousseau exhibits *The Rock Oak (Forest of Fontainebleau)* at the Salon (no. 2734; pl. 59).

APRIL 14: An imperial decree designates 1,097 hectares of the Forest of Fontainebleau as a "réserve artistique." It is the first act of natural preservation in history.

MAY – AUGUST: Gaillard and Alphonse Jeanrenaud exhibit forest views at SFP.

12 SEPTEMBER TO MID-OCTOBER: Corot is in Fontainebleau.

1862

22 JUNE: The Hippodrome de la Solle is inaugurated in the presence of Emperor Napoleon III and Empress Eugénie.

1863

EARLY APRIL: Claude Monet and Frédéric Bazille are in Chailly. Auguste Renoir and Sisley are also in Fontainebleau.

1864

Millet receives a first-class medal at the Salon for his painting *Shepherdess Tending Her Flock* (Musée d'Orsay, Paris).

APRIL: Monet returns to Fontainebleau.

MAY – AUGUST: Eugène Cuvelier exhibits twelve photographs of the forest at SFP; Gaillard exhibits four.

SUMMER: Renoir is in Marlotte with Jules Le Coeur.

1865

Henri Fantin-Latour is in Fontainebleau where he produces a number of landscape studies.

Le Coeur purchases a house in the village of Marlotte. Renoir is a regular visitor.

SPRING: Monet goes to Chailly where he remains until the fall; Bazille joins him there in August.

EARLY JUNE: Gustave Courbet is briefly in Fontainebleau.

15 – 29 AUGUST: Corot is in Fontainebleau.

1866

At the Salon, Karl Bodmer exhibits *A Band of Wild Boar beneath the Haute Futaie* (no. 189, Museum of Fine Arts, Boston), Monet exhibits *Forest of Fontainebleau* (no. 1387), and Sisley exhibits *Women Going to the Woods: Landscape* and *Village Street in Marlotte* (nos. 1785 and 1786; pl. 66).

FEBRUARY: Renoir, Sisley, and Le Coeur are all together in Marlotte. Renoir returns in July.

SPRING/SUMMER: Taine is in Fontainebleau.

LATE 1866/EARLY 1867: Thomas Moran is sketching in Fontainebleau.

1867

At the Exposition Universelle in Paris, Millet exhibits nine works, including *The Potato Harvest* (no. 478; pl. 83), and Rousseau exhibits eight works, three of the Forest of Fontainebleau, including *The Rock Oak (Forest of Fontainebleau)* (no. 504; pl. 59).

The Auberge Siron (now the Hôtellerie Bas-Bréau) opens in Barbizon.

The Goncourt brothers' *Manette Salomon* (written between December 1864 and August 1865 and drawing upon a sojourn to Barbizon in 1865) is published.

Millet exhibits *Winter (A View of Plain of Chailly)* at the Salon (no. 1080).

JUNE: Rousseau's work is exhibited at the Cercle des Arts in Paris. A total of 109 works are shown, including numerous works executed at Fontainebleau (see pl. 24).

22 DECEMBER: Rousseau dies in Barbizon and is interred at the Chailly cemetery.

1869

Flaubert's *L'Education sentimentale* is published. It includes a highly fictionalized account of Musset and George Sand's visit to Fontainebleau in 1833.

MAY – OCTOBER: Eugène Cuvelier and Charles Harrison exhibit numerous photographs of the forest at the SFP. Harrison also exhibits enlargements of photographs of the forest made by Olympe Aguado.

LATE 1860S: Alfred Sensier writes an unpublished history of the Forest of Fontainebleau.

1870

A fire breaks out in the Forest of Fontainebleau.

MAY – AUGUST: Eugène Cuvelier, Harrison, and Maurice Delondre exhibit photographs of the forest at the SFP.

19 JULY: France declares war on Prussia.

4 SEPTEMBER: The Third Republic is proclaimed.

6 SEPTEMBER: The forest is restored to the French state under whose authority it remains today.

1871

24 FEBRUARY: Aligny dies.

1872

The Committee for the Artistic Protection of the Forest of Fontainebleau is established. Millet is the president of honor; Daubigny and Corot are also members.

Julia Kavanagh's novel *Bessie* is published. It is set in large part in the Forest of Fontainebleau.

Sensier's *Souvenirs sur Th. Rousseau* is published. Millet provides much of the material used.

1 – 7 SEPTEMBER: Corot is staying at the Auberge de la Sirène in Fontainebleau.

26 OCTOBER: A letter written by Philip Burty in defense of the Forest of Fontainebleau is published in *La renaissance littéraire et artistique*.

13 NOVEMBER: A letter written by George Sand in support of the Committee for the Artistic Protection of the Forest of Fontainebleau is published in *Le Temps*. It is republished the following year in *Impressions et souvenirs*, a volume of her collected writings.

7 DECEMBER: A letter written by Victor Hugo in support of the Committee for the Artistic Protection of the Forest of Fontainebleau is published in *La renaissance littéraire et artistique*.

1873

Eugène Cuvelier exhibits photographs in Arras.

Paul Domet's *Histoire de la forêt de Fontainebleau* is published.

AUGUST: Will Hickok Low makes his first excursion to Fontainebleau and stays at the Auberge Siron in Barbizon.

1875

Jules Levallois' *Mémoires d'une forêt: Fontainebleau* is published.

20 JANUARY: Millet dies and is interred at the Chailly cemetery near Rousseau.

22 FEBRUARY: Corot dies and is interred at Père Lachaise cemetery in Paris.

24 MARCH: Denecourt dies and is interred in the cemetery of Fontainebleau.

SPRING: Robert Louis Stevenson is in Barbizon and resides at the Auberge Siron. He later publishes two essays describing the artists' colonies in Fontainebleau.

MAY: Odilon Redon is in Fontainebleau.

25 JUNE: Barye dies.

1876

7 – 12 FEBRUARY: Barye's studio is sold after his death. Seventy-three paintings inspired by the Forest of Fontainebleau are included in the sale.

MAY: Stevenson's "Forest Notes" is published in *The Cornhill Magazine*. It recounts his experiences in the Forest of Fontainebleau.

NOVEMBER 18: Diaz dies.

1877

SUMMER: Theodore Robinson is at the artists' colony at Grez-sur-Loing. He returns there in 1879.

1879

Paul Cézanne is in Melun for several months. He paints in the environs, including in the Forest of Fontainebleau, where he works in the snow.

22 – 24 JANUARY: An ice storm causes severe damage to the trees in Fontainebleau.

1883

Stevenson's "Fontainebleau: Village Communities of Painters" is published in *Magazine of Art*.

OCTOBER 6 – 10: Georges Seurat and Edmond-François Aman-Jean are at the Auberge Ganne.

1884

21 APRIL: A monument devoted to Millet and Rousseau is dedicated in Fontainebleau near the village of Barbizon where they had resided.

1890

The term "Barbizon School" first appears in David Croal Thomson's *The Barbizon School of Painters*.

1892

The artistic reserve in the Forest of Fontainebleau is expanded to 1,692 hectares.

Cézanne acquires a house in Marlotte and works in the forest through 1893.

1893

The oak Henri IV is destroyed in a fire.

1899

JANUARY: The oak Briarée is felled in a windstorm.

1900

Eugène Cuvelier dies at Thoméry.

Notes

Landscapes, Legends, Souvenirs, Fantasies

The Forest of Fontainebleau in the Nineteenth Century

KIMBERLY JONES

1 Julia Kavanagh, *Bessie* (London, 1872), 1.

2 Chateaubriand to Mme Récamier, November 1834, *Souvenirs et correspondance tirés des papiers de Madame Récamier...*, ed. Amélie Cyvoct Lenormant (Paris, 1859), 441; George Sand "Fragment d'une lettre écrite à Fontainebleau," in Claude-François Denecourt, *Fontainebleau. Paysages, légendes, souvenirs, fantasies. Hommage à C. F. Denecourt* (Paris, 1855b), 82, and Sand to Gustave Flaubert, 31 July 1868, *Correspondance, 1812–1876* (Paris, 1884), 5:270; and *Victor Hugo Correspondance (1867–1873)* (Paris, 1952), 3:341.

3 Albert de la Fizelière, "Les auberges illustrées," *L'Illustration* 22, no. 565 (24 December 1853): 424–425; Philippe Burty, "La forêt de Fontainebleau," *La Renaissance littéraire et artistique*, no. 27 (26 October 1872): 211; and Frédéric Henriet, *Le paysagiste aux champs* (Paris, 1876), 13.

4 According to a study undertaken in 1967–1968, this was nine times the number of people who visited the Musée du Louvre. See OTAM—SARES—District de la Région Parisienne, Ministère de l'Agriculture, ONF, "La fréquentation des Forêts de la Région Parisienne," April 1969, cited in Bernard Kalaora, *Le musée vert, ou, le tourisme en forêt. Naissance et développement d'un loisir urbain. Le cas de la forêt de Fontainebleau* (Paris, 1981), 99.

5 Paul Domet, *Histoire de la forêt de Fontainebleau* (Paris, 1873), 2. Domet's text is the most authoritative examination of the forest published in the nineteenth century and is an invaluable contemporary study.

6 Denecourt recounts this story in his popular guidebooks. See, for example, Claude-François Denecourt, *Guide du voyageur et de l'artiste à Fontainebleau, itinéraire du palais et de la forêt avec les promenades les plus pittoresques* (Paris, 1850a), 23. See also Frédéric Bernard, *Fontainebleau et ses environs* (Paris, 1853), 90. Remarkably, even scholarly texts repeated this fictional account. See Jules Clavé, "Etudes forestières. La forêt de Fontainebleau," *Revue des deux mondes* 45 (1 May 1863): 144.

7 Domet 1873, 4.

8 Antoine Fontanon, *Les edicts et ordonnances des roys [sic] de France*, 2d ed. (Paris, 1585), 2:259, cited in L. F. Alfred Maury, *Histoire des grandes forêts de la Gaule et de l'ancienne France* (Paris, 1850), 234 n. 2.

9 Domet 1873, 3, 5–6, 9, 11.

10 Domet 1873, 31. The *liste civile* (based on the civil list of the British monarchy) is the sum that is allotted to a sovereign for expenses related to the performance of his state duties. This includes state visits, official entertainment, personal staff, and the upkeep of his household. It also encompasses properties and residences designated for his use.

11 Domet 1873, 37–39. On the size of the forest and information about the decree of 6 September 1870, see Gérard Tendron, *La forêt de Fontainebleau. De l'écologie à la sylviculture* (Fontainebleau, 1983), 21.

12 Fontainebleau is 4.56 times the size of the forest of Saint-Germain-en-Laye, 6.4 times the size of Sénart, and 15 times the size of Meudon. Kalaora 1981, 98.

13 Clavé 1863, 155.

14 Tendron 1983, 12–14. See also Clavé 1863, 145–146.

15 Clavé 1863, 169.

16 The first paved streets in Paris date from the reign of Philippe-Auguste in 1184. It is possible that some of those paving stones came from Fontainebleau; however, other scholars date the export of paving stones from Fontainebleau to Paris to c. 1388. Domet 1873, 212.

17 *Dictionnaire de l'industrie, manufactère, commerciale et agricole* (Paris, 1837), 16:130. See also Domet 1873, 217; and Tendron 1983, 23.

18 From a diary entry, 7 March 1644, *The Diary of John Evelyn* (London, 1906), 1:88.

19 Addison to William Congreve, December 1699, *The Works of Joseph Addison*, ed. George Washington Greene (New York, 1853), 2:463.

20 From an entry dated 2 September [1814], Percy Bysshe Shelley, Mary Wollstonecraft Shelley, and John Davis, *Essays, Letters from Abroad, Translations, and Fragments* (London, 1840), 104.

21 From a journal entry, 1 July 1834, *A Portion of the Journal Kept by Thomas Raikes, Esq. from 1831 to 1847* (London, 1856), 1:254.

22 See E. Jamin, *Fontainebleau, ou notice historique et descriptive sur cette résidence royale*, 2d. ed. (Fontainebleau, 1838), 250; "Forêt de Fontainebleau," *Magasin pittoresque* 17 (March 1849): 75; and "Résidences royales. Fontainebleau—La forêt," *L'Illustration* 6, no. 141 (8 November 1845): 151.

23 *Extracts from the Journals and Correspondence of Miss Mary Berry: From the Year 1783 to 1852*, ed. Lady Theresa Lewis (London, 1865), 1:220.

24 From an entry dated 10 April 1837, Stendhal, *Mémoires d'un touriste*, new ed. (Paris, 1854), 25.

25 John Ruskin, "Fontainebleau," in *The Works of John Ruskin*, ed. Ernest Thomas Cook and Alexander Wedderburn (London, 1908), 35:314. The passage is from Ruskin's incomplete autobiography, *Praeterita*, which was published in 1881 and 1886.

26 Seward to F., August 1833, *The Works of William H. Seward*, ed. George E. Baker (New York, 1853), 3:580. From 1861 to 1869, Seward was U.S. secretary of state under Presidents Abraham Lincoln and Andrew Johnson.

27 Etienne Pivert de Senancour, *Obermann*, with a preface by George Sand, new ed. (Paris, [1840?]), 74.

28 Sand's preface appeared in at least five editions published between 1840 and 1874.

29 George Sand, *Impressions et souvenirs*, ed. Eve Sourian (Paris, 2005), 279, 280.

30 Sand in Denecourt 1855b, 82.

31 For more on Flaubert's novel, see Jean Borie, *Une forêt pour les dimanches. Les romantiques à Fontainebleau* (Paris, 2003), 297–343.

32 Gustave Flaubert, *L'Education sentimentale* (Paris, 1985), 396.

33 Hue offered the painting *View Taken in the Forest of Fontainebleau* (no. 212) as his reception piece on 30 November 1782. Georgel 2007, 19. He would exhibit this piece at the Salon of 1783, and he exhibited a third forest scene at the Salon of 1785. For an overview of artists in Fontainebleau prior to the nineteenth century, see Georgel 2007, 19–27.

34 Bidauld traveled to Fontainebleau in late 1783. He returned there in 1793. See Georgel 2007, 29. Le Gillon was there in the summer of 1783, "spending all his days making sketches of beautiful sites." *Biographie des hommes remarquables de la Flandre Occidentale* (Bruges, 1843), 1:283. He exhibited *View of the Forest of Fontainebleau, Several Figures and Animals near a Fountain* (no. 8) at the Salon of 1791.

35 Charles Rémard, *Le guide du voyageur à Fontainebleau* (Fontainebleau and Paris, 1820), 130–131.

36 François-Hippolyte Paillet, *Description physique de la forêt de Fontainebleau* (Versailles, 1806), 24; and Jacques-Antoine Dulaure, *Histoire physique et morale de Paris depuis les premiers temps historiques jusqu'à nos jours* (Paris, 1825), 62. See also Georgel 2007, 26.

37 Pierre-Henri de Valenciennes, *Eléments de perspective pratique, à l'usage des artistes, suivis de réflexions et conseils à un élève sur la peinture, et* *particulièrement sur le genre du paysage* (Paris, [1800?]; reprint, Geneva, 1973), 626.

38 On Valenciennes and plein-air practice, see Paula Rea Radisich, "Eighteenth-Century *Plein-Air* Painting and the Sketches of Pierre-Henri de Valenciennes," *The Art Bulletin* 65, no. 1 (March 1982): 98–104. See also Philip Conisbee, "The Early History of Open-Air Painting," in *In the Light of Italy: Corot and Early Open-Air Painting* [exh. cat., National Gallery of Art] (Washington, 1996), 29–47.

39 These paintings include *View Taken at Essonnes* (c. 1805; Musée du Louvre) and *Entrance to the Park at Saint Cloud* (c. 1800; Museum of Fine Arts, Boston).

40 Alfred Robaut and Etienne Moreau-Nélaton, *L'oeuvre de Corot, par Robaut. Catalogue raisonné et illustré, précédé de l'histoire de Corot et de ses oeuvres* (Paris, 1905), vol. 5, no. 5.

41 Vincent Pomarède and Gérard de Wallens, *L'école de Barbizon. Peindre en plein air avant l'impressionnisme* [exh. cat., Musée des Beaux-Arts] (Lyon, 2002), 277.

42 See Marie-Madeleine Aubrun, *Théodore Caruelle d'Aligny, 1798–1871. Catalogue raisonné de l'œuvre peint, dessiné, gravé* ([Paris], 1988).

43 See Washington 1996; and *Paysages d'Italie. Les peintres du plein air (1780–1830)* [exh. cat., Galeries nationales du Grand Palais] (Paris, 2001).

44 On Corot's associates in Italy, see Peter Galassi, *Corot in Italy: Open-Air Painting and the Classical-Landscape Tradition* (New Haven and London, 1991), 136. Galassi provides an excellent overview of the artistic community in Rome during the early nineteenth century.

45 Etienne Moreau-Nélaton, *Corot raconté par lui-même* (Paris, 1924), 1:29.

46 See Félix Herbet, *Stamati Bulgari* (Fontainebleau, 1905), quoted in Georgel 2007, 31.

47 From an article by M. Carro in the *Chronique* of Seine-et-Marne, quoted in H. Mion, *La salamandre, ou l'histoire abrégée et la description complète de la ville* (Fontainebleau, 1839), 137, 139.

48 On Rousseau's sojourns to Fontainebleau, see Alfred Sensier, *Souvenirs sur Th. Rousseau* (Paris, 1872), 51–52, 95, 98, 117, 119, 121, 170.

49 Cabat exhibited a painting at the Salon that year entitled *View of the Gorges-aux-Loups (Seine-et-Marne)* (no. 285). Diaz exhibited *View Taken in the Gorges d'Appremont* [*sic*] (no. 352) at the Salon of 1837.

50 See Marie-Thérèse Forges, *Barbizon* (Paris, 1962), 70–74.

51 On the village of Barbizon and its artist colony, see Nicholas Green, *The Spectacle of Nature: Landscape and Bourgeois Culture in Nineteenth-Century France* (Manchester and New York, 1990), 116–120.

52 Bernard 1853, 119.

53 Marie-Thérèse Caille, *L'Auberge Ganne: Musée Municipal de l'Ecole de Barbizon* (Moisenay, 1994), 40. Sensier claimed that it was Aligny who advised Ganne to open his inn in 1824. However, this is suspect since, according to Aubrun, Aligny was in Italy from 1822 to 1827. The lack of any extant works—the earliest known drawings of Fontainebleau by Aligny date to 1828—argues against this as well. See Alfred Sensier, "Historique de Barbizon" (unpublished manuscript, Bibliothèque municipale de Fontainebleau), 50; and Georgel 2007, 159–163.

54 Bernard 1853, 119. This was the rate for guests who were lodging a month or more. For shorter stays, the price was four francs. Adolphe Joanne, *Fontainebleau. Son palais, ses jardins, sa forêt* (Paris, [1856]), 193. See also Caille 1994, 48.

55 Henry Murger, *Scènes de campagne; Adeline Protat* (Paris, n.d.), 305–306.

56 Charles Sprague Smith, *Barbizon Days* (New York, 1902), 19–20. See also Forges 1962, 70–74.

57 A number of other artists identified Barbizon as their place of residence between the years 1850 and 1875, including Eugène Lavieille, Adolphe-André Wacquez, Ferdinand Chaigneau, Georges-Etienne Prieur, Vincent Chevillard, Camille Paris, Jean-Baptiste Millet (the brother of Jean-François Millet), and Eugène Masson. See the catalogues of the Paris Salon from 1850 to 1875. These are only a fraction of the artists who were affiliated with the village.

58 De la Fizelière 1853, 426.

59 David Croal Thomson is generally credited with coining the term "Barbizon School" in his book *The Barbizon School of Painters: Corot, Rousseau, Diaz, Millet, Daubigny, etc.* (New York, 1890).

60 Théophile Thoré, "Par monts et par bois," pt. 2, *Le Constitutionnel*, no. 532 (28 November 1847): 1, col. 5.

61 Sensier 1872, 118.

62 See Mariana Starke, *Information and Directions for Travelers on the Continent*, 5th ed. (Paris, 1826), 331–333.

63 See Claude-François Denecourt, *Nouvel indicateur de Fontainebleau* (Fontainebleau, 1843b), n.p.

64 The Paris-Corbeil line opened on 20 September 1840, and the Paris-Tonnerre section was inaugurated on 17 August 1849. Adolphe Joanne, *Atlas historique et statistique des chemins de fer* (Paris, 1859), 50, 62.

65 See Joanne [1856], 2.

66 It should be noted that three of those trains were "direct" and only accommodated first- and second-class passengers. Those desiring the less expensive third-class seats were understandably more limited in their options. In 1850, a first-class ticket between Paris and Fontainebleau cost 6F10, second class cost 4F60, and third class cost 3F40. Denecourt 1850a, n.p.

67 Denecourt 1850a, n.p.; Joanne [1856], 1; Adolphe Joanne, *Fontainebleau. Son palais, ses jardins, sa forêt et ses environs* (Paris, 1867), 1; and Joanne 1859, 69.

68 The *trains de plaisir* between Paris and Fontainebleau operated only on Sundays. In 1850, trains left Paris promptly at 10 AM; the return train left Fontainebleau at ten the same evening. See Denecourt 1850a, n.p.

69 "Aperçu biographique de l'auteur," in Claude-François Denecourt, *L'Indicateur de Fontainebleau. Visite du palais et de la forêt*, 10th ed. (Fontainebleau, [1855a]), 50, 45–53. See also Auguste Luchet, "Pour qui ce livre est fait," in Denecourt 1855b, 1–25.

70 For a thorough study of tourist literature and Fontainebleau, see Green 1990, 167–181.

71 Denecourt even included the text of Jamin's "Description physique et topographique de la forêt de Fontainebleau" in his *Nouvel indicateur de Fontainebleau*. See E. Jamin, *Quatre promenades dans la forêt de Fontainebleau, ou description physique et topographique de cette forêt royale* (Fontainebleau, 1837); and Denecourt 1843b.

72 Claude-François Denecourt, *Camp de Fontainebleau, sa position topographique.... Avec une carte.... Cet opuscule fait suite au "Guide du voyageur dans la forêt de Fontainebleau"* (Fontainebleau, September 1839).

73 Claude-François Denecourt, *Guide du voyageur dans le palais et la forêt de Fontainebleau, ou histoire et description abrégées de ces lieux rémarquables et pittoresques*, pt. 2 (Fontainebleau, 1843a), 11.

74 The standard guides were generally priced from 1F to 1F50 while the *Délices* typically sold for 50 centimes. Guides with good quality maps were more expensive.

75 Claude-François Denecourt, *L'Indicateur de Fontainebleau. Itinéraire descriptif du palais, de la forêt et des environs* (Fontainebleau, 1868).

76 Claude-François Denecourt, *Guide of the English Traveller, Fontainebleau.* (Fontainebleau, 1856).

77 See Pecheux-Herbenville, *Fontainebleau et les charmantes promenades aux sites et aux rochers qui l'environnent. Edition ornée de cartes et vues et comprenant un aperçu historique et artistique du palais et de ses dependances* (Fontainebleau, 1850).

78 Rémard 1820, 121–122; and Denecourt 1840, 29; also Jean-Baptiste-Alexis Durand, "La forêt de Fontainebleau, poème en 4 chants, suivi de poésies diverses" (Fontainebleau, 1836), 28; Jamin 1838, 255; and Dencourt 1840, 27. Rocher des Deux Soeurs is named for Anais and Félicie de Larminat and bears an inscription with its name and a date of 1829. See Denecourt 1840, 24; Claude-François Denecourt, *Les délices de la forêt de Fontainebleau*, 3d ed. (Fontainebleau, [1845a]), 42–43; and Félix Herbet, *Dictionnaire historique et artistique de la Forêt de Fontainebleau. Routes, carrefours, cantons, gardes, monuments, croix, fontaines, puits, mares, environs, moulins, etc.* (Fontainebleau, 1903), 163.

79 Neither tree still stands. Pharamond fell in 1909, and Charlemagne in 1925. René Alleau, *Guide de Fontainebleau mystérieux* (Paris, 1967), 60.

80 Denecourt 1840, 26; and Denecourt [1845a], 15. The Henri IV was destroyed by a fire in 1893. Herbet 1903, 205.

81 Denecourt 1840, 112.

82 Denecourt [1845a], 24, 35, 45.

83 Denecourt [1855a], 8, 9, 11, 12, 26, 27, 72.

84 Denecourt [1855a], 18.

85 Flaubert 1985, 395.

86 Jean-Pierre Hervet and Patrick Mérienne, *La forêt de Fontainebleau* (Rennes, 1997), 12.

87 See Denecourt 1850a.

88 Kalaora 1981, 114.

89 Claude-François Denecourt, *Petit indicateur du voyageur à Fontainebleau, ou renseignements indispensables pour séjourner agréablement dans ce pittoresque rendez-vous de plaisance* (Paris, 1850b), 15.

90 Kavanagh 1872, 87–88.

91 The original Fort de l'Empereur was destroyed by an earthquake in 1878 and was subsequently rebuilt by Claude Charles Colinet, Denecourt's successor. See Herbet 1903, 431.

92 Herbet 1903, 169. Sanguinède, a former merchant in Paris, was one of Denecourt's most generous subscribers, donating 322 francs to his enterprise. Denecourt [1855a], 63. The Fontaine Dorly, also built in 1852, was named for another of Denecourt's generous subscribers.

93 See Herbet 1903, 78.

94 Denecourt [1845a], 13–14. See also Denecourt 1850a, 34.

95 Herbet 1903, 78.

96 Joanne openly acknowledges this practice. He described the Grotte de Serment as "the most surprising of M. Denecourt's creations," and recounted that Denecourt engaged fifteen quarrymen to carve it out. The nearby Grotte de Parjure is also one of Denecourt's "follies," as is the Rendez-vous du Chasseur-noir. Joanne [1856], 160, 161, 162.

97 Denecourt 1850b, 6.

98 Denecourt 1850b, 9–10. See, for example, Denecourt 1843a; and Claude-François Denecourt, *Les délices de la forêt de Fontainebleau, ou itinéraire descriptif de tous les sites et points de vue remarquables de cette forêt royale* (Fontainebleau, [1855c]). For the "genévrines," see Jean-Claude Polton, *Tourisme et nature au XIXe siècle. Guides et itinéraires de la forêt de Fontainebleau (vers 1820–vers 1880)* (Paris, 1994), 214.

99 Green 1990, 177.

100 Karl Baedeker, *Paris and Its Environs, with Routes from London to Paris, and from Paris to the Rhine and Switzerland: Handbook for Travellers* (Leipzig, 1878), 319. There is still a snack stand near that site today.

101 Jules Levallois, *Mémoires d'une forêt. Fontainebleau* (Paris, 1875), 168.

102 Anonymous, "Of the Picturesque Beauty around Us," *The Monthly Religious Magazine and Independent Journal* 17, 2d ser., vol. 15 (Boston, 1857), 254.

103 From an agenda entry, 23 March 1856, George Sand, *Agendas (1852–1856)* (Paris, 1990), 1:367.

104 Levallois 1875, 53.

105 Burty 1872, 212.

106 Robert Louis Stevenson, "Fontainebleau: Village Communities of Painters," in *Virginibus Puerisque and Other Papers: Later Essays* (Edinburgh, 1895), 209–210.

107 A.S., "La forêt de Barbizon — Dévastations," *L'artiste* 3, 2d ser. (1839): 290.

108 Sensier 1872, 18.

109 Thoré 1847, pt. 2, 1, col. 3.

110 A draft version of this petition is reproduced in its entirety in Greg M. Thomas, *Art and Ecology in Nineteenth-Century France: The Landscapes of Théodore Rousseau* (Princeton, 2000), 214–217. Thomas also provides a thorough account of Rousseau's petition along with its content, implications, and consequences on pages 173–186. See also Sensier 1872, 211–212.

111 Petition to Napoleon III, quoted in Thomas 2000, 215.

112 Tendron 1983, 28.

113 See A.S. 1839, 292. See also Joanne 1856, 185; and Du Pays, "Le château et la forêt de Fontainebleau: La forêt," *Le Tour du monde* 16, no. 393 (1867): 22.

114 Burty 1872, 212.

115 Thoré 1847, pt. 2, col. 2.

116 "Résidences royales" 1845, 154.

117 Most of the trees from this planting died from cold during the winter of 1788–1789. Domet 1873, 140–141.

118 Domet 1873, 141.

119 See Charles d'Orbigny, ed., *Dictionnaire universel d'histoire naturelle* (Paris, 1847), 10:195, "pin sylvestre."

120 Tendron 1983, 28.

121 Denecourt [1845a], 68–69.

122 Clavé 1863, 154. Four years later, Du Pays estimated that it was closer to 5,000 hectares. Du Pays 1867, 27. By the late twentieth century, pines accounted for 41 percent of the trees that populate the Forest of Fontainebleau, second only to oak at 44 percent. Kalaora 1981, 98.

123 René-Richard Castel, "La forêt de Fontainebleau. Poème" (Paris, 1805), quoted in Jamin 1838, 255.

124 A.S. 1839, 292.

125 Thoré 1847, pt. 1, col. 5.

126 Du Pays 1867, 26.

127 "La forêt de Fontainebleau," *Magasin pittoresque* 31 (May 1863): 154.

128 Thomas 2000, 215.

129 Sensier 1872, 359.

130 On Denecourt and his detractors, see Polton 1994, 206–207.

131 Claude-François Denecourt, "La guerre déclarée à mes sentiers," in Denecourt 1855a, 66.

132 Joanne [1856], 180. See also Du Pays 1867, 30. The effects of tourism on this site had been noted as early as 1845: "all around the Roche Qui Pleure, the ground is trampled, tread underfoot like on a highway; the rock is covered with names and inscriptions. This universal plague called tourism has tarnished all of that." "Résidences royales" 1845, 154.

133 Adolphe Joanne, *Les environs de Paris illustrés*, 2d ed. (Paris, 1878), 506. Another tree was later given this name. It too met a tragic fate in 1893, when it was toppled by a windstorm. Herbet 1903, 368.

134 Petition to Napoleon III, quoted in Thomas 2000, 216, 217.

135 For a more thorough discussion of this decree and the studies leading up to its creation, see Thomas 2000, 173–178.

136 Polton 1994, 222.

137 This *réserve artistique* was discontinued in 1967. The majority of its most interesting trees had long since died, and the most important parcels of land had already been integrated into the newer *réserve biologique* in 1953. Tendron 1983, 36.

138 Polton 1994, 223. For a more complete discussion of this commission, see pages 223–228.

139 Burty 1872, 211–212. Sand's letter was published in *Le Temps* on 13 November. It is reproduced in Sand 2005, 285–298. Hugo's letter was published in *La Renaissance littéraire et artistique* on 7 December 1872. It is reproduced in Hugo 1952, 341.

140 Burty 1872, 212.

141 Polton 1994, 227.

142 "Le Salon," *Journal des artistes* 1, no. 40 (1844): 74.

143 Thoré 1847, pt. 1, 1, col. 2.

144 Henriet 1876, 4. Saint-Cyr is the French military academy founded by Napoleon I in 1802.

145 Murger's description of the Mare aux Fées was published in extracted form in Denecourt 1855b, 97–102.

146 Murger n.d., 196.

147 Clavé 1863, 170.

148 For information on the Auberge de la Mère Anthony, see Henriet 1876, 15; and Edmond and Jules de Goncourt, *Journal: Mémoires de la vie littéraire* (Monaco, 1956), 6:101.

149 For a partial list of artists who worked in Barbizon and Fontainebleau during the second half of the nineteenth century, see Forges 1962, 70–74.

150 Sharman Wallace McGurn, "William Morris Hunt: A Chronology," in *The Late Landscapes of William Morris Hunt* [exh. cat., University of Maryland Art Gallery] (College Park, 1976), 61.

151 The works were titled *View Taken in the Forest of Fontainebleau*, *Highway* and *View of Bas-Bréau in the Forest of Fontainebleau* (nos. 649 and 650).

152 Letter dated 19 July 1858, no. 1047, *The Letters of William Cullen Bryant, 1858–1864*, ed. William Cullen Bryant II and Thomas G. Voss (Bronx, 1994), 4:68. The letter is an incomplete draft presumed to have been intended for publication in *The Evening Post*.

153 See Anne Morand, *Thomas Moran: The Field Sketches, 1856–1923* (Norman, OK, 1996), 130–132. Moran first traveled to Yellowstone in the summer of 1871. I wish to thank Nancy Anderson for bringing this to my attention.

154 Will H. Low, *A Chronicle of Friendship, 1873–1900* (New York, 1908), 123.

155 See "Montigny and Grez — Summer of '76," in Low 1908, 172–183. See also Robert Louis Stevenson, "Forest Notes," in *Essays of Travel and in the Art of Writing* (New York, 1905), 179–182.

156 On the artists who traveled to Grez, see H. Barbara Weinberg, "Summers in the Country," in *Americans in Paris, 1860–1900* [exh. cat., National Gallery] (London, 2006), 133–135. See also pages 248, 254, 263.

157 Charles Lenormant, *Les artistes contemporains: Salons de 1831 et 1833* (Paris, 1833), 158.

158 The first painting of this site was Eugène Ciceri's *Mare aux Fées* (no. 379). It appeared at the Salon of 1850.

159 For Giverny, see *Impressionist Giverny: A Colony of Artists, 1885–1915* [exh. cat., Musée d'Art Américain] (Giverny, 2007). For Old Lyme, see Jeffrey W. Andersen, *Old Lyme: The American Barbizon* (Old Lyme, 1982).

160 Stevenson 1895, 223–224.

Plates

Discovery

1 Corot to Abel Osmond, July 1831, *Corot, raconté par lui-même et par ses amis* (Vésenaz-Geneva, 1946), 1:191.

2 Murger n.d., 2–3.

3 Stevenson 1895, 215; Georgel 2007, 159, 161. The Auberge Siron opened on 7 July 1867. See Henriet 1876, 14.

4 Frédéric Bazille to his mother, 8 April 1863, Bazille 1992, 51; Goncourt 1956, 6:101.

5 Clavé 1863, 170.

Topography

1 "Fontainebleau: The Forest," pt. 4, *Littell's Living Age* 21, no. 257 (21 June 1849): 140; Herbet 1903, 196. The Mare à Piat is named for a garde général of the forests. Herbet 1903, 258.

2 Clavé 1863, 155.

3 In 1661, Paul Barillon d'Amoncourt was charged with conducting an examination of the forests of the French crown; he submitted the report of his findings in 1664. Bas-Bréau is named for the medieval fiefdom to which this region once belonged. See Domet 1873, 17–19, 22.

4 For a list of works depicting Bas-Bréau, see Herbet 1903, 26–28.

5 This road is part of route nationale no. 7, which stretches from Paris to Antibes. Herbet 1903, 306.

6 Robaut 1905, 2, no. 8; Sensier 1872, 18.

7 On artists and the Pavé de Chailly, see Georgel 2007, 68–71.

8 Domet 1873, 238, 239.

9 Herbet 1903, x. A *toise* is a measurement used in prerevolutionary France. It is equivalent to about 1.949 meters.

10 Kalaora 1981, 114.

Trees

1 For a thorough discussion of the plant life in Fontainebleau during the nineteenth century, see E. Jamin, "Description physique et topographique de la forêt de Fontainebleau," in Denecourt 1843b, 41–61. At present there are an estimated eighty species of trees in the Forest of Fontainebleau. See Jean-Pierre Hervet and Patrick Mérienne, *Fontainebleau. Une forêt de légendes et de mystères* (Rennes, 2004), 100. *Pissat du lapin* was created by infusing juniper berries in brandy, to which sugar was then added. See Denecourt 1843b, 54–55.

2 Denecourt 1843b, 51.

3 Bazille to his mother, 8 April 1863, Bazille 1992, 51.

4 Stevenson 1895, 208.

5 Thoré 1847, pt. 1, 1, col. 6.

6 On the association of the oak trees of Fontainebleau and the Druids, see "Résidences royales" 1845, 152; and Du Pays 1867, 22.

7 Flaubert 1985, 398.

8 "Fontainebleau" 1849, pt. 4, 140.

9 Bodmer exhibited three paintings; each entitled *Forest Interior* (nos. 268–270). It is unclear when the name "Bodmer" became widely associated with this oak tree, but it was at least by 1855, when it appeared as part of a litany of oak trees Denecourt proudly claimed to have brought to light. See "La guerre déclarée à mes sentiers," in Denecourt [1855a], 66.

Rocks

1 "Résidences royales" 1845, 154.

2 Comte de Buffon, *L'histoire naturelle des minéraux* (Paris, 1783), 1:138–149.

3 Lyell to his father, 10 August 1823, *Life, Letters, and Journal of Sir Charles Lyell, Bart . . .*, ed. Katherine M. Lyell (London, 1881), 1:137.

4 Journal entry, 26 June 1818, Lyell 1881, 1:64.

5 Denecourt [1845a], 25.

6 Joanne [1856], 172.

7 The Elephant is located in the Gorges d'Apremont, the Tortoise is on the Massif des Trois Pignons, and the Hippopotamus is near Rocher Cassepot. See Denecourt [1855a], 26, 72.

8 Thoré 1847, pt. 1, 2, cols. 1–2.

9 See Denecourt [1855a] for additional examples.

10 "When the sun gilds the sands and illuminates the arid rock with its warm rays, one believes oneself to be in the solitude of Palestine." Clavé 1863, 156.

11 A. Hugo, *France pittoresque, ou description pittoresque, topographique et statistique des départements et colonies de la France* (Paris, 1838), 3:149.

12 "Forêt de Fontainebleau," in George Sand, *Impressions et souvenirs* (Paris, 1873), 320.

Village Life

1 Joanne 1878, 532.

2 Millet to Sensier, [February 1851], Musée du Louvre, Départment des arts graphiques, fonds des autographes, A 1716, reproduced in Alfred Sensier and Paul Mantz, *La vie et l'œuvre de Jean-François Millet* (Bricquebosq, 2005), 116.

3 See Jones essay this volume.

4 Domet 1873, 200, 202. There were rare exceptions to this rule. Following the French Revolution, there was a brief period during which sheep grazed freely in the forest. This, however, was due to lack of policing rather than a change in the forest code. In 1870, an extreme drought led Napoleon III to loosen restrictions temporarily and allow unlimited grazing in the forest for all domestic animals, including sheep. See Domet 1873, 210.

5 A[dolphe] Hugues, ed., *Inventaire des Archives départementales postérieures à 1789. Seine-et-Marne. Période révolutionnaire* (Melun, 1904), 1:172.

6 On the Forest Code of 1827, see Peter Sahlin, *Forest Rites: The War of the Desmoiselles in the Nineteenth Century* (Cambridge, MA, 1994), 18–19.

7 Domet 1873, 207. See also Thomas 2000, 154–156.

8 Polton 1994, 42.

9 Domet 1873, 210–211.

Nature and Observation

1 Théophile Thoré, "Salon of 1844," in *Salons de T. Thoré*, 2d ed. (Paris, 1870), 73.

2 M. de Sen . . ., "Sur Fontainebleau," *Mercure de France* 5 (January 1812): 15.

3 Tendron 1983, 11.

4 Millet to Sensier, c. 1850, Sensier and Mantz 2005, 109; Millet to Sensier, c. 24 February 1853, Valentine de Chillaz, *Inventaire général des autographes. Musée du Louvre* (Paris, 1997), 235, Aut. 1742.

5 Millet to [Emile] Gavet, 28 December 1865, cited in Alfred Sensier, "Jean-François Millet—Peasant and Painter," pt. 5, *Scribner's Monthly* 21, no. 3 (January 1881): 397.

6 Jules Michelet, *L'Insecte*, 5th ed. (Paris, 1863): XXVIII–XXIX.

7 Thoré 1847, pt. 2, 1, col. 5.

8 Sensier 1872, 117.

9 Charles Clément, *Etudes sur les beaux-arts en France* (Paris, 1865), 382.

The Mystery of the Forest

Paintings of Fontainebleau at the Salon

SIMON KELLY

The title for this essay is taken from Charles Blanc, "Salon of 1846," pt. 3, *La Réforme*, 10 April 1846. All translations are the author's unless otherwise noted.

1 Henriet 1876, 13.

2 See Nelda Damiano, "Landscapes in the Salon," in *Renoir Landscapes, 1865–1883* [exh. cat., National Gallery] (London, 2007), 280.

3 See Georgel 2007, 111–117. See also the valuable listing on pages 176–187. There are some omissions, including, for example, Rousseau's *The Oak Tree of the Rock (Forest of Fontainebleau)*, which was exhibited in 1861, or Millet's *Winter*, a view of the plain of Chailly, which was shown in 1867.

4 See Chantal Georgel, lecture presented at the Forest of Fontainebleau colloquium, Musée d'Orsay, 27 April 2007.

5 The Gorges d'Apremont appeared forty-six times from 1836 to 1881, the Bas-Bréau fifty-two times from 1835 to 1881, the Belle-Croix fifty-six times from 1840 to 1881, and the Gorges aux Loups thirty-eight times from 1827 to 1881. Views of Barbizon appeared sixty-nine times from 1835 to 1881. See J. Whiteley, "Subject Index to Paintings Exhibited at the Paris Salon, 1673–1881," Sackler Library, University of Oxford.

6 The first artist to exhibit a forest painting at the Salon was Jean-François Hue in 1781. In 1796, Théodore Rousseau's great-uncle, Pau de Saint-Martin père, exhibited two views of the forest.

7 Lenormant, for example, noted of Bertin: "The young painter seems to us to have rendered perfectly the austerity of the sandstone of Fontainebleau." Lenormant 1833, 2:158.

8 Aubrun 1988, D131; Auguste Jal, *Salon de 1833. Les causeries du Louvre* (Paris, 1833), 354.

9 "The painting of M. Corot seems to me the perfect landscape of the exhibition this year." See Lenormant 1833, 2:105.

10 Félix Pyat, *Diogène au Salon* (Paris, 1846), 96–97. For Charles Blanc, Corot was the "Scheffer du paysage." See Blanc 1846.

11 See Théophile Gautier, "Salon de 1846," *La Presse*, 4 April 1846.

12 See also Richard Shiff, "Natural, Personal, Pictorial: Corot and the Painter's Mark," in Burmester, Heilmann, and Zimmermann 1999, 120–138.

13 See Théophile Thoré, "Le Salon de 1844. Précédé d'une lettre à Théodore Rousseau" (Paris, 1844), 34. The talented etcher Louis Marvy reproduced Diaz' forest views. See "Paysage d'après M. Diaz, gravé par M. Marvy," *L'Artiste* 5, 3d ser., no. 14 (1844); and "Paysage d'après M. Diaz, gravure de M. L. Marvy," *L'Artiste* 6, 4th ser., no. 2 (15 March 1846).

14 "The painting of M. Diaz is a dream in enchanted lands. These forests and voluptuous creatures only appear in visions. Diaz owes his success to this magical charm; because his painting itself, or rather his execution, is a little frightening for the bourgeoisie, who in general love finished, tidy and easily comprehensible painting." See Théophile Thoré, "Le Salon de 1846. Précédé d'une lettre à George Sand" (Paris, 1846), 109.

15 Clément de Ris, "Salon de 1848, IV," *L'Artiste* 1, 5th ser., no. 4 (2 April 1848): 59.

16 The vertical composition of this painting is reminiscent of Rousseau's *La descente des vaches* (Museum Mesdag, The Hague). Diaz' work for the Salon of 1847—*The Bas-Bréau, Forest of Fontainebleau* (Musée d'Orsay)—shows a group of cows in this ancient wood and arguably looks to a similar view by Rousseau, *Forest Interior* (Musée d'Orsay), which was begun in 1837 and completed at the end of Rousseau's life.

17 Blanc 1846.

18 Théophile Gautier, *La Presse*, 17 April 1845. At the same Salon, Thoré described Troyon's landscape (location unknown) as "perhaps the best landscape of the Salon." See Théophile Thoré, *Salon de 1845* (Paris, 1845), 144.

19 Charles Blanc included a laudatory biography on Troyon in his later publication, *Les artistes de mon temps* (Paris, 1876), 313–323.

20 Rousseau included views of the Forest of Fontainebleau in nine of the eleven Salons in which he participated, from 1850 until his death in 1867 (1850, 1852, 1855, 1857, 1859, 1861, 1863, 1866, and 1867).

21 Théophile Gautier, "Salon de 1850–1," *La Presse*, 24 April 1851.

22 The work was exhibited as *Forest Edge, Sunset*. The dimensions of the painting in the register of Salon works (Archives des Musées nationaux) are 1.80 × 1.15 meters (with frame) and thus do not correspond to the Louvre painting, but examination of Salon criticism (such as that of François Sabatier-Ungher or Gabriel de Ferry) clearly indicates that this was indeed the painting that was shown and that the measurements must be mistaken. De Ferry, for example, described the painting thus: "A group of three mossy, rough and contorted hundred-year-old oaks form with another oak an arch-shaped opening of foliage at the end of which the round disk of the sun—a pale red like white-hot iron—appears through the purple of the horizon." See Gabriel de Ferry, *L'Ordre*, 23 April 1851.

23 De Ferry 1851.

24 See François Sabatier-Ungher, *Salon de 1851* (Paris, 1851), 13.

25 Alfred Dauger, "Salon de 1851," *Le Pays*, 13 March 1851.

26 Gautier 1851.

27 The measurements of the work are listed in the Enregistrement des ouvrages (Archives des Musées nationaux) as 4475, *Paysage, forêt de Fontainebleau*, 1.35 × 1.60 meters (with frame). In his review of the Salon of 1851, François Sabatier-Ungher described the work this way: "The sky, bright with warm and colored light, gives a strange power to the tree masses.... Sheltered and almost hidden between these trees is a small woodcutter's hut made from debris like the hut of a savage.... a woman is seated next to the door. In front and in the middle ground, in the very center of the painting, two cows, marked with patches, come down to drink at the most attractive pond imaginable that has been left behind in the fields after rainfall.... here and there tips of gray rocks emerge from the earth like bones in a cemetery." See Sabatier-Ungher 1851, 15. Rousseau also sent a small pen-and-ink sketch of the work to a prospective collector (Musée des Beaux-Arts, Dijon, Donation Granville).

28 Rousseau to M. Sériyes, quoted in *Donation Granville, Musée de Dijon*, ed. Serge Lemoine (Dijon, 1975), 225. Two drafts of this letter are in the Département des arts graphiques, Musée du Louvre. See Valentine de Chillaz, *Inventaire général des autographes, Musée du Louvre* (Paris, 1997), Aut. 3832. BS. bs. L168.

29 Rousseau to Sensier, c. 1850, quoted in Sensier 1872, 200, where he also noted, "When it's needed, when I've used up all the resources offered by colors, I use the scraper, my thumb, a cigarette and, if it's still necessary, the butt end of my brush."

30 Paul Mantz, "Le Salon," *L'Evénement*, 26 March 1851.

31 Sabatier-Ungher 1851, 15.

32 "His [Corot's] naïve incompetency does not incite the same rebellion as the natural or exaggerated ruggedness of M. Rousseau.... both inferior in the science of finish to a crowd of even mediocre landscape painters, they simplify and sum up their subject in order to grasp it better." See Alexandre du Pays, "Salon de 1850," *L'Illustration*, 22 March 1850, 180.

33 Charles Blanc considered that Rousseau's method was informed by Rembrandt: "Following the example of Rembrandt, Théodore Rousseau only begins his landscape in the middle ground. ... The very finished work of the foreground indicates a man who looks at his feet." Blanc 1876, 438.

34 "If M. Th. Rousseau, who has such a skillful and solid execution, who pushes finish as far as it is possible, leaves so many approximations and areas of obvious emptiness in the foregrounds, it is on purpose and following a system. In his landscapes... the foregrounds are ill-defined and ignored, as they are in nature; he does not see them and does not want to see them: his eye carries forward, studies and fixes on all the succeeding planes, reaches the most distant, extreme points on the horizon; it follows that, while all perspective is retained, his backgrounds are more precise and finished than his foregrounds." See Prosper Haussard, "Salon de 1850–1851," *Le National*, 19 March 1851.

35 "Have you finished your small paintings? It's just that you have only a month to do your forest and it is very important that this painting is at the Salon: it absolutely must be there." Millet to Rousseau, [1852], quoted in Sensier and Mantz 2005, 148.

36 Mathilde Stevens, *Impressions d'une femme au Salon de 1859* (Paris, 1859), 125.

37 "It's the wildest and most savagely desolate site in the environs of Paris." See Théophile Gautier, "Salon de 1859," *Le Moniteur universel*, 4 September 1859.

38 Quoted in Sensier 1872, 289.

39 See Zacharie Astruc's Salon review, which includes a description of the work: "The Edge of the Wood, Plain of Barbizon. See these red trees on the right; on the left, gray, uncultivated, rocky ground. Oh! The good small donkey which follows the path, loaded with wood, carrying also his carefree mistress. How I would like to be in her place! The sky is luminous with overlapping pink clouds. You can imagine nothing more pleasing than this charming canvas." Zacharie Astruc, *Les quatorze stations au Salon* (Paris, 1859), 246.

40 G. Bourdin, ed., *L'Autographe au Salon de 1864 et dans les ateliers* (Paris, 1864).

41 Rousseau to Martinet, 22 August 1861. See Norssen, catalogue of the letters auction, spring 1976, no. 227.

42 Olivier Merson, *La peinture en France. Exposition de 1861* (Paris, 1861), 336.

43 Théophile Thoré-Bürger, "Salon de 1861," in *Salons de W. Bürger, 1861 à 1868* (Paris, 1870), 50–51.

44 During the 1850s and 1860s, Millet frequently listed his address in the Salon catalogue as "à Barbison (Seine-et-Marne)," while also including the Paris contact address, "chez M. A. Sensier, rue-Fontaine-Saint-Georges, 19."

45 Pierre Millet remembered a walk taken by these two artists in the forest. Rousseau affirmed, "Look, Millet, at the grand, admirable character of this old oak and how the rock behind is well situated! How that is all so well composed! Millet turned towards the Chailly plain: 'How great it is, how immense it is.'" Pierre Millet, "Millet's Life at Barbizon," *Century* 47 (April 1894): 908–915, quoted in Robert Herbert, *Jean-François Millet* [exh. cat., Galeries nationale d'exposition du Grand Palais] (Paris, 1975), 229.

46 Rousseau to Millet, [January 1852], Chillaz 1997, Aut. 1729. Cote BS.b12.L20.

47 On 20 January 1863, following reforms in the Salon administration, Millet wrote: "I shall now be able to exhibit my *Man with the Hoe*, which would most certainly have been refused by the jury whom we know but too well! . . . It is good all the same to feel yourself free and able to say what you like. But how I shall be attacked!" Millet to Sensier, 20 January 1863, quoted in Julia Cartwright, *Jean-François Millet* (New York, 1896), 237–238.

48 Paul de Saint-Victor, "Salon de 1863," *La Presse*, quoted in Etienne Moreau-Nélaton, *Millet raconté par lui-même* (Paris, 1921), 2:134.

49 Jules Castagnary, "Salon de 1863," in *Salons de 1857–1870* (Paris, 1892), 152.

50 Moreau-Nélaton 1921, 2:129.

51 It is possible that *November* may represent a site in Normandy. Alexandre Piedagnel described the work as a "memory of Gruchy, his [Millet's] birthplace." See Alexandre Piedagnel, *Jean-François Millet. Souvenirs de Barbizon* (Paris, 1876), 63.

52 In early 1852, he wrote to Rousseau: "There have been frost effects in the past few days that I am not going to try to describe, not feeling the ability to do so. . . . I only wish you had seen them." Millet to Rousseau, [1852], quoted in Sensier and Mantz 2005, 148.

53 Edmond About, "Salon de 1867," *Le Temps*, 30 June 1867.

54 Alfred Sensier, "Les peintres de la nature," *Revue de l'art et de la curiosité* (15 May 1870): 383. The artist Jules Dupré noted: "It's the most beautiful landscape that has been painted. For twenty years, I have known nothing that surpasses it." See Sensier to Millet, 9 April 1872, Chillaz 1997, Aut. 3039.

55 Théodore Duret, "Salon de 1870," in *Critique d'avant-garde, Théodore Duret* (Paris, 1998), 47.

56 See Georgel 2007, 100.

57 In a letter of 1892, Sisley reminisced: "It's only in 1866 that I sent two canvases to the Salon that were accepted. As I had put several women in one of my canvases, one witty critic treated me as an animal painter!" Sisley to Adolphe Tavernier, 19 January 1892, quoted in Richard Shone, *Sisley* (New York, 1992), 216.

58 This work was probably informed by preparatory oil studies (such as the Ordrupgaard work), but Daniel Wildenstein has dated it to 1864. Daniel Wildenstein, *Claude Monet. Biographie et catalogue raisonné* (Lausanne and Paris, 1974–1991), 1:423.

59 Monet to Amand Gautier, 22 May 1866, in Wildenstein 1974, 1:423.

60 Thoré-Bürger 1870, 2:325. His friend Bazille wrote, "Monet has come out of the blue with a collection of magnificent canvases, which will be highly successful at the Exposition." Bazille to his mother, Wednesday [1866], quoted in J. Patrice Marandel, *Frédéric Bazille and Early Impressionism* [exh. cat., Art Institute of Chicago] (Chicago, 1978), 173.

61 Emile Zola, *Salons*, ed. Frederick W. J. Hemmings and Robert J. Neiss (Geneva, 1959), 59.

An Infinite Museum

Photography in the Forest of Fontainebleau

SARAH KENNEL

I wish to acknowledge the assistance of the following individuals: Sylvie Aubenas, Malcolm Daniel, Sarah Greenough, Charles Isaacs, Kimberly Jones, Gérard Lévy, Russell Lord, Chris Mahoney, Rolf Mayer, Michael Sachs, and Gary Sokol. All translations are the author's unless otherwise noted.

1 This was a camera with folding bellows that held plates, an iodine box, a mercury box with spirit lamp, a plate holder (often called an "apparatus"), a thermometer, and assorted chemicals. Helmut Gernsheim and Alison Gernsheim, *The History of Photography from the Camera Obscura to the Beginning of the Modern Era* (London, 1969), 74.

2 Although William Henry Fox Talbot had invented the paper negative process in 1840, he patented it in 1841, thus obviating its widespread use until 1847 when Louis Désiré Blanquart-Evrard published a process for making paper negatives and prints. See Richard R. Brettel, *Paper and Light: The Calotype in Britain and France, 1839–1870* (London, 1984).

3 Le Gray visited Fontainebleau in September–October of 1849 in the company of fellow painter-photographer Charles Nègre. See Sylvie Aubenas, *Gustave le Gray, 1820–1884* [exh. cat., Bibliothèque Nationale] (Paris, 2002), 46. Chantal Georgel reports that Charles Marville first visited the Forest of Fontainebleau on 28 August 1848. See Georgel 2007, 54. By 1849, Théodore Rousseau and Narcisse-Virgile Diaz de la Peña were already living in Barbizon and Corot was a frequent visitor.

4 Noël-Marie-Paymal Lerebours, "Plaque, Papier, ou Verre?" *La Lumière* (1 May 1852): 75.

5 See Margaret Denton, "Francis Wey and the Discourse of Photography as Art in France in the Early 1850s: 'Rien n'est beau que le vrai; mais il faut le choisir,'" *Art History* 25, no. 5 (November 2002): 622–648.

6 Francis Wey, "De l'influence de l'héliographie sur les beaux-arts," *La Lumière* (9 February 1851): 2–3.

7 André Jammes and Eugenia Parry Janis, *The Art of French Calotype, with a Critical Dictionary of Photographers, 1845–1870* (Princeton, 1983), 86–87.

8 Aubenas 2002, 45.

9 As Greg Thomas notes, Rousseau's petition was made in 1852. Sometime thereafter, the land was set aside, but the official decree declaring it an artistic preserve was not issued until 1861. Several other areas were also protected by the decree, including the Gorges d'Apremont, the Plateau of Belle-Croix, and the Gorges aux Loups. See discussion in Thomas 2000, 175–176, 216–217.

10 Gautier 1851.

11 For a discussion of Rousseau's reception at the Salon of 1850, see Simon Kelly's essay in this volume.

12 See Aubenas 2002, 45–46.

13 Marc-Antoine Gaudin, "Visite à l'atelier de M. Le Gray," *La Lumière* (10 December 1853): 198.

14 Paul Nibelle, "Fontainebleau," *La Lumière* (8 and 15 April 1853): 55, 59–60. Roger Taylor discusses the importance of individual trees to nineteenth-century British society and especially to landowning classes, who saw the trees as symbols of their own ancient lineage. See Roger Taylor, "British Sensibilities," in *Impressed by Light: British Photographs from Paper Negatives, 1840–1860* [exh. cat., Metropolitan Museum of Art] (New York, 2007).

15 Denecourt 1840, 6.

16 Denecourt 1850a, 70–71. See also Eugenia Parry Janis, *The Photography of Gustave Le Gray* [exh. cat., Art Institute of Chicago] (Chicago 1987), 45–53.

17 Denecourt 1840, 5.

18 A.S. 1839, 290. For further discussion of this issue, see Thomas 2000 and Caroline Ford, "Nature, Culture, and Conservation in France and Her Colonies, 1840–1940," *Past and Present* 183 (May 2004): 173–198.

19 Rousseau's petition is reproduced in Thomas 2000, 214–217.

20 "Résidences royales" 1845, 152. I wish to thank Kimberly Jones for alerting me to this passage.

21 Janis 1987, 53.

22 Laurie Dahlberg, *Victor Regnault and the Advance of Photography: The Art of Avoiding Errors* (Princeton and Oxford, 2005), 7.

23 Le Gray, along with other photographers, used combination printing as a means of avoiding the blank sky that often resulted from long exposures.

24 Paul Périer, "Exposition Universelle," pt. 3, *Bulletin de la Société Française de Photographie* (1855): 191. For Périer's role as patron of Barbizon art, see Simon Kelly, "Early Patrons of the Barbizon School: The 1840s," *Journal of the History of Collections* 16, no. 2 (2004): 161–172.

25 For a general overview of most of the nineteenth-century photographers who worked in the Forest of Fontainebleau, see Daniel Challe and Bernard Marbot, *Les photographes de Barbizon. La forêt de Fontainebleau* [exh. cat., Bibliothèque Nationale] (Paris, 1991).

26 See Kermit S. Champa, ed. *The Rise of Landscape Painting in France: Corot to Monet* [exh. cat., Currier Gallery of Art] (Manchester, NH, 1991).

27 See Dahlberg 2005, 141.

28 Périer 1855, 191.

29 The rise of landscape representation, the emergence of "nature tourism," and the transformations of the capital (and of the capital as a dominant market force) are explored in Green 1990.

30 Périer 1855, 190.

31 Marbot and Challe 1991 identify this site as the Mare à Dagneau, which is located in the canton of Rocher Cuvier Chatillon.

32 Chauvel's collection was acquired by the Musée d'Orsay. See Marie-Thérèse Caille and Philippe Neagu, *Photographies. Barbizon d'hier et d'aujourd'hui. La collection du peintre Théophile Chauvel au Musée d'Orsay* [exh. cat., Musée Municipale de l'Ecole de Barbizon] (Barbizon, 1998).

33 André was long presumed to have worked with his father, Alphonse Giroux, a well-known art dealer. In fact, André and his brother, Alphonse-Gustave, bought the firm from their parents in 1838, making them the sole owners. See Vincent Pomèrade, Alexander Grishin, and Denis Canguilhem, *André Giroux* (London, 2004), 177.

34 Edmond Fierlants, "Rapport sur la section de photographie à l'exposition des arts industriels de Bruxelles," *Bulletin de la Société Française de Photographie* 4 (April 1858): 107, cited in Pomèrade, Grishin, and Canguilhem 2004, 179.

35 Ernst Lacan, "Exposition Universelle—Photographie," pt. 4, *La Lumière* (6 October 1855): 157.

36 "Rapport sur l'exposition de la Société Française de Photographie en 1857," *Bulletin de la Société Française de Photographie* 3 (September 1857): 281.

37 Périer 1855, 196.

38 Michèle Auer and Michel Auer, *Encyclopédie internationale des photographes de 1839 à nos jours* (Hermance, c. 1985), "Jeanrenaud."

39 After his death, Corot's studio contained more than two hundred photographs "after nature, by various artists." For more on the relationship between painters and photographers during the nineteenth century, see Aaron Scharf, "Camille Corot and Landscape Photography," *Gazette des beaux-arts*, 6th ser., 59 (February 1962): 99–102; Margaret Stuffmann, "Between the Barbizon School and the Beginnings of Impressionism: The Landscape Photography of Gustave Le Gray," in *Pioneers of Landscape Photography: Gustave le Gray, Carleton E. Watkins, Photographs from the Collection of the J. Paul Getty Museum* [exh. cat., Städtische Galerie] (Frankfurt, 1993). For the rise of the photographic study, see Ken and Jenny Jacobson, *Etude d'après nature: Nineteenth-Century Photographs in Relation to Art* (Essex, 1996).

40 Ernst Lacan, "Publications photographiques de M. Blanquart-Evrard," *La Lumière* (9 April 1853): 57.

41 See Monique Le Pelley Fonteny, *Adolphe et Georges Giraudon. Une bibliothèque photographique* (Paris, 2005).

42 Steven Adams argues that by the 1870s, when these photographs were made, the symbolic image of the peasant had changed from one of threatening disorder to one of rural nostalgia; it may also account for the focus on women in the series. See Steven Adams, "Signs of Recovery: Landscape Painting and Masculinity in Nineteenth-Century France," in *Gendering Landscape Art* (New Brunswick, 2001), 13–25. An overview of peasant imagery can be found in *The Peasant in Nineteenth-Century French Art* [exh. cat., The Douglas Hyde Gallery, Trinity College] (Dublin, 1980).

43 An alternative technique, which Corot sometimes employed, involved painting directly on the bare sheet of glass. See Elizabeth Glassman and Marilyn Symmes, *Cliché-Verre: Hand-Drawn, Light-Printed, A Survey of the Medium from 1839 to the Present* [exh. cat., Detroit Institute of Arts] (Detroit, 1980).

44 The best source of information on the circle of artists working in Arras during the nineteenth century is found in Gaston-Louis Marchal and Patrick Wintrebert, *Arras et l'art au XIXe siècle. Dictionnaire des peintres, sculpteurs, graveurs, architectes, photographes, critiques et amateurs d'art (1800–1914)* (Arras, 1987).

45 As Malcolm Daniel notes, several photographs inscribed "E.C. 1852" appear to have been made by Adalbert. They were initialed A.C. but were later amended, perhaps to reflect Eugène's collaborative role in their creation. See Malcolm Daniel, *Eugène Cuvelier: Photographer in the Circle of Corot* [exh. cat., Metropolitan Museum of Art] (New York, 1997), 16. It is also possible that Adalbert made the negatives and Eugène printed them at some later date.

46 Cuvelier returned to the forest in 1858, this time listing his profession as "mécanicien," meaning mechanic or engineer. Cuvelier's work as an engineer is briefly discussed in Daniel 1997, 7.

47 For reasons unknown, Cuvelier appears to have ceased photographing sometime in the 1870s. Later in life, he retired to the small village of Thoméry on the edge of the forest, where he lived until his death in 1900. The most comprehensive account of Cuvelier's career is Ulrike Gauss, Daniel Challe, and Henning Weidemann, *Eugène Cuvelier* (Stuttgart, 1996).

48 Challe and Marbot 1997, 15.

49 Cuvelier was relatively well-off and pursued scientific research; among his inventions are a machine gun, a fabric dye, and a steam engine that he exhibited in 1873 at the Exposition artistique, agricole et industrielle d'Arras. See Gauss, Challe, and Weidemann 1996, 20–21.

50 Millet to Rousseau, 31 December 1861, quoted in Sensier 1881, 105. Two portraits of Millet by Cuvelier are reproduced in Sensier's biography. See also Robert Herbert, "Millet et la photographie," in *L'Ecole de Barbizon: Peindre en plein air avant l'impressionisme* [exh. cat., Musée des Beaux-Arts] (Lyon, 2002), 66–79.

51 Flaubert 1985, 349.

52 At the time that Cuvelier made this photograph, the self-sustainability of the forest was not known. See Thomas 2000, 217.

53 The Pavé de Chailly's importance as a motif is discussed in Georgel 2007, 68–71.

54 Tendron 1983, 23.

55 Du Pays 1867, 30.

56 Claude-François Denecourt, *Promenade dans la forêt de Fontainebleau* (Fontainebleau, 1844), quoted in Challe and Marbot 1997, 23. The discourse of catastrophe in describing the forest's geological features was common. In *L'Education sentimentale*, Flaubert described how the forest's rocks evoked "dreams of volcanos, floods, great unknown cataclysms." That the forest fueled a fascination with catastrophe as a form of national history is linked to broader nineteenth-century trends in historiography that increasingly aligned geographic and environmental history with identity. See Ford 2004.

The Impressionists at Fontainebleau

HELGA AURISCH

1 See Robert Herbert, *Barbizon Revisited* [exh. cat., California Palace of the Legion of Honor] (San Francisco, 1962), 16; Christoph Heilmann, Michael Clarke, and John Sillevis, *Corot, Courbet und die Maler von Barbizon. "Les amis de la nature"* [exh. cat., Haus der Kunst] (Munich, 1999), 12–13; and Georgel 2007, 99.

2 André Billy, *Les beaux jours de Barbizon* (Paris, 1947), 77, cited in *Alfred Sisley*, ed. MaryAnn Stevens (London, 1992), 260.

3 Michel Schulman, *Frédéric Bazille, 1841–1870, catalogue raisonné. Peintures—dessins, pastels, aquarelles, sa vie, son oeuvre, sa correspondence* (Paris, 1995), 103.

4 Daniel Wildenstein, *Monet, or the Triumph of Impressionism* (Cologne, 1996), 1:48. As Wildenstein points out, Gleyre's advice may simply have been an encouragement for his pupils to work on their own, outside the hours spent at his studio.

5 Schulman 1995, 325–326.

6 Dianne W. Pitman, "The Art of Frédéric Bazille (1842–1870)" (Ph.D. diss., Johns Hopkins University, 1989), 81–82.

7 Schulman 1995, 121.

8 Marandel 1978, 17.

9 François Daulte, *Frédéric Bazille et son temps* (Geneva, 1952), 170–171; and Schulman 1995, 120–121.

10 Schulman 1995, 121.

11 Richard Kendall, ed. *Monet by Himself* (London, 1989), 23.

12 Bazille's *Valley in the Forest of Fontainebleau* was sold at Sotheby's New York, 23 May 1997 (no. 43). The exact date of Bazille's departure is unknown, but Schulman speculates that it took place in early September. See Schulman 1995, 121.

13 Schulman 1995, 121.

14 Schulman 1995, 127.

15 Wildenstein 1996, 1:21–24, 27.

16 Wildenstein 1996, 1:49–52. Although Wildenstein states that Gleyre's studio was closed permanently in 1864, William Hauptman argues that the studio continued to function until 1870, after a temporary closure in 1864. See William Hauptman, "Delaroche's and Gleyre's Teaching Ateliers and Their Group Portraits," *Studies in the History of Art* 18 (1985): 79–119.

17 George T. M. Shackelford and Fronia E. Wissman, *Impressions of Light: The French Landscape from Corot to Monet* [exh. cat., Museum of Fine Arts] (Boston, 2002), 12.

18 See Millet's *The Wood Gatherers* of 1850–1851 (Art Gallery of Ontario, Toronto) and *The Faggot Gatherers Returning from the Forest* of 1862–1863 (Museum of Fine Arts, Boston).

19 Shackelford and Wissman 2002, 98. Shackelford points out that Monet used the same device in his *Rue de la Bavolle, Honfleur* of 1864 (Museum of Fine Arts, Boston).

20 Shackelford and Wissman 2002, 19.

21 Georgel 2007, 71. See also Wildenstein 1996, vol. 2, nos. 19 and 17.

22 Virginia Spate, *Claude Monet, Life and Work* (New York, 1992), 30.

23 Jean Bouret, *L'Ecole de Barbizon et le paysage français au XIXe siècle* (Neuchâtel, 1972), 140–141.

24 Spate 1992, 31. See also the Kelly essay in this volume.

25 Wildenstein 1996, 1:59. See also James Ganz and Richard Kendall, *The Unknown Monet, Pastels and Drawings* [exh. cat., Sterling and Francine Clark Art Institute] (Williamstown, 2007), 96–99.

26 Ganz and Kendall 2007, 96.

27 Spate 1992, 31.

28 Georgel 2007, 71.

29 Georgel 2007, 69–71.

30 Quotation and information about Monet's preparatory sketches in this paragraph are from Ganz and Kendall 2007, 96.

31 Ganz and Kendall 2007, 99.

32 Wildenstein 1996, 1:59.

33 Wildenstein 1996, 2:34 and 1:397.

34 François Daulte, *Auguste Renoir. Catalogue raisonné de l'oeuvre peint* (Lausanne, 1971), 1:32.

35 There is a discrepancy as to the date of this encounter. Daulte 1971, 32, gives it as 1863, but Bernard Denvir dates it at 1864. See Bernard Denvir, *The Chronicle of Impressionism: A Timeline History of Impressionist Art* (Boston, 1993), 30.

36 Daulte 1971, 1:33.

37 Georgel 2007, 99–100.

38 Colin B. Bailey, et al., *Renoir Landscapes, 1865–1883* [exh. cat., National Gallery] (London, 2007), 86.

39 Bailey et al. 2007, 51, 52.

40 Daulte 1971, 33.

41 Anne Distel, "1860s," in *Renoir* [exh. cat., Hayward Gallery] (London, 1985), 184.

42 Barbara Ehrlich White, *Impressionists Side by Side: Their Friendships, Rivalries, and Artistic Exchanges* (New York, 1996), 25. According to White, the waitress Nana flanks the group at the left, while Mother Anthony is the woman in a kerchief at the back. Renoir even mentions the canine companion Toto, the dog with a wooden leg, and he speaks about the graffiti on the walls—drawings by Henri Mürger, author of *Scènes de la vie de bohème*, which served as inspiration for Puccini's opera *La Bohème*.

43 White 1984, 21; and Bailey et al. 2007, 88.

44 John Oliver Hand, ed., *National Gallery of Art: Master Paintings from the Collection* (Washington, 2004), 312. See also White 1984, 24.

45 Daulte 1971, 34.

46 White 1984, 26–28.

47 Stevens 1992, 86.

48 Georgel 2007, 99–100.

49 Stevens 1992, 94.

50 Stevens 1992, 12.

51 Stevens 1992, 10, 91.

52 Ian Crofton, *A Dictionary of Art Quotations* (New York, 1988), 177.

Bibliography

A. S. "La forêt de Barbizon—Dévastations." *L'Artiste*, 2d ser., 3 (1839): 290–292.

Adams, Steven. *The Barbizon School and the Origins of Impressionism*. London, 1994.

———. "Signs of Recovery: Landscape Painting and Masculinity in Nineteenth-Century France." In *Gendering Landscape Art*, 13–25. New Brunswick, 2001.

Aigoin, Julien. *Fontainebleau sous le Second Empire*. Fontainebleau, 1931.

Alleau, René. *Guide de Fontainebleau mystérieux*. Paris, 1967.

Arnold, Matthew. *The Poetical Works of Matthew Arnold*. New York, 1897.

Aubenas, Sylvie. *Gustave le Gray, 1820–1884*. Exh. cat., Bibliothèque Nationale. Paris, 2002.

Aubrun, Marie-Madeleine. *Théodore Caruelle d'Aligny, 1798–1871. Catalogue raisonné de l'œuvre peint, dessiné, gravé*. [Paris], 1988.

———. *Théodore Caruelle d'Aligny (1798–1871) et ses compagnons*. Exh. cat., Musée des Beaux-Arts. Orléans, 1979.

Baedeker, Karl. *Paris and Its Environs, with Routes from London to Paris, and from Paris to the Rhine and Switzerland: Handbook for Travellers*. Leipzig, 1878.

———. *Paris et ses environs. Manuel du voyageur*. 5th ed. Leipzig, 1878.

Bailey, Colin B. *Renoir's Portraits: Impressions of an Age*. New Haven, London, and Ottawa, 1997.

———, Christopher Riopelle, John House, Simon Kelly, and John Zarobell. *Renoir Landscapes, 1865–1883*. Exh. cat., National Gallery. London, 2007.

Baillo, Joseph. *The Wild Kingdom of Antoine-Louis Barye, 1795–1875*. New York, 1994.

Bailly-Herzberg, Janine. *L'art du paysage en France au XIXe siècle. De l'atelier du plein-air*. Paris, 2000.

Bajou, Valérie. *Frédéric Bazille*. Aix-en-Provence, 1993.

Barnes, Rachel, ed. *Renoir by Renoir*. New York, 1990.

Bazille, Jean-Frédéric. *Correspondance*. Compiled by Guy Barral and Didier Vatuone. Montpellier, 1992.

Bazille: Exposition organisée au profit du Musée de Montpellier. Exh. cat., Galerie Wildenstein. Paris, 1950.

Bernard, Bruce, ed. *The Impressionist Revolution*. London, 1986.

Bernard, Frédéric. *Fontainebleau et ses environs*. Paris, 1853.

Berson, Ruth. *The New Painting: Impressionism, 1874–1886, Documentation*. 2 vols. San Francisco, 1996.

Billy, André. *Les beaux jours de Barbizon*. Paris, 1947.

Blanc, Charles. "C. Troyon." In *Les artistes de mon temps*. Paris, 1876.

Boime, Albert. "The Instruction of Charles Gleyre and the Evolution of Painting in the Nineteenth Century." In *Charles Gleyre ou les illusions perdues*, 102–124. Zurich, 1974.

Borie, Jean. *Une forêt pour les dimanches. Les romantiques à Fontainebleau*. Paris, 2003.

Bouret, Jean. *The Barbizon School and Nineteenth-Century French Landscape Painting*. Greenwich, CT, 1973. Originally published as *L'Ecole de Barbizon et le paysage français au XIXe siècle*. Neuchâtel, 1972.

Brettell, Richard R. *Paper and Light: The Calotype in Britain and France, 1839–1870*. London, 1984.

———, et al. *A Day in the Country: Impressionism and the French Landscape*. Exh. cat., Los Angeles County Museum of Art. Los Angeles, 1984.

Brockedon, William. *Road-Book from London to Naples*. London, 1835.

Burmester, Andreas, Christoph Heilmann, and Michael F. Zimmermann, eds. *Barbizon. Malerei der Natur—Natur der Malerei*. Munich, 1999.

Burty, Philippe. "Camille Corot." In *Exposition de l'œuvre de Corot à l'Ecole nationale des beaux-arts*. Exh. cat., L'Ecole nationale des beaux-arts. Paris, 1875. Reproduced in Reff 1981, no. 3, 5–26.

———. "La forêt de Fontainebleau." *La Renaissance littéraire et artistique*, no. 27 (26 October 1872): 211–212.

———. *Notice des études peintes par M. Théodore Rousseau exposées au Cercle des Arts*. Exh. cat., Cercle des Arts. Paris, June 1867. Reproduced in Reff 1981, no. 11, 3–14.

Caille, Marie-Thérèse. *L'Auberge Ganne: Musée Municipal de l'Ecole de Barbizon*. Moisenay, 1994.

———, and Philippe Neagu. *Photographies. Barbizon d'hier et d'aujourd'hui. La collection du peintre Théophile Chauvel au Musée d'Orsay*. Exh. cat., Musée Municipale de l'Ecole de Barbizon. Barbizon, 1998.

Callias, Hector de. "L'Ecole de Barbizon." *L'Artiste*, no. 3 (15 December 1866): 57–58.

Cartwright, Julia. *Jean-François Millet*. New York, 1896.

Castel, René-Richard. "La forêt de Fontainebleau. Poème." Paris, 1805.

Castellan, Antoine-Laurent. *Fontainebleau. Etudes pittoresques et historiques sur ce château, considéré comme l'un des types de la renaissance des arts en France, au XVIe siècle*. 2 vols. Paris, 1840.

Challe, Daniel, and Bernard Marbot. *Les photographes de Barbizon. La forêt de Fontainebleau*. Exh. cat., Bibliothèque Nationale. Paris, 1991.

Champa, Kermit S. *Studies in Early Impressionism*. New Haven and London, 1973.

———, ed. *The Rise of Landscape Painting in France: Corot to Monet*. Exh. cat., Currier Gallery of Art. Manchester, NH, 1991.

Champfleury. *Oeuvres nouvelles de Champfleury. Les amis de la nature*. Paris, 1859.

Chillaz, Valentine de. *Inventaire général des autographes. Musée du Louvre*. Paris, 1997.

Claretie, Jules. "N. Diaz de la Peña." In *Exposition des œuvres de N. Diaz de la Peña à l'Ecole nationale des beaux-arts*. Exh. cat., L'Ecole Nationale des Beaux-Arts. Paris, 1877. Reproduced in Reff 1981, no. 5, 9–27.

———. *Peintres et sculpteurs contemporains*. 2 vols. Paris, 1882–1884.

Clark, T. J. *The Absolute Bourgeois: Artists and Politics in France, 1848–1851*. 2nd ed. Princeton, 1982.

Clarke, Michael. *Corot and the Art of Landscape*. New York, 1991.

Clavé, Jules. "Etudes forestières. La forêt de Fontainebleau." *Revue des deux mondes* 45 (1 May 1863): 142–170.

Conisbee, Philip. "The Early History of Open-Air Painting." In *In the Light of Italy: Corot and Early Open-Air Painting*. Exh. cat., National Gallery of Art. Washington, 1996.

Corot, raconté par lui-même et par ses amis. 2 vols. Vésenaz-Geneva, 1946.

Cros, Philippe. *Pierre-Auguste Renoir*. Paris, 2003.

Dahlberg, Laurie. *Victor Regnault and the Advance of Photography: The Art of Avoiding Errors*. Princeton and Oxford, 2005.

Daniel, Malcolm. *Eugène Cuvelier: Photographer in the Circle of Corot*. Exh. cat., Metropolitan Museum of Art. New York, 1997.

Daulte, François. *Alfred Sisley. Catalogue raisonné de l'oeuvre peint*. Lausanne, 1959.

———. *Auguste Renoir. Catalogue raisonné de l'oeuvre peint*. Vol. 1, *Figures, 1860–1890*. Lausanne, 1971.

———. *Frédéric Bazille et les débuts de l'impressionnisme. Catalogue raisonné de l'oeuvre peint*. Paris, 1992.

de Font-Réaulx, Dominique. "Reproducing Reality: Landscape Photography of the 1850s and 1860s." In *Courbet and the Modern Landscape*, 39–53. Exh. cat., J. Paul Getty Museum. Los Angeles, 2006.

De la Fizelière, Albert. "Les auberges illustrées." *L'Illustration* 22, no. 565 (24 December 1853): 423–426.

Denecourt, Claude-François. *Carte-guide du voyageur à Fontainebleau. Visite du palais et de la forêt*. 8th ed. Fontainebleau, [1853].

———. *Délices de Fontainebleau. Itinéraire des toutes les promenades parcourables à l'aide de voiture*. Fontainebleau, [1852].

———. *Délices de Fontainebleau. Promenades à la Vallée de la Solle et au rocher des cristaux, par C.-F. Denecourt*. Fontainebleau, [1851].

———. *Délices de Fontainebleau. Promenades au rocher d'Avon et au Chêne des Fées, par C.-F. Denecourt*. Fontainebleau, [1851].

———. *Délices de Fontainebleau. Promenades aux Gorges d'Apremont et au Mont-Aigu, par C.-F. Denecourt*. Fontainebleau, [1851].

———. *Délices de Fontainebleau. Promenades de la Gorge-aux-Loups et vers Thomery et Moret, par C.-F. Denecourt*. Fontainebleau, [1851].

———. *Les délices de la forêt de Fontainebleau*. 3d ed. Fontainebleau, [1845a].

———. *Fontainebleau. Paysages, légendes, souvenirs, fantasies. Hommage à C. F. Denecourt*. Paris, 1855b.

———. *The Forest of Fontainebleau*. London, 1866.

———. *La forêt de Fontainebleau, ses beautés pittoresques . . . aperçu des travaux Denecourt*. 17th ed. Paris, 1860.

———. *Guide du voyageur dans le Château de Fontainebleau, ou précis historique et descriptif de ce magnifique séjour de plaisance. Avec carte topographique*. Fontainebleau, 1840.

———. *Guide du voyageur dans le palais et la forêt de Fontainebleau, ou histoire et description abrégées de ces lieux rémarquables et pittoresques*. Fontainebleau, 1843a.

———. *Guide du voyageur et de l'artiste à Fontainebleau, itinéraire du palais et de la forêt avec les promenades les plus pittoresques*. Paris, 1850a.

———. *Guide of the English Traveller, Fontainebleau*. Fontainebleau, 1856.

———. *L'Indicateur de Fontainebleau. Itinéraire descriptif du palais, de la forêt et des environs*. Fontainebleau, 1868.

———. *L'Indicateur de Fontainebleau. Visite du palais et de la forêt*. 10th ed. Fontainebleau, [1855a].

———. *Itinéraire historique et descriptif de Franchard. La promenade aux cent vues pittoresques. Nouvelles découvertes dans la forêt de Fontainebleau*. Fontainebleau, 1867.

———. *La merveille des rochers de Fontainebleau, ou la roche du cinq mai*. Fontainebleau, November 1866.

———. *Nouvel indicateur de Fontainebleau*. Fontainebleau, 1843b.

———. *Petit indicateur du voyageur à Fontainebleau, ou renseignements indispensables pour séjourner agréablement dans ce pittoresque rendez-vous de plaisance*. Paris, 1850b.

———. *Souvenirs historiques et pittoresques de Fontainebleau*. Fontainebleau, 1845b.

Denton, Margaret. "Francis Wey and the Discourse of Photography as Art in France in the Early 1850s: 'Rien n'est beau que le vrai; mais il faut le choisir.'" *Art History* 25, no. 5 (November 2002): 622–648.

Denvir, Bernard. *The Chronicle of Impressionism: A Timeline History of Impressionist Art*. Boston, 1993.

Doignon, Pierre. *Répertoire bibliographique et analytique du massif du Fontainebleau et de la basse vallée du Loing (Travaux historiques et scientifiques)*. Fontainebleau, 1958.

Domet, Paul. *Histoire de la forêt de Fontainebleau*. Paris, 1873.

Du Pays. "Le château et la forêt de Fontainebleau. La forêt." *Le Tour du monde* 16, no. 393 (1867): 17–32.

Durand, Jean-Baptiste-Alexis. "La forêt de Fontainebleau, poème en 4 chants, suivi de poésies diverses." Fontainebleau, 1836.

———. *Indicateur. Quatre promenades historiques et pittoresques dans la forêt de Fontainebleau.* Fontainebleau, 1851.

Engel de Janosi, Carlette. "The Forest of Fontainebleau in Painting and Writing." *The Journal of Aesthetics and Art Criticism* 11, no. 4 (June 1953): 390–396.

Fanica, Pierre-Olivier. *Charles Jacque, 1813–1894. Graveur original et peintre animalier.* Montigny-sur-Loing, c. 1995.

Flaubert, Gustave. *L'Education sentimentale.* Paris, 1985.

"Fontainebleau: The Forest." Part 4. *Littell's Living Age* 21, no. 257 (21 June 1849): 138–140.

Ford, Caroline. "Nature, Culture, and Conservation in France and Her Colonies, 1840–1940." *Past and Present* 183 (May 2004): 173–198.

"Forêt de Fontainebleau." *Magasin pittoresque* 17 (March 1849): 75–78.

"La forêt de Fontainebleau." *La Causerie* 2, no. 29 (18 September 1859): 33–39.

"La forêt de Fontainebleau." *Magasin pittoresque* 31 (May 1863): 153–155.

Forges, Marie-Thérèse. *Barbizon.* Paris, 1962.

Galassi, Peter. *Before Photography: Painting and the Invention of Photography.* Exh. cat., Museum of Modern Art. New York, 1981.

———. *Corot in Italy: Open-Air Painting and the Classical-Landscape Tradition.* New Haven and London, 1991.

Galiègue, Josette. *De l'école de la nature au réve symboliste. L'esprit d'une collection, La donation Marie-Thérèse Laurenge au Musée départemental de l'Oise.* Beauvais and Paris, 2004.

Ganz, James, and Richard Kendall. *The Unknown Monet, Pastels and Drawings.* Exh. cat., Sterling and Francine Clark Art Institute. Williamstown, 2007.

Gassies, Georges. *Le vieux Barbizon. Souvenirs de jeunesse d'un paysagiste, 1852–1875.* Paris, 1907; reprint, 1998.

Gauss, Ulrike, Daniel Challe, and Henning Weidemann. *Eugène Cuvelier.* Stuttgart, 1996.

Georgel, Chantal. *La forêt de Fontainebleau. Un atelier grandeur nature.* Exh. cat., Musée d'Orsay. Paris, 2007.

Gernsheim, Helmut, and Alison Gernsheim. *The History of Photography from the Camera Obscura to the Beginning of the Modern Era.* London, 1969.

Glassman, Elizabeth, and Marilyn Symmes. *Cliché-Verre: Hand-Drawn, Light-Printed, A Survey of the Medium from 1839 to the Present.* Exh. cat., Detroit Institute of Arts. Detroit, 1980.

Goncourt, Edmond de, and Jules de Goncourt. *Journal. Mémoires de la vie littéraire.* Vol. 6. Monaco, 1956.

———. *Manette Salomon.* Paris, 1996.

Green, Nicholas. *The Spectacle of Nature: Landscape and Bourgeois Culture in Nineteenth-Century France.* Manchester and New York, 1990.

Guibert, Abbé. *Description historique des château, bourg, et forest* [sic] *de Fontainebleau.* 2 vols. Paris, 1731.

Hauptman, William. *Charles Gleyre, 1806–1874.* 2 vols. Zurich, Princeton, and Basel, 1996.

———. "Delaroche's and Gleyre's Teaching Ateliers and Their Group Portraits." *Studies in the History of Art* 18 (1985): 79–119.

Heilbrun, Françoise. *Les paysages des impressionnistes.* Paris, c. 1986.

Heilmann, Christoph, Michael Clarke, and John Sillevis. *Corot, Courbet und die Maler von Barbizon. "Les amis de la nature."* Exh. cat., Haus der Kunst. Munich, 1999.

Henriet, Frédéric. *Le paysagiste aux champs.* Paris, 1876.

———. *Le paysagiste aux champs, croquis d'après nature.* Paris, 1866.

Herbert, Robert. *Barbizon Revisited.* Exh. cat., California Palace of the Legion of Honor. San Francisco, 1962.

———. *Impressionism: Art, Leisure, and Parisian Society.* New Haven and London, 1988.

———. *Jean-François Millet.* Exh. cat., Galeries Nationales d'Exposition du Grand Palais. Paris, 1975.

———. "Millet et la photographie." In *L'Ecole de Barbizon. Peindre en plein air avant l'impressionnisme,* 66–79. Exh. cat., Musée des Beaux-Arts. Lyon, 2002.

Herbet, Félix. *Dictionnaire historique et artistique de la Forêt de Fontainebleau. Routes, carrefours, cantons, gardes, monuments, croix, fontaines, puits, mares, environs, moulins, etc.* Fontainebleau, 1903.

Hervet, Jean-Pierre, and Patrick Mérienne. *Fontainebleau. Une forêt de légendes et de mystères.* Rennes, 2004.

———. *La forêt de Fontainebleau.* Rennes, 1997.

House, John. *Monet: Nature into Art.* New Haven and London, 1986.

———, Anne Distel, and Lawrence Gowing. *Renoir.* Exh. cat., Hayward Gallery. London, 1985.

Hugo, A. *France pittoresque, ou description pittoresque, topographique et statistique des départements et colonies de la France.* Vol. 3. Paris, 1838.

Jacobson, Ken, and Jenny Jacobson. *Etude d'après nature: Nineteenth-Century Photographs in Relation to Art.* Essex, 1996.

Jamin, E. *Fontainebleau, ou notice historique et descriptive sur cette résidence royale.* Fontainebleau, 1834; 2d ed., 1838.

———. *Quatre promenades dans la forêt de Fontainebleau, ou description physique et topographique de cette forêt royale.* Fontainebleau, 1837.

Jammes, André, and Eugenia Parry Janis. *The Art of French Calotype, with a Critical Dictionary of Photographers, 1845–1870.* Princeton, 1983.

Janis, Eugenia Parry. *The Photography of Gustave Le Gray*. Exh. cat., Art Institute of Chicago. Chicago, 1987.

Johnston, William R., and Simon Kelly. *Untamed: The Art of Antoine-Louis Barye*. Exh. cat., Walters Art Gallery. Baltimore, 2006.

Joanne, Adolphe. *Atlas historique et statistique des chemins de fer*. Paris, 1859.

———. *Les environs de Paris illustrés*. 2d ed. Paris, 1878.

———. *Fontainebleau. Son palais, ses jardins, sa forêt*. Paris, [1856].

———. *Fontainebleau. Son palais, ses jardins, sa forêt et ses environs*. Paris, 1867.

———. *Itinéraire général de la France. Environs de Paris*. Paris, 1887.

Kalaora, Bernard. *Le musée vert, ou, le tourisme en forêt. Naissance et développement d'un loisir urbain. Le cas de la forêt de Fontainebleau*. Paris, 1981.

———. "Les salons verts. Parcours de la ville à la forêt." In *La théorie du paysage en France, 1974–1994*, 109–132. Edited by Alain Roger. Seyssel, 1995.

Kavanagh, Julia. *Bessie*. London, 1872.

Kelly, Simon. "Early Patrons of the Barbizon School: The 1840s." *Journal of the History of Collections* 16, no. 2 (2004): 161–172.

———. "The Landscapes of Théodore Rousseau and Their Market." In Burmester, Heilmann, and Zimmermann c. 1999, 419–436.

Küster, Bernd. *Monet. Seine Reisen in den Süden*. Hamburg, 1992.

La Fosse, G. "Train de plaisir à Fontainebleau. " *Le journal amusant*, no. 994 (18 September 1875): 1–7.

Laughton, Bruce. "Marks and Meaning: Some Responses to the Forest by Rousseau and Millet." In Burmester, Heilmann, and Zimmermann c. 1999, 160–177.

Lebart, Luce. "Photographes et peintres sur le motif à Barbizon." In *Autour du symbolisme. Photographie et peinture aux XIXe siècle*. Exh. cat., Palais des Beaux-Arts. Brussels, 2004.

Lemoine, Serge, ed. *Donation Granville, Musée de Dijon*. Dijon, 1975.

Lenormant, Charles. *Les artistes contemporains. Salons de 1831 et 1833*. 2 vols. Paris, 1833.

Le Pelley Fonteny, Monique. *Adolphe et Georges Giraudon. Une bibliothèque photographique*. Paris, 2005.

Levallois, Jules. *Mémoires d'une forêt. Fontainebleau*. Paris, 1875.

Low, Will H. *A Chronicle of Friendship, 1873–1900*. New York, 1908.

MacWilliam, Neil. "Mythologising Millet." In Burmester, Heilmann, and Zimmermann c. 1999, 437–447.

Mantz, Paul. "Jean-François Millet." In *Catalogue descriptif des peintures, aquarelles, pastels, dessins rehaussés croquis et l'eau-fortes de J.-F. Millet*. Exh. cat., L'Ecole Nationale des Beaux-Arts. Paris, 1887. Reproduced in Reff 1981, no. 10, 7–35.

Marandel, J. Patrice. *Frédéric Bazille and Early Impressionism*. Exh. cat., Art Institute of Chicago. Chicago, 1978.

Marchal, Gaston-Louis, and Patrick Wintrebert. *Arras et l'art au XIXe siècle. Dictionnaire des peintres, sculpteurs, graveurs, architectes, photographes, critiques et amateurs d'art (1800–1914)*. Arras, 1987.

Marionneau, Charles. *Brascassat, sa vie et son oeuvre*. Paris, 1872.

Marryat, Florence. *Too Good for Him*. Boston, 1867.

Maury, L. F. Alfred. *Histoire des grandes forêts de la Gaule et de l'ancienne France*. Paris, 1850.

Michel, Emile. *La forêt de Fontainebleau dans la nature, dans l'histoire, dans la littérature et dans l'art*. Paris, 1909.

Michelet, Jules. *L'Insecte*. 5th ed. Paris, 1863.

Mion, H. *La salamandre, ou l'histoire abrégée et la description complète de la ville*. Fontainebleau, 1839.

Miquel, Pierre. *Paysage et société, 1800–1900*. Maurs-la-Jolie, 1985.

———. *Le paysage français au XIXe siécle*. 4 vols. Maurs-la-Jolie, 1975.

———, and Rolande Miquel. *Narcisse Diaz de La Peña (1807–1876)*. 2 vols. Courbevoie, 2006.

Moreau-Nélaton, Etienne. *Corot raconté par lui-même*. 2 vols. Paris, 1924.

———. *Histoire de Corot et de ses œuvres*. Paris, 1905.

———. *Millet, raconté par lui-même*. 3 vols. Paris, 1921.

Morton, Mary, and Charlotte Eyerman. *Courbet and the Modern Landscape*. Exh. cat., J. Paul Getty Museum. Los Angeles, 2006–2007.

Muller, Eugène. *La forêt: Son histoire, sa légende, sa vie, son rôle, ses habitants*. Paris, 1878.

Murger, Henry. *Le sabot rouge*. Paris, n.d.

———. *Scènes de campagne. Adeline Protat;* Paris, n.d.

Murphy, Alexandra R. *Jean-François Millet: Drawn into the Light*. Exh. cat., Sterling and Francine Clark Art Institute. Williamstown, 1999.

Musset, Alfred de. *La confession d'un enfant du siècle*. Paris, 1995.

Nibelle, Paul. "Fontainebleau." *La Lumière* (8 and 15 April 1853): 55, 59–60.

Nigro, Carol. *The Figure and the Forest: Nineteenth-Century French Photographs and Drawings*. Exh. cat., Jill Newhouse Gallery. New York, 2004.

Nochlin, Linda. *The Politics of Vision: Essays on Nineteenth-Century Art and Society*. New York, 1989.

Nodier, Charles, and Louis Lurine. *Les environs de Paris. Paysage, histoire, monuments, moeurs, chroniques et traditions*. Paris, 1844.

Paillet, François-Hippolyte. *Description physique de la forêt de Fontainebleau*. Versailles, 1806.

Pantazzi, Michael, Vincent Pomaréde, and Gary Tinterow. *Corot, 1796–1875*. Exh. cat., Galeries Nationales du Grand Palais. Paris, 1996–1997.

Parinaud, André. *Les peintres et leur école Barbizon et les origines de l'impressionnisme*. Vaduz and Paris, c. 1994.

Paulet, Jean-Jacques. *Observations sur la vipère de Fontainebleau, et sur les moyens de remédier à sa morsure*. Fontainebleau, 1805.

Pecheux-Herbenville. *Fontainebleau et les charmantes promenades aux sites et aux rochers qui l'environnent. Edition ornée de cartes et vues et comprenant un aperçu historique et artistique du palais et de ses dependances*. Fontainebleau, 1850.

Périer, Paul. "Exposition Universelle." Part 3. *Bulletin de la Société Française de Photographie*. July 1855, 187–201.

Pitman, Dianne W. "The Art of Frédéric Bazille (1842–1870)." Ph.D. diss., Johns Hopkins University, 1989.

———. *Bazille: Purity, Pose, and Painting in the 1860s*. University Park, 1998.

———. "Overlapping Frames." In *Monet and Bazille: A Collaboration*, 19–65. Edited by David A. Brenneman. Exh. cat., The High Museum of Art. Atlanta, 1999.

Pohlmann, Ulrich. "Barbizon und die Photographie." In *Corot, Courbet und die Maler von Barbizon*. Exh. cat., Haus der Kunst. Munich, 1996.

Polton, Jean-Claude. *Tourisme et nature au XIXe siècle. Guides et itinéraires de la forêt de Fontainebleau (vers 1820–vers 1880)*. Paris, 1994.

Pomarède, Vincent, Alexander Grishin, and Denis Canguilhem. *André Giroux*. London, 2004.

———, and Gérard de Wallens. *L'école de Barbizon. Peindre en plein air avant l'impressionnisme*. Exh. cat., Musée des Beaux-Arts. Lyon, 2002.

Reff, Theodore, ed. *Exhibitions of Barbizon and Landscape Art*. New York, 1981.

Rémard, Charles. *Le guide du voyageur à Fontainebleau*. Fontainebleau and Paris, 1820.

"Résidences royales. Fontainebleau—La forêt." *L'Illustration* 6, no. 141 (8 November 1845): 151–154.

Rewald, John. *The History of Impressionism*. New York, 1946; rev. ed., 1961; 4th rev. ed., 1973.

———, and Frances Weitzenhoffer, ed. *Aspects of Monet*. New York, 1984.

Robaut, Alfred, and Etienne Moreau-Nélaton. *L'oeuvre de Corot, par Robaut. Catalogue raisonné et illustré, précédé de l'histoire de Corot et de ses oeuvres*. 5 vols. Paris, 1905.

Rosenblum, Robert. *Paintings in the Musée d'Orsay*. New York, 1989.

Ruskin, John. *The Works of John Ruskin*. Edited by Ernest Thomas Cook and Alexander Wedderburn. London, 1908.

Sahlin, Peter. *Forest Rites: The War of the Desmoiselles in the Nineteenth Century*. Cambridge, MA, 1994.

Sand, George. *Agendas (1852–1856)*. Vol. 1. Paris, 1990.

———. *Correspondance, 1812–1876*. Vol. 5. Paris, 1884.

———. *Elle et lui*. Paris, 1859.

———. *La filleule*. New ed. Paris, 1890.

———. *Impressions et souvenirs*. Edited by Eve Sourian. Paris, 2005.

Sarraute, Gabriel. "Catalogue de l'oeuvre de Frédéric Bazille." Thesis, Ecole du Louvre, Paris, 1948.

Schama, Simon. *Landscape and Memory*. New York, 1995.

Schapiro, Meyer. *Impressionism: Reflections and Perceptions*. New York, 1997.

Scharf, Aaron. "Camille Corot and Landscape Photography." *Gazette des beaux-arts*, 6th ser., 59 (February 1962): 99–102.

Schulman, Michel. *Frédéric Bazille, 1841–1870, catalogue raisonné. Peintures—dessins, pastels, aquarelles, sa vie, son oeuvre, sa correspondence*. Paris, 1995.

———. *Théodore Rousseau, 1812–1867*. 2 vols. Paris, 1997–1999.

———. *Théodore Rousseau: The Language of Nature*. Exh. cat., Salander-O'Reilly Galleries. New York, 2002.

The Second Empire, 1852–1870: Art in France under Napoleon III. Exh. cat., Philadelphia Museum of Art. Philadelphia, 1978.

Sen..., M. de. "Sur Fontainebleau." *Mercure de France* 5 (January 1812): 15.

Senancour, Etienne Pivert de. *Obermann*. Preface by George Sand. New ed. Paris, [1840?].

Sensier, Alfred. "Historique de Barbizon." Unpublished manuscript. Bibliothèque municipale de Fontainebleau, n.d.

———. "Jean-François Millet—Peasant and Painter." Parts 1–5 (parts 3–5 with Paul Mantz). *Scribner's Monthly* 20, no. 5 (September 1880): 732–750; 20, no. 6 (October 1880): 825–840; 21, no. 1 (November 1880): 104–110; 21, no. 2 (December 1880): 189–200; 21, no. 3 (January 1881): 392–407.

———. "Les peintres de la nature." *Revue de l'art et de la curiosité* (15 May 1870): 383.

———. *Souvenirs sur Th. Rousseau*. Paris, 1872.

———, and Paul Mantz. *La vie et l'œuvre de Jean-François Millet*. Bricqueboscq, 2005.

Shackelford, George T. M., and Fronia E. Wissman. *Impressions of Light: The French Landscape from Corot to Monet*. Exh. cat., Museum of Fine Arts. Boston, 2002.

———. *Monet, Renoir, and the Impressionist Landscape*. Exh. cat., National Gallery of Canada. Ottawa, 2000.

Shaw, Jennifer. "French Landscape Painting and Modern Life." In *Paris and the Countryside: Modern Life in Late-Nineteenth-Century France*. Exh. cat., Portland Museum of Art. Portland, ME, 2006.

Shone, Richard. *Sisley*. New York, 1992.

Sillevis, John, and Hans Kraan. *De School van Barbizon. Franse meesters van de 19de eeuw*. Exh. cat., Museum voor Schone Kunsten. Ghent, 1985–1986.

Smith, Charles Sprague. *Barbizon Days*. New York, 1902.

Spate, Virginia. *Claude Monet, Life and Work*. New York, 1992.

Starke, Mariana. *Information and Directions for Travelers on the Continent*. 5th ed. Paris, 1826.

Stendhal. *Mémoires d'un touriste*. New ed. Paris, 1854.

Stevens, MaryAnn, ed. *Alfred Sisley*. London, 1992.

Stevenson, Robert Louis. "Fontainebleau: Village Communities of Painters." In *Virginibus Puerisque and Other Papers: Later Essays*, 201–226. Edinburgh, 1895.

———. "Forest Notes." In *Essays of Travel and in the Art of Writing*, 162–195. New York, 1905.

Stuffmann, Margaret. "Between the Barbizon School and the Beginnings of Impressionism: The Landscape Photography of Gustave Le Gray." In *Pioneers of Landscape Photography: Gustave le Gray, Carleton E. Watkins, Photographs from the Collection of the J. Paul Getty Museum*. Exh. cat., Städtische Galerie. Frankfurt, 1993.

Taine, Hippolyte. *Notes sur Paris. Vie et opinions de M. Frédéric Thomas Graindorge ... recueillies et publiées par H. Taine, son exécuteur testamentaire*. Paris, 1857; 3d ed., 1867.

Tendron, Gérard. *La forêt de Fontainebleau. De l'écologie à la sylviculture*. Fontainebleau, 1983.

Théodore Rousseau, 1812–1867. Exh. cat., Musée du Louvre. Paris, 1967–1968.

Thomas, Greg M. *Art and Ecology in Nineteenth-Century France: The Landscapes of Théodore Rousseau*. Princeton, 2000.

———. "The Practice of 'Naturalism': The Working Methods of Théodore Rousseau." In Burmester, Heilmann, and Zimmermann c. 1999, 437–447.

Thomson, David Croal. *The Barbizon School of Painters: Corot, Rousseau, Diaz, Millet, Daubigny, etc.* New York, 1890.

Thoré, Théophile. "Par monts et par bois." Parts 1 and 2. *Le Constitutionnel*, no. 531 (27 November 1847): 1–2; no. 532 (28 November 1847): 1–2.

———. *Salon de 1845*. Paris, 1845.

———. *Salons de T. Thoré*. 2d ed. Paris, 1870.

Tinterow, Gary, and Henri Loyrette. *Origins of Impressionism*. Exh. cat., Galeries Nationales du Grand Palais. Paris, 1994.

Valenciennes, Pierre-Henri de. *Eléments de perspective pratique, à l'usage des artistes, suivis de réflexions et conseils à un élève sur la peinture, et particulièrement sur le genre du paysage*. Paris, [1800?]; reprint, Geneva, 1973.

Vollard, Ambroise. *Renoir: An Intimate Record*. Translated by Harold L. Van Doren and Randolph T. Weaver. New York, 1930.

White, Barbara Ehrlich. *Impressionists Side by Side: Their Friendships, Rivalries, and Artistic Exchanges*. New York, 1996.

———. *Renoir: His Life, Art, and Letters*. New York, 1984.

Wildenstein, Daniel. *Claude Monet: Biographie et catalogue raisonné*. 5 vols. Lausanne and Paris, 1974–1991.

———. *Monet, or the Triumph of Impressionism*. 4 vols. Cologne, 1996.

Wilkin, Karen. "Photography's Painter." *The New Criterion* 23 (January 2005): 40–43.

Zola, Emile. *L'œuvre*. Paris, 1886.

Index

Illustrations are indicated by italic type.

R

S

T

U

V

W

Y

Z

Photography Credits

PLATES

pl. 2: Wildenstein & Co., New York; pl. 3: Musée de l'Oise, Beauvais (photographer: Fabrice Gousset); pls. 4, 96: Réunion des Musées Nationaux [RMN hereafter] / Art Resource, NY (photographer: René-Gabriel Ojeda); pl. 6: The National Museum of Fine Arts, Stockholm; pls. 7, 16, 25, 76: RMN / Art Resource, NY (photographer: Hervé Lewandowski); pl. 8: Bibliothèque-Musée Marmottan, Boulogne-Billancourt; pls. 9, 17, 19, 29, 33, 36, 44, 48, 56, 69, 73, 74, 77, 79, 90: © 2007 Board of Trustees, National Gallery of Art, Washington (photographer: Lorene Emerson); pls. 10, 58, 94: © 2007 Board of Trustees, National Gallery of Art, Washington (photographer: Greg Williams); pls. 12, 24, 39, 93: The Museum of Fine Arts, Houston; pl. 13: Pernille Klemp; pl. 14: Victoria and Albert Museum, London; pls. 15, 23: Digital Images © The Museum of Modern Art / Licensed by SCALA / Art Resource, NY; pl. 18: The Cleveland Museum of Art; pl. 20: Southampton City Art Gallery, Hampshire, UK / The Bridgeman Art Library; pls. 21, 42: Sotheby's, New York; pl. 22: The J. Paul Getty Museum, Los Angeles; pl. 26: Kunsthalle Bremen (photographer: Lars Lohrisch / Abdruck nur mit Genehmigung der Kunsthalle); pl. 27: Chrysler Museum of Art, Norfolk; pl. 28: Photograph © 1993 The Detroit Institute of Arts; pls. 30, 60: © 2007 Board of Trustees, National Gallery of Art, Washington; pls. 31, 37, 65, 75, 81, 82: Photograph © 2007, Museum of Fine Arts, Boston; pl. 34: Minneapolis Institute of Arts; pl. 35: Jack Kilgore & Co. Inc., New York City; pl. 38: Wilson Centre for Photography, London; pls. 41, 53: © Musée des Beaux-Arts de la Ville de Reims (photographer: C. Devleeschauwer); pls. 43, 62, 99: Image © The Metropolitan Museum of Art; pl. 47: Kunstmuseum Winterthur; pl. 49: Yale Center for British Art, Paul Mellon Collection, New Haven, CT / The Bridgeman Art Library; pls. 50, 98: Photograph © 2006 Museum Associates / LACMA; pls. 51, 95: The City of Fontainebleau; pls. 52, 102: RMN / Art Resource, NY (photographer: Gerard Blot); pl. 54: © Musée de l'Oise, Beauvais (photographer: Jean-Louis Bouché); pl. 55: Staatliche Kunsthalle Karlsruhe; pl. 57: Photography © The Art Institute of Chicago; pl. 61: Van Gogh Museum, Amsterdam; pl. 63: Museum Boijmans Van Beuningen, Rotterdam; pl. 64: ICN, Rijswijk / Amsterdam (photographer: Tim Koster); pl. 66: Albright-Knox Art Gallery, Buffalo; pls. 67, 80: Bibliothèque Nationale de France, Paris; pl. 70: Murray Riss; pl. 71: Brooklyn Museum; pls. 72, 86: Bildarchiv Preussischer Kulturbesitz / Art Resource, NY; pl. 78: © Sterling and Francine Clark Art Institute, Williamstown, MA; pls. 83, 89: The Walters Art Museum, Baltimore; pls. 84, 85: Cincinnati Art Museum; pls. 87, 92: Courtesy of the Philadelphia Museum of Art; pl. 88: The Baltimore Museum of Art; pl. 91: RECOM, GmbH, Ostfildern; pl. 97: © The National Gallery, London; pl. 100: San Diego Museum of Art; pl. 101: Middlebury College Museum of Art; pl. 103: Wadsworth Atheneum Museum of Art; pl. 104: Yale University Art Gallery.

FIGURES

Jones fig. 4: RMN / Art Resource, NY (photographer: Hervé Lewandowski); fig. 5: Photograph © 2006 Museum Associates / LACMA; fig. 6: RMN / Art Resource, NY (photographer: Madeleine Coursaget); fig. 11: Ole Haupt; fig. 17: Sipa, Paris; fig. 18: Didier Michalet; fig. 24: RMN / Art Resource, NY (photographer: Gerard Blot); fig. 32: Image © The Metropolitan Museum of Art. *Kelly* fig. 2: Pernille Klemp; fig. 3: RMN / Art Resource, NY (photographer: Jacques Quecq d'Henripret); fig. 4: RMN / Art Resource, NY (photographer: Daniel Arnaudet); fig. 8: reproduced with the permission of the Saint Louis University Pius XII Memorial Library. *Kennel* figs. 2 and 10: Image © The Metropolitan Museum of Art; figs. 3 and 4: RMN / Art Resource, NY (photographer: Patrice Schmidt).